AN INTRODUCTION TO CRIME AND JUSTICE

Edited by
John W. Silva
Cerro Coso Community College

MSS Information Corporation
655 Madison Avenue, New York, N. Y. 10021

This is a custom-made book of readings prepared for the courses taught by the editor, as well as for related courses and for college and university libraries. For information about our program, please write to:

MSS INFORMATION CORPORATION
655 Madison Avenue
New York, New York 10021

MSS wishes to express its appreciation to the authors of the articles in this collection for their cooperation in making their work available in this format.

Library of Congress Cataloging in Publication Data

Silva, John W comp.
An introduction to crime and justice

1. Criminal justice, Administration of--United States--Addresses, essays, lectures. I. Title.
KF9223.A75S5 345'.73'05 72-86200
ISBN 0-8422-5049-2
ISBN 0-8422-0223-4 (pbk.)

CONTENTS

Gauging Public Opinion about the Crime Problem

Don C. Gibbons
Joseph F. Jones
Peter G. Garabedian

Because punitive and correctional actions against lawbreakers are often undertaken in the name of the public, it is frequently said that the citizenry demands that some specific penalty be visited upon offenders. Only in recent years, however, as pollsters and social scientists began to take soundings on citizen opinions regarding the crime problem and the handling of lawbreakers, have we come to learn anything about public sentiments on these matters.

Previous Studies

One study of citizen attitudes by Rose and Prell asked a number of persons to indicate the most serious offenses from a list of thirteen minor felonies.[1] Examination of the sentences actually handed out to offenders indicated that many of the crimes regarded as *least* serious by citizens

[1]Arnold E. Rose and Arthur E. Prell, "Does the Punishment Fit the Crime? A Study in Social Valuation," *American Journal of Sociology*, November 1955, pp. 247-59.

CRIME AND DELINQUENCY, 1972, Vol. 18, pp.134-146.

were the ones which received the heaviest penalties in the courts.

Newman examined food, drug, and cosmetic violations by asking a sample of adults to indicate the punishment they considered appropriate for cases of these offenses taken from federal files.[2] Most of the respondents thought that these activities should be more heavily punished than they actually had been.

A third study, by Gibbons, dealt with citizen knowledge of criminality and correction.[3] Few of the laymen had any detailed understanding of the workings of the correctional system. Similar results were obtained in a survey commissioned by the California state legislature, which found that few citizens had any detailed knowledge of the correctional machinery, and the majority thought that penalties for most crimes were less severe than they actually are.[4]

Another study by Rooney and Gibbons questioned citizens regarding abortion, homosexuality, and drug addiction.[5] The respondents held that abortion laws should be liberalized, but they were not so tolerant of homosexuality, and they were particularly strident in their demands for severe penalties for drug addicts.

Gibbons also conducted an inquiry in which California citizens were asked about the degree of punishment they considered appropriate for twenty different crimes.[6] The most visible and coercive offenses received the most severe penalty choices, often exceeding in harshness the dispositions actually pronounced for similar offenses in the state.

McIntyre has summarized the studies of public attitudes undertaken for the President's Commission on Law Enforcement and Administration of Justice.[7] These indicated that most people throughout the nation see crime as a growing problem in their own communities, although they do not feel unsafe near their own homes, even when they live in high crime areas. The majority of them asserted that such things as the "breakdown of moral standards" rather than deleterious social conditions are responsible for increased crime. Many of them recommended repressive rather than ameliorative steps to curb crime, and many claimed that the courts are too lenient with offenders. Large numbers of citizens favored "get tough" policies of the police, but many were simultaneously ambivalent about increasing other powers of the police in law enforcement.

A nation-wide survey of citizen views of the correctional system authorized by the Joint Commission on Correctional Manpower and Training showed that only about a quarter of the respondents held that the law enforcement system is efficient in deterring crime, while half thought that the courts are too lenient, and half believed that the national prison system is doing an inadequate job.[8]

Some related observations were ob-

---

[2]Donald J. Newman, "Public Attitudes toward a Form of White-Collar Crime," *Social Problems,* January 1957, pp. 228-32.

[3]Don C. Gibbons, "Who Knows What about Correction?" *Crime and Delinquency,* April 1963, pp. 137-44.

[4]Assembly Committee on Criminal Procedure, *Deterrent Effects of Criminal Sanctions* (Sacramento: California State Legislature, 1968).

[5]Elizabeth A. Rooney and Don C. Gibbons, "Social Reactions to 'Crimes without Victims,'" *Social Problems,* Spring 1966, pp. 400-10.

[6]Don C. Gibbons, "Crime and Punishment: A Study in Social Attitudes," *Social Forces,* June 1969, pp. 391-97.

[7]Jennie McIntyre, "Public Attitudes toward Crime and Law Enforcement," *Annals of the American Academy of Political and Social Science,* November 1967, pp. 34-46.

tained in a survey of the readers of *Psychology Today.*[9] These relatively young and well-educated citizens were of the opinion that crime rates are currently higher than in the past. Most of them held that some kind of treatment rather than punishment should be given to drug addicts, alcoholics, prostitutes, and homosexuals. Many of them said that white-collar criminals are dealt with too leniently, most of them opposed the death penalty, and most asserted that penalties for juveniles should be different from and less harsh than those for adults. Liberal respondents voiced approval of Supreme Court decisions concerning due process, while conservatives opposed these rulings. Most of the respondents held that responsibility for crime rests on the individual, not on adverse societal conditions.

One indication of historical changes in public attitudes is found in a study by Pattison, Bishop, and Linsky which examined perceptions of drug addiction in a sample of popular magazines.[10] Their data indicated that, in contrast to opinions expressed in 1900, contemporary views regard drug addicts as less responsible for their behavior, give greater attention to the social milieu, and stress rehabilitation rather than a strictly punitive approach.

In addition to these studies, which have focused on adults, some reports are available concerning public perceptions of the juvenile justice system. In one of these, Lentz surveyed a sample of Wisconsin adults concerning attitudes toward juvenile control.[11] Most of the citizens favored swift and impartial justice, punishment that fits the crime, and probation in place of institutional commitment. Over half advocated publishing the names of juvenile offenders, and many asserted that juvenile offenders are "ill" and in need of expert treatment.

A study made by Parker dealt with citizen views of the juvenile court in four Washington state communities.[12] Many of the respondents asserted that the juvenile court was not tough enough in its dealings with offenders. But when these same laymen were asked how they would punish offenders, the penalties they chose were similar to or less severe than the ones actually handed out by the juvenile courts!

The study reported here is a continuation of the line of research reviewed above. In it, citizens in San Francisco, Calif., and Portland, Oreg., were surveyed regarding their attitudes on the crime problem, personal fear of crime, due process for adults and juveniles, and punitive measures.

Study Design and Procedures

This investigation employed a relatively short, self-administered questionnaire[13] dealing with (1) opinions on the seriousness of the crime problem; (2) perceptions of personal

[8]Joint Commission on Correctional Manpower and Training, *The Public Looks at Crime and Corrections* (Washington, D.C.: Joint Commission on Correctional Manpower and Training, 1968).

[9]"Your Thoughts on Crime and Punishment," *Psychology Today,* May 1969, pp. 53-58.

[10]E. M. Pattison, L. A. Bishop, and A. S. Linsky, "Changes in Public Attitudes on Narcotic Addiction," *American Journal of Psychiatry,* August 1968, pp. 160-67.

[11]William P. Lentz, "Social Status and Attitudes toward Delinquency Control," *Journal of Research in Crime and Delinquency,* July 1966, pp. 147-54.

[12]Howard A. Parker, "Juvenile Court Actions and Public Response," *Becoming Delinquent,* P. G. Garabedian and D. C. Gibbons, eds. (Chicago: Aldine, 1970), pp. 252-65.

[13]Copies of the questionnaire are available on request from the authors.

safety from crime; (3) attitudes toward due process for adult offenders; (4) attitudes toward due process for juvenile offenders; (5) attitudes toward punitive measures; and (6) related attitudes and information, including questions on the socio-demographic characteristics of the respondents. The questionnaire was pretested and then administered by a group of trained interviewers. These workers, advanced sociology students at San Francisco State College and Portland State University, sought out respondents and remained present while the questionnaire was completed so as to be available to deal with queries concerning the questions. The questionnaires were administered during the spring of 1970.

A total of 466 persons in San Francisco and 353 in Portland completed questionnaires.[14] No formalized sampling procedure such as stratified random sampling was employed; instead, interviewers were sent to widely separated areas and neighborhoods in Portland and San Francisco, including adjacent suburbs. The intent was to obtain a broad cross section of citizens within the two communities, although areas of very low income were avoided. The social characteristics of the two samples are shown in Table 1.

Table 1 indicates that the two samples were similar in age, educational status, and residential stability; however, the Portland group had greater numbers of older individuals and persons with high incomes. In both areas, the higher levels of education are overrepresented.

This study differs from those cited previously in several ways. For one, it involves responses of a rather large number of persons in two cities of different size and character in states that are adjacent but unlike in a number of important ways; thus, the data allow an opportunity for comparative analysis. Second, the questionnaire utilized here was multidimensional, so that opinions concerning a number of facets of the crime problem, law enforcement, correc-

TABLE 1
BACKGROUND CHARACTERISTICS OF SAMPLES

Characteristics	Per cent S.F. (N = 466)	Per cent Port. (N = 353)
Sex		
Male	50.0	49.0
Female	50.0	50.1
No response	0	.9
Age		
45 and over	20.6	35.1
35–44	17.2	15.6
25–34	30.9	26.6
Under 25	30.0	21.8
No response	1.3	.9
Education		
College graduate	24.0	25.8
Some college	42.3	36.5
High school graduate	23.4	27.5
Some high school	7.7	7.4
Grade school	1.7	2.0
No response	.9	.9
Income		
$15,000 and over	13.5	22.9
$10,000–$14,999	27.3	30.3
$6,000–$9,999	33.9	30.6
Under $6,000	21.2	13.3
No response	4.1	2.8
Residence		
10 years or more in state	68.2	76.8
5–10 years in state	16.3	8.5
1–5 years in state	10.9	10.2
Under 1 year in state	3.6	3.1
No response	.9	1.4

[14]Actually, more than 466 and 353 individuals completed questionnaires. In the case of married couples, both often filled out questionnaires. One person from each of these married pairs was randomly selected for inclusion in the final sample to eliminate husband-wife bias of responses.

TABLE 2
PERCEPTIONS OF THE CRIME PROBLEM

Questions	Per cent San Francisco (N = 466)	Per cent Portland (N = 353)
1. Crime problem in California [Oregon] compared with 1950		
Somewhat or much worse now than in 1950	89.1	85.6
About the same or better than in 1950	9.0	12.2
No response	1.9	2.3
2. Crime problem in California [Oregon] compared with Oregon [California]		
Worse in home state	79.0	3.1
Same in both states	16.3	20.1
Worse in other state	1.9	75.6
No response	2.8	1.1
3. Crime problem in California [Oregon] compared with the East		
Worse in home state	11.8	1.1
Same in both areas	53.0	15.0
Worse in the East	33.5	83.0
No response	1.7	.8
4. Crime problem in California [Oregon] compared with Washington State		
Worse in home state	63.5	6.2
Same in both states	25.2	81.0
Worse in other state	8.2	12.0
No response	2.8	.8
5. Seriousness of crime problem in California [Oregon] these days		
Not very serious	6.7	14.4
Quite serious	62.9	73.9
Most serious problem in state	28.3	10.8
No response	2.1	.8

tion, and related matters were tapped. Third, the study involved some questions regarding citizen preferences for due process standards for juveniles, which is a matter that has not been probed in other investigations.

The general working hypotheses of this study were that California respondents would view the crime problem as more serious and would exhibit greater personal fear of crime than would citizens in Oregon. It was anticipated that persons in both samples would show considerable willingness to suspend due process standards in the interest of repressing crime and would show relative insensitivity to the rights of juveniles. Finally, we expected to find that many citizens would opt for punitive responses to lawbreakers rather than for ameliorative ones.

Results

PERCEPTIONS OF THE CRIME PROBLEM

The distribution of responses to the items tapping public conceptions of the current crime problem are shown in Table 2.[15] Although most citizens

[15]These items are shown in an abridged form of the wording in the questionnaire.

in both cities considered the crime problem in their state to be worse than in 1950, marked differences showed up on other items. The San Francisco residents held that the crime problem was worse in their state than in Oregon or Washington, and many of them also perceived crime to be as marked in California as in the East. The Portland respondents asserted that their state was less ridden with crime than California or the East. We would argue that the Portland citizens were probably fairly accurate in their view that they live in a less crime-filled city than San Francisco residents.

Another indication of public perceptions of the crime problem can be found in Table 3. These results were obtained by asking persons to rank the eight social problems listed in that table.[16] More than two-thirds of the respondents in both cities asserted that crime was a leading social problem, a result in accord with the findings of other investigations cited in this paper. A slightly greater percentage of Portland respondents considered juvenile delinquency a major social problem. Poverty was identified as a major social problem by a larger share of San Francisco respondents. Somewhat surprisingly, student protests were identified as a major problem by more Portlanders even though their city has experienced few major student demonstrations.

TABLE 3
RANK ORDER OF EIGHT SOCIAL PROBLEMS

Social Problems	Per cent S.F. (N = 466)	Per cent Port. (N = 353)
Crime		
Ranked in top three	69.5	67.6
Ranked in lower five	25.1	28.3
No response	5.4	4.0
Poverty		
Ranked in top three	60.3	41.3
Ranked in lower five	35.6	54.7
No response	4.1	4.0
Drug Use		
Ranked in top three	54.5	62.6
Ranked in lower five	41.2	35.0
No response	4.3	2.3
Air Pollution		
Ranked in top three	40.3	50.1
Ranked in lower five	55.0	47.2
No response	4.7	2.5
Juvenile Delinquency		
Ranked in top three	26.8	39.4
Ranked in lower five	68.2	56.7
No response	4.9	4.0
High Taxes		
Ranked in top three	26.0	17.3
Ranked in lower five	69.7	78.6
No response	4.3	4.0
Student Protests		
Ranked in top three	7.7	10.7
Ranked in lower five	86.3	84.5
No response	6.0	4.8
Traffic Congestion		
Ranked in top three	6.4	8.2
Ranked in lower five	88.2	87.8
No response	5.4	4.0

PERCEPTIONS OF PERSONAL SAFETY

Three items on the questionnaire dealt with feelings of personal safety from crime, the results of which are shown in Table 4. Responses to all three questions showed Portland citizens as somewhat less fearful of being robbed or burglarized in their neighborhoods or of being the victim of a crime somewhere in the wider community. In both cities, respondents said they were less apprehensive for their safety in their own neighbor-

[16]These items are presented in Table 3 in order of decreasing frequency of being listed as one of the top three major social problems. In the questionnaire, they were presented in the following order: air pollution, traffic congestion, juvenile delinquency, poverty, student protests, drug use, crime, and high taxes.

TABLE 4
PERCEPTIONS OF PERSONAL SAFETY

Questions	Per cent San Francisco (N = 466)	Per cent Portland (N = 353)
1. How safe in your neighborhood from being beaten up or robbed?		
Quite safe or reasonably safe	69.2	87.6
Somewhat or very fearful	30.7	12.5
No response	.1	0
2. How safe from being burglarized?		
Quite safe or reasonably safe	53.2	68.5
Somewhat or very fearful	46.4	30.9
No response	.4	.6
3. How safe in general San Francisco [Portland] area from being beaten up or robbed?		
Quite safe or reasonably safe	41.8	67.4
Somewhat or very fearful	57.8	31.8
No response	.4	.8

hoods than they were in the rest of the city. These findings are also in accord with results of previous investigations. We would contend that here again the respondents were accurately reflecting the realities of crime, so that it probably was the case that people were generally safer in Portland than in San Francisco.

ATTITUDES TOWARD DUE PROCESS FOR ADULTS

Table 5 presents the findings on eight items dealing with due process for adult offenders. These data indicated that more than half of the respondents from each city agreed that the Supreme Court has hindered the police through such decisions as *Mapp* and *Miranda.* But only about a quarter of the citizens believed that the police should be allowed to conduct periodic searches of the houses of known criminals, and most of the respondents agreed that the police should warn suspects of their right to remain silent. From one viewpoint, it might optimistically be reported that only a few persons disagreed with the Court regarding admonitions about citizen rights and that, similarly, only a few persons were willing to allow the police to "rough up" suspects. However, a civil libertarian might find these same figures alarming; he would be appalled that *any* citizens sanctioned the use of police tactics identified in these questions. Nearly half of the respondents held that when a person is apprehended for a crime, the police should be allowed to conduct general searches of him, his property, etc., for evidence of other crimes. Over half agreed that the police ought to use whatever technique is expedient in catching criminals. Due process considerations appear to have had only a tenuous hold on the allegiance of many persons. Our own view of these results is pessimistic, particularly when we consider the relatively high educational level of these respondents, who might, therefore, be expected to be the most liberal. As can be seen from Table 5, respondents in the two communities did not differ markedly in their opinions on these issues.

Attitudes toward Due Process for Juveniles

The *Kent* and *Gault* decisions of the Supreme Court in 1966 and '67 laid down substantial rights of due process for juveniles, holding that accused offenders must be notified of charges, allowed lawyers, given the right of appeal, and so on, while the 1970 *Winship* decision requires juvenile courts to observe the "be-

Table 5
Attitudes toward Due Process for Adults

Questions	Per cent San Francisco (N = 466)	Per cent Portland (N = 353)
1. Supreme Court decisions have hindered the police in efforts to fight crime		
Agree or strongly agree	54.3	67.7
Disagree or strongly disagree	44.4	30.1
No response	1.3	2.3
2. Police should periodically search houses of known criminals		
Agree or strongly agree	26.8	26.3
Disagree or strongly disagree	72.1	73.4
No response	1.1	.3
3. Police should not question suspects without advising them of right to be silent		
Agree or strongly agree	82.7	77.7
Disagree or strongly disagree	16.4	21.8
No response	1.1	.6
4. When police catch a person for a crime, should search him, his car, etc., for evidence of other crimes		
Agree or strongly agree	43.4	54.1
Disagree or strongly disagree	55.6	44.7
No response	1.1	1.1
5. Police should use any necessary technique to catch criminals who commit robberies, etc.		
Agree or strongly agree	54.9	55.5
Disagree or strongly disagree	43.0	43.0
No response	2.1	1.4
6. Police should be allowed to "rough up" rape suspect to get confession from him		
Agree or strongly agree	13.1	10.4
Disagree or strongly disagree	85.6	88.7
No response	1.3	.8
7. State should provide lawyer to person arrested for *serious* crime		
Agree or strongly agree	87.5	87.5
Disagree or strongly disagree	10.9	11.6
No response	1.5	.8
8. State should provide lawyer to person arrested for *minor* crime		
Agree or strongly agree	77.1	69.7
Disagree or strongly disagree	21.6	29.4
No response	1.3	.8

yond a reasonable doubt" standard of evidence in court proceedings. In addition, several states in recent years have initiated reforms in juvenile court practice to ensure due process and legal safeguards for juveniles. Finally, many social scientists have begun to voice skepticism about the rehabilitative potential of the juvenile court and have begun to agitate against such relaxed procedures as informal probation. In all of this, there is a growing suspicion that even though the juvenile court operates out of good intentions, its effects may often be less than beneficial. If this is so, the reasoning goes, juvenile courts ought to become more legalistic in operation than they have been in the past.

Table 6 shows the distribution of responses to questions dealing with matters of due process in juvenile proceedings. As can be seen in the first item, more than two-thirds of the respondents favored policies of "informal probation," in which the court retains control over children who have not been given a hearing or been adjudicated. Along the same line, nearly all the respondents asserted that the courts should continue to handle offenders who fall within the omnibus part of delinquency laws—that is, ungovernability, waywardness, immorality, and the like. Clearly, citizen views have not yet been influenced by criticisms that have pointed out the hazards of utilizing the crude machinery of the court for

TABLE 6

ATTITUDES TOWARD DUE PROCESS FOR JUVENILES

Questions	Per cent: San Francisco (N = 466)	Per cent: Portland (N = 353)
1. Juvenile court should not hold formal hearing for petty delinquent but should give him treatment		
Agree or strongly agree	66.5	70.8
Disagree or strongly disagree	31.9	27.5
No response	1.5	1.7
2. Juvenile court should work with ungovernable, wayward, or immoral conduct cases		
Agree or strongly agree	78.3	89.3
Disagree or strongly disagree	19.7	10.5
No response	1.9	.3
3. Judge should remand "tough guy" delinquent to criminal court, without holding a hearing		
Agree or strongly agree	19.9	22.9
Disagree or strongly disagree	78.3	76.5
No response	1.7	.6
4. Juveniles should not have jury trials in juvenile court		
Agree or strongly agree	38.6	47.0
Disagree or strongly disagree	58.6	51.8
No response	2.8	1.1
5. Juveniles should have lawyers in juvenile court		
Agree or strongly agree	74.5	66.6
Disagree or strongly disagree	23.9	30.8
No response	1.7	2.5

children who fall under these rubrics.

But citizen approval apparently does not extend to informal procedures of the sort that have characterized juvenile courts in the past. Less than a quarter of the respondents agreed that judges should remand delinquents to criminal court without holding hearings. Therefore, the majority were in accord with the principle enunciated in *Kent.* While more than a third of the citizens thought that juveniles should not have jury trials, over half of them contended that they should. Finally, two-thirds or more of the respondents agreed that lawyers should be provided for juveniles in court hearings. On all of these items, the differences between San Francisco and Portland respondents did not appear to be marked.

Attitudes toward Punitive Measures

The questions that probed the punitive orientations of the citizens are shown in Table 7. Over half of the respondents in both samples asserted that offenders should serve three years or less in prison; at the same time, a considerable number refrained from offering any estimate of the appropriate time to be served. It should be noted that prisoners in these two states spend markedly different periods of time in prison: terms in California run about three years

Table 7
Attitudes toward Punitive Measures

Questions	Per cent: San Francisco (N = 466)	Per cent: Portland (N = 353)
1. How much time should prisoners serve, on the average?		
1½ years or less	29.6	24.9
3 years	25.3	29.5
5 years	21.9	20.4
10 years	6.0	7.1
No response	17.2	18.1
2. Circumstances under which crime is least likely		
Likely to be caught, mild penalty	49.6	49.6
Severe penalty, unlikely to be caught	46.1	45.6
No response	4.3	4.8
3. Opinion on proportion of offenders sent to prison		
Not enough get prison terms	24.5	51.0
About right number get prison	23.4	28.0
Too many are put in prison	47.9	16.7
No response	4.3	4.2
4. Criminals should not be executed		
Agree or strongly agree	56.0	51.0
Disagree or strongly disagree	41.4	42.4
No response	2.6	6.6
5. Which programs would help most to reduce the crime problem in California [Oregon]		
Better education or employment opportunities, social and psychiatric help, more study of crime causes	70.4	64.9
Emphasis on moral standards, pass more laws, stiffer penalties, put religion back into schools	20.1	31.5
No response	9.5	3.6

on the average; those in Oregon, about a year and a half.[17]

Table 7 shows the samples equally divided on the question of whether certainty or severity of punishment is the more effective deterrent. Also, about equal proportions in both samples opposed the death penalty.[18]

More Portland residents held that not enough offenders get prison sentences. This is a curious finding, given the earlier observation that San Franciscans were more concerned than Portlanders about the crime problem. Actually, a larger proportion of the offender population was placed on probation in California than in Oregon. Several conjectures can be offered to account for this finding. One is that Oregon residents are generally more conservative than Californians and for this reason adopt a harsher posture toward offenders. It is also possible that the hearings of the Assembly Committee on Criminal Procedure in California had directed the public's attention to parole policies and the high costs of operating prisons in that state.

The respondents were also asked to identify from a list of seven possibilities the procedure which they thought would make the most impact upon crime control. These are enumerated in the final question in Table 7. About two-thirds of the respondents chose some type of ameliorative or therapeutic approach, while only a third or less took refuge in a popular belief such as "Religion should be put back into the schools."

[17]*Op. cit. supra* note 4, p. 44.

[18]The death penalty was abolished by referendum in Oregon in 1964. It might be noted that 60.1 per cent of the voters approved abolition in that election, so that it appears that support for abolition may have declined somewhat in Oregon.

Additional Questions on Crime

The questionnaire used in this study included a number of items related to crime and correction which do not fit into the previous categories. These items are shown in Table 8.

About one-third of the respondents in both groups thought that prison inmates served less than two years in prison, while nearly half of the Portland citizens thought that prisoners serve three-year terms. As we have already noted, California inmates do spend three years on the average in institutions, while the average term in Oregon is about eighteen months. Thus, most of the Portland residents were incorrect in naming three years or more as the average prison term, while a fair number of San Francisco respondents thought prison terms were shorter than they actually are.

More than half of the Portland residents asserted that juvenile correctional workers were doing a good job of rehabilitating offenders, but less than half of them judged that adult correctional agents were performing well. On the other hand, about two-thirds of the San Francisco respondents asserted that neither the adult nor juvenile workers were doing a good job.

Negotiated pleas of guilty as a means of disposing of criminal cases failed to receive the support of very many of the respondents, even though "plea copping" does account for most of the convictions that are obtained in the courts. Two-thirds of the respondents in both communities said that they would support a halfway house located in their neighborhood. Furthermore, about two-thirds of the citizens asserted that the police ought to handle skid row drunks in some other way than arresting them for drunkenness. Two-thirds of them also

Table 8
Additional Questions on Crime

Questions	Per cent	
	San Francisco (N = 466)	Portland (N = 353)
1. How much time do prisoners serve in state prisons, on the average?		
1½ years or less	35.9	31.7
3 years	38.0	45.3
5 years	19.3	16.1
10 years	1.9	2.0
No response	4.9	4.8
2. How well are state juvenile correctional workers doing their job?		
Very well or reasonably well	33.5	53.3
Somewhat poorly or very poorly	65.2	44.7
No response	1.3	2.0
3. How well are state adult correctional workers doing their job?		
Very well or reasonably well	31.9	44.2
Somewhat poorly or very poorly	66.9	53.2
No response	1.1	2.5
4. Opinion on "plea copping"		
Approve or strongly approve	28.4	20.9
Disapprove or strongly disapprove	70.1	77.1
No response	1.5	2.0
5. Opinion on halfway house in own neighborhood		
Support or strongly support	66.7	62.3
Oppose or strongly oppose	31.7	36.2
No response	1.5	1.4
6. Police should not arrest skid row drunks solely for drunkenness		
Agree or strongly agree	65.6	60.6
Disagree or strongly disagree	33.1	38.8
No response	1.5	1.1
7. Police and courts are almost always fair with accused persons		
Agree or strongly agree	41.6	56.4
Disagree or strongly disagree	57.3	42.5
No response	1.1	1.1
8. Opinion on release on "own recognizance"		
Approve or strongly approve	63.1	67.2
Disapprove or strongly disapprove	34.7	31.4
No response	2.1	1.4
9. Police know who the people are that make their living committing burglaries, robberies, etc.		
Agree or strongly agree	54.7	62.6
Disagree or strongly disagree	44.2	35.7
No response	1.1	1.7
10. Know anyone who has been arrested for a major crime?		
Yes	42.9	35.7
No	56.0	62.3
No response	1.1	2.0
11. Any close friends been the victim of a major crime?		
Yes	30.7	23.2
No	68.0	73.9
No response	1.3	2.8

said that they approved of releasing persons on their own recognizance.

The two samples differed widely on the question of whether the police and courts are fair in their dealings with accused persons. Over half of the Portland residents contended that they were fair, while over half of the San Francisco respondents believed they were not fair.

The final observation from Table 8 is that while a sizable proportion of persons—43 per cent in San Francisco and 36 per cent in Portland—said that they knew someone who had been arrested for a major crime, a markedly smaller percentage—31 per cent in San Francisco and 23 per cent in Portland—asserted that any of their close friends had been the victim of a major crime.

Summary

This study deals with public attitudes and opinions on a number of matters involving the crime problem. Many of the results are consistent with findings reported in previous studies.

In general, Portland citizens appeared to be less concerned about the crime problem and their own personal safety than San Francisco residents. The respondents from the two communities differed little in their attitudes on due process and civil liberties. However, on one or two items, Portland residents appeared to favor more repressive tactics directed at offenders.

UNIFORM CRIME REPORTS–1970 *(EXCERPTS)*

Federal Bureau of Investigation

Chart 2

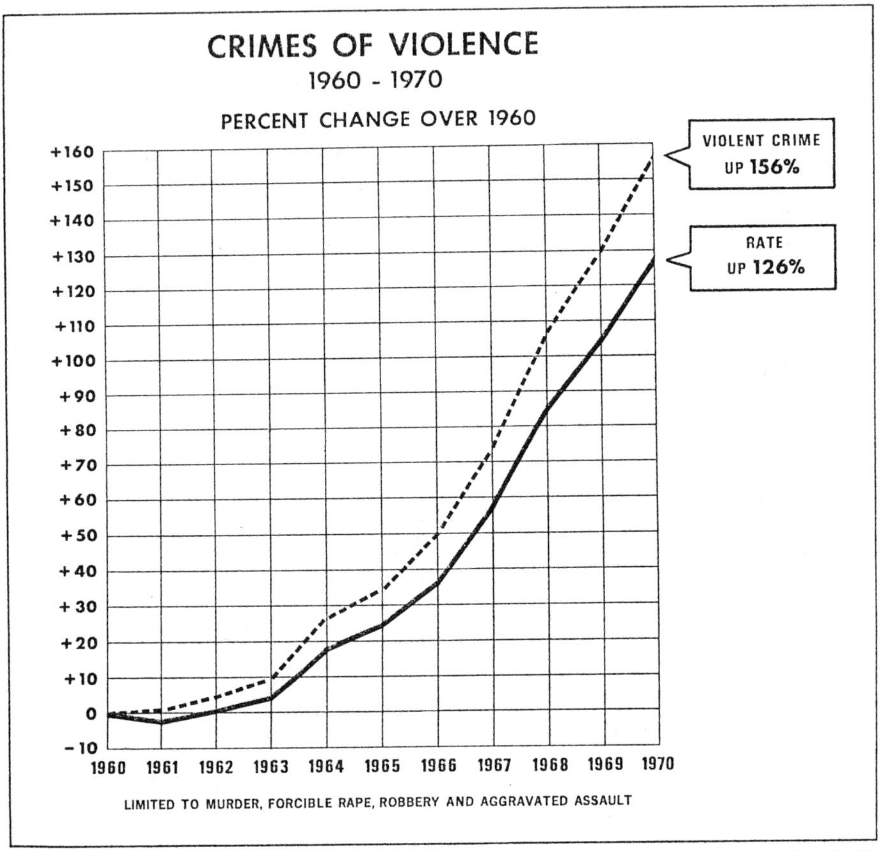

FBI CHART

CRIME IN THE UNITED STATES: UNIFORM CRIME REPORTS--1970, Washington, D.C.: U.S. Government Printing Office, pp. 3, 8, 31, 32, 39, 40, 41, 119.

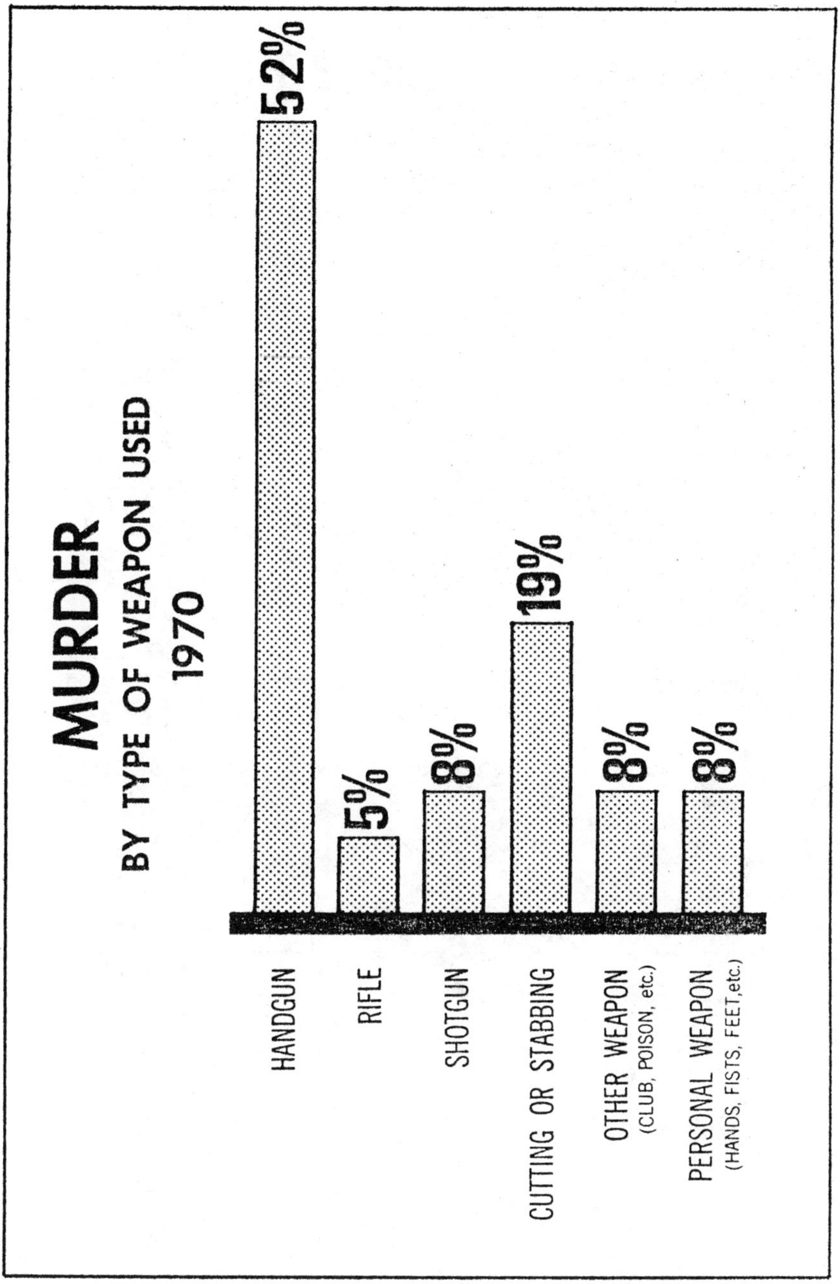

FBI CHART

Chart 5

Chart 16

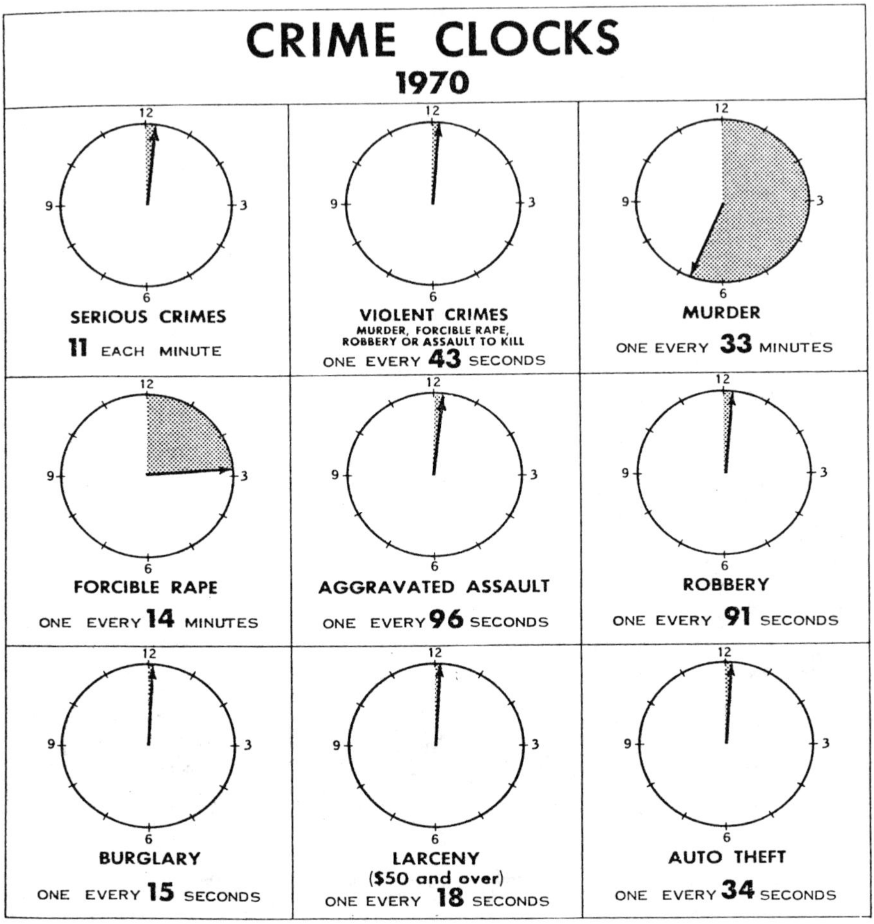

FBI CHART

Chart 17

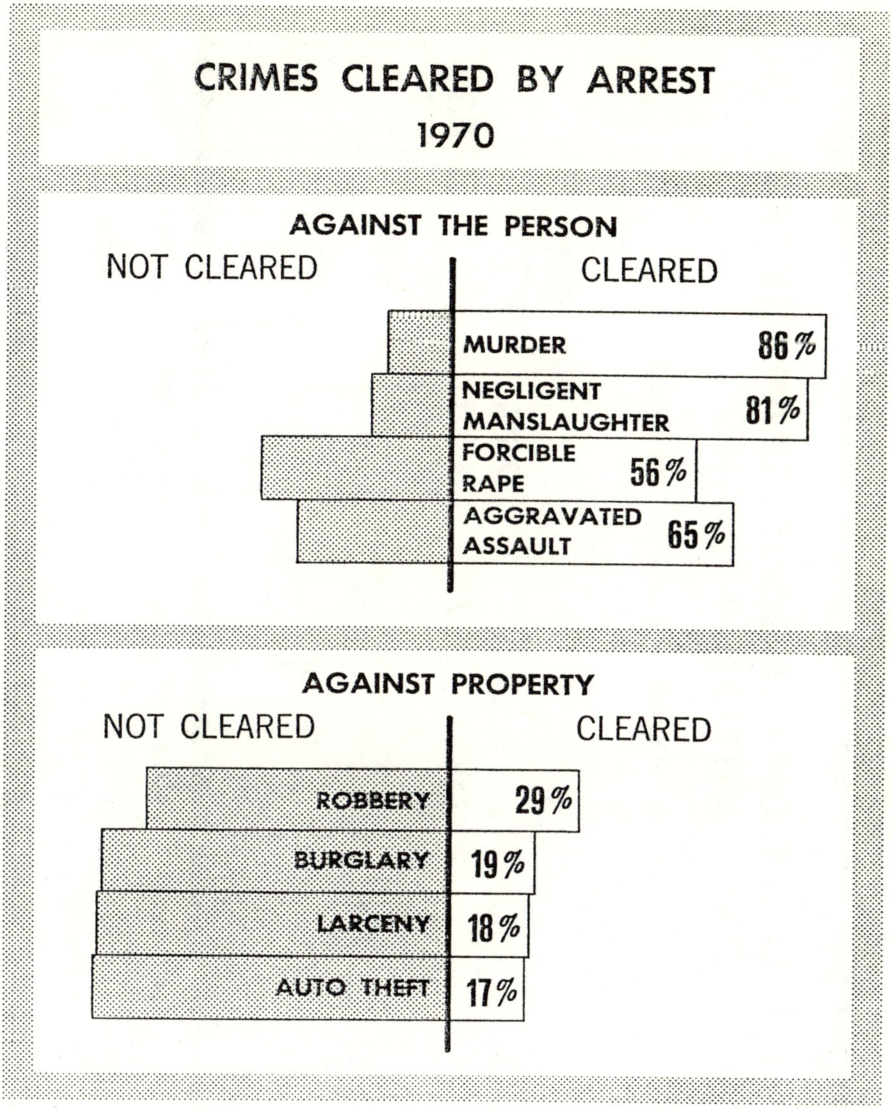

FBI CHART

Chart 19

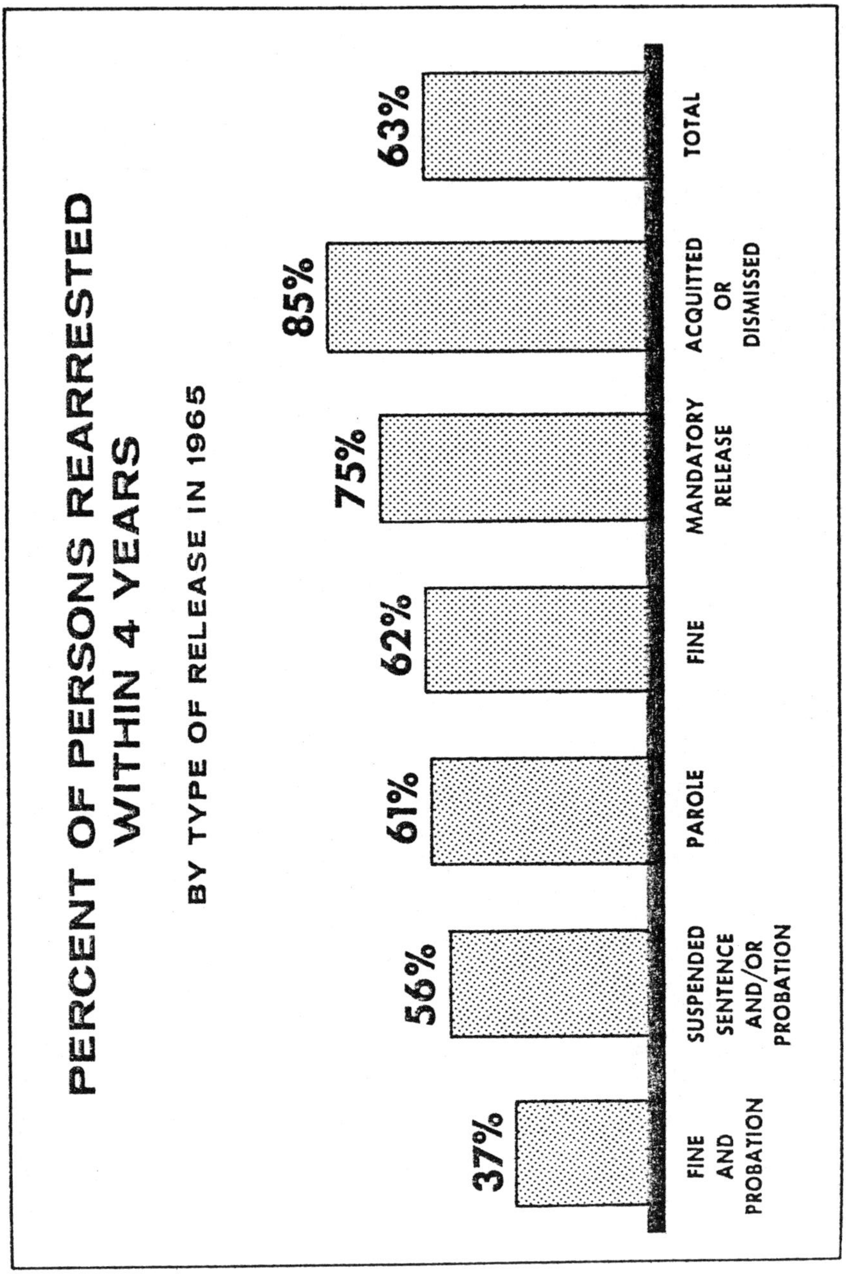

FBI CHART

Chart 20

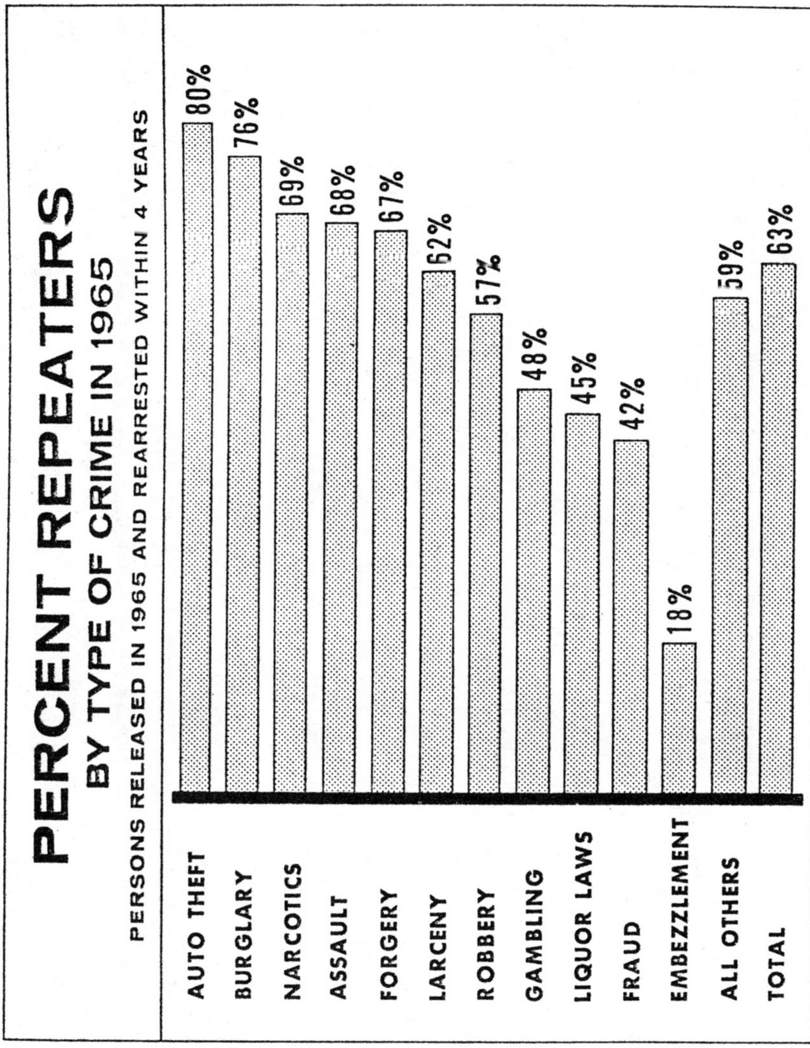

FBI CHART

Chart 21

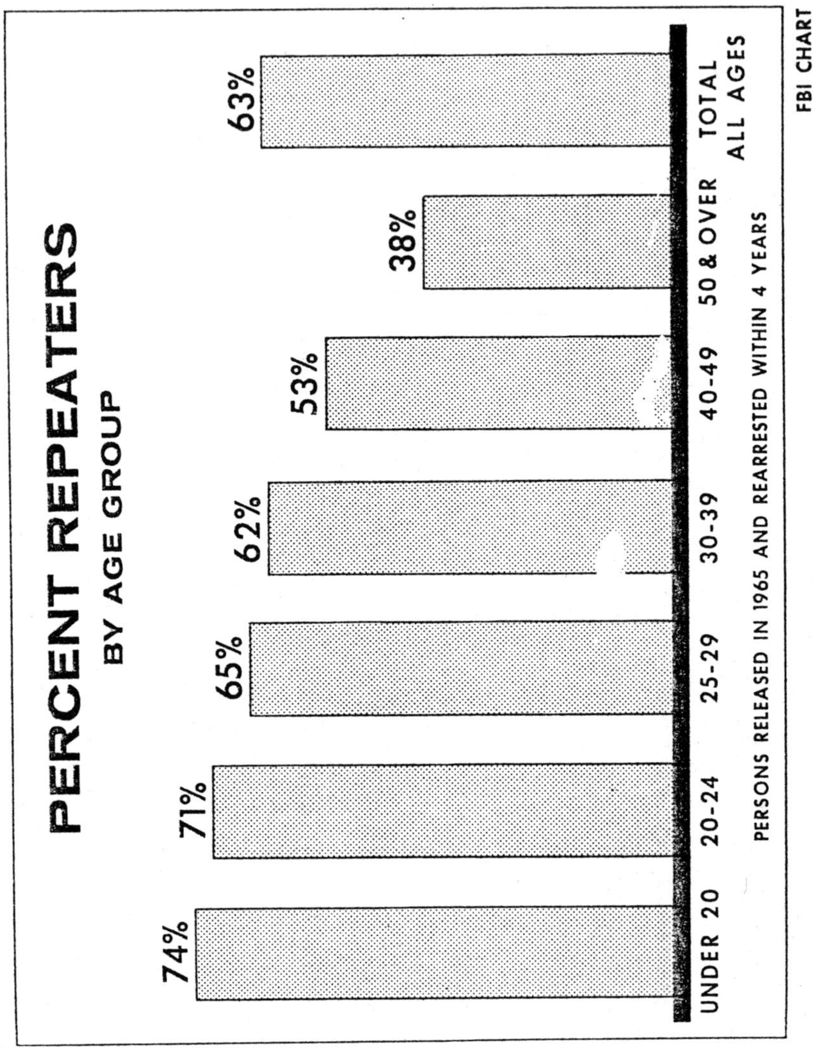
PERCENT REPEATERS
BY AGE GROUP
74%
71%
65%
62%
53%
38%
63%
UNDER 20
20-24
25-29
30-39
40-49
50 & OVER
TOTAL ALL AGES
PERSONS RELEASED IN 1965 AND REARRESTED WITHIN 4 YEARS
FBI CHART

Total Estimated Arrests,[1] United States, 1970

Offense	Arrests	Offense	Arrests
Total	8,117,700	Arson	11,900
		Forgery and counterfeiting	55,500
Criminal homicide:		Fraud	104,600
Murder and nonnegligent manslaughter	15,230	Embezzlement	10,000
Manslaughter by negligence	4,190	Stolen property; buying, receiving, possessing	74,000
Forcible rape	19,050	Vandalism	141,900
Robbery	98,210	Weapons; carrying, possessing, etc.	120,400
Aggravated assault	155,060	Prostitution and commercialized vice	51,700
Burglary—breaking or entering	358,100	Sex offenses (except forcible rape and prostitution)	59,700
Larceny—theft	748,200	Narcotic drug laws	415,600
Auto theft	153,300	Gambling	91,700
		Offenses against family and children	78,500
Violent crime	287,550	Driving under the influence	555,700
Property crime	1,259,600	Liquor laws	309,000
		Drunkenness	1,825,500
Subtotal for above offenses	1,551,300	Disorderly conduct	710,000
		Vagrancy	113,400
Other assaults	348,900	All other offenses (except traffic)	1,042,600
		Suspicion	83,500
		Curfew and loitering law violations	129,600
		Runaways	232,700

[1] Arrest totals based on all reporting agencies and estimates for unreported areas.

TASK FORCE REPORT: THE POLICE *(EXCERPT)*

The President's Commission on Law Enforcement and Administration of Justice

POLICE CONTACTS WITH CITIZENS ON THE STREET

It is extremely difficult for a policeman to maintain his composure in all street situations even though this is expected and demanded of him in nearly all police departments. For example, the Law Enforcement Code of Ethics, which has been adopted by nearly all departments and police associations, requires the following: [304]

> I will * * * maintain courageous calm in the face of danger, scorn, or ridicule; develop self-restraint; and be constantly mindful of the welfare of others.
>
> I will never act officiously or permit personal feelings, prejudices, animosities or friendships to influence my decisions * * *. I will enforce the law courteously and appropriately without fear or favor, malice or ill will, never employing unnecessary force or violence * * *

But the capability of a policeman, and particularly one who works in a high-crime rate or slum neighborhood, to act in a restrained manner is constantly tested. There are countless pressures which increase the difficulty of performing police work calmly and with restraint. Typically, an officer is expected to maintain order on the street, to keep "a clean beat," to disperse mobs, to remove "undesirables," whether or not legal tools for accomplishing these results are available. A policeman's authority is daily challenged by unruly juveniles anxious to detect any weakness or fear. In dangerous neighborhoods, he may be mocked, threatened, or even spat upon. Police work requires that policemen continually see the tragedy of victimized citizens and the sordid lives of the reprehensible and unfortunate elements of the community. And, a policeman must always live with the prospect that he may be subject to attack without warning.

Even if an officer is of the highest quality, his work and the people with whom he must deal may cause him to become disillusioned or angry. If he is not of the highest quality or if he has not been properly trained, if he is

TASK FORCE REPORT: THE POLICE, 1967, Washington, D.C. U.S. Government Printing Office, pp. 179-190.

prejudiced or hotheaded, he may succumb to his anger or resentment and physically or verbally abuse someone who offends him.

The problems of police-citizen contacts are multiplied and exacerbated when the citizens involved are youths. Youths commit a large and increasing proportion of crimes. They are out and around, noticeable to the patrolling officer. They travel in groups, which may make them appear more suspicious and at least potentially harder to control. They spend time in such local gathering places as pool halls, recreation centers, record shops, and street corners, and they often acquire information useful to the police. The antipathy toward the police that they might have at any age by virtue of race, neighborhood, or experience is heightened by youth's natural dislike for authority.

It is hardly surprising that youths and policemen are not always on the best of terms. Various factors influence their reactions to and relations with each other. Informal street contacts are rarely recorded, and little factual information is available about their real extent and nature. Several recent studies and field research projects, however, have begun to explore the causes of friction between police and juveniles.

In one study, a series of interviews was conducted with San Francisco gang boys—white, Mexican, and Negro—over a 2-year period.[305] While the survey was limited to gang members, it has broader significance both because its observations and analyses deal with activities of the boys independent of their gangs and because gangs and their members probably have greater contact than other youths with the police.

As the San Francisco observers point out, besides needing to obtain information from youths and to apprehend them when they have violated the law, the police also feel an obligation to receive respectful behavior from them, both to symbolize their law-abiding attitude and to attest their acceptance of the particular police officer's authority. The youths in question, however, feel an equal need to establish and maintain their autonomy—a need that, in the case of many lower class gang boys, has been a way of life since they were children and successfully asserted their independence of overworked, ineffectual, or absent parents. One of the most tangible ways in which gang boys assert autonomy is their claim to control of a street corner, city block, or other geographical area as the inviolable site of their activities. But the gang's private hangout is also the policeman's beat and:[306]

Although the boys attempt either subtly or violently to convince outsiders that their behavior at the hangout is a strictly private affair, the police tend to insist with equal conviction that all behavior on public property is their legitimate concern.

According to one sociologist, the Chicago police illustrate the conflict by saying, when displeased by a gang's hangout behavior, "Give me that corner!" [307]

The struggle for street corner control may be the backdrop for encounters between police and juveniles, but it is the more pointed, circumscribed encounters—stops, searches, trips to the stationhouse—that shape their views of each other. As the San Francisco sociologists point out, when policemen are suspicious of youths in a strange neighborhood, or their furtive actions, or their gathering together in groups, they are often supported in their suspicions by common sense and experience, as well as by want of alternative means to solve crimes and preserve public order. But feeling themselves both demeaned and challenged, the youths may react with more or less open defiance and hostility, slouching or smirking or answering the officers in an offhand or uncooperative manner, thereby challenging the policeman, in turn, to "put-up-or-shut-up." In that situation the officers, fearful of losing face and sacrificing authority on future occasions, may feel virtually forced either to arrest the juveniles for a vague or minor offense (suspicion of robbery, loitering, disturbing the peace, violating curfew regulations) or to make it appear that they are being let go out of the goodness of the officer's heart. The San Francisco study concludes that "this is why criminal records of many gang boys are often heavily laced with such charges as 'suspicion of robbery' and 'suspicion of rape.' " [308] Similarly, a study of disorderly conduct arrests of both adults and juveniles in the District of Columbia found that in almost a quarter of them the arrest had been made only for loud and boisterous talking or obscene remarks to the police. [309]

The San Francisco gang study, in taped interviews of youths, found that the appearances of authority thereby gained is more than offset by the resentment and disrespect created: [310]

> One day we were standing on the corner about three blocks from school and this juvenile officer comes up. He say, "Hey you boys! Come here!" So everybody else walked over there. But this one stud made like he didn't hear him. So the cop say, "Hey punk! Come here!" So the stud sorta look up like he hear him and start walking over. But he walking over real slow. So the cop walk over there and grab him by the collar and throw him down and put the handcuffs on him, saying, "When I call you next time come see what I want!" So everybody was standing by the car, and he say, "All right you black * * *! Get your * * * home!" Just like that. And he handcuffed the stud and took him to juvenile hall for nothing. Just for standing there looking at him.

Demeanor appears to affect police disposition after arrest as well as arrest in the first instance. Juvenile officers and patrolmen interviewed in the San Francisco study estimated that demeanor is the major factor in 50 to 60 percent of juvenile dispositions.[311] Another study of juvenile offenders reports police officials in agreement that "defiance on the part of a boy will lead to juvenile court quicker than anything else." [312] The more general significance of demeanor is illustrated by a study of a western police department, in which it was found that charges against speeders, prostitutes, and other offenders depended in large part on the suspect's demeanor.[313]

Not all policemen equate unusual attire or surroundings with actual or potential lawlessness, and not all interpret defiance as need or justification for custody. This distinction is not lost on youths: [314]

> Those two studs out in Lakeview wouldn't always be on our back for playing neither. We'd be standing on the corner pulling some kinda phoney (!) * * *, and they'd pull up to find out if we was up to something. But they talked to us nice. They wouldn't let us get away with nothing, and, I mean, them cats would bust you if they had to. But they talked to us nice.

Such officers—as the gang boy himself points out—are not necessarily softer, more lenient, or less effective. But by avoiding ethnic slurs, by recognizing and making allowance for the exuberance and the naturally combative and nonconforming attitudes of adolescents, these policemen allow adolescents to escape the uncomfortable spotlight of constant suspicion. Such a spotlight is not only frequently undeserved but it may encourage the youths to act as their audience, the police officers, appear to expect.

Verbal Abuse and Discourtesy

Commission studies reveal that there are abuses in some cities which range from simple discourtesy to clearly unwarranted excessive use of force against persons of all ages. In focusing on such abuses, it is important to bear in mind that in the large majority of instances officers were observed to handle themselves with courage and often with restraint. Therefore, it is important that the following material not be read as a general description of the conduct of all police officers, but rather as a description of certain conduct which cannot be tolerated regardless how frequent or infrequent it may be.

No matter is more important to police-community relations than the manner in which police officers talk to people on the street. The Michigan State survey found that while allegations of excessive physical force receive the most attention, verbal abuse and discourtesy were probably greater irritants to community relations.[315] If officers are abusive, insulting, or condescending, the most insignificant contact can become an occasion which arouses hostility against the police. On the other hand, if police officers are polite, forthright, respectful, and, where appropriate, friendly, a field interrogation, a traffic ticket, or even an arrest can actually increase the respect of the citizen, as well as others who see the incident, for the police.

Commission surveys revealed that a number of officers treat citizens in a demeaning manner. In one Commission study, observations were made in several cities of several hundred routine contacts between police and citizens, usually in a home or on the street. Most of the persons interviewed were witnesses, bystanders, and victims, rather than suspects. The study showed 9 percent of the persons received a polite request from the officers; 5 percent received an impersonal summons which was neither polite nor nasty; 66 percent were interrogated without introduction; and 15 percent of the interrogations began with a brusque or nasty command like "Come 'ere, punk" or "Get your * * * over here, pork chop." [316]

Discriminatory statements, in particular, produce both anger and strong counterprejudice among minority groups.[317] The use of racial epithets, such as "nigger," "coon," "boy," and "Pancho" appears to be widespread, even though their use is condemned by responsible police administrators. The President's Commission on Crime in the District of Columbia found that "offensive terms such as 'boy' or 'nigger' are too often used by officers of the Department" and that "in most cases, the language is chosen deliberately to demean the citizen and demonstrate the superiority of the officer." [318] And a study of police handling of juveniles in two police departments stated that, while the observer never heard derogatory remarks made to Negroes by officers on the professionalized force, he heard dozens of insults and derogatory remarks by officers in the less professionalized department.[319] It is precisely this type of language which solidifies the conflict between minority groups and the police.

Many police departments have regulations which require that citizens be treated with courtesy and respect and train their officers accordingly. One of the most far-reaching is that of the San Diego Police Department: [320]

> *We should treat all juveniles as we would want our own children treated, even the "hard core young hoodlum,"* for our job is to help juveniles toward good citizenship and build respect for the police and not to create "cop-haters" and criminals. *Always be fair, impartial, honest, and constructive.* [Emphasis in original.]

A similar rule might properly be applied to adults as well.[321]

But the general instructions of most departments are neither sufficiently forceful nor specific as to the manner in which police officers should conduct themselves with regard to citizens. General police statements concerning the need for courtesy are not enough. All departments, for example, should formulate clear policies which prohibit the use of racial epithets. A similar recommendation was made by the President's Commission on Crime in the District of Columbia:[322]

> The chief of police should issue a directive concerning verbal abuse of citizens by police officers, which identifies and prohibits the use of trigger words such as "boy" or "nigger." The Metropolitan Police Department should make it clear that violation of its order will be cause for disciplinary procedures. Current department statements on the subject, which urge that "undue familiarity with the use of such terms as 'bud,' 'Junior,' 'Mac,' be avoided," are neither sufficiently forceful nor directly related to the problems of the community.

Shortly after that report, the chief of police issued a more specific directive than had previously existed.

Other police departments also prohibit certain forms of address. For example, the Chicago Police Department has the following policy:[323]

> At all times Departmental personnel will:
>
> 1. Never show any bias or prejudice against race, religion, or any other group or individual.
>
> 2. Act, speak, and conduct themselves in such a manner as to treat all persons with complete courtesy and with that respect due to every person as a human being.
>
> 3. Never "talk down" to any group or individual or engage in the use of derogatory terms such as "nigger," "boy," "wop," "kike," "chink," "shine," "burrhead," "dago," "polack," "bohunk," and the like * * *.

Some departments, such as Baltimore, require that their officers address persons as Mr. ----------, Mrs. ----------, Sir, or Madam.[324] Such forms of address should be used as a matter of common courtesy.

Of course, it is often difficult for officers to be respectful when dealing with citizens who are abusive or disrespectful. But, as was expressed by the President's Commission on Crime in the District of Columbia after it deplored the use of abusive language both by police and citizens: "Officers must be held to a higher standard of conduct in performing their official duties."[325] This view was also expressed by O. W. Wilson, the superintendent of police in Chicago:[326]

> The officer * * * must remember that there is no law against making a policeman angry and that he cannot charge a man with offending him. Until the citizen acts overtly in violation of the

law, he should take no action against him, least of all lower himself to the level of the citizen by berating and demeaning him in a loud and angry voice. The officer who withstands angry verbal assaults builds his own character and raises the standard of the department.

Consequently, if citizens show disrespect for an officer, such conduct, alone, while reprehensible, does not justify making an arrest or taking other action.

Finally, police officers should be encouraged to talk to citizens about nonpolice matters while on duty, as they are in New York, rather than prohibited from conducting such conversations with citizens.[327] The BSSR survey of three Washington, D.C., precincts shows that hostility in Negro males declines as informal contacts with the police increase.[328] These contacts allow the police to establish friendships rather than having solely the role of making arrests and interrogations.

Physical Misconduct

Unjustified use of force, like verbal abuse, cannot be tolerated in law enforcement. Many persons, and particularly those from minority groups, believe that police officers sometimes or even frequently engage in excessive or unnecessary physical force. The Commission was not able to determine the extent of physical abuse by policemen in this country since recent studies have generally not been systematic. Earlier studies, however, found that police brutality was a significant problem. For example, the National Commission on Law Observance and Enforcement (the Wickersham Commission), which reported to President Hoover in 1931, found considerable evidence of police brutality.[329] The President's Commission on Civil Rights, appointed by President Truman, made a similar finding in 1947.[330] And in 1961, the U.S. Civil Rights Commission concluded that "police brutality is still a serious problem throughout the United States." [331]

The Commission believes that physical abuse is not as serious a problem as it was in the past. The few statistics which do exist suggest small numbers of cases involving excessive use of force.[332] Although the relatively small number of reported complaints cannot be considered an accurate measure of the total problem, most persons, including civil rights leaders, believe that verbal abuse and harassment, not excessive use of force, is the major police-community relations problem today.[333] It is clear, however, that excessive force remains a serious problem in parts of the South. There are too many well-documented instances of brutality against Negroes and civil rights workers in the recent past to doubt that it still occurs today. For example, during the Mississippi march in the summer of 1966, State, county and local law enforcement officers on several occasions struck demonstrators.[334] On numerous other occasions, law enforcement officers have watched white citizens attack civil rights demonstrators or have otherwise failed to prevent or halt private violence.[335]

Moreover, one study undertaken by the Commission also determined that excessive use of force still remains as a significant problem outside the South as well. During this study, Commission observers systematically accompanied police officers on regular patrol in a number of major cities—primarily in high crime and slum precincts—for periods ranging from 5 to 8 weeks. During the survey, observers witnessed, during 850 8-hour patrols, 5,339 police-citizen encounters—encounters which included police contacts with suspects, witnesses, victims, and bystanders. While watching these encounters, Commission observers reported that there were 20 instances where officers used force where none was clearly required or where its use was plainly excessive. Of the incidents observed, most did not appear to be based upon racial prejudice. More than half of those subjected to excessive force were white. Almost all of the victims appeared to be poor. They included drunks, sexual deviates, or juveniles who were regarded by the police as hoodlums, and most appeared to contest verbally the police officer's authority.[336] Three of the 20 examples of the incidents observed are as follows: [337]

> White officers responded to a man with a gun * * * and heard three shots fired. Then the white man with the gun got a drop on the officer—somehow they got the gun away and handcuffed him (gun was a 12 gauge 1905 musket). When they got him to the station garage, they kicked him all over, but the principal one was the officer who had been in danger when the man had the drop on him. He beat him as the others held him up. I got to the scene and the lockup man whistled for them to stop but they didn't. The Lieutenant arrived with everyone else and said there's going to be a beef on this one so cover it up and go find the empty shells. Someone call an ambulance (he needed it badly). Then the Lieutenant took complete control. They got the shells, got a complainant who said the three shots were an attempt to kill the officer, and he would sign a complaint, say he called an ambulance, etc. They wrote a cover for the incident. The officer who beat the man most was shaken by then but the others gave him support, telling him how brave he was and how wise he had been not to kill the guy at the scene, etc. They then set about to put all the stories in order and I was carefully notified of it in detail so I would have it straight. I had enough rapport with these officers that they talked about it even after. The man was in pretty bad shape when he got to the hospital.

* * * * *

The officers were flagged down by a white man and woman. "The man who flagged us down said a Negro was inside the (public transportation station) causing trouble. The woman said he had sworn at her as did the man. One said: 'What's a nigger doing here; he should be down on * * *' The two white officers went in and grabbed him. They shoved him into a phone booth. Both officers beat him with fists and a flashlight and also hit him in the groin, then they dragged him out and kept him on his knees. He said he had just been released from a mental hospital that day. He begged them not to hit him again and let him go back to the hospital. One officer said: 'Don't you like us Nigger; we're here to help you! You're a crazy nigger.' They took him to the car and he kept begging them not to hurt him. Then they put him on the wrong bus—he wanted to go to the hospital and they sent him the wrong way. The last thing the Negro man said was: 'You police just like to shoot and beat people.' Officer No. 1 said: 'Get moving nigger or I'll shoot you.' The offender was crying and bleeding as he was put on the bus. Officer No. 2 said: 'He won't be back.' "

* * * * *

The dispatch was drunks in a cemetery. "We found the drunks sleeping in the cemetery. They were white men between 25 and 45 years of age. Officer No. 1 (white) ripped the shirt off one drunk in searching him. He also hit him in the groin with his nightstick. Officer No. 2 ripped back of pants of another drunk. The officers laughed as they forced them to climb over the fence and they laughed because the buttocks of the one was completely exposed. One officer said: 'I ought to run you * * * in.' As they left over the fence, another said: 'Those * * * * * won't be back—a bunch of * * * winos.' "

While this limited study gave the Commission no basis for stating the extent to which police officers use force, it did confirm that such conduct still exists in the cities where observations were made.

One other study conducted in a large city revealed that when juveniles show disrespect to officers, many of the officers prefer to settle the challenge to their authority by physical means. This study indicated that certain officers would justify their use of force by deliberately provoking the juvenile until he could be considered to be resisting arrest. This technique is described in the statements of one police officer and one juvenile taken during interviews in this city: [338]

For example, when you stop a fellow for a routine questioning, say a wise guy, and he starts talking back to you and telling you that you are no good and that sort of thing. You know you can take a man in on a disorderly conduct charge, but you can practically never make it stick. So what you do in a case like this is to egg the guy on until he makes a remark where you can justifiably slap him, and then if he fights back, you can call it resisting arrest.

* * * * *

Another reason why they beat up on you is because they always have the advantage over you. The cop might say, "You done this." And you might say, "I didn't!" And he'll say, "Don't talk back to me or I'll go upside your head!" You know, and then they say they had a right to hit you or arrest you because you were talking back to an officer or resisting arrest, and you were merely trying to explain or tell him that you hadn't done what he said you'd done. One of those kinds of things. Well, that means you in the wrong when you get downtown anyway. You're always in the wrong.[339]

A survey of policemen in one midwestern city in 1951 also indicated that many officers had misconceptions about when they are justified in using force. Officers were asked to respond to this question: "When do you think a policeman is justified in roughing a man up?" They gave the following responses: [340]

Reason	*Percentage*
Disrespect for police	37
To obtain information	19
For the hardened criminal	7
When you know the man is guilty	3
For sex criminals	3
When impossible to avoid	23
To make an arrest	8

The interviews provided considerable detail concerning the officers' rationale. They believed that the use of force to obtain evidence which would justify an arrest in a felony case was acceptable—"to rough him up a little, up to a point * * * You feel that the end justifies the means." [341] Force was seen to be permissible with sex criminals when the officer knew that a person was guilty, did not have enough evidence, and considered it necessary to ensure that the criminal was punished. The officers said that force was justified in cases involving disrespect such as: [342]

I was on the beat, and I was taking [a man] down to the station. There were people following us. He kept saying that I wasn't in the army. Well, he kept going on like that, and I finally had to bust him one. I had to do it. The people would have thought I was afraid otherwise.

The officers believed that the only way to treat certain groups of people, including Negroes and the poor, is to treat them roughly.[343] On the other hand, this study did conclude that illegal force was not used as frequently and with as little provocation as the officers' statements would suggest.

To prevent physical abuse by police officers requires that all police departments take great care in selecting personnel, formulate strong policies on permissible conduct, dismiss officers who engage in physical misconduct, regularly review personnel practices, comprehensively investigate all complaints made against individual officers, and strongly discipline those officers who misbehave. Methods for accomplishing this are described in chapters 2 and 3 of this volume. Policies should be formulated to bar not only unnecessary force but describe, to the extent possible, the amount of force which is permissible for making arrests and carrying out other police activities. Such policies can best be enforced if all officers who use physical force for any reason are required to report in writing the circumstances under which the force was used.[344]

Discrimination

The University of California study found that members of minority groups in Philadelphia and San Diego generally believed that discrimination is practiced against both middle class and poor persons from minority groups.[345] Polls of minority groups show similar results.[346] It is extremely difficult to establish the extent to which such allegations are accurate since discrimination is likely to be only one of several factors which affect an officer's decision in any particular situation. Negroes, other minority groups, and the poor are arrested and probably stopped in disproportion to their numbers. However, these groups frequently live in high-crime areas. Consequently, normal, completely fair police work would doubtless produce the arrest or stopping of larger numbers of these groups.

Two studies of referrals to juvenile courts in several cities found that the police referred significantly more Negro than white juveniles for the same types of offenses, particularly for minor offenses.[347] Another study of police handling of juveniles in two large cities found that the eastern, nonprofessional police force referred three times as many Negro juveniles to court as whites. On the other hand, the western, more professional police force tended to treat similar types of offenders alike.[348] And, the Commission's study, based on observation of routine police work in several northern cities, found that the police did not discriminate between whites and Negroes of the same economic class; instead, police conduct seemed to depend on economic status and on whether the person was a drunk, a homosexual, or otherwise an outcast.[349]

As was described earlier, a high percentage of Negroes believe that the police provide inadequate protection in minority communities.[350] Lack of protection can take the form of police being slow to respond to calls, having inadequate personnel, or tending to ignore offenses by one minority person against another in contrast to those by members of minority groups against whites or whites against whites. While the lack of attention paid to investigating violations against others of the same race is probably decreasing, it still exists in many localities.[351] For example, the American Bar Foundation study undertaken in mid-1950's found that it exists especially in large cities and particularly as to serious offenses such as aggravated assault.[352]

Police officers should not base decisions to arrest, stop, use force, or the like, in whole or in part, on race, poverty, or civil rights activity. All decisions must be based on objective evidence which creates suspicion, proof of guilt, or threat of danger to the officer or public, as the law requires.

Field Interrogation

In many communities, field interrogations are a major source of friction between the police and minority groups. Many minority group leaders strongly contend that field interrogations are predominantly conducted in slum communities, that they are used indiscriminately, and that they are conducted in an abusive and unfriendly manner.

The police consider field interrogations to be an important method of preventing and investigating crime, since they rarely encounter a crime in progress. Normally, by the time a police officer has arrived at a crime scene. the perpetrator has fled, people have gathered, and confusion has ensued. Further, the police believe that they can prevent much crime if they are permitted to stop and question persons whose behavior strongly suggests that a criminal act is being contemplated:[353]

> A law enforcement officer in the performance of his duties will be confronted with innumerable situations in which it seems necessary to make some inquiry of a person whose name he does not know, and whom, if further action is not taken, he is most unlikely ever to find again. An inquiry may appear appropriate because such a person is behaving in a suspicious or unusual manner which suggests a possible involvement in crime. Thus, he may be a person running with a heavy package at 2:00 a.m. in a business neighborhood. Or he may correspond to a description of the perpetrator of a recent crime, but because he is traveling in an automobile it is impossible to be sure. Or he may be walking slowly down a street at night, looking into the windows of parked cars.
>
> The person to whom the officer would like to direct an inquiry may clearly not be involved in criminality. He may be a person who was near the scene of a crime, and thus a potential source of information. Or it may be impossible to tell in advance whether the person to be stopped is a suspect or a source of information.

The limits of police authority to stop persons briefly for purposes of criminal investigation are unclear in most jurisdictions. In some States, there is specific statutory authority for officers to stop suspicious persons. For example, a recently enacted statute in New York gives an officer authority to stop for questioning a person whom "he reasonably suspects is committing, has committed, or is about to commit" a felony or other specified crimes and authorizes the officer to use whatever force is necessary to effectuate such stops.[354]

In most States, however, there is no specific statute which defines this authority. As a result, police departments are given little guidance as to when a person may be stopped, whether or how long he may be detained, whether force may be used to detain him, what degree of force may be used, whether a person may be searched, whether he may be compelled to answer certain questions, and under what circumstances he must be advised of his legal rights.

A few police departments have policies governing the conduct of field interrogations. Training materials of the Oakland, Calif. Police Dept., for example, carefully describe the types of persons who should be stopped;[355] the San Diego, Calif. Police Dept. specifically forbids officers to restrain persons being questioned against their will;[356] and the Tampa, Fla. Police Dept. defines conditions under which a person may be searched.[357]

The Commission believes that there is a definite need to authorize the police to stop suspects and possible witnesses of major crimes, to detain them for brief questioning if they will not voluntarily cooperate, and to search such suspects for dangerous weapons when such a precaution is necessary. This need was also recognized by the reporters for the American Law Institute Model Pre-Arraignment Code Project:[358]

> If, as some have argued, the only power to restrain a person, even briefly, is by arresting him on reasonable grounds to believe him guilty of a crime, the police will be foreclosed from responding to confused, emergency situations in the way that seems most natural and rational. For in such circumstances, where a crime may have been committed and a suspect or important witness is about to disappear, it seems irrational to deprive the officer of the opportunity to "freeze" the situation for a short time, so that he may make inquiry and arrive at a considered judgment about further action to be taken. To deny the police such a power would be too high a price in effective policing and in the police's respect for the good sense of the rules that govern them, in order to avoid brief inconveniences that most innocent persons would be prepared to undergo.

Misuse of field interrogations, however, is causing serious friction with minority groups in many localities. This is becoming particularly true as more police departments adopt "aggressive patrol" in which officers are encouraged routinely to stop and question persons on the street who are unknown to them, who are suspicious, or whose purpose for being abroad is not readily evident. The Michigan State survey found that both minority group leaders and persons sympathetic to minority groups throughout the country were almost unanimous in labelling field interrogation as a principal problem in police-community relations:[359]

> * * * race has an undue influence on who is stopped.
>
> * * * practice is o.k., but the way it was carried out was unfriendly, abusive, etc. Not against method, but how it is used.
>
> Personally, I found it offensive and was affronted on occasions of its use in New York.
>
> Spanish-Americans are picked up sooner.
>
> Many Negroes stopped in other neighborhoods and questioned. Happens more to Negroes than to others.

The Commission has found that field interrogations, used sometimes in conjunction with aggressive, preventive patrol, are often conducted on a broad-scale basis by many police departments. First, field interrogations are often conducted with little or no basis for suspicion. In San Diego, written reports were made of over 200,000 stops in 1965 and there were probably about as many stops which were not recorded.[360] The effect on attitudes which can result is revealed by the following comment of a lower income Negro:[361]

> When they stop everybody, they say, well, they haven't seen you around, you know, they want to get to know your name, and all this. I can see them stopping you one time, but the same police stopping you every other day, and asking you the same old question.

A study of juvenile offenses in a western city with high police standards found that Negroes were stopped more frequently than other juveniles "often even in the absence of evidence that an offense had been committed."[362]

Second, field interrogations are sometimes used in a way which discriminates against minority groups, the poor, and the juvenile. For example, the Michigan State survey found, on the basis of riding with patrol units in two cities, that members of minority groups were often stopped, particularly if found in groups, in the company of white people, or at night in white neighborhoods, and that this caused serious problems.[363] Similarly, in a midwestern city, using aggressive patrol and field interrogations seems to cause, as in San Diego, the major problem in police-community relations.[364] In contrast, in Philadelphia the field interrogation is used less and is not a major item of criticism by minority groups or others.[365]

Finally, field interrogations are frequently conducted in a discourteous or otherwise offensive manner which is particularly irritating to the citizen. For example, even in San Diego, where officers are instructed specifically and at length to give the citizen an explanation and to act courteously,[366] the University of California study found that an explanation is frequently not given. In some cities, searches are made in a high proportion of instances not for the purpose of protecting the officer but to obtain drugs or other incriminating evidence. In New York, for example, where searches are permitted only when the officer reasonably believes he is in bodily danger, searches were made in 81.6 percent of stops reported.[367] However, a Commission survey of police practices in several large cities, found that one out of every five persons frisked was carrying a dangerous weapon—10 percent were carrying guns and another 10 percent knives.[368]

While the same problems exist as to field interrogations of juveniles as with adults, there are also additional difficulties. As was described earlier, juveniles are subjected to particularly close scrutiny by police officers. The study in San Francisco, for example, found that juveniles are frequently stopped when they travel outside their own neighborhoods:[369]

> If we go someplace, they tell us to go on home. Because every time we go somewhere we mostly go in big groups and they don't want us. One time we was talking in Steiner Street. So a cop drove up and he say, "Hey! Hanky and panky! Come here!" And he say, "You all out of bounds, get back on the other side of Steiner Street."
>
> * * * * *
>
> If boys from Hunter's Point or Fillmore [Negro neighborhoods in San Francisco] go in all white districts, the police will stop you and ask you where you from. If you say Fillmore or Hunter's Point, they'll take you down to the station and run checks on you. Any burglaries, any purse snatchings, anything.

The same study also found that the police are suspicious and make field interrogations of certain individuals because of clothing, hair, and walking mannerisms:[370]

> Why do they pick us up? They don't pick everybody up. They just pick up on the ones with the hats on and trench coats and conks [a Negro hair style]. If you got long hair and hats on, something like this one, you gonna get picked up. Especially a conk. And the way you dress. Sometimes, like if you've got on black pants, better not have on no black pants or bends [a kind of trouser] or levis. They think you going to rob somebody. And don't have a head scarf on your head. They'll bust you for having a head scarf.
>
> * * * * *
>
> The way you walk sometimes. * * * Don't try to be cool. You know. They'll bust you for that. * * * Last night a cop picked me up for that. He told me I had a bad walk. He say, "You think you're bad."

White youths who wear the clothes and have the look of possible delinquents are likewise stopped sometimes without evidence of criminality.[371]

The study concluded that the juveniles understood being sought and interrogated for their illegal activity: [372]

> If you done something and you be lying and yelling when the boys from juvy come around and they catch you lying, well, what you gonna do? You gonna complain 'cause you was caught? Hell man, you can't do that. You did something and you was caught and that's the way it goes.

But they were indignant about field interrogation for offenses they did not commit—when "we were just minding our own business when the cops came along." And they particularly resented being singled out because of their clothes or hair: "Hell man, them cops is supposed to be out catching criminals! They ain't paid to be lookin' after my *hair!*" [373] The juveniles consider this harassment by the police as a policy of confinement by a "foreign army of occupation." [374]

In order to balance the need for field interrogations and the harmful effect on police-community relations which may result from their indiscriminate use, State legislatures should define the extent of police authority to stop and question persons, and police departments should adopt detailed policies governing this authority whether or not legislation exists. Such legislation and policies should have the following principles:

- ☐ Field interrogations should be conducted only when an officer has reason to believe that a person is about to commit or has committed a crime, or that a crime has been committed and he has knowledge of material value to the investigation.
- ☐ Field interrogations should not be used at all for minor crimes like vagrancy and loitering.
- ☐ Adequate reason should be based on the actions of the person, his presence near the scene of a crime, and similar factors raising substantial suspicion, and not on race, poverty, or youth.
- ☐ The stop should be limited in time.[375] The sole purposes should be: (*a*) to obtain the citizen's identification; (*b*) to verify it by readily available information; (*c*) to request cooperation in the investigation of a crime; and (*d*) to verify by readily available information any account of his presence or any other information given by the person.
- ☐ The citizen should be addressed politely and should receive a suitable explanation of the reason for the stop.
- ☐ An officer should be allowed to conduct a search of the person only if he has reason to believe that his safety or the safety of others so requires.
- ☐ Officers should be required to file a report each

time a stop is made in order to record the circumstances and persons involved.[376] Even greater care should be taken with these records, than with arrest records so that the police do not use them to establish the delinquency or bad character of the person stopped. Moreover, the records should not be available to persons outside of public law enforcement agencies.

One of the most difficult questions in connection with a stop and attendant search is whether the results or fruits of a search other than weapons, should be used by police. While there are serious objections to barring evidence of crime discovered in a lawful search, the admissibility of evidence such as betting slips or narcotics found during a stop may encourage the misuse of the search power.[377]

EXERCISE OF THE ARREST POWER

Arrests for Investigation

Although there is no legal basis for arresting persons simply as a means of detaining them while an investigation of their possible involvement in crime is conducted, this has been a common practice in a number of departments.

The American Bar Foundation study of police practices in three midwestern States found that in cities with substantial crime problems, arrests are often made on suspicion—such as refusing to answer questions or giving an equivocal answer during a field interrogation.[378] In 1960, the Washington, D.C. Police Department made 4,684 arrests for investigation, but only 257 (5.5 percent) of the arrested persons were ever charged with the commission of a specific offense. Of those arrested, 1,349 were held for 8 hours or more. This practice was abolished in 1963 as a result of a study in 1962 condemning it.[379]

In Detroit, from 1947 to 1956, 219,053 arrests of a total of 658,808 nontraffic arrests were listed by the police department as arrests for investigations.[380] In 1956, of 73,827 arrests, only 40,641 persons were formally charged with commission of an offense; 33,186, or 45 percent, were arrested for investigation. Of the latter, only 6,490 were subsequently charged with a crime and the others were released without charge. The suspect would be detained for an average of at least 3 days before release or before being brought before a magistrate. Authority for the practice was provided in the police manual.[381] The 1964 police department statistics still showed that 8,140 arrests out of 63,125 nontraffic arrests were classified merely as "detention."[382]

Sixteen of fifty-five departments responding to a Commission survey in 1966 admitted the use of investigative arrests.[383] In Baltimore, for example, 3,719 (6.6 percent) of the 56,160 nontraffic arrests during 1964 were recorded as arrests for investigation. Of those arrested on this basis, 98 percent were dismissed without going before a magistrate.[384]

Occasionally, police departments engage in dragnet arrests on suspicion after serious crimes have been committed. In Detroit, in December 1960 and January 1961, after a series of rapes and murders of women, persons were stopped on the street, searched, and in about 1,000 cases arrested.[385] In 1964, after two brothers killed one policeman and seriously wounded another, Baltimore police officers searched more than 300 homes, most belonging to Negroes, looking for the gunman. The searches were often made in the middle of the night and were based almost entirely on anonymous tips. The U.S. Court of Appeals for the Fourth Circuit stated: [386]

> Lack of respect for the police is conceded to be one of the factors generating violent outbursts in Negro communities. The invasions so graphically depicted in this case "could" happen in prosperous suburban neighborhoods, but the innocent victims know only that wholesale raids do not happen elsewhere and did happen to them. Understandably they feel that such illegal treatment is reserved for those elements who the police believe cannot or will not challenge them.

As reported in the Uniform Crime Reports prepared by the Federal Bureau of Investigation, 76,346 arrests for suspicion were listed for the year 1965, in jurisdictions with approximately 70 percent of the Nation's population.[387] These statistics almost certainly understate the number of investigative arrests in the country. In jurisdictions where the practice is not permitted, such arrests are frequently made by using the drunkenness, vagrancy, and other petty offense laws. [388] Similarly, the American Bar Foundation found that in the three States it studied, a common practice was to arrest a suspicious person and then book him for an offense which occurs frequently in the area or for an offense for which he resembled generally the person wanted.[389] A captain in a Kansas sheriff's department said that it was no problem to arrest a person without a specific offense in mind since "it is no difficult matter to find some sort of a 'want' on the State teletype that will fit the man's description." [390] An instructor in a training session said that "[It] is a poor policeman who cannot find a description to fit the suspect, as you officers have at least 30 days of daily bulletins in your notebooks." [391]

One nationally recognized governmental consulting firm, which has done considerable consulting with police agencies, recently reported that the widespread use of investigative arrests demonstrates inadequate policy, supervision, and investigative personnel: [392]

> The practice of allowing or perhaps even condoning such arrests reflects an unawareness of the impropriety and, in fact, the illegality of most such arrests. It has developed as a result of failure to formulate policy and adequate procedures on the part of the chief and the command staff.
>
> Aside from the legal and constitutional implications of arrests for "suspicion" or "for investigation," the frequency of occurrence of such arrests tends to reflect upon the competency and attitude of the investigator, and quality of investigations surrounding the cases for which these arrests are made * * *.
>
> Thus, it may be seen that departments and individual investigators who tend to rely heavily upon indiscriminate and casual arrests of known criminals, suspects, and others will generally perform rather inadequate and unprofessional investigations.

Arrests for investigation or on suspicion, whatever label is attached, should be abolished by all departments that now utilize them. This practice has long been a source of justified community hostility. They not only seriously inconvenience the citizen or even result in his incarceration, but they result in an arrest record which may greatly affect his present or future employment.

Arrests for Harassment

The police in some cities use their arrest power to harass persons whom they do not intend to prosecute because of insufficient evidence or because of the practice of the courts in giving light sentences. The harassment arrest is primarily used as a mechanism for annoying persons who are allegedly involved in vice practices such as prostitution, gambling, or illegal liquor sales. The American Bar Foundation study found in Detroit, during 1956–57, for example, over 1,000 arrests were made for gambling and liquor violations during a 6-month period in one precinct. Ultimately, however, only 60 cases were presented for prosecution.[393] These arrests were made because, as an assistant prosecutor commented: "the prosecutor's office and the police department are forced to find other means of punishing, harassing, and generally making life uneasy for the gamblers." [394]

The same study found that as many as 40 or 50 prostitutes a night were arrested and released the next day because they were found on the street in an area where prostitution was practiced and they had a prior record of arrests for prostitution. Negro women with white men were almost always charged. A police official asserted that the arrests were part of "a harassment program. The police department has no other means of dealing with prostitution." [395]

Similarly, in Cleveland, of 1,202 women arrested and taken to a particular precinct in a Negro area of Cleveland for investigation in connection with prostitution, 1,075 were Negro. Only 96 were charged. The 224 white men arrested were all released on the stated ground that they were needed to testify against the women. The uniform release of these men has been a cause of great resentment in the Negro community.[396]

While the police are under considerable pressure to contain vice within a community and to keep undesirable persons off the streets, the current practice of using the arrest power in situations in which there is no intent to submit the case for prosecution is deplorable. Police departments, therefore, should establish policies which specifically prevent illegal harassment arrests, and which direct that arrests be made only if probable cause exists that a crime has been committed.

Arrests for Minor Crimes

Arrests for minor crimes, such as vagrancy, disorderly conduct, use of obscene language, loitering, failure to move on, blocking the street or sidewalk, drunkenness, drinking in public, and curfew violations, constitute almost one-half of all arrests made each year in the United States.[397] There is evidence that such arrests create great antagonism against police officers in slum communities. For example, many complaints filed with the review board in Philadelphia involve such ordinances and not a single complaint has involved an incident during commission of a felony.[398] The reason for hostility resulting from minor crimes is probably that while most offenders know when they have committed major crimes and expect that they will be arrested for them, the issue as to most alleged minor crimes is not as clear and the offender does not usually believe, whether or not he has acted illegally, that he has done anything sufficiently wrong to justify arrest. The comments of two men in Harlem suggest the antagonism that can result: [399]

> A bunch of us could be playing some music, or dancing, which we have as an outlet for ourselves. We can't dance in the house, we don't have clubs or things like that, so we're out on the sidewalk, right on the sidewalk; we might feel like doing dancing, or one might want to play something on his horn. Right away here comes a cop. "You're disturbing the peace!" No one has said anything, you understand; no one has made a complaint. Everyone is enjoying themselves. But here comes one cop, and he'll want to chase everyone. And gets mad. I mean, he gets mad! We aren't mad. He comes into the neighborhood, aggravated and mad.
>
> * * * * *
>
> Last night, for instance, the officer stopped some fellas on 125th

Street * * *. [T]he officer said, "All right, everybody get off the street or inside!" Now, it's very hot. We don't have air-conditioned apartments in most of these houses up here, so where are we going if we get off the streets? We can't go back in the house because we almost suffocate. So we sit down on the curb, or stand on the sidewalk, or on the steps, things like that, till the wee hours of the morning, especially in the summer when it's too hot to go up. Now where were we going? But he came out with his nightstick and wants to beat people on the head, and wanted to—he arrested one fellow. The other fellow said, "Well, I'll move, but you don't have to talk to me like a dog."

Minor crime statutes are frequently misused. They are employed as a means of clearing undesirables or unsightly persons from the street or driving them out of town, aiding the police in detaining a suspected person during an investigation of a more serious crime, and regulating street activity in slum neighborhoods. Often, under pressure from the community, the police will "declare a war on bums, prostitutes, homosexuals, and narcotic traffickers" by making wholesale arrests for vagrancy, disorderly conduct, drunkenness, or loitering.[400] Justice William O. Douglas found that in Tucson, between 1958 and 1960, the poor were discouraged to come to the city for employment by the policy of picking "up any vags spotted within the city limits." [401] In 1966, a District of Columbia judge found that "the typical accused under [the vagrancy] law is a miserable derelict whose principal offense is poverty and affinity for cheap wine, or an individual, male or female, suspected of engaging in prostitution or homosexuality." [402] The court concluded that the "basic design" of the vagrancy law is "preventive conviction imposed upon those who because of their background and behavior are more likely than the general public to commit crimes and * * * the statute contemplates such convictions even though no overt criminal act has been committed or can be proved." [403] Recent studies of the use of public drunkenness statutes in two cities found that they were often employed to arrest skid row types who were not drunk but were aesthetically displeasing.[404] Until 1965, one department was arresting women under an ordinance which made it a crime for a "woman of notorious character" to walk or ride up "the streets of this city." [405]

This practice is even more harmful to a person than an unwarranted field interrogation, since the suspect is not merely stopped, but he is arrested and confined, at least until he can make bail. While such arrests may serve some investigative value to the police, there is grave question as to their propriety.

The American Bar Foundation, in its study of 1956–57, found that the "Police assume that these [vagrancy] statutes are intended primarily as aids to investigation." [406] For example, if the police desire to undertake an in-custody investigation of a person, and investigative arrests are not used, they often arrest a person for violating a vagrancy-type statute. In one observation made during the American Bar Foundation study, a man was seen near a pawn shop with a jacket on his arm. When questioned, he said that he was unemployed because he had just come to the city to find work and that he had no identification because his wallet had been stolen; he also gave other evasive answers. The officers arrested him for vagrancy because they suspected him of burglary but lacked evidence. Similarly, a man suspected of homicide was arrested for vagrancy so that a prolonged investigation could be made while he served his sentence.[407] Other statutes were found to be used for the same purpose. A man suspected of carrying narcotics, whom the officers did not have evidence to arrest, was arrested for a minor traffic violation which would ordinarily result in a warning and his car was searched.[408]

Arrests for failure to move on, loitering, blocking the sidewalk, or public drinking are predominantly made in slum neighborhoods. One reason is that more officers are stationed in these neighborhoods because of the greater amount of serious crime. As a result, residents sometimes charge "over policing" at the same time they seek more protection from crimes such as robbery and burglary. Minor crime statutes, however, are also more used in poor areas because it is harder to keep order there. As a precinct captain in Washington, D.C. stated: [409]

> We do tend to enforce the drunk laws more rigidly on 14th Street than in, say, Crestwood, a better part of the precinct. If we overlooked things on 14th Street, we would have a more serious problem.

The source of these difficulties in enforcement of minor crime statutes reaches beyond the police. The community often demands that the police rid the city of undesirable persons, harass persons engaged in vice activities, and keep the unsightly off the streets, even though the police do not have legal means of doing so.[410] Thus, until the public recognizes the dilemma facing the police in regulating such behavior, the police will continue to be placed in an untenable position.

As recommended in chapter 5 of the General Report, the content and use of minor crime statutes should be carefully reexamined in all communities. Obviously, certain minor crime statutes are necessary in order to regulate reasonable conduct on the street. If persons are disorderly and disturb others, if they block the streets and sidewalk, if they use obscene language in public, police action is warranted. Many existing statutes, however, which base criminality on suspicious conduct, a prior record, or poverty, are of questionable legal validity and usually of considerable harm to community relations.

At least some minor crime statutes should be eliminated. In chapter 9 of the General Report, the Commission recommended the abolition of criminal drunkenness statutes. Besides its other virtues, this would reduce the tension which frequently results, particularly in minority communities, from the arrest of drunks. The neighborhood reaction would doubtless be different if citizens knew, as the Commission recommends, that drunks were merely taken to a sobering up facility and then released or treated.

Most statutes which are used to regulate street conduct are so broad that almost unlimited discretion is given to the police officer to arrest persons on the street or, as with a failure-to-move-on statute, to regulate conduct by the threat of arrest. Such statutes should be amended to cover only conduct which reasonably disturbs the public or is an immediate threat to the peace. Even if this is done, however, there would still be a need for police departments to formulate guidelines concerning their permissible use.[411] The guidelines should clearly bar discriminatory enforcement of minor crime statutes either against individuals or in particular neighborhoods. The District of Columbia Crime Commission Report noted that "until recently, there were no criteria issued by the police to assist the officer in exercising * * * discretion wisely." [412]

Arrest Quotas

It is often alleged that police officers and perhaps even precincts have arrest quotas. As a result, it is contended, officers who have not made a sufficient number of arrests begin to make frivolous or marginally warranted arrests relating to minor crimes and that supervising officers order patrolmen to clear the streets of drunks and the like. The police, on the other hand, generally deny that such quotas exist.[413]

The difficulty in determining whether arrest quotas exist is that they need not be absolute requirements. The effect is virtually the same if precincts and individual officers are expected to make an approximate number of arrests as evidence that they are carrying out their responsibilities in a diligent and effective manner. Such expectations can be as effective as a regulation.

The Commission has little evidence that police forces use quotas for evaluating officers. Two Commission surveys did find, however, that, in both a midwestern and a western city, one means by which superior officers evaluated officers was by the number of field interrogations each had made.[414] In one of those cities a ranking officer stated: [415]

> Our first line supervisors [Sergeants] have a responsibility to keep statistics on each officer's production—not an average, but his production—to find out whether a particular officer's performance is consistent with what his [s]quad's average might be. As a result, if a particular man is low, we expect an explanation.

Police work is far too complicated and delicate a job to judge an officer's work or qualifications for promotion on the number of arrests he has made. Furthermore, arrest quotas, if they exist as either explicit requirements or implied expectations, can lead to improper activity by policemen. Patrolling officers have the complex and difficult responsibility of exercising their discretion based on the circumstances of the particular case. No part of this calculation should consist of the number of arrests the officer has made in comparison to a preestablished quota or expectation set by the department.

USE OF FIREARMS TO APPREHEND OR ARREST SUSPECTS

Police use of firearms to apprehend suspects often strains community relations or even results in serious disturbances. For example, the San Francisco riot of 1966 started after a juvenile was shot and killed while fleeing from a stolen car.[416] Severe tensions were aroused in Los Angeles during May 1966, after an officer's firearm accidentally discharged and killed a man who had refused to stop his automobile until it was forced to the curb.[417] In St. Louis, disturbances began in September 1966 after police officers shot and killed a person who had his hands handcuffed behind him in a police car located in the courtyard of police headquarters. The police assert that the suspect threatened officers in the car with a tear gas pistol he had in his belt behind him which the officers had failed to find in a search earlier.[418]

When studied objectively and unemotionally, particular uses of firearms by police officers are often unwarranted. For example, an American Bar Foundation study revealed one instance where a foot patrolman signaled a speeding driver to stop. When the driver did not, the officer fired five times at the speeding car.[419]

A study by an American Civil Liberties Union affiliate in a medium-sized city found that officers fired guns more than 300 times in a 2-year period and over one-third were during automobile chases involving juveniles.[420] An average of 240 persons per year were fatally injured by police between 1950 and 1960.[421] The Michigan State study concluded that police officers often use guns indiscriminately and that this was due, in large part, to overemphasis of danger in police work.[422] While the murder of a single police officer is a tragedy, as of 1955, the rate of total police fatalities while on duty (including accidents) was 33 fatalities per 100,000 officers which was less than the rate of deaths on duty in mining (94), agriculture (55), construction (76), and transportation (44).[423]

It is surprising and alarming that few police departments provide their officers with careful instruction on the circumstances under which the use of a firearm is permissible. For example, a 1961 survey of Michigan police forces found that 27 out of 49 had no firearms policies.[424] A survey in 1964, of 45 of the 51 American cities of over 250,000 population, found that 3 had no written firearms policy,[425] and, while others had comprehensive policy statements, many were quite limited. For example, one simply prohibited warning shots, one instructed its officers to "exercise the greatest possible caution," and 10 urged officers to use "good judgment."[426] While it is true that many departments have oral firearms policies, these policies have normally developed through customary practices that rarely are the product of careful analysis and are usually not well understood by patrolmen.[427]

It is essential that all departments formulate written firearms policies which clearly limit their use to situations of strong and compelling need. A department should even place greater restrictions on their use than is legally required. Careful review of the comprehensive firearms use policies of several departments and discussions with police administrators indicate that these guidelines should control firearms use:

1. Deadly force should be restricted to the apprehension of perpetrators who, in the course of their crime threatened the use of deadly force, or if the officer believes there is a substantial risk that the person whose arrest is sought will cause death or serious bodily harm if his apprehension is delayed. The use of firearms should be flatly prohibited in the apprehension of misdemeanants, since the value of human life far outweighs the gravity of a misdemeanor.[428]

2. Deadly force should never be used on mere suspicion that a crime, no matter how serious, was committed or that the person being pursued committed the crime. An officer should either have witnessed the crime or should have sufficient information to know, as a virtual certainty, that the suspect committed an offense for which the use of deadly force is permissible.

3. Officers should not be permitted to fire at felony

suspects when lesser force could be used; when the officer believes that the suspect can be apprehended reasonably soon thereafter without the use of deadly force; or when there is any substantial danger to innocent bystanders. Although the requirement of using lesser force, when possible, is a legal rule, the other limitations are based on sound public policy. To risk the life of innocent persons for the purpose of apprehending a felon cannot be justified.

4. Officers should never use warning shots for any purpose. Warning shots endanger the lives of bystanders, and in addition, may prompt a suspect to return the fire. Further, officers should never fire from a moving vehicle.

5. Officers should be allowed to use any necessary force, including deadly force, to protect themselves or other persons from death or serious injury. In such cases, it is immaterial whether the attacker has committed a serious felony, a misdemeanor, or any crime at all.

6. In order to enforce firearms use policies, department regulations should require a detailed written report on all discharges of firearms. All cases should be thoroughly investigated to determine whether the use of firearms was justified under the circumstances.

If all departments formulated firearms use policies which include the above principles and these policies were consistently enforced, many of the tragic incidents which had a direct bearing upon community relations could have been avoided.

---

[304] Law Enforcement Code of Ethics. See ch. 7, Police Integrity.

[305] Carl Werthman and Irving Piliavin, "Gang Members and the Police," in David Bordua, ed., "The Police" (New York: John Wiley & Sons, 1967), pp. 56–98. The study of the police reported in this chapter was conducted by the Survey Research Center at the University of California under a grant from the National Institute of Mental Health. The study of gangs was carried out by the Survey Research Center and the Center for the Study of Law and Society at the University of California under grants from the Ford Foundation and the Department of Health, Education, and Welfare. Aaron V. Cicourel, whose recent study of police handling of juveniles in two California cities will appear in a forthcoming book, states that the "actual encounters [he] witnessed over a 4-year period support the Werthman analysis of the problem of police authority." ("The Social Organization of Juvenile Justice" ch. 7, p. 73, of unpublished manuscript.)

[306] Id. at p. 62.

[307] Ibid.

[308] Id. at p. 91.

[309] Patricia M. Wald and Joel E. Hoffman, "Report on the Disorderly Conduct Statute of the District of Columbia" (unpublished manuscript: July 16, 1966), p. 25.

[310] Supra, note 305 at p. 90–91.

[311] Id. at p. 74.

[312] Nathan Goldman, "The Differential Selection of Juvenile Offenders for Court Appearances" (Washington: National Council on Crime and Delinquency, 1963), p. 106.

[313] Supra, note 1 at pp. 90, 94, 95, 108, 111. See also the similar accounts of Philadelphia police officers in supra, note 21, vol. I, p. 112; vol. II, pp. 145, 146, 156, 168, and 169.

[314] Supra, note 305 at p. 68.

[315] Supra, note 22 at p. 17.

[316] Supra, note 184 at table 14.

[317] Supra, note 171 at pp. 46–48, 253, 257–258, 283, 301.
[318] Supra, note 77 at pp. 66–67.
[319] Supra, note 172 at p. 30.
[320] J. R. Laffoon, "Field Interrogation" (San Diego, Calif.: San Diego Police Department, July 1965), p. 38.
[321] Id. at pp. 41–44.
[322] Supra, note 77 at p. 74.
[323] Supra, note 22 at p. 187.
[324] Richard Severo, "Strong Police Command Vital to Avert More City Violence," the Washington Post, June 30, 1966, sec. A, p. 6, cols. 1, 2, 3.
[325] Supra, note 77 at p. 74.
[326] Supra, note 96 at p. 188.
[327] Thomas A. Johnson, "New Police Plan Used on Crowds," New York Times, July 25, 1966, p. 16, col. 6.
[328] For a similar result, see Donald Lowell Johns, "A Study of Some Factors Related to the Formation of Attitudes Toward the Police" (unpublished masters thesis, University of California at Berkeley, School of Criminology, 1966), pp. 122, 144.
[329] National Commission on Law Observance and Enforcement "Report on Lawlessness in Law Enforcement" (Washington: U.S. Government Printing Office, 1931).
[330] President's Commission on Civil Rights, "To Secure These Rights" (New York: Simon & Schuster, 1947), pp. 25–27.
[331] "The 50 States Report," submitted to the Commission on Civil Rights by the State Advisory Committees, 1961 (Washington: U.S. Government Printing Office, 1961), 687 p.
[332] In fiscal year 1965, FBI statistics show that there were only 9 convictions out of 1,787 cases of excessive force investigated and in fiscal 1966 there were 1,671 excessive force complaints investigated and only 3 resulted in convictions. These data were provided by Jerome Daunt, Chief, Uniform Crime Reporting Section, FBI, Mar. 7, 1967.
[333] Supra, note 22 at p. 66; Walter Gellhorn, "When Americans Complain" (Cambridge, Mass.: Harvard Press, 1966), pp. 176–177; William Raspberry, "Physical Violence May Be Gone, But Police Brutality Still Exists," the Washington Post, May 27, 1966, sec. B, p. 1, cols. 1, 2, 3.
[334] Gene Roberts, "Police Seize 11 in Rights March," New York Times, June 24, 1966, sec. 21, col. 4; "175 Negroes Are Pursued and Clubbed," the Washington Post, July 11, 1966, p. 1, col. 3. See supra, note 331 at p. 1.
[335] U.S. Commission on Civil Rights, "Law Enforcement: A Report on Equal Protection in the South" (Washington: U.S. Government Printing Office, 1965), pp. 174–175; "Court Told How Police Ignored Negro Beatings," the Washington Post, Sept. 16, 1966, sec. A, p. 6, cols. 1, 2. See also supra, note 331 at pp. 29–44, 105–109.
[336] Supra, note 207 at pp. 16–17.
[337] Id. at pp. 1, 2, and 8 of appendix.
[338] William A. Westley, "Violence and the Police," American Journal of Sociology, 59; 34–41, 38, as quoted in Werthman and Piliavin, supra, note 305 at pp. 92–93.
[339] Supra, note 305 at p. 93.
[340] Supra, note 338 at p. 38. Only one reason was counted—either that first mentioned or that given most heatedly or at greatest length—for each officer. Dr. Westley believed that the officers were cautious with him because of recent criticism by the chief of police and the community about the use of violence.
[341] Id. at p. 36.
[342] Id. at p. 39.
[343] Id. at p. 40.
[344] This was also recommended by Chief Stanley R. Schrotel in "Supervising the Use of Police Authority," Journal of Criminal Law, Criminology and Police Science, 47; 590–591.
[345] Supra, note 21 at vol. I, p. 78, 107; vol. II, pp. 105, 153.
[346] Supra, note 14 at 138.
[347] Supra, note 312 at pp. 42–44, 57–58, 65–67, 73–75, 88–89; supra, note 177 at p. 212.
[348] Supra, note 172 at pp. 9–10, 29–30.
[349] Supra, note 305; supra, note 184 at pp. 9–10, 14–17.
[350] Supra, note 21 at vol. I, p. 139.
[351] Supra, note 1 at p. 172; report to the U.S. Commission on Civil Rights, Delaware Advisory Committee, "50 States Report" (Washington: U.S. Government Printing Office, 1961), p. 92; George E. Simpson and J. Milton Yinger, "Racial and Cultural Minorities" (rev. ed.; New York: Harper & Brothers, 1958), pp. 511–512.
[352] Wayne R. LaFave, "Arrest: The Decision to Take a Suspect into Custody" (Boston: Little, Brown and Co., 1965), pp. 110–114.
[353] American Law Institute, "A Model Code of Pre-Arraignment Procedure; Tentative Draft No. 1," 1965, p. 95.
[354] New York Code Criminal Procedure § 180–a(1); see Uniform Arrest Act, § 2; supra, note 353 at pp. 6–10.
[355] Oakland Police Department, "Departmental Training Bulletin," Mar. 7, 1966.
[356] Supra, note 320 at pp. 41, 44.
[357] Tampa Police Department, "Training Bulletin," vol. XII, No. 6, Dec. 10, 1962, p. 3.
[358] Supra, note 353 at pp. 96–97.
[359] Supra, note 22 at pp. 333–334.
[360] San Diego Police Department, "Field Interrogation—Burglary Graph," (San Diego: San Diego Police Department, 1966); supra, note 21 at vol. I, p. 127.

361 Supra, note 21 at vol. I, p. 86.
362 Supra, note 177 at p. 212.
363 Supra, note 22 at pp. 327–336.
364 Supra, note 21 at vol. I, pp. 85, 127–128, 142.
365 Supra, note 21 at vol. II, pp. 170, 173.
366 Supra, note 1 at pp. 87–88; supra, note 360 at pp. 29–30, 43–44. The San Diego Department explicitly requires an explanation because of the sensitive community relations problems involved in field interrogations. The same is true of Oakland. See supra, note 355 at p. 8.
367 New York City Police Department, Quota Circular, Misc. 15, Oct. 13, 1965.
368 Albert J. Reiss, Jr., "Personal and Property Searches in Radio Dispatched Police Work: An Overview of the Data from Three Cities," (Ann Arbor: University of Michigan, 1966) pp. 4–6. A report prepared for the President's Commission on Law Enforcement and Administration of Justice. This report is a preliminary draft which is being included with the Commission's records in the National Archives. It is presently being revised and supplemented by the University of Michigan and will be embodied in research studies to be published by the Commission.
369 Supra, note 305 at pp. 77, 79.
370 Id. at p. 80.
371 Supra, note 177 at pp. 212, 213.
372 Supra, note 305 at p. 71.
373 Supra, note 305 at p. 82.
374 Supra, note 305 at p. 98.
375 Supra, note 353 at p. 6. The American Law Institute draft model statute specifies 20 minutes.
376 Some police forces now have such a requirement. See, e.g., St. Louis Police Department, "Special Order 60–S–122," Aug. 9, 1965, p. 1; New York Police Department Circular Order No. 25.
377 Supra, note 353 at p. 10. Reporters of the American Law Institute Pre-Arraignment Code have this issue under further study.
378 Supra, note 352 at pp. 249–250, 295.
379 "The Report and Recommendations of the Commissioner's Committee on Police Arrests for Investigation, Washington, D.C., July, 1962.
380 Harold Norris, "Arrests Without Warrant," "Crisis," October 1958, 65: 486.
381 Supra, note 352 at pp. 302, 306; Detroit Bar Association Committee on Civil Rights, "Report on Detroit Police Department Policy of 'Arrests For Investigation' " as published in "United States Commission on Civil Rights, hearings held in Detroit, Michigan," (Washington: U.S. Government Printing Office, 1961), p. 505.
382 See also Michigan Civil Rights Commission, "Report on Investigations of Law Enforcement Claims Against the Detroit Police Department," June 24, 1966, p. 4.
383 Supra, note 22 at p. 338.
384 Baltimore Police Department, "Annual Report" (1964), p. 33–43.
385 Arnold S. Trebach, "The Rationing of Justice" (New Brunswick: Rutgers University Press, 1964), p. 6.
386 *Lankford* v. *Gelston*, Fourth Cir., No. 10, 384, decided June 23, 1966, pp. 2, 3, 16, 17.
387 Federal Bureau of Investigation, "Uniform Crime Reports, 1965" (Washington: Department of Justice, 1966), p. 109.
388 The use of these statutes for investigative purposes is described more fully later in this chapter.
389 Supra, note 352 at p. 296.
390 Ibid.
391 Id. at p. 297.
392 Public Administration Service, "The Savannah Police Department, Part V: Guidelines to Measurement and Evaluation" (Chicago: Public Administration Service, 1964), p. 21, 22.
393 Supra, note 352 at p. 473.
394 Id. at p. 478.
395 Id. at p. 456.
396 U.S. Civil Rights Commission, staff memorandum. "Police-Community Relations, Cleveland, Ohio" (Feb. 21, 1966), pp. 3–4.
397 Supra, note 387 at pp. 108–109.
398 Supra, note 21, vol. II, at p. 232.
399 Kenneth B. Clark, "Dark Ghetto" (New York: Harper & Row, 1965), pp. 4–5.
400 Caleb Foote, "Vagrancy Type Law and Its Administration," University of Pennsylvania Law Review, 104: 603–650, 613.
401 Tucson Daily Citizen, Jan. 4, 1960, quoted in William O. Douglas, "Vagrancy and Arrest on Suspicion," Yale Law Journal, 70: 1–14.
402 *District of Columbia* v. *Ricks*, No. D.C. 3050–66, decided June 16, 1966, p. 10.
403 Id. at p. 2, 3.
404 Emory University, Department of Psychiatry, "Alcohol Project," Sept. 23, 1963, p. 18.
405 "Atlanta Prostitutes Win Fight to Curb Arrests on Streets," New York Times, Dec. 10, 1965, p. 38, col. 5.
406 Supra, note 352 at p. 88.
407 Id. at p. 151.
408 Ibid.
409 Supra, note 134 at p. 35, col. 5.
410 See, ch 2, Law Enforcement Policy: The Police Role.
411 For example, the Corporation Council in the District of Columbia has recently issued a ruling, construing the move-on statute to mean that the person does not commit an offense when he fails to move after being ordered by an officer unless there are circumstances which "(a) amount to an actual obstruction of

vehicular or pedestrian traffic, or (b) constitute an immediate threat to public safety, public peace, or public order." Milton D. Korman, Letter to the Commissioners, "Authority of Police Officers to Order Persons Congregating on Public Streets to Move On," June 7, 1966, p. 13.

[412] Supra, note 77 at p. 67.

[413] Supra, note 21 at vol. I, pp. 126–127, 162.

[414] Supra, note 22 at pp. 335–336; supra, note 21 at vol. I, p. 142.

[415] Supra, note 21 at vol. I, p. 126.

[416] Lawrence E. Davies, "Calm is Restored in San Francisco," New York Times, Sept. 30, 1966, p. 1, col. 5.

[417] Peter Bart, "Inquest Tightens Tension in Watts," New York Times, May 21, 1966, p. 13, col. 1.

[418] Donald Janson, "St. Louis Orders Riot Crackdown," New York Times, Sept. 29, 1966, p. 39, col. 3.

[419] Supra, note 352 at p. 213.

[420] American Civil Liberties Union, "Police Power vs. Citizens' Rights" (New York: The American Civil Liberties Union, 1966), pp. 4–5.

[421] Gerald D. Robin, "Justifiable Homicide by Police Officers," Journal of Criminal Law, Criminology and Police Science, 54: 228–229. Robin also notes that an average of 240 persons per year were fatally injured by police intervention between 1950 and 1960—approximately six times the number of officers killed by criminals.

[422] Supra, note 22 at pp. 344–346.

[423] Supra, note 421 at pp. 228–231.

[424] Samuel G. Chapman and Thompson S. Crockett, "Gunsight Dilemma: Police Firearms Policy," Police, May–June 1963, p. 54.

[425] Cincinnati Police Department, "Police Regulations Governing Use of Firearms Survey," Apr. 22, 1964, p. 1.

[426] Id. pp. 9–54.

[427] Supra, note 424 at p. 22.

[428] This is already prohibited in many States by statute.

Crime Victims: Recovery for Police Inaction and Underprotection

In recent years criminal activity has been increasing throughout the country.[1] Although there is wide disagreement regarding the accuracy of reported crime rates,[2] and varied opinions regarding the methods to be utilized in solving the crime problem, there is little doubt that the public needs increased protection. The populations of our major cities are the most readily accessible

1. Fandel, *Operational Problems of a Local Police Precinct*, 13 POLICE no. 3, 74, 80 (1969): "The Federal Bureau of Investigation Crime Reports indicate that crime has increased many times the rate of our population growth in recent years and that most transgressions are committed by persons under 25 years of age." According to a recent Harris poll, 81 percent of the public "is convinced that 'law and order has broken down in this country'." *The Police and the Law*, 4 TRIAL no. 6, 11 (1968). Reported violent, physically injurious crimes are substantial every year. In 1967, 12,093 murders and nonnegligent manslaughters, 253,321 aggravated assaults, and 27,096 forcible rapes were reported in this country. FEDERAL BUREAU OF INVESTIGATION, UNIFORM CRIME REPORTS—1967, 60 (1968).
2. The statistical validity of the UNIFORM CRIME REPORTS, *supra* note 1, has not been accepted without challenge. Each issue of the reports includes a disclaimer of responsibility for accuracy, and the reports themselves represent only those crimes known to the police. By accepting their correctness, it is assumed that all crimes reported to the police were also subsequently reported by the police to those responsible for compiling the reports. This may not be a valid assumption, and if it is not, it would detract from the validity of the reports. For the argument that the UNIFORM CRIME REPORTS cannot adequately answer the question whether criminal activity is increasing and are at best a census of reported crimes see Wolfgang, *Uniform Crime Reports: A Critical Appraisal*, 111 U. PA. L. REV. 708 (1963). Concern has also been registered regarding the indiscriminate acceptance of the reports by legislators and social science investigators and the subsequent inferences drawn by the public from news releases. *See, e.g.* Robison, *A Critical View of the Uniform Crime Reports*, 64 MICH. L. REV. 1031 (1966).

   It has been suggested that what is needed in the area of crime statistics is a reformulation of the "underlying conception of crime, and therefore [in] the nature of the materials that are gathered as a result of this underlying conception," rather than refinements in the methodology of crime reporting. Wheeler, *Criminal Statistics: A Reformulation of the Problem*, 58 J. CRIM. L.C. & P.S. 317, 324 (1967), argues that in constructing a useful crime rate, the "characteristics of the police system and the nature of victims or the citizen population" should be included to facilitate understanding of crime and make the collected data more meaningful.

LAW AND THE SOCIAL ORDER, Vol. 1970, No. 2, pp. 279-303.

criminal targets. Urban dwellers have constituted, to a greater extent than the rest of the country, the many victims of the growing crime rate.[3] The urban environment itself with its inherent complexities and overcrowded living conditions is undoubtedly a major cause of this dilemma. Another factor not as self-evident but just as basic to the problem is the inadequacy of police protection afforded many urban inhabitants.

For various reasons, many sectors of the public are not being provided the kind of protection needed to adequately insure their safety. Existing methods of protecting potential crime victims have proven ineffective in many instances. Allegations of discriminatory practices in providing police protection have been voiced by racial minorities throughout the country. Certainly these aspects of underprotection in our cities merit consideration.

The first portion of discussion examines the inequalities of law enforcement provided racial minority areas.[4] This practice is characterized by the discriminatory manner in which the protection afforded the whole community is rationed to certain minority segments of the city. Related to this problem is the practice of giving existing laws unequal enforcement in so-called "inner-city" areas. The second portion of discussion focuses upon police "inaction" as it affects the individual. This problem is characterized by the failure of police to respond to citizen complaints or requests for individual protection. These two practices combine in some cases to produce a general condition of police inaction. Unfortunately, the injured victims are generally left without recourse from the municipality. This aspect compounds the gravity of the whole subject of underprotection; once a victim has suffered criminal abuses, he may never recover for what would be considered municipal negligence.

This Comment discusses the general problem of police underprotection as it affects the minority group and the individual urban dweller. The following

---

3. The crime rate in the more populous cities has increased substantially faster than the rate in the country as a whole. *E.g.*, President's Commission on Law Enforcement and Administration of Justice, The Challenge of Crime in a Free Society 22-29 (1967). This report also indicates that lower income groups supply the most frequent victims of violent crimes. *Id.* at 38. The characteristics of the most susceptible crime victims have been aptly described: "[I]t is those factors that tend to disadvantage a person in general that make him more vulnerable to crime. . . . The persons most vulnerable to crime are the less intelligent, the very young, the very old, the female, the *nonwhite,* the *poor,* the foreign born, and the *urban dweller.*" (Emphasis added.) Lamborn, *Toward a Victim Orientation in Criminal Theory,* 22 Rutgers L. Rev. 733, 757-58 (1968).

4. Inadequate police protection of minority group ghetto areas is not the only example of municipal discrimination observed in minority areas. It has been conceded that the quality of education, street cleaning and paving, garbage collection, and other municipal services has not been uniform in different residential areas of many cities. *E.g.*, Ratner, *Inter-Neighborhood Denials of Equal Protection in the Provision of Municipal Services,* 4 Harv. Civ. Rights-Civ. Lib. L. Rev. 1 (1968). The particular inequity of discriminatory police protection, however, is one of the most disturbing to the residents of these areas. *See, e.g.*, Report of the National Advisory Commission on Civil Disorders, 81 (1968). [hereinafter cited as *The Kerner Report*].

topics will be incorporated into the general discussion: discriminatory police practices in providing protection to minority areas, police inaction to requests for aid from individuals, sovereign immunity and other major bars to crime victim recovery, existing remedies for victims of police inaction and discriminatory enforcement policies and practices, and police justifications for underprotection.

I. Discriminatory Police Practices In Providing Protection To Minority Areas

Ideally, equal police protection should be provided to all citizens, and the laws of a jurisdiction should be enforced equally in every segment of the community. This would provide uniformity of law enforcement and police protection. Unfortunately, the ideal may be neither practical nor desirable because of the nature of cities and the fact that areas of higher crime rates will require a greater amount of police supervision. When these ideals are not met, and police resources are allocated in a discriminatory or arbitrary fashion, substantial inter-neighborhood inequities in the provision of police services may result. Individual studies have demonstrated the existence of such unequal conditions by comparing the protection afforded minority group areas with that provided the more affluent residential neighborhoods.[5]

A major product of these discriminatory police practices has been a growing resentment toward policemen. It is well known that many inner-city residents harbor an aversion toward the police.[6] As the most visible symbol of a

---

5. In Cleveland it was reported that police knowingly allow gambling and prostitution to thrive in Negro areas while responding very slowly, if at all to calls for help from predominately Negro neighborhoods. Testimony in Boston suggested that law enforcement in the poorer neighborhoods with minority group populations was insufficient. This was evidenced by the fact that prostitution, gambling and narcotics traffic thrived in these neighborhoods while being stifled by police in other parts of the city. Ratner, *supra* note 4, at 8-9.

In Hartford, Connecticut, it has been found that:

> [T]he residents of a large area in the center of the Negro ghetto are victims of over one-third of the daylight residential burglaries in the city. Yet during the daytime only one of Hartford's eighteen patrol cars and none of its eleven foot patrolmen is assigned to this area. Sections in the white part of town about the same size as the central ghetto area receive slightly more intensive daytime patrol even though the citizens in the ghetto area summon the police about six times as often because of criminal acts.

Comment, *Program Budgeting for Police Departments,* 76 Yale L.J. 822 (1967). The existence of higher crime levels in the cities may be a major factor in some people's decision to move to the suburbs. If discriminatory practices in allocating police services existed before this exodus of the more affluent to the suburbs, the problem may be compounded by their move. Resources that previously had been directed to the "inner-city" are possibly being rechanneled to the outskirts of the community in pursuit of the wealthier people who have relocated.

6. *See generally* Bordva, *Comments On Police-Community Relations,* 1 Conn. L. Rev. 306, 308-09 (1968). Fandel, *supra* note 1, explains that:

> In recent years, an atmosphere of dislike for law enforcement has been built up within large segments of the public. This has been especially true in depressed areas. The surge for civil rights among minority groups, their attitude toward authority, has produced friction with law enforcement. The role the police necessarily play in restricting the activities of these groups creates ani-

society from which ghetto residents increasingly feel alienated, the policeman in the inner-city symbolizes not only the local law but the whole spectrum of law enforcement and criminal justice.[7] Thus, a strong bias against police and municipal governmental authority is formulated by people living in these areas. Aside from hindering general police relations, this added factor compounds the problem of police inaction and underprotection.[8]

The bias against police is influenced by a firm belief that police brutality and harassment occur to a disproportionately greater extent in the minority areas of cities. Despite this substantial resentment towards police, however, inner-city residents want increased police protection. It has been suggested that "[t]he strength of ghetto feelings about hostile police conduct may even be exceeded by the conviction that ghetto neighborhoods are not given adequate police protection."[9] This conviction is founded on universally held complaints. Included are the suppositions that police maintain a less rigorous standard of law enforcement in the ghetto and that police treat complaints and calls for help from minority areas much less urgently than from white areas.[10]

One of the more blatant forms of police discrimination is the failure of police

---

mosity toward the police. Groups often feel that the officer is trying to thwart their efforts. This leaves them with the feeling that police are antagonistic and unsympathetic.

7. It is probable that in the de facto segregated portions of an "inner-city," the policeman is often one of the most frequently encountered white persons. It is not hard to visualize the nature of these confrontations. When a policeman is faced by local residents obsessed with the supposition that "white government" is the source of all their trouble, he readily becomes the accessible symbol of that source. *See* Doig, *Police Problems, Proposals, and Strategies for Change*, 28 PUB. AD. REV. 393, 394 (1968).

8. The resulting effect of general police misconduct to which minorities are subjected has been aptly described:

   > Where, as is often the case, police misconduct focuses largely on classes of people who are politically powerless to protect themselves, the Constitution's promise of equal protection is mocked, and a community is divided into those whom the police protect and those whom the police victimize. Such police misconduct, unredressed and undeterred, has often been blamed for the frustrations which have recently erupted into violence in many large American cities.

   Comment, *The Federal Injunction as a Remedy for Unconstitutional Police Conduct*, 78 YALE L.J. 143, 144 (1968). This statement depicts the possible societal consequences that may occur when minorities activate the ill will they feel toward police. Further evidence of the explosive tensions existing between black ghetto residents and police can be found in the seven major riots experienced by this country's cities in the summer of 1964. All of the riots were started by confrontations between these two groups. Comment, *Black Power Advocacy: Criminal Anarchy or Free Speech*, 56 CALIF. L. REV. 702, 727 (1968); PRESIDENT'S COMMISSION ON LAW ENFORCEMENT AND ADMINISTRATION OF JUSTICE, TASK FORCE REPORT: CRIME AND ITS IMPACT — AN ASSESSMENT, 118 (1967).

9. *The Kerner Report* at 161.

10. Residents of "inner-city" areas often complain that the police are slow in responding to requests for help and often their pleas are left completely unanswered. *See generally* J. HERSEY, THE ALGIERS MOTEL INCIDENT (1968). A New Haven community group reported: "The problem of the adequacy of current police protection ranked with 'police misconduct' as the most serious sore points in police-community relations. . . . When calls for help are registered, it is all too frequent that police respond too slowly or not at all." *The Kerner Report* at 161.

to enforce certain laws that would otherwise be enforced if minority people were not involved. Because of the continuous barrage of news reports of violent crime in the inner-city areas, many people seriously believe that most minority group ghetto dwellers are crooks and deviates and therefore welcome lax law enforcement. Although this may be true for individual offenders and potential law-breakers, the majority of inner-city residents are not habitual criminals and may not concur. The majority of these people are caught up in a "vicious circle" of crime breeding crime and are constantly subjected to the brunt of criminal activity. Minority group members have recognized the futility resulting from police policies of allowing offenses of members of their group to go noticed but not acted upon:

> Equality of treatment implies that there will be one standard of law enforcement in all areas within the community. Respectable members of a minority group do not appreciate the fact that minor criminals in their areas are sometimes treated like children, or are laughed at, when their violations are the type that run down the minority community, but do not seriously annoy the police or vocal complainants. . . . They sometimes allege the police make or fail to make arrests of their members to suit police convenience rather than the ends of justice.[11]

Considering the substantial discriminatory police practices with which inner-city residents have had to cope, it is not difficult to understand why they visualize the existing inequities as providing a dual standard of law enforcement. It has been suggested that this dual standard continues to plague the ghetto community because it is assumed by some law enforcement officials that inner-city residents have a greater tolerance for certain kinds of antisocial conduct, and thus a different standard of law enforcement is justified.[12] Similarly, it is felt that minority groups living in substandard conditions have a much higher propensity to commit crime because of factors such as lower social values, and this propensity accounts for the difference in crime norms. Considering his environment, the supposed greater tolerance of the inner-city resident for certain kinds of antisocial conduct may be an unavoidable concession.

This concession may be derived from imposed unequal law enforcement, living conditions, and social customs to which the inner-city resident has in the past grown accustomed and accepted as a burden of life. Whatever the reason for the higher crime rate of the inner-city, however, it is questionable

---

11. Brown, The Police and Community Conflict 19-20 (1962), cited in W. LaFave, Arrest 111 n.37 (1965). (The author of the textual quote is a retired inspector of the New York City Police Department who had twenty-two years of service.)
    It is arguable that any distinction based on race has a psychologically demeaning effect regardless of the good faith intention of the police in making the racial distinction. *See*, Kaplan, *Equal Justice in an Unequal World: Equality for the Negro—The Problem of Special Treatment*, 61 Nw. U.L. Rev. 363 (1966).
12. *Cf.*, W. LaFave, *supra* note 11, at 114.

whether the customs, practices, and prevailing standard of conduct of an identifiable subculture should determine the degree to which the law is enforced.[13]

In some cases, the discriminatory attitude of the individual officer affects to a substantial degree the manner in which the law is enforced in these areas.[14] A policeman with racial prejudices may be influenced by his own bias when faced with a discretionary decision involving minorities.[15] In a confrontation involving a minority group member and a policeman, the degree of impartiality displayed in the policeman's actions would be partially determinative of the outcome. Even if equality in general police enforcement policies is eventually achieved, discriminatory practices may not be fully abated until individual police attitudes are changed.[16] While directly changing the personal beliefs of municipal employees is probably not a duty of the legal system, the courts should make every possible effort to help create an atmosphere more conducive to equitable treatment of minorities by police.[17]

Unequal protection may be the result of community demand, particularly

---

13. Conversely, it is arguable that as a matter of necessity the police must be allowed to follow certain racial classifications in the inner-city in order to enforce laws adequately and efficiently. Otherwise, the police would be swamped with the enforcement of "unimportant" laws in the higher crime areas while major crime ran rampant. *See* Comment, *Equal Protection as a Defense to Selective Law Enforcement by Police Officials,* 14 J. PUB. L. 223 (1965). It would seem that when such racial classifications are necessary, their utilization should be kept to a minimum and then only in a reasonable manner. If these safeguards are not followed the implementation of such racial classifications could be subject to attack as a violation of the equal protection clause. *E.g.*, Yick Wo v. Hopkins, 118 U.S. 356, 373-74 (1886).

14. For a discussion of the basic hostility of white officers toward blacks in general see A REPORT OF A RESEARCH STUDY SUBMITTED TO THE PRESIDENT'S COMMISSION ON LAW ENFORCEMENT AND ADMINISTRATION OF JUSTICE, THE POLICE AND THE COMMUNITY, 192-94 (1966). For the reasoning behind the prejudices entertained by police in black ghetto areas see Riley, *Should Communities Control Their Police?*, 2 CIVIL RIGHTS DIGEST, no. 4, 27, 28 (1969). According to one study "[o]ver three-fourths of the white officers serving in predominantly black precincts expressed either 'prejudiced' or 'highly prejudiced' attitudes toward Negroes." *Id.*

15. A strong racial bias could affect both the patrolman's decision whether to act in providing protection in a given situation and it could influence the manner in which that protection were employed. One solution to this problem is the use of psychological testing to screen out candidates for police work who may have prejudicial attitudes. This method of selection is currently being used by some departments. *See*, PRESIDENT'S COMMISSION ON LAW ENFORCEMENT AND ADMINISTRATION OF JUSTICE, TASK FORCE REPORT: THE POLICE 128-30, 164 (1967).

16. It would seem that one easy answer to the problem of racial prejudices of policemen would be to have black policemen patrol Negro areas. This method, however, has not proven to be entirely successful. In Baker v. City of St. Petersburg, 400 F.2d 294 (5th Cir. 1968), black officers brought an action to enjoin the department from exclusively assigning black patrolmen to the Negro district. The Court of Appeals for the Fifth Circuit held that the practice of assigning black patrolmen solely on the basis of race violated the equal protection clause of the fourteenth amendment. Not only has this theoretically attractive solution encountered its own inherent difficulties but its effectiveness is also questionable: "It is not clear today that departments with large numbers of Negroes patrolling Negro areas have experienced less community tension than departments with few Negroes, or that in any given encounter a Negro officer behaves much differently from a white one." Wilson, *Police Dilemmas,* 4 TRIAL, no. 6, 12-13 (1968).

17. See Bordva, *supra* note 6, for an excellent discussion of the ways in which the police can improve police-community relations in the urban ghetto. The Article also examines court support of such police practices.

where the minority area population is significantly less in number than that of the whole city. The argument that those people who are paying the taxes to support the police force should be the ones to whom initial concern is directed when police protection is afforded, gains strength when it is vocalized by the voters and supporters of city officials. This is suggested as an explanation for the practice, found in many communities, of police constantly patrolling the suburbs while generally neglecting crime reports in the poorer areas.[18] While this viewpoint may have some validity if comparative property values are considered of paramount interest, it is certainly questionable whether a person's safety should depend on the amount of municipal taxes he has paid.

The simplest answer to the underprotection problem would seem to be to provide those areas of a community where the crime rate is highest a proportionately greater amount of police supervision. This is not, however, the situation that has developed in many of our major cities. Nor does this initial impression answer the underlying question of what constitutes equality in the disposition of this municipal service. Equal police protection may mean the attainment of an equal crime rate for all sectors of society. This will of necessity require that more resources go to certain classes because of their greater propensity for crime. On the other hand, it may mean that equal resources are devoted to each individual. Arguably, one portion of society should not necessarily be afforded more police supervision than another, whose members are more law abiding, merely because the former commits more crimes per capita. These issues are fundamental to the whole problem of underprotection and should be considered when the municipal practice of providing different levels of protection to different areas is examined. Existing remedies and proposed solutions for this institutional problem on the minority area level will be discussed in a later portion of this Comment.

II. Police Inaction To Requests For Aid From Individuals

In the previous discussion, those subjected to underprotection and discriminatory practices in the provisions of police services, were considered as a class, a subgroup of the urban population. Another dimension of the underprotection problem is that of police inaction — failure to provide protection even though police may have knowledge of the need. A typical case of police inaction is one in which a person, believing himself to be in danger, calls the police requesting protection, and the officer receiving the call either ignores the plea altogether or discounts the gravity of the danger that has been

18. An analogous example of this "comparative economic discrimination" is the lower quality of school and educational facilities provided minority group areas. *See, e.g.*, Hobson v. Hansen, 269 F. Supp. 401 (D.D.C. 1967); Manjares v. Newton, 64 Cal. 2d 365, 411 P.2d 901, 49 Cal. Rptr. 805 (1966). For the argument that police protection, fire protection, public school, or any other municipal service being distributed unequally by public officials is a denial of equal protection guaranteed by the fourteenth amendment, see Abascal, *Municipal Services and Equal Protection: Variations on a Theme by* Griffin v. Illinois, 20 HASTINGS L.J. 1367 (1969).

related to him.[19] Other situations may arise in which, although no formal solicitation for police aid is made, the police are aware of existing dangerous conditions. This type of situation may be one of constructive notice to the police that someone is in danger and may suffer personal injury.

The two types of underprotection coexist and interrelate in some instances. If an individual making a request for protection resides in a minority area already receiving a disproportionately small amount of police service, the chances of having his request fulfilled will probably be influenced by this factor. Another aspect common to both levels is that adequate recovery for the individual victim and abatement of discriminatory practices for minority areas may both hinge on municipal liability doctrines. These doctrines may prove to be substantial barriers to recovery in jurisdictions where they still enjoy judicial recognition.

In *Riss v. City of New York*,[20] the plaintiff, a young woman, was repeatedly threatened by a rejected suitor, but was denied aid from the police. When she became engaged to another man the threats became immediate, but again her plea for police protection was refused. Subsequently, the threats were fulfilled and as a result she was maimed for life. Prompt response by the police possibly could have avoided this result. The trial court denied recovery against the municipality for the police department's alleged negligence in failing to provide protection. The Court of Appeals affirmed 4-3, with a strong dissent by Judge Keating. The significance of the *Riss* case is that crime victims have no adequate legal remedy against a municipality for a failure to provide police protection.[21]

Had this factual setting arisen in another jurisdiction it probably would not have been litigated. Municipalities generally recognize no duty to protect the individual, and in many jurisdictions the doctrine of sovereign immunity is a complete barrier to recovery regardless of whether municipal negligence can be shown. New York State, however, has abolished by statute the doctrine of sovereign immunity,[22] and New York City has, by municipal charter provision, imposed on the police department the duty to "protect . . . persons and property."[23] Apparently the plaintiff in *Riss* was hopeful that these

19. It has been suggested that only on rare occasions do police satisfactorily help people requesting assistance. *See generally* A. NIEDERHOFFER, BEHIND THE SHIELD (1967).

20. 22 N.Y.2d 579, 240 N.E.2d 860, 293 N.Y.S.2d 897 (1968).

21. Arguably, the crime victim has an adequate remedy against his assailant. This argument assumes that the offender has been found and is in custody or is available for service of process. This is somewhat illusory, however, because few offenders possess sufficient funds to make adequate restitution or pay money damages. *See* Mueller, *Compensation for Victims of Crime: Thought Before Action*, 50 MINN. L. REV. 213 (1965).

22. N.Y. CT. CL. ACT § 8 (McKinney 1963). This statutory waiver has been extended by the court to include local government units. Bernardine v. City of New York, 294 N.Y. 361, 62 N.E.2d 604 (1945).

23. NEW YORK CITY CHARTER, § 435a (1963):

The police department and force shall have the power and it shall be their

two factors, coupled with the unfortunate circumstances of her case, would create liability even though it had not been found in similar cases in the past.[24]

Tort actions against municipalities have traditionally proven an ineffective remedy for recovery in circumstances of pure inaction as was the case in *Riss*.[25] The tort theory of recovery — liability for negligence of police in failing to provide protection — has been unsuccessful unless combined with other factors that enhance the duty owed the plaintiff by the municipality.

The courts have historically distinguished between a municipality's duty to the individual and its duty to the general public in providing services such as police protection or fire control. An example of this distinction can be found by comparing cases holding the state liable to individuals for failure to maintain highways[26] with cases denying recovery for negligent failure to provide adequate police and fire protection.[27] These cases explain that the duty to provide police and fire protection runs only to the public in general whereas the duty of maintaining highways inures to the individual victim. The rationale for this dichotomy and the foundation for liability is the common law principle that a person who positively or actively attempts to confer a benefit on another, has a duty to act with reasonable care. In this sense, the maintaining of highways is considered an affirmative act in its inception whereas providing protection is considered initially, an inactive function. The conceptual framework of the duty analysis has been offered as justification for the judicial interpretation that the police duty created by legislation or municipal charter such as that found in New York City[28] is designed primarily to protect the public as a whole rather than individuals.[29]

> duty to preserve the public peace, prevent crime, detect and arrest offenders, . . . protect the rights of persons and property, . . . [and] enforce and prevent the violation of all laws and ordinances in force in the city.

Jurisdictions without a similar statute have no trouble asserting that the municipal corporation is under no duty to provide police or fire protection and therefore is not liable to individuals for losses suffered because of the failure to so provide. *See, e.g.*, Thon v. City of Los Angeles, 203 Cal. App. 2d 186, 21 Cal. Rptr. 398 (Dist. Ct. App. 1962); City of Purcell v. Hubbard, 401 P.2d 488 (Okla. 1965).

24. *E.g.*, Motyka v. City of Amsterdam, 15 N.Y.2d 134, 204 N.E.2d 635, 256 N.Y.S.2d 595 (1965); Steitz v. City of Beacon, 295 N.Y. 51, 64 N.E.2d 704 (1945).

25. *E.g.*, note 36, *infra* and accompanying text.

26. *E.g.*, Eastman v. State, 303 N.Y. 691, 103 N.E.2d 56 (1951).

27. *E.g.*, Gilbertson v. City of Fairbanks, 262 F.2d 734 (9th Cir. 1959); Woodford v. City of St. Petersburg, 84 So. 2d 25 (Fla. 1955); Conway v. Humbert, 82 S.D. 317, 145 N.W.2d 524 (1966).

28. New York City Charter § 435a (1963).
While courts usually establish this duty through a statute, there are decisions finding the municipal corporation, through its agent the police, liable in situations not directly involving statutory duties. In Lubelfeld v. City of New York, 4 N.Y.2d 455, 151 N.E.2d 862, 176 N.Y.S.2d 302 (1958), negligence was established when police failed to take into custody an intoxicated policeman who shot a cab driver.

29. Motyka v. City of Amsterdam, 15 N.Y.2d 134, 204 N.E.2d 635, 256 N.Y.S.2d 595 (1965). *See also* Massengill v. Yuma County, 104 Ariz. 518, 456 P.2d 376 (1969). In Riss v. City of New York, 22 N.Y.2d 579, 240 N.E.2d 860, 293 N.Y.S.2d 897

The courts have commonly distinguished the inaction of the *Riss* situation from those cases in which a duty to the victim had been established before the crime.[30] Similarly distinguished by the courts are those cases in which, although a prior duty did not exist, the police undertook to provide protection but were negligent in their attempt.[31]

In *Schuster v. City of New York,*[32] the victim recognized an escaped criminal and notified police. Subsequently he received threats of physical violence, and ultimately was shot to death on a public street. The victim's estate recovered from the city because partial protection had been extended by the police. This created an active duty to protect the victim which the police were negligent in performing.

Although the municipality has no specific duty of affording protection to the individual, if the individual can establish a "special relationship" with the police department, the police may have a duty to protect him. In *Schuster,* one of the grounds for liability was that such a special duty was created. When the victim collaborated as an informer in the arrest of a known criminal and it became evident that protection was needed, the police acquired an obligation to exercise due care in protecting the victim.[33] It has been suggested that the special relationship category be expanded to create a duty to protect whenever the police become aware of impending danger to an individual and continued inaction would be unreasonable.[34] Although Judge Keating, dissenting in *Riss,* feels the law is moving in this direction,[35] it is evident in light of the majority opinion that mere knowledge by the police

---

(1968), it would seem that the court assumed that, prima facie, because the city owes a duty to protect everyone, it owes it to no single individual. No substantial reasons were given as to why this police duty was so limited. It is questionable whether this interpretation of the statutory duty will stand without further substantiation when compelling circumstances necessitate an extension of the duty to include the individual.

30. *See* Abraham v. Boat Center, Inc., 146 So. 2d 23 (La. Ct. App. 1962); *Cf.* Motyka v. City of Amsterdam, 15 N.Y.2d 134, 139, 204 N.E.2d 635, 637, 256 N.Y.S.2d 595, 597 (1965); Honeycutt v. Bass, 187 So. 848, 851 (La. Ct. App. 1939). *See generally* Comment, *Tort Liability of Law Enforcement Officers: State Remedies,* 29 La. L. Rev. 130 (1968).

31. *See,* Town of Mount Dora v. Bryant, 128 So. 2d 4 (Fla. Ct. App. 1961); Wimberly v. City of Paterson, 75 N.J. Super. 584, 183 A.2d 691 (1962); *Cf.* Wilson v. City of Tucson, 8 Ariz. App. 398, 446 P.2d 504 (1968).

32. 5 N.Y.2d 75, 154 N.E.2d 534, 180 N.Y.S.2d 265 (1958).

33. Other authority exists for the creation of a higher duty to protect people engaging in activity that society wishes to encourage, such as that of informing on criminals. *See, e.g., In re* Quarles, 158 U.S. 532 (1895); Gardner v. Village of Chicago Ridge, 71 Ill. App. 2d 373, 219 N.E.2d 147 (1966).

34. *See, e.g.,* Comment, *Municipality Liable for Negligent Failure to Protect Informer: The* Schuster *Case,* 59 Colum. L. Rev. 487, 503 (1959).

35. Judge Keating felt that no liability arose by mere inaction when police knew nothing about the validity of the claim. But he said liability should be imposed when it was established that the victim was a reputable person, other verifiable attempts to injure her or intimidate her had taken place, and that other witnesses were available to support her claim that her life was being threatened. Riss v. City of New York, 22 N.Y.2d 579, 590, 240 N.E.2d 860, 866, 293 N.Y.S.2d 897, 905 (1968) (dissenting opinion).

of a probable danger to an individual is not enough to establish municipal liability for police inaction.

Previously, courts considering police negligence cases have made a distinction between nonfeasance and misfeasance in the failure to provide protection. Earlier decisions involving municipal liability held that nonfeasance or omission was not enough to establish a duty, the breach of which is a basis for recovery.[36] This is in line with the traditional rule in cases of this type that, absent a prior duty to the victim-plaintiff, relief may be denied when a defendant's negligence consists of passive rather than active conduct.[37] Modern courts have done away with this distinction in cases of omission when the police have played a role in the creation of the danger.[38] Nevertheless, the *Riss* decision makes it clear that absent any prior involvement by the police, failure to respond to a request for help will not result in liability.

In *Adamczyk v. Zambelli*,[39] a minor plaintiff alleged that the city's policemen were negligent in failing to suppress the unlawful explosion of fireworks by participants in a church parade. The court denied recovery with very traditional language: "[T]he exercise of a city's police power is a governmental function for the benefit of the people and general welfare. A municipality is not liable in tort for the failure of its policemen to prevent and stop others from violating the law."[40] The court distinguished similar cases that had found liability saying that they "involve[d] affirmative negligent or wilful acts by municipal employees."[41] The dissent disagreed, finding that the case involved "something more than mere omission" — more than just failure to act. They felt that the case called "for a further step in the direction of the trend away from governmental immunity."[42]

While it is apparent from these recent cases that mere inaction by police is not enough to support municipal liability, many observers feel that a remedy should exist that would allow recovery for police nonfeasance in the proper

36. *E.g.*, Koerth v. Borough of Turtle Creek, 355 Pa. 121, 49 A.2d 398 (1946). Generally, liability in tort for an "ommission" results only when a statutory duty exists to protect a certain class of individuals as members of the class and not as members of the general public. *See* Lloyd, *Le Roi-Est Mort; Vive Le Roi! (Municipal Tort Liability in New York—Sequel)*, 24 N.Y.U.L. Rev. 38 (1949).

37. *E.g.*, Hurley v. Eddingfield, 156 Ind. 416, 59 N.E. 1058 (1901) (no recovery for doctor's refusal to attend person in critical condition); Osterlind v. Hill, 263 Mass. 73, 160 N.E. 301 (1928) (defendant on dock watching person in capsized boat drown). It is noted by some that the misfeasance-nonfeasance distinction has been eroding recently in the law of torts. *See, e.g.*, W. Prosser, Torts § 54, 334-35 (3d ed. 1964).

38. *E.g.*, Lubelfeld v. City of New York, 4 N.Y.2d 455, 151 N.E.2d 862, 176 N.Y.S.2d 302 (1958); Meistinsky v .City of New York, 285 App. Div. 1153, 140 N.Y.S.2d 212 (1955), *aff'd mem.*, 309 N.Y. 998, 132 N.E.2d 900 (1956).

39. 25 Ill. App. 2d 121, 166 N.E.2d 93 (1960).

40. *Id.* at 128, 166 N.E.2d at 97.

41. *Id.* at 127, 166 N.E.2d at 97.

42. *Id.* at 129, 166 N.E.2d at 98.

circumstances. Even though municipal charter provisions requiring affirmative acts by police are construed as being solely for the benefit of the public as a whole, it would seem that they could be interpreted to impose a duty on the municipality and its police force to actively insure an individual's safety.[43]

III. Sovereign Immunity And Other Major Bars To Crime Victim Recovery

The doctrine of sovereign immunity is one of the major obstacles confronting the victim seeking civil redress from a municipality whose police have neglected to provide protection. Sovereign immunity has traditionally barred recovery for municipal negligence in performing a "governmental function." Police activity has commonly been regarded a "governmental" function rather than a "proprietary" one and thus has enjoyed the immunity privilege.[44] Many jurisdictions, however, have either waived or modified their sovereign immunity in one form or another and provide for relief in certain instances.[45] Contemporary schemes for abolishing sovereign immunity include striking

---

43. In other areas of the law, courts have implied a right of individual action from the express provision of broader public duties. The Restatement (Second) of Torts § 286 (1965), implies a civil remedy in favor of anyone injured by violation of a statute enacted for the protection of the class of persons of which he is a member. The implication of a private civil remedy was first recognized by the Supreme Court in Texas & Pac. Ry. v. Rigsby, 241 U.S. 33 (1916). It was held that an employee could recover damages under the Federal Safety Appliance Act, 27 Stat. 531 (1893), *as amended,* 45 U.S.C. §§ 1-16 (1958). In the area of securities regulation, there is no provision in Securities Exchange Act of 1934, ch. 404, § 1, 48 Stat. 881, *as amended,* 15 U.S.C. § 78j(b) (1958), for a civil remedy. It has repeatedly been held, however, that a right of action exists in favor of an injured purchaser or seller of securities. *E.g.,* Ellis v. Carter, 291 F.2d 270 (9th Cir. 1961); Hooper v. Mountain States Sec. Corp., 282 F.2d 195 (5th Cir. 1960). For implied remedies in the area of airline regulations see Fitzgerald v. Pan Am. World Airways, 229 F.2d 499 (2d Cir. 1956); Mortimer v. Delta Air Lines, 302 F. Supp. 276 (N.D. Ill. 1969). For a general history of the implied civil remedy in the federal area see Note, *Implying Civil Remedies from Federal Regulatory Statutes,* 77 Harv. L. Rev. 285 (1963).

44. *See, e.g.,* 18 E. McQuillin, The Law of Municipal Corporations § 53.51 (3d ed. rev. 1963). The court in Arms v. City of Knoxville, 32 Ill. App. 604 (1889) said that the negligence of police in failing to stop the firing of a cannon, known to be dangerous, upon the streets of a city, did not render the city liable: "For failure to exercise *governmental* power cities are not liable." *Id.* at 611. (Emphasis added)

The governmental-proprietary test for recognizing sovereign immunity is currently under attack. It is argued that distinguishing between governmental and proprietary functions has resulted in many unjust and arbitrary decisions of who may recover. Blades, *A Comment on Governmental Tort Immunity in Kansas,* 16 Kan. L. Rev. 265, 271 (1968): The governmental-proprietary test for determining ". . . who can recover from those who cannot is too arbitrary and haphazard to be considered a fair and satisfactory means of ameliorating the harsh impact of governmental immunity. . . . In a word, [it] leaves unremedied too many wrongs where recovery is justified."

45. *See generally* Hargrove v. Town of Cocoa Beach, 96 So. 2d 130 (Fla. 1957); *cf.* Muskopf v. Corning Hosp. Dist., 55 Cal. 2d 211, 359 P.2d 457, 11 Cal. Rptr. 89 (1961); Molitor v. Kaneland Community Unit District No. 302, 18 Ill. 2d 11, 163 N.E.2d 89 (1959); Williams v. City of Detroit, 364 Mich. 231, 111 N.W.2d 1 (1961). The waiver of sovereign immunity, however, will in no way benefit an injured party unless the sovereign is found to have breached a duty owed to that party. *Cf.* Restatement (Second) of Torts § 4 (1965).

immunity provisions from state statutes, establishing a statutory system of liability, and judicial imposition of liability.[46]

Incidental to the question of waiving sovereign immunity, is the issue of whether judicial or legislative action is the proper vehicle for reform in this area. Many feel that because the judiciary lacks adequate facilities for an examination of the social, economic and political considerations involved, and because a uniform standard of liability is desirable, legislative action would be more desirable.[47] The language of the *Riss* decision supports this view: "Before such extension of responsibilities should be dictated by the indirect imposition of tort liabilities, there should be a legislative determination [of] the scope of public responsibility."[48]

This rationale of the court in *Riss*, well precedented and seemingly valid, is a familiar one. It has been employed by the courts in almost every field of the law in which judicial alteration of the law has been urged prior to legislative change. It is likely, however, that before legislators exercise their power to alter the law and thus subject the state's budget to a new liability, they will require more demanding reasons than have been advanced for abolishing sovereign immunity and establishing municipal liability in this area. In spite of the natural legislative reluctance to implement change and the disagreement concerning the method to employ in abolishing sovereign immunity and introducing liability, the law has definitely undergone a transition in the direction of increased liability for municipal negligence.[49]

Related to the municipal shield of sovereign immunity is the defense of

---

46. A summary of methods of state liability is provided in F. SPIEGEL, THE ILLINOIS COURT OF CLAIMS: A STUDY OF STATE LIABILITY 40-59 (1962).

47. *See, e.g.*, Muskopf v. Corning Hosp. Dist., 55 Cal. 2d 211, 359 P.2d 457, 11 Cal. Rptr. 89 (1961) (dissenting opinion). For the argument that a comprehensive legislative solution is the only acceptable alternative to making inroads on the doctrine of sovereign immunity see Van Alstyne, *Governmental Tort Liability: A Public Policy Prospectus*, 10 U.C.L.A.L. REV. 463, 467 (1963); Note, *Municipal Corporations—Liability in Tort—Prospective Judicial Abrogation of the Sovereign Immunity Concept*, 60 MICH. L. REV. 379, 382 (1962). The cases utilizing the judicial vehicle as the means of abrogating the doctrine of governmental sovereign immunity cited *supra* note 45, are supported by L. GREEN, THE LITIGATION PROCESS IN TORT LAW 47, 52 (1965). Professor Green expounds upon the doctrine of judicial *stare decisis* and the propriety of judge-made law.

48. Riss v. City of New York, 22 N.Y.2d 579, 582, 240 N.E.2d 860, 861, 293 N.Y.S.2d 897, 898 (1968).

49. Judge Gibson, concurring in Hack v. City of Salem, 174 Ohio St. 383, 397, 189 N.E.2d 857, 868-69 (1963), aptly voices the doctrine that has been expounded for the abrogation of governmental immunity involving the negligence of municipal corportions:

> The municipal corporation is of no more a legal concept than a private corporation. Both arise by operation of law, both necessarily act through agents, and both necessarily are going to have agents who at times are negligent in the performance of their duties. The ordinary rules of liability applicable to private corporations should give municipalities all the protection they require against unreasonable claims. The defenses [of contributory negligence and voluntary assumption of risks are available and] . . . are consistently upheld by the courts. Moreover, under the doctrine of *respondeat superior* the liability of municipal corporations would be as limited as that of a private corporation

"official immunity" provided to public officers while engaged in discretionary functions. Policemen have been included in the spectrum of public officers protected by this doctrine.[50] If a policeman is confronted with a request for aid and he decides not to provide it, his decision is discretionary; his official immunity thus protects him from liability. The police commissioner is afforded the same immunity along with "all executive public officers when performing within the scope of their power, acts which require the exercise of discretion or judgment."[51] Since this immunity is applicable whenever an officer acts within the scope of his authority, it is an absolute bar to recovery by individuals who are victims of police inaction or discriminatory policies. This is illustrated by cases holding police officers immune from tort liability for failing to arrest a person committing a crime in their presence even though the person then proceeds to injure someone by his criminal act.[52]

In certain circumstances, a municipality may be liable to an injured plaintiff for negligent acts of an officer notwithstanding the officer's personal immunity.[53] This liability normally arises in situations in which a duty to the individual victim had been established prior to the crime and the jurisdiction has abandoned the defense of sovereign immunity.[54]

> by the requirement that the municipal employees act within the scope of their employment.

Cf. Muskopf v. Corning Hosp. Dist., 55 Cal. 2d 211, 359 P.2d 457, 11 Cal. Rptr. 89 (1961); Hargrove v. Town of Cocoa Beach, 96 So. 2d 130 (Fla. 1957); Molitor v. Kaneland Community Unit Dist., 18 Ill. 2d 11, 163 N.E.2d 89 (1959); Williams v. City of Detroit, 364 Mich. 231, 111 N.W.2d 1 (1961).

50. *See, e.g.*, Tomlinson v. Pierce, 178 Cal. App. 2d 112, 2 Cal. Rptr. 700 (Dist. Ct. App. 1960); Rubinow v. County of San Bernadino, 169 Cal. App. 2d 67, 336 P.2d 968 (Dist. Ct. App. 1959).

51. Hardy v. Vial, 48 Cal. 2d 577, 582, 311 P.2d 494, 496 (1957).

52. *See, e.g.*, cases cited note 50 *supra*.

53. Justice Gibson has expounded on the criteria for these circumstances:

> Although it may not be possible to set forth a definitive rule which would determine in every instance whether a governmental agency is liable for discretionary acts of its officials, various factors furnish a means of deciding whether the agency in a particular case should have immunity, such as the importance to the public of the function involved, the extent to which governmental liability might impair free exercise of the function, and the availability to individuals affected of remedies other than tort suits for damages.

Lipman v. Brisbane Elementary School Dist., 55 Cal. 2d 224, 230, 359 P.2d 465, 467, 11 Cal. Rptr. 97, 99 (1961). *See generally* Foote, *Tort Remedies for Police Violations of Individual Rights*, 39 MINN. L. REV. 493 (1955); Jaffe, *Suits Against Governments and Officers: Damage Actions*, 77 HARV. L. REV. 209 (1963); Mathes & Jones, *Toward a "Scope of Official Duty" Immunity for Police Officers in Damage Actions*, 53 GEO. L.J. 889 (1965).

54. When the conduct of police officers on duty is deliberate and not merely negligent, the state, under the doctrine of "state action," has not been relieved of responsibility merely because the officer in question exceeded the authority granted him. Identifying an instance of state action, the court in Baldwin v. Morgan, 287 F.2d 750 (5th Cir. 1961), stated:

> If city policemen, with the color of office which their uniform, badge, display of authority and available arms reflects, undertake as policemen to subject persons to treatment which denies them a constitutionally protected right, it is state action. It is state action though in excess of actual legal authority or even if done without formal authorization.

The concept of state action is usually attributable to private individuals or groups that

IV. Existing Remedies For Victims Of Police Inaction And Discriminatory Enforcement Policies And Practices

If police inaction results in a discriminatory application of the law, an injured plaintiff has a possibility of recovering under section 1983 of the Civil Rights Act of 1867.[55] In *Huey v. Barloga*,[56] a Negro plaintiff brought an action seeking damages for the death of his son who, while walking down a city street, was beaten by a group of white youths.[57] The plaintiff tried to show discriminatory practices of the police as not providing equal protection, but was denied recovery because he failed to ". . . allege any specific acts or omissions by defendants, any causal connection between such acts or omissions and the deprivations suffered by Huey, or that the alleged acts or omissions were unreasonable in light of the circumstances."[58] If in the future a plaintiff can satisfy the requirements of both the statute and the language of the *Huey* court, a similar action against the state or the officers involved may be successful.

Several recent lower court decisions have interpreted section 1983 as not authorizing damages against a police department head for failure to prevent section 1983 torts committed by his subordinates.[59] It has, however, been

---

are endowed by the state with powers or functions governmental in nature so they become instruments of the state and subject to the same constitutional limitations. *See* Marsh v. Alabama, 326 U.S. 501 (1946); Smith v. Allwright, 321 U.S. 649 (1944).

55. 42 U.S.C. § 1983 (1964):

> Every person who, under color of any statute, ordinance, regulation, custom, or usage, of any State or Territory, subjects or causes to be subjected, any citizen of the United States or other person within the jurisdiction thereof to the deprivation of any rights, privileges, or immunities secured by the Constitution and laws, shall be liable to the party injured in an action at law, suit in equity, or other proper proceeding for redress.

For the general applicability of § 1983 see Monroe v. Pape, 365 U.S. 167 (1961). *Monroe* concerned the illegal activities of police officers who conducted an unlawful search. Liability was imposed for the benefit of the search victim when the officers' argument that they did not act "under color of any statute, ordinance, regulation, custom, or usage, of any State or Territory" was rejected by the court. *Monroe* was distinguished in Pierson v. Ray, 386 U.S. 547, 556-57 (1967), which held that the defense of good faith and probable cause which is available to police officers in a common-law action for false arrest and imprisonment is also available in an action under § 1983. For recent developments of § 1983 see Note, *Limiting the Section 1983 Action in the Wake of* Monroe v. Pape, 82 Harv. L. Rev. 1486 (1969); and Comment, *Civil Actions for Damages Under the Federal Civil Rights Statutes,* 45 Texas L. Rev. 1015 (1967).

56. 277 F. Supp. 864 (N.D. Ill. 1967).

57. Although no actual notice existed as a result of a direct plaintiff appeal to police for protection (as in *Riss*) there was constructive notice. The court felt the police should have been cognizant of the active prejudicial conditions in the area creating precarious situations for blacks traveling on predominantly white streets.

58. 277 F. Supp. at 873.

59. *E.g.*, Runnels v. Parker, 263 F. Supp. 271 (C.D. Cal. 1967) (police official immune with respect to rules set for police department subordinates); Salazar v. Dowd, 256 F. Supp. 220 (D. Colo. 1966); Jordan v. Kelly, 223 F. Supp. 731 (W.D. Mo. 1963). Even a judge, who enjoys absolute immunity from a section 1983 damage suit, *see, e.g.*, Pierson v. Ray, 386 U.S. 547 (1967), has been held to be a proper defendant in an injunction action. *See also* United States v. McLeod, 385 F.2d 734 (5th Cir. 1967).

shown that a federal action for an injunction is available for police misconduct.[60] This form of relief could possibly be utilized by either individuals or minority group neighborhood coalitions to effect changes in a particular type of police inaction or discriminatory protection policy.[61] Such plaintiffs could argue that they were being deprived of their right of equal protection by the police "under color of any statute, ordinance, regulation, custom, or usage," thus satisfying the requirements of the statute. There are other methods for correcting police inaction, but their effectiveness may be questionable. The common-law writ of quo warranto is available to the plaintiff seeking to remove an officer for discriminatory practices and has been used in the past to challenge police inaction.[62] Its effect, however, is limited to the prevention of future abuses and it is difficult to acquire standing to bring this action in some jurisdictions. Mandamus, another extraordinary writ, is a possible remedy available to challenge either a particular instance or a general policy of nonenforcement.[63] It will not be issued, however, if the court is required to supervise the daily activities of the police,[64] or if the complaint states only a general allegation of nonenforcement and no specific instances are alleged.[65] Although there are state statutes making neglect of duty a criminal offense[66] and others dealing with police inaction through failure to enforce a particular law,[67] provisions granting a plaintiff civil relief do not exist.

---

60. Under 28 U.S.C. § 1343(3), the federal courts have jurisdiction over section 1983 suits for injunctions without regard to the amount in controversy. *See* Hague v. Committee for Indus. Organization, 307 U.S. 496, 519 (1939) (Court approved a federal injunction against police constitutional violations); Lankford v. Gelston, 364 F.2d 197 (4th Cir. 1966); Houser v. Hill, 278 F. Supp. 920 (M.D. Ala. 1968); Cottonreader v. Johnson, 252 F. Supp. 492 (M.D. Ala. 1966).

61. In Newark, New Jersey, a class action has been filed on behalf of all of the black residents of the city. They are seeking a federal injunction under section 1983 against the Chief of Police, the Mayor, and other public officials. A main objective of the suit is to have alleged racially discriminatory police practices enjoined. Included in the list of specific acts upon which the complaint is based are: beating or intimidating members of plaintiffs' class, habitually referring to members of plaintiffs' class with derogatory, humilitating, and obscene racial epithets, and of particular importance here, the refusing to give members of plaintiffs' class proper protection from criminal acts perpetrated against them. Kidd v. Addonizio, Civil No. 899-67 (D. N.J., filed Aug. 24, 1967).

62. *E.g.*, Parker v. McKnaught, 152 Kan. 689, 107 P.2d 693 (1940) (chief of police was ousted from office because of inaction while in a hotel room where intoxicating liquor was being illegally consumed); *cf.* Anderson v. Engler, 181 Kan. 1040, 317 P.2d 432 (1957).

63. *E.g.*, 17 E. McQuillin, The Law of Municipal Corporations § 51.28 (3d ed. rev. 1968).

64. *E.g.*, Walsh v. La Guardia, 269 N.Y. 437, 199 N.E. 652 (1936).

65. *E.g.*, State v. Brewer, 39 Wash. 65, 80 P. 1001 (1905).

66. *E.g.*, Mich. Stat. Ann. § 28.746 (1954); Wis. Stat. Ann. § 946.12(1) (1958).

67. For example, in Michigan it is a misdemeanor to neglect or refuse to enforce the Liquor Control Act, Mich. Stat. Ann. § 18.971 (1957). There is also a statute in Michigan that makes it a misdemeanor for an officer not to make an arrest under a warrant, Mich. Stat. Ann. § 28.388 (1962). For citations and comment on various provisions making the failure to take action or the neglect of duty punishable, see Goldstein, *Police Discretion Not to Invoke the Criminal Process: Low-Visibility Decisions in the Administration of Justice,* 69 Yale L.J. 543, 592-94 (1960).

It is apparent that the present legal remedies available for police inaction are inadequate as regards the victim of crime. Bars to recovery against the municipality, such as the discretionary immunity, protect the individual policeman and administrator when their actions are within the scope of their duties. Even if a policeman's negligence were found to be outside the scope of his authority and a judgment were obtained against him, it is probable that his personal resources would cover only a small fraction of the total disability suffered by the victim. The combined effect of providing immunities for both the municipality and the individual policeman has been to leave the victim of crime, even in cases of clear police negligence, without a successful tort remedy.[68] The effectiveness of section 1983 is limited when dealing with omissive negligence. Initially the plaintiff must have a cause of action wherein he could or would have recovered in that jurisdiction but for his being deprived of some right or privilege by police implementation of existing laws and enforcement policies.

Some authorities feel that the victim of a crime should be compensated by the state for his injury regardless of the state's negligence.[69] With this type of solution, the distinction between misfeasance and nonfeasance in police negligence cases loses its significance and the duty to provide protection is expanded to include the individual crime victim.[70] Recovery rests not on the showing of municipal liability, but on state recognition of the duty to protect the individual.[71] Underlying the rationale for state compensation is the realistic admission that all crime is not preventable; regardless of the amount of police protection provided, a certain amount of crime is inevitable.

A convincing argument for state compensation[72] is that while the state does nothing for the victim of a crime, the tort feasor-criminal may be provided

68. *See* Mathes & Jones, *Toward a "Scope of Official Duty" Immunity for Police Officers in Damage Actions,* 53 GEO. L.J. 889 (1965). The authors argue for an extension of financial responsibility to the public agency for police officer offenses committed during the scope of "official duty".

69. *See, e.g.,* Goldberg, *Equality and Governmental Action,* 39 N.Y.U.L. REV. 205, 224 (1964). This author feels that the victim of a crime has been denied the "protection" of the law, and ". . . society should assume some responsibility for making him whole."

70. *See* Comment, *Compensation for Victims of Crime,* 33 U. CHI. L. REV. 531, 536 (1966).

71. A derivative of this viewpoint is the notion that people who live in areas subject to high crime rates do not share equally in the general welfare of the community and therefore should be compensated for their injuries resulting from this inequity. *See* Kutner, *Crime-Torts: Due Process of Compensation For Crime Victims,* 41 NOTRE DAME LAW. 487, 488 (1965).

72. Advocates of state compensation plans argue that the state should note the lack of satisfactory alternative sources of relief and assume the obligation of compensating the victim of crime. *See, e.g.,* Wolfgang, *Victim Compensation in Crimes of Personal Violence,* 50 MINN. L. REV. 223, 240-41 (1965). When consideration is given to what happens to the victim's chances of recovery from the criminal when the state imposes criminal sanctions, this argument is given added validity. The state probably impairs the victim's civil remedy when it imposes prison confinement on the criminal and puts him in a nonproductive situation where he has no opportunity to provide restitution to his victim.

with food, shelter, medical attention and rehabilitative services. Liability has has been imposed without fault in analogous areas of the law, such as workmen's compensation, warranty, and extrahazardous activity. In these areas the victims are members of an enterprise and their loss is distributed among all the beneficiaries of the enterprise that created the risk. Similarly, it is argued that society is such an enterprise and that the loss suffered by crime victims should be distributed among all members of society. Yet another argument is that in return for a citizen's payment of taxes, the government agrees to provide certain services; when police protection is inadequate, a breach of implied contract occurs. Moreover, criminally inflicted injuries are reasonably foreseeable incidental damages from the breach of such a contract.

Five states have compensation plans in effect at the present time,[73] and many other jurisdictions are considering their adoption, including the District of Columbia.[74] Support for the theoretical basis of these statutes can be found by considering the rationalization for state statutes currently in existence that provide general recovery for property damage and personal injury of victims of mob and riot damages.[75] These statutes, which have been in effect for several years, are justified by the same major premise that supports the current compensation plans: the state has a general duty to prevent these acts of lawless violence.[76]

One major drawback of a crime compensation plan is that such a system

---

73. California—CAL. GOV'T CODE §§ 13960 to 66 (West Supp. 1970); Hawaii—HAWAII REV. STAT. § 351 (1968); Maryland—MD. ANN. CODE art. 26A, §§ 1-17 (Supp. 1969); Massachusetts—MASS. GEN. LAWS ch. 258A, §§ 1-7 (Supp. 1970); New York—N.Y. EXEC. LAW §§ 620-35 (McKinney Supp. 1969-70).

74. For a comprehensive discussion of the peculiarities in the compensation plans of California, New York, Maryland, Hawaii, Massachusetts and those jurisdictions where their initiation is under consideration, including the District of Columbia, see Geis, *Compensation for Crime Victims and the Police,* 13 POLICE no.5 at 56-57 (1969). For their general relative propriety see Comment, *But What About the Victim? The Forsaken Man in American Criminal Law,* 22 U. FLA. L. REV. 1 (1969).

75. In Darlington v. New York, 31 N.Y. 163, 186-87 (1865), the court stated the underlying policy of the law respecting mob and riot statutes:

> [t]o make good at the public expense, the losses of those who may be so unfortunate, as, without their own fault, to be injured in their property by acts of lawless violence of a particular kind, which it is the general duty of the government to prevent; and, further, and principally, we may suppose, to make it the interest of every person liable to contribute to the public expenses, to discourage lawlessness and violence, and maintain the empire of the laws established to preserve public quiet and social order.

For typical state statutes see, *e.g.*, CONN. GEN. STAT. ANN § 7-108 (1958); ILL. STAT. ANN. ch. 24 1-4-8 (Smith-Hurd Supp. 1970); KAN. STAT. ANN. § 12-201 (1964); WIS. STAT. ANN. § 66.091 (1965). *See generally* Baylor, *The Ghetto's Need for Liability Insurance,* 57 KY. L.J. 676, 678-80, 682-86 (1969); Lefkowitz, *Municipal Liability for Damage Caused by Riot,* 35 BROOKLYN L. REV. 412 (1969).

76. Further support for victim compensation plans is found in the argument that by imposing criminal sanctions the state not only impairs the victim's private remedy, but frequently leaves him completely without a remedy. This is particularly true if the state convicts the offender and sentences him to life imprisonment or death. *See* Comment, *Victims of Violent Crime: Should They be an Object of Social Effection?,* 40 MISS. L.J. 92 (1968).

might require substantial tax increases to meet the newly created financial burden.[77] Because of this factor, many state legislatures are probably unwilling to establish compensation systems. Even if state insurance could be obtained, its cost may not be considered presently feasible. The economic outlay could be reduced if a system other than one of absolute liability were adopted. One alternative would be to subject the state to liability only when a state employee has been negligent to some degree. In cases in which the employee has acted outside the scope of his authority, the state could pay the plaintiff's claim but retain a right of indemnification against the employee. Such a variation of the concept of strict compensatory state liability would seem to be more acceptable to the budgetary minded legislator whose state does not presently have sufficient resources to invoke a total compensation plan.

It could be argued that if an adequate tort remedy were available to crime victims for a municipality's negligence, this would provide an increased incentive for police to provide as much protection as possible in a nondiscriminatory manner. This expanded municipal duty would not necessarily mean the imposition of strict liability. It is not expected that the police could provide protection to everyone who requests aid. In deciding whether to provide individual protection in a given situation, the officer should become aware of the comparative gravity of the situation and determine his actions accordingly. A practice could be initiated whereby a policeman's response to a given situation would be compared to that of a reasonable man in similar circumstances. He would make his decision whether to act by comparing the present circumstances with suggested procedures for like situations, rather than by arbitrary convenience. For example, if someone complained that he was being threatened, the policeman would attempt to ascertain the credibility of the claim by questioning the individual as to its validity. If the claim were substantiated or considered justified and reasonable, then the police would acquire a duty to provide a reasonable amount of protection, taking into account the magnitude of the task involved in relation to available resources. The added financial burden placed on the municipality because of the imposition of this extended liability could be met by obtaining liability insurance.[78] Thus an individual's

---

77. The chief objection to such a plan seems to be the cost to the public. *See, e.g.*, Covey, *Alternatives to a Compensation Plan for Victims of Physical Violence*, 69 DICK. L. REV. 391, 392 (1965); Schultz, *The Violated: A Proposal to Compensate Victims of Violent Crime*, 10 ST. LOUIS U.L.J. 238, 246 (1965). This lack of adequate financing has been the biggest defect in victim compensation plans. *See* Note, *The Ghetto Disorders: A Reconsideration of Post-Riot Remedies*, 21 U. FLA. L. REV. 84, 91 (1968).

78. For the view that the trend is toward implementing liability insurance, risk-spreading, and protection of individual security, see Lloyd, *The Rising Tide of Liability*, 17 SYRACUSE L. REV. 127 (1965): "The most significant phenomenon of judicial lawmaking in the last twenty-five years has been the positive, accelerating trend toward the extension of liability . . . in all areas of the law . . . ." It is arguable that if the economic burden of providing insurance is too great for the municipality, a practice whereby the potential victim purchases the insurance could be initiated. This type of special individual crime risk policy does not appear to be practical because few

loss or injury as the result of a crime would be spread over the entire municipal population.

The problem with this standard of reasonableness[79] analysis is that the amount of protection currently capable of being provided may not be enough to meet the demands and requirements of society. Thus, although this solution would probably induce the police to be more conscious of individual requests for protection, and more equitable in distribution of existing resources, it would not solve the overall problem of underprotection, but neither would an automatic crime compensation system.[80] Although a total crime compensation plan may pay for resulting injuries, it is not an adequate substitute for efficient police protection of the potential victim. Crime compensation plans, while aiding the injured victim, do very little in terms of "preventative maintenance." Lacking is the motivating incentive factor found in the threat of an impending tort suit. Ideologically, although a system of crime compensation does not necessarily imply a direct notion of admitted police defeat to criminal activity, it does suggest that respect for law and order and the right of an individual to be secure in his person from unlawful acts have been compromised to a certain degree.

V. Police Justifications For The Existence Of The Underprotection Problem

It has been suggested that "[t]here is no way to measure the number of crimes prevented by police activity; but the number of crimes prevented is not likely to be large."[81] There are many reasons behind the underprotection problem; two of these are most basic: First, police are given grossly inadequate resources; second, the resources actually provided are inefficiently and inequitably allocated.

In some instances these two factors interrelate, causing discriminatory enforcement situations, derivatives of the major problem of underprotection. Ideally, discretionary enforcement would occur in attempting to obtain the best results from the limited available resources. The police may be granted some reprieve for their inaction and subsequent disregard of individual re-

---

people would consider the possibility of being victimized sufficient reason to purchase a separate insurance policy. *See*, Starrs, *A Modest Proposal to Insure Justice for Victims of Crime,* 50 MINN. L. REV. 285, 301 (1965).

79. A simple reasonableness test is somewhat inadequate in the traditional sense, because it does not provide for a uniform standard. Cases involving police inaction, however, are usually peculiar in their facts and as a matter of necessity this test could provide one guideline for municipal tort recovery.

80. An argument could be made that, in some less physically damaging situations, this type of system would encourage two people with criminal tendencies to get together and collude, whereby one would perpetrate a staged crime on the other and then the two would split the compensation award. For a discussion of collusion in cases of intrafamily claims see Comment, *Compensation for Victims of Crime—Some Practical Considerations,* 15 BUFFALO L. REV. 645, 650-51 (1966).

81. Wilson, *Police Dilemmas,* 4 TRIAL no. 6, 12 (1968).

quests for protection because of the limited resources they have to work with and the discretionary manner in which these resources have to be allocated. This justification, however, has not satisfied the claim of the ghetto resident that the available resources are allocated in an unequal and discriminatory fashion.

When a policeman learns of the possibility of a crime being committed and he decides to investigate further, or when a police commissioner decides how many officers to assign to a certain area in the city, discretionary functions are being performed. Whether police inaction is a single omissive act, the consequences of which fall on an individual, or it is a whole conglomeration of events and practices combining to subject different municipal areas to unequal amounts of police protection, part of the justification and responsibility for such conditions rests with the practice of police discretion. Police discretion occurs at both the individual officer level and at the administrative level. Discretionary decisions at the administrative level involve such matters as the laws to be given the most strict enforcement, the methods to be employed in their enforcement, and the allocation of limited available enforcement resources to the various areas of the municipality according to their needs. It is evident that an unwise decision influenced by racial or political bias on any of these matters could severely compound the underprotection problem for residents of adversely affected municipal areas.

The practice of police discretion runs contrary to the concept of "full enforement." This concept implies that the police enforce all statutes at all times against every possible offender.[82] This idea is physically impossible. Discretion is utilized, therefore, to decide which laws will be rigidly enforced and what kind of effort will be exerted to enforce them.

State statutes and city ordinances are explicit in defining criminal conduct, but the legislators who voted the statutes into law probably did not expect them to be strictly or literally enforced in all cases without exception. Consequently, though few statutes actually provide for any police discretion,[83] it

---

82. The concept of full enforcement is explained in Goldstein, *Police Discretion: The Ideal Versus the Real*, 23 PUB. AD. REV. 140 (1963):

> It [full enforcement] suggests that the police are without authority to ignore violations, to warn offenders when a violation has in fact occurred, or to do anything short of arresting the offender and placing a charge against him for the specific crime committed.

Some state statutes impose a duty upon law enforcement officers to arrest "all" violators of the criminal law. For sheriffs see ARIZ. REV. STAT. ANN. § 11-441 (A) (2) (1956); ARK. STAT. ANN. § 12-1110 (1947); CAL. GOV'T CODE § 26601 (West 1968); IDAHO CODE § 31-2202 (2) (1963); N.D. CENT. CODE § 11-15-03 (1960); WASH. REV. CODE § 36.28.010 (1969). For city police see COLO. REV. STAT. § 139-3-15 (1963); IOWA CODE ANN. § 748.4 (1950); NEB. REV. STAT. § 16-323 (1962); WYO. STAT. ANN. § 7-155 (1959).

83. Partial recognition of police discretion is found in N.M. STAT. § 39-1-1 (1953), which makes it a police duty:

> . . . to investigate all violations of the criminal laws . . . which are called to the attention of any such officer or of which he is aware, and it is also declared

is an irreplaceable tool, the use of which is essential if police are to be expected to achieve the results expected by lawmakers. The indispensable nature of police discretion was recognized years ago by the Michigan Supreme Court:

> [T]he [police] commissioner is bound to use the discretion with which he is clothed . . . . To enable him to perform the duties imposed upon him by law, he is supplied with certain limited means. It is entirely obvious that he must exercise a sound discretion as to how those means shall be applied for the good of the community.[84]

Police do not like to publicly acknowledge the exercise of discretion because it belies the image of total objectivity and impartiality in enforcement that they attempt to project. This attitude exists because of a fear that a formally expressed discretion policy would be too vulnerable to public charges of discrimination in its application. It would seem that if police officers were impartial in their enforcement policies and openly exercised equitable discretion, a public recognition of this practice would do much to improve public relations. Although police do not claim to have been granted discretionary powers, they exercise a wide range of discretion without offering any justification for its practice. Formal legislative recognition of these informal discretionary practices would provide useful guidelines for implementing standards for discretion policies and would result in a better public understanding and appreciation of their value.

The allocation of resources has become a mandatory police function because of the limited manpower and other resources available to police departments. There are not enough resources and personnel at police disposal to detect all the crime flourishing in a city or to suppress all conduct the legislature has deemed unlawful. Consequently, the municipality, acting through the police administrative level, must exercise discretion in determining how to allocate the limited resources that do exist. This municipal function was recognized in the *Riss* decision: "[t]he amount of protection that may be provided is limited by the resources of the community and by a considered legislative-executive decision as to how those resources may be deployed."[85]

Various factors included in the limited resource problem are responsible

---

> the duty of every such officer to diligently file a complaint or information, if the circumstances are such as to indicate to a reasonable prudent person that such action should be taken. . . .

For the legal justification of police discretion see W. LaFave, *supra* note 11, at 68:

> There has been no express legislative delegation of discretion to the police, although it is arguable that such a delegation would be constitutional because police are in a position comparable to other administrative agencies. Such a delegation might even be implied, particularly where the substantive criminal law is ambiguous.

84. Gowan v. Smith, 157 Mich. 443, 473, 122 N.W. 286, 297 (1909). For the argument that discretion is a necessary aspect of the allocation of limited resources see Kadish, *Legal Norm and Discretion in the Police and Sentencing Processes*, 75 Harv. L. Rev. 904 (1962).

85. Riss v. City of New York, 22 N.Y.2d 579, 581-82, 240 N.E.2d 860, 861, 293 N.Y.S.2d 897, 898 (1968).

for the creation of insufficient available police protection and subsequent police inaction. Many police departments simply do not have enough resources, including manpower and finances, to adequately protect everyone. Other departments with abundant resources allocate them in such a way that, contemplated or not, certain areas are deprived of equal protection. Some police departments, with substantial resources and the potential for providing equal protection, fall short of this standard because inefficient resource allocation methods are employed by police administrators.

When the legislature declares that a particular form of conduct is criminal, this mandate is usually not accompanied by an appropriation to provide the resources necessary for its enforcement. When appropriations are made, it is by a different segment of the legislature and no guidelines are issued to assist in the direction of their disposal. The police administrator is left with the task of combining these, often conflicting, legislative mandates into an adequate enforcement system. Frustrating his position further is the fact that although there has been a marked increase in total expenditures for law enforcement services in recent years, this increase is comparatively less than the substantial increase provided other public services.[86]

If any progress is to be made in alleviating the problems of underprotection, municipal governmental policies should be reviewed and police operating systems should be evaluated.[87] Policies adopted and promulgated by municipal administrators should reflect the desire to treat all areas of the community equally. Until municipal governments are resigned to the fact that minority and ghetto areas should be provided an equal share of governmental services, existing inequalities will continue to plague these areas, regardless of the police resources available. Police departments should develop definite operating standards that would serve as guidelines for individual officers and patrolmen to follow. Enforcement priorities should be formulated and made part of standard enforcement procedure to insure that manpower is not being wasted on the enforcement of laws the public has little interest in upholding.[88]

---

86. *See, e.g.*, B. OLSON, POLICE EXPENDITURES 3 [submitted to the PRESIDENT'S COMMISSION ON LAW ENFORCEMENT] (1967); PRESIDENT'S COMMISSION ON LAW ENFORCEMENT, TASK FORCE REPORT: CRIME AND ITS IMPACT—AN ASSESSMENT 55 (table 9) (1967).

87. For an analysis of the methods employed in reviewing complaints directed toward the police see Note, *The Administration of Complaints by Civilians Against the Police*, 77 HARV. L. REV. 499 (1964). Because the utilization of the courts has proven somewhat ineffective as a check for police activity, some observers favor the creation of civilian review boards to hear citizen complaints of police misconduct. *E.g.*, Burger, *Who Will Watch the Watchman?*, 14 AM. U.L. REV. 1 (1964). For a bibliography of works discussing police review boards see Cray, *Annotated Bibliography on Police Review Boards*, 3 LAW IN TRANSITION Q. 197 (1966).

88. Often the complaint is made by both police personnel and others that too much of a policeman's time is spent doing routine clerical chores, such as filling out and filing reports, thus providing less time for the protection function. "Studies have indicated that perhaps 90 percent of police contacts with the public are non-criminal in nature." Fandel, *supra* note 1, at 78. Perhaps better utility of a policeman's time could be

One alternative that has been suggested to help initiate these proposals is the "program budget."[89] The objective of this proposal is a systemized method of allocating police department resources in an efficient and equitable manner, insuring that each municipal area will receive equal police protection and attention. Attractive features of the program budget include the following: allowing the public to observe and modify police practices, illustrating where allocated money goes and how it is spent, showing the emphasis that police give to each major task, and publicly acknowledging the exercise of discretion. Implementation of these and similar programs by police departments across the country will improve police public relations and lead to a solution of the underprotection problem.

Conclusion

Clearly, there are substantial barriers to recovery from the municipality for the victim of a crime. Barriers to judicial recovery such as sovereign immunity, discretionary immunity, lack of a duty to protect the individual, and the rule of no liability for omissive conduct, confront crime victims in many jurisdictions. The doctrine of sovereign immunity has been abolished or signififantly altered in many jurisdictions, but as long as the courts fail to impose a duty on the municipality to protect the individual, the crime victim is without recourse to recover for his injuries.

When the police, under reasonable circumstances, ignore a notice of a possible criminal attack, as was the case in *Riss*, the municipality should be held accountable for the inaction of its police. Society created the circumstances giving rise to the victim's plight; society should bear the burden of making the victim whole. The amount of attention and resources given the victim of a crime should compare more favorably with that given the criminal. Judicial promulgation of a municipal duty to protect the individual would encourage society to search for more effective policing methods, dedicate more of its resources to crime prevention, and better allocate existing resources.

The state crime compensation plan seems the most attractive of the possible methods for providing relief to the crime victim. The two major criticisms of such systems are the increased financial burden on the state, and that simply providing monetary relief to the victim does nothing to cure the overall problem of underprotection and increasing crime.

The plight of minority groups residing in the "inner-city" is similar to that of the individual crime victim. The substandard quality and quantity of pro-

---

obtained by employing civilian personnel to do some of the less critical tasks, thus leaving the policeman more time to concentrate on his primary duty (the one for which he has been specifically trained), that of ensuring law and order and protecting the citizen.

89. Comment, *Program Budgeting for Police Departments*, 76 YALE L.J. 822 (1967).

tection that these minority people are subjected to is a product of discriminatory police policies and practices. The Constitutional and local statutory tools presently available adequately guarantee the rights of equal police protection and other municipal services. What is lacking is enforced judicial recognition of these rights. The alienated residents of the "inner-city" need an improved image of the police and local government. Jurisdictions that recognize these facts may well have fewer racial disturbances and incidents of crime as a result.

Imprisonment For Debt And The Constitution

Imprisonment for civil debt[1] originated in ancient times and is part of our western legal heritage.[2] The punishment for debt under early Roman law was especially savage. Following judgment, the debtor could be arrested and held in the creditor's home or private prison. If the debt was not paid within a specified length of time, the creditor could either kill the debtor or sell him and his family into slavery. If there were more than one creditor, the law allowed them to divide the debtor's body among them according to the relative amount owed to each creditor.[3]

In the early Middle Ages imprisonment for debt was common; with the rise of feudalism, however, the practice dwindled because feudal lords disliked losing the service of their vassals.[4] In England, by the beginning of the

1. This Comment will deal only with imprisonment for civil debt, as opposed to criminal debt – fines imposed for crimes. Imprisonment for nonpayment of fines was the subject of a recent Supreme Court decision in which the Court held it a denial of equal protection to limit punishment to payment of a fine for those who are able to pay but to convert the fine to imprisonment for those who are unable to pay. Tate v. Short, 39 U.S.L.W. 4301 (1971). The subject has also received much treatment in legal periodicals. Comment, *Fines, Imprisonment, and the Poor: "Thirty Dollars or Thirty Days,"* 57 CALIF. L. REV. 778 (1969); Comment, *Jail Fees and Court Costs for the Indigent Criminal Defendant: An Examination of the Tennessee Procedure,* 35 TENN. L. REV. 74 (1968); Note, *Imprisonment for Nonpayment of Fines and Costs: A New Look at the Law and the Constitution,* 22 VAND. L. REV. 611 (1969); Note, *Criminal Costs Assessment in Missouri – Without Rhyme or Reason,* 1962 WASH. U.L.Q. 76; Note, *The Assessment and Collection of the Costs of a Criminal Prosecution in Wyoming,* 13 WYO. L.J. 178 (1959).
2. Ford, *Imprisonment for Debt,* 25 MICH. L. REV. 24 (1927) [hereinafter cited as Ford]; Shaiman, *The History of Imprisonment for Debt and Insolvency Laws in Pennsylvania as They Evolved from the Common Law,* 4 AM. J. LEGAL HIST. 205 (1960); Washer, *Imprisonment for Debt,* 7 GREEN BAG 410, 411 (1895) (compares early practices in Greece, Rome, England and America).
3. Ford at 24-25.
4. *Id.* at 25; Note, *Present Status of Execution Against the Body of the Judgment Debtor,* 42 IOWA L. REV. 306 (1957).

LAW AND THE SOCIAL ORDER, Vol. 1970, No. 2, pp. 659-677.

13th century, no arrests were allowed at any stage of civil proceedings except in actions of trespass *vi et armis*. Nevertheless, arrests for nonpayment of a judgment were accomplished in many situations by bringing sham actions of trespass along with the principal action. While courts were expanding by fiction the right to arrest a defendant for nonpayment of a judgment, Parliament was expanding the right to arrest a defendant before trial. One popular method was the use of a writ of *capias ad respondendum*, which commanded the sheriff to take the debtor into custody until security for the creditor's claim was furnished.[5] By 1503 a writ of *capias ad respondendum* was available for nearly every civil action. Moreover, courts used this as grounds for holding that in cases in which the defendant could have been arrested before trial, he could also be arrested after the trial for nonpayment of the judgment by a writ of *capias ad satisfaciendum*.[6]

The colonization of America benefited from the harsh English practices of imprisoning for debt. Many of the settlers came to America to avoid arrest and imprisonment at the hands of their creditors. The colonial laws of civil arrest prohibited many of the most abusive of the English practices.[7] In the drafting stage of early state constitutions, however, provisions prohibiting imprisonment for debt were proposed, but few changes from the English law were actually made.[8] As a result, many debtors were imprisoned during this country's early history.[9]

A reform movement swept the nation in the 1830's, and statutes were passed restricting, and in some cases prohibiting imprisonment for debt.[10] There have been few legislative changes in this area since that time.[11]

---

5. For a discussion of the history and development of *capias ad respondendum* or imprisonment by mesne process as it relates to imprisonment for debt see Freedman, *Imprisonment for Debt*, 2 TEMP. L.Q. 330, 333-39 (1928).

6. *Id.;* Washer, *supra* note 2, at 412. The practice of imprisoning for debt grew to such proportions in England that separate prisons were established for debtors. The deplorable conditions of these prisons were written about by protest writers of that time. *E.g.*, C. DICKENS, PICKWICK PAPERS (1836); C. DICKENS, DAVID COPPERFIELD (1849).

7. An example is the "Concessions and Agreements" of West New Jersey of 1677; *see* Ford at 28 & n.23.

8. Pennsylvania is one of the few states that granted some relief to the debtor in its first Constitution. PA. CONST. § 28 (1776) *cited in* Shaiman, *supra* note 2, at 214.

9. It is estimated that in the years preceeding 1850, fifty thousand people annually were imprisoned for debt in the northern and middle states. Approximately fifteen percent of those imprisoned owed debts of less than five dollars. Ford at 29 & n.27.

10. This came about through the influence exerted by groups such as the Prison Discipline Society. *Id.* at 32.

11. Generally, states admitted to the Union after 1830 adopted imprisonment for debt provisions similar to those of the older states. *E.g.*, ARIZ. CONST. art. II, § 18 (allows imprisonment only for debts incurred by fraud); HAWAII CONST. art. I, § 17 (completely prohibits imprisonment for debt); KAN. CONST. Bill of Rights § 16 (allows imprisonment for debts incurred by fraud); UTAH CONST. art. I, § 16 (allows imprisonment of absconding debtors only).

I. Present Status Of The Law

The United States Constitution contains no express provision prohibiting imprisonment for debt. The only federal statute that refers to this subject is part of the Conformity Act, which directs each federal court to follow the applicable law of the state in which it sits.[12]

The remedy of imprisonment for debt has been influenced not only by legislation but also by case law. Courts have traditionally allowed imprisonment for debt according to the category within which each case falls. The two basic categories of debtors in this area are those who owe a contract debt and those who owe a debt on a tort.[13] A further distinction is made by the courts of a few states between those debtors who are able to pay the debt in question and those debtors who are unable to pay it, or are indigent.[14]

A. *State Constitutional and Statutory Provisions*

The constitutions of ten states completely prohibit imprisonment for debt,[15] while nine states have no constitutional provisions on the subject.[16] Most of the other states have general prohibitions against imprisonment for debt, with certain specific exceptions.[17] The most commonly enumerated exceptions are for debts arising from tort actions,[18] cases of fraud by debtor,[19] and situations where the creditor believes the debtor is about to abscond.[20] Some of the states that allow imprisonment for debts arising from tort actions further narrow the category to willful torts.[21]

Some states have chosen a few specific torts which they except from the general prohibition. For example, Nevada allows imprisonment for debts

---

12. 28 U.S.C. § 2007 (1964).
13. *See* p. 662 & notes 28 & 29 *infra.*
14. *See* p. 677 & note 113 *infra.*
15. Ala. Const. art. I, § 20; Ga. Const. art. I, para. XXI; Hawaii Const. art. I, § 17; Md. Const. art. III, § 38; Miss. Const. art. III, § 30; Mo. Const. art. I, § 13; N.M. Const. art. II, § 21; Okla. Const. art. II, § 13; Tenn. Const. art. I, § 18; Tex. Const. art. I, § 18. Some of these provisions except imprisonment for nonpayment of fines or limit the prohibition to civil actions.
16. Connecticut, Delaware, Louisiana, Maine, Massachusetts, New Hampshire, New York, Virginia, and West Virginia.
17. The States have been classified according to the circumstances in which they allow imprisonment for debt, with each state constitution cited for the exceptions it allows in Legislative Drafting Research Fund of Columbia University, Index Digest of State Constitutions 35051 (2d ed. 1959, Supp. 1964) [Hereinafter cited as Index Digest] and Note, *Supra* note 4.
18. *E.g.*, Colo. Const. art. II, § 12; Mont. Const. art. III, § 12; N.D. Const. art. I, § 15; Idaho Code Ann. § 8-102 (1948); Pa. Stat. Ann. tit. 12, § 257 (Purdon 1970).
19. *See* p. 662 & note 25 *infra.*
20. *See* p. 662 & note 27 *infra.*
21. *E.g.*, Cal. Const. art. I, § 15; Colo. Rev. Stat. Ann. § 77-9-3 (1963); Idaho Code Ann. § 8-102 (1948); Ill. Ann. Stat. ch. 77, § 5 (Smith-Hurd 1966). The exception for wilful torts is probably a reflection of old English laws by which imprisonment was allowed only in actions for trespass *vi et armis.* In such cases imprisonment was considered a punishment for the wrongful act. Ford at 26. *See also* Ky. Rev. Stat. § 426.390 (1969).

arising from actions in libel or slander.[22] Michigan allows the use of this remedy to enforce payment of debts from actions for breach of trust.[23]

Contractual debtors are protected from imprisonment in some states by constitutional provision.[24] Such provisions are often weakened, however, by exceptions for fraud.[25] The definition of "fraud" has been expanded to include almost every instance in which a person owes a contractual debt and does not pay.[26] In this context, fraud usually refers to fraudulent inducement of a contract or fraudulent evasion of a contractual debt. Although absconding debtors often fall within the general exception of fraud, many states have separate provisions that allow for imprisonment if the debtor is about to leave the jurisdiction to avoid payment.[27] This remedy against absconding debtors is often available before as well as after judgment.

B. *Judicial Interpretation of Legislation*

Although statutes authorizing arrests in civil actions are penal in nature and are generally strictly construed,[28] "debt" is often interpreted to thwart prohibitions against imprisonment. Courts have found that the easiest way to avoid the prohibition is to say that the sum owed is not a debt. The definition most commonly used by courts limits "debt" to obligations arising out of contract.[29] An exemplary definition is found in the following language:

> It is well settled that "imprisonment for debt," . . . applies only to debts arising on contract and has no reference to liabilities imposed by law originating in tort or actions ex delicto.[30]

This definition greatly narrows the category of persons covered by state laws designed to protect debtors from incarceration.

---

22. NEV. CONST. art. I, § 14.
23. MICH. CONST. art. I, § 21.
24. *See id.;* S.D. CONST. art. VI, § 15; WIS. CONST. art. I, § 16. In many states, courts interpret the word "debt" to mean only debts on a contract. This is often done even when the prohibition may not be expressly limited to such. *See* note 29 *infra.*
25. *E.g.,* ARIZ. CONST. art. II, § 18; FLA. CONST. art. I, § 11; IDAHO CONST. art. I, § 15; WYO. CONST. art. I, § 5.
26. Fraud in the creation of a debt or obligation may bring the debtor within the fraud exception as may any element of misrepresentation as to the basis of indebtedness. *See, e.g.,* People v. Neal C. Oester, Inc., 154 Cal. App. 2d 888, 891, 316 P.2d 784, 786-87 (1957); Allied Financial Corp. v. Steel Panel Sales Corp., 86 N.J. Super. 65, 75, 205 A.2d 904, 909-10 (1964); Jordan v. Hoffman, 126 N.J.L. 100, 105, 18 A.2d 607, 609 (1941); Comment, *Enforcement of Divorce Decrees and Settlements by Contempt and Imprisonment in California,* 9 HASTINGS L.J. 57, 61 (1957); Comment, *Contempt Enforcement of "Integrated" Divorce Settlements in California,* 10 STAN. L. REV. 321, 324 (1958).
27. *E.g.,* ALASKA CONST. art. I, § 7; ORE. CONST. art. I, § 19; UTAH CONST. art. I, § 16; WASH. CONST. art. I, § 17.
28. *See, e.g.,* Baker Wholesale Co. v. Fleming, 227 S.C. 312, 317, 87 S.E.2d 876, 878 (1955); North Central Inv. Co. v. Vander Vorste, 81 S.D. 340, 350-51, 135 N.W.2d 23, 30 (1965).
29. *E.g.,* Davis v. State, 237 Ala. 143, 144, 185 So. 774, 776 (1938); *Ex parte* Silvas, 16 Ariz. 41, 44, 140 P. 988, 989 (1914); Reese v. Baker, 98 Fla. 52, 56, 123 So. 3, 4 (1929); Cox v. Rice, 375 Ill. 357, 361-62, 31 N.E.2d 786, 788 (1941).
30. Reese v. Baker, 98 Fla. 52, 56, 123 So. 3, 4 (1929).

Courts have been consistent in calling a monetary obligation something other than a "debt" when they find that the integrity of the judicial process might be threatened by nonpayment. The most common examples are imprisonment for contempt upon failure to pay a judgment when specifically ordered to do so,[31] and failure to pay alimony[32] or child support.[33]

Two main reasons are given for differentiating between simple debt and alimony or support payments. One reason is that in most civil suits "the judgment of the court is merely a declaration of an amount owing,"[34] whereas alimony and support payments are obligations imposed by direct court order to pay. Disobedience of such orders is an affront to the dignity of the court and threatens the effectiveness of the judicial process. Unless the court has some method of enforcing its orders, they are meaningless.[35]

A second reason for treating alimony and child support differently is the belief that the obligations arising from the marital bond are unique and not to be classified as ordinary "debts." The family is one of the most highly protected institutions in American society.[36] As such, it is argued that when a man enters matrimony, he assumes socially imposed obligations that cannot be lightly disposed of. Society has traditionally felt that a woman should be secure upon abandonment of her premarital means of support. By enforcing alimony and support payments society ensures the security of women, encourages their participation in marriage, and protects the institution most basic to society, the family. Furthermore, society has a pecuniary interest in enforcing these payments. If the wife and children are left without the husband's support, they are more likely to become wards of society — recipients of welfare. Thus, it is the sanction of society that induces courts to define debt so as to exclude alimony and child support payments, allowing imprisonment for those who fail to meet these obligations.[37]

Imprisonment on mesne process presents another case in which courts allow imprisonment of a debtor on the grounds that it is necessary for the

---

31. *E.g.*, United States *ex rel.* Griffin v. Martin, 409 F.2d 1300, 1302 (2d Cir. 1969); Cutting v. Van Fleet, 252 F. 100, 102 (9th Cir. 1918); Harrison v. Harrison, 239 Ark. 756, 759-60, 394 S.W.2d 128, 130 (1965); Zeitinger v. Mitchell, 244 S.W.2d 91, 97 (Mo. 1951). *See also* Reeves v. Crownshield, 274 N.Y. 74, 77, 8 N.E.2d 283, 285 (1937). *But cf.* Leonard v. State, 170 Ark. 41, 49-50, 278 S.W. 654, 657 (1926).

32. *E.g.*, State *ex rel.* Krueger v. Stone, 137 Fla. 498, 499-500, 188 So. 575, 576 (1939); Howard v. Howard, 130 So. 2d 83, 85 (Fla. Ct. App. 1961); Clausen v. Clausen, 250 Minn. 293, 301, 84 N.W.2d 675, 681 (1957); *Ex parte* Phillips, 43 Nev. 368, 187 P. 311, 311-12 (1920).

33. *E.g.*, Johnson v. Johnson, 241 Md. 416, 419, 216 A.2d 914, 916 (1966); Freeland v. Freeland, 313 S.W.2d 943, 946 (Tex. Civ. App. 1958); Decker v. Decker, 52 Wash. 2d 456, 458, 326 P.2d 332, 333 (1958).

34. Decker v. Decker, 52 Wash. 2d 456, 458, 326 P.2d 332, 333 (1958).

35. *Id.*

36. H. Clarke, Social Legislation 27, 73 *et seq.* (1957).

37. Howard v. Howard, 130 So. 2d 83, 85 (Fla. Ct. App. 1961). *See generally* H. Clarke, *supra* note 36.

proper functioning of the court. This process, sometimes executed by a writ of *ne exeat,* developed from the common law writ of *capias ad respondendum*[38] and the chancery writ of *ne exeat regno.*[39] Both of these writs resulted in the imprisonment of the debtor even before a judgment on the debt and were considered mesne processes — auxiliary steps necessary for the court to proceed with the main action.[40]

In modern times almost all states use procedures similar to the old writs but known by different names. In California, and elsewhere, the term used is simply mesne process.[41] Illinois is an example of the states using a writ of *ne exeat.*[42] Pennsylvania issues writs of *capias ad respondendum*[43] for the same purpose. An Illinois court, in discussing at length the history and use of writs of *capias ad respondendum,* decided that the use of such writs does not constitute imprisonment for debt.[44]

Like the court above, most courts hold that imprisonment under a writ of *ne exeat* or mesne process is not imprisonment for debt,[45] but is more analagous to imprisonment for contempt. When a person is arrested under a writ of *ne exeat,* he is being held not to enforce payment of any money owed, but to enforce his appearance in court, thus insuring that the judicial proceeding is meaningful and functional.[46] However, the fact remains that if the defendant posts bond, he will be released, and if he cannot or does not post bond, he will be held in jail. Although this raises some of the same problems as imprisonment for nonpayment of fines or penalties,[47] it is relevant to imprisonment for debt since the defendant is involved in a civil suit and he is imprisoned before the rendering of judgment.

---

38. Since judgment by default was unknown in the early common law, it was essential that the defendant appear in court. By obtaining a writ of *capias ad respondendum,* the plaintiff could ensure the defendant's appearance. This writ ordered the sheriff to arrest and hold the defendant until the trial. The defendant could post bond and be released, but since the sheriff could be held liable for the debt if he failed to appear for trial, the bond was usually equal to or higher than the amount in dispute. Freedman, *supra* note 5, at 330-31.

39. A writ of *ne exeat regno* was an order by the chancery court for the defendant not to leave the kingdom or the court's jurisdiction. If the plaintiff presented facts showing that the defendant was about to leave the jurisdiction, the defendant could be arrested and held until trial, unless he posted bond. *Id.*

40. *See, e.g.,* Shatz v. Paul, 7 Ill. App. 2d 223, 236, 129 N.E.2d 348, 355 (1955); Elkay Steel Co. v. Collins, 392 Pa. 441, 443 n.2, 141 A.2d 212, 214 n.2 (1958).

41. CAL. CONST. art. I, § 15.

42. ILL. ANN. STAT. ch. 97, § 1 (Smith-Hurd 1958).

43. PA. STAT. ANN. tit. 12, § 171 (Purdon 1970).

44. Shatz v. Paul, 7 Ill. App. 2d 223, 129 N.E.2d 348 (1955).

45. *E.g.,* Gooding v. Reid, Murdock & Co., 177 F. 684, 686 (7th Cir. 1910); and cases cited note 40 *supra.*

46. Anderson v. Anderson, 315 Ill. App. 380, 387, 43 N.E.2d 176, 179 (1942); Cohen v. Cohen, 319 Mass. 31, 64 N.E.2d 689 (1946); Nixon v. Nixon, 39 Wis. 2d 391, 397, 158 N.W.2d 919, 923 (1968). Statutes that allow imprisonment of absconding debtors are very similar in purpose and effect to arrests under writ of *ne exeat.*

47. Note 1 *supra.*

II. Constitutional Questions

A. Unenumerated Rights

In addition to the specific rights enumerated in the Bill of Rights, other rights originating from the concept of democratic government are also retained by the people. The task of defining these unenumerated rights has never been easy. Courts have been reluctant to base the reasoning in their decisions on such vague terms as natural rights, preferring to find the protection sought in one of the specific limitations of the constitutional amendments. Nevertheless, certain rights have been recognized by the Supreme Court which cannot be grounded in the "plain words" of the Constitution.[48] These rights have been based on "principle[s] of justice so rooted in the traditions and conscience of our people as to be ranked as fundamental," and therefore "implicit in the concept of ordered liberty."[49]

The question remaining to be determined is whether the practice of imprisonment for debt violates any of these fundamental rights. There are two general tests for determining whether a statute or regulation contravenes these basic rights. The first is the social purpose test,[50] which implies that since liberty and freedom are primary in our system of government, any regulation circumscribing that freedom must have a demonstrable social need or socially useful purpose. No law or regulation may be made unless some definite social need or purpose is demonstrated.[51]

The second test is an extension of the first. Social benefit is balanced against the detriment resulting from impairment of natural rights.[52] If the benefit to society outweighs the detriment, the regulation may be upheld as a proper exercise of police power. However, if the detriment proves to be greater than the benefit, the regulation is invalid as beyond police powers.[53]

Thus the benefit to society of imprisonment for debt and the social purpose of statutes allowing this practice must be determined. The definite purpose of these statutes is difficult to ascertain. Essentially this is because

---

48. *See, e.g.,* Loving v. Virginia, 388 U.S. 1, 12 (1967) (freedom to marry); United States v. Laub, 385 U.S. 475, 481 (1967) (right to travel); Griswold v. Connecticut, 381 U.S. 479, 485 (1965) (right of privacy); Aptheker v. Secretary of State, 378 U.S. 500, 505 (1964) (right to travel abroad); Kent v. Dulles, 357 U.S. 116, 125-27 (1958) (right to travel); Skinner v. Oklahoma, 316 U.S. 535, 541 (1942) (right to procreate).

49. Palko v. Connecticut, 302 U.S. 319, 325 (1937), *quoting* Snyder v. Massachusetts 291 U.S. 97, 105 (1934).

50. Ratner, *The Function of the Due Process Clause,* 116 U. Pa. L. Rev. 1048, 1070 (1968) [hereinafter cited as Ratner].

51. *Id.;* Note, *Substantive Due Process and Felony Treatment of Pot Smokers: The Current Conflict,* 2 Ga. L. Rev. 247, 254 (1968). *See also* Griswold v. Connecticut, 381 U.S. 479, 497-99 (1965) (Goldberg, J. concurring); Goldblatt v. Hempstead, 369 U.S. 590, 594-95 (1962); Shelton v. Tucker, 364 U.S. 479, 488-89 (1960); Bates v. Little Rock, 361 U.S. 516, 524 (1960).

52. Ratner at 1071.

53. *Id.*

the statutes themselves have existed for so long, and because many of society's basic values have drastically changed since the time when the practice of imprisoning for debt was initiated.[54] The original purpose may have been to punish a person, since being in debt was once considered a sin and a crime.[55] Today this is no longer a valid purpose since the state does not purport to punish sin, and indebtedness is not considered a crime. Another purpose may have been to punish the debtor for the act from which the debt arose, as in the ancient tort cases.[56] Yet imprisonment occurs today only if the defendant fails to pay the debt, making it apparent that it is the failure to pay, rather than the act of incurring the debt, which is being punished.

A more likely purpose may have been to enforce payment of debts. Although this goal would seem reasonable, the method employed was unrealistic. The threat of imprisonment may prod some of those capable of paying into making payment, but debtors who are unable to pay remain so despite the threat. Those capable of paying, however, are not forced to pay by most imprisonment for debt statutes, but are only forced to post bond until they can litigate whether their circumstances actually fit within the exceptions to the general prohibition against imprisonment for debt. Nor is it likely that this threat will discourage the prospective tortfeasor from incurring the tort-related debt, since it is unlikely that he will have the possibility of imprisonment in mind when he commits the tort. If he commits an intentional tort without being deterred by the criminal liability, he is not likely to be deterred by the existence of this additional civil remedy.

Probably neither of the alleged benefits to society is so great as to outweigh the detriment of taking a man's liberty. Moreover, the concept of depriving one of his freedom because of an unpaid debt could be considered repulsive by modern standards. The contention that imprisonment for debt does not violate fundamental values because it has been accepted and practiced in the United States since this nation's beginning carries little weight; it is well known that the standards for determining what is reasonable and right change and evolve with the advancement of society.[57]

B. Cruel and Unusual Punishment

The eighth amendment prohibiting cruel and unusual punishment[58] is recited in all state constitutions,[59] and in addition, is made applicable to the

---

54. *See* pp. 659-60 *supra.*
55. Persons dying with unpaid debts were denied Christian burial. Ford at 25.
56. Ford at 26.
57. Wolf v. Colorado, 338 U.S. 25, 27 (1949).
58. "Excessive bail shall not be required, nor excessive fines imposed, nor cruel and unusual punishments inflicted." U.S. CONST. amend. VIII.
59. INDEX DIGEST 342-43.

states through the fourteenth amendment.[60] The source of the eighth amendment is the English Bill of Rights of 1680, which prohibited excessive fines and cruel and unusual punishment in almost the same words.[61] While cruel and unusual punishment is difficult to define, it is generally thought to be any inhuman or barbarous punishment.[62] Public opinion and contemporary attitudes generally guide courts in deciding what is cruel and unusual.[63] Thus, "[t]he Amendment must draw its meaning from the evolving standards of decency that mark the progress of a maturing society."[64]

For evidence of our changing concepts of "cruel and unusual punishment" one may examine the change in attitudes toward death sentences. Capital punishment, like imprisonment for debt, was once completely accepted by society. Recently, however, there has been a growing trend away from this practice, possibly bringing it within the realm of cruel and unusual punishment.[65] Fifteen states have abolished the death penalty or severely restricted it.[66] States which retain the penalty seldom apply it.[67] It may be argued that a similar change in attitude[68] has evolved regarding imprisonment for debt, and that this practice may now also approach the status of "cruel and unusual."[69]

---

60. Robinson v. California, 370 U.S. 660 (1962); *cf.* Molloy v. Hogan, 378 U.S. 1 (1964); Gideon v. Wainwright, 372 U.S. 335 (1963).

61. "[E]xcessive fines have been imposed; and illegal and cruel punishment inflicted. . . . [E]xcessive bail ought not to be required, nor excessive fines imposed; nor cruel and unusual punishments inflicted." 1 W. & M. 2, c. 2 (1688); Note, *Imprisonment for Nonpayment of Fines and Costs: A New Look at the Law and the Constitution,* 22 VAND. L. REV. 611, 634 n.107 (1969).

62. *In re* Kemmler, 136 U.S. 436, 447 (1890); Wilkerson v. Utah, 99 U.S. 130, 134-36 (1878). But for a modern view of what is cruel and unusual see Robinson v. California, 370 U.S. 660 (1962); Trop v. Dulles, 356 U.S. 86 (1958).

63. *See* Weems v. United States, 217 U.S. 349 (1910) for a general discussion of the definition of cruel and unusual punishment and how that definition changes with the advance of civilization. The recent cases of Robinson v. California, 370 U.S. 660 1962) and Driver v. Hinnant, 356 F.2d 761 (4th Cir. 1966) are examples of this change.

64. Trop v. Dulles, 356 U.S. 86, 101 (1962) (divestiture of citizenship violates eighth amendment).

65. Note, *Constitutional Law – Cruel and Unusual – Capital Punishment,* 42 N.C.L. REV. 909, 914 (1964); Comment, *Capital Punishment,* 29 TENN. L. REV. 534, 541 (1962).

66. Comment, *Witherspoon – Will the Due Process Clause Further Regulate the Imposition of the Death Penalty,* 7 DUQUESNE L. REV. 414, n.6 (1969); Comment, *The Capital Punishment Controversy,* 60 J. CRIM. L.C. & P.S. 360, 364 n.42 (1969).

67. THE PRESIDENT'S COMMISSION ON LAW ENFORCEMENT AND THE ADMINISTRATION OF JUSTICE, THE CHALLENGE OF CRIME IN A FREE SOCIETY 143 (1967). "[T]here were no executions in 1968, two in 1967 and one in 1966." Comment, *The Capital Punishment Controversy, supra* note 66, at 364 n.45 (1969).

68. The change in attitude toward capital punishment has been reflected by legislative mandate rather than judicial abrogation. Similarly it is arguable that legislative rather than judicial reform is a more appropriate method of prohibiting imprisonment for debt, should its abolition prove desirable.

69. There are older cases, however, which specifically state that imprisonment for debt is not cruel and unusual punishment. *E.g.,* Tatlow v. Bacon, 101 Kan. 26, 165 P. 835, 837 (1917).

C. Involuntary Servitude

The thirteenth amendment states that "[n]either slavery nor involuntary servitude, except as a punishment for crime whereof the party shall have been duly convicted, shall exist within the United States, or any place subject to their jurisdiction."[70] This amendment, unlike many of the others, had a specific purpose and meaning when it was created and ratified. It was directed at the abolition of slavery and of all the badges and incidents of slavery. Though originally concerned with Black Americans, it has been enlarged by courts to include all persons of whatever race, color, or estate. One major purpose of this amendment was to "maintain a system of completely free and voluntary labor throughout the United States."[71] In *Pollock v. Williams,*[72] the Supreme Court applied the amendment to collection of debts and said, "[w]hatever of social value there may be, . . . no indebtedness warrants a suspension of the right to be free from compulsory service."[73] The question remains whether mere imprisonment can be equated with slavery or involuntary servitude.[74] Imprisonment — total restriction of a man's liberty and freedom — could be considered an act of slavery or servitude. If mere imprisonment is servitude, then imprisonment for debt, as long as it is classed as a civil remedy, would violate the thirteenth amendment.

The prohibition of the thirteenth amendment may, however, be limited to enforced labor, excluding mere confinement, in which case the thirteenth amendment would not prohibit imprisonment for debt.[75] What is enforced labor? It is clear that a prisoner may be required to do some necessary maintenance chores such as making his bunk, cleaning his cell, and even working in the kitchen preparing meals or washing dishes.[76] Since this limited type of work in prison is incidental to the act of imprisonment and not for the purpose of working off a debt, it probably would not be considered enforced labor.

---

70. U.S. CONST. amend. XIII.
71. Pollock v. Williams, 322 U.S. 4, 17 (1944). *See also* Baily v. Alabama, 219 U.S. 219, 243-44 (1911); Hodges v. United States, 203 U.S. 1, 16-17 (1906); Jobson v. Henne, 355 F.2d 129 (2d Cir. 1966).
72. 322 U.S. 4 (1944). This case involved the use of criminal sanctions to force persons to work for private employers.
73. *Id.* at 18.
74. *See* Jones v. Alfred Mayer Co., 392 U.S. 409 (1968).
75. *See* County of Milwaukee v. Horvath, 31 Wis. 2d 490, 143 N.W.2d 466 (1966).
76. This view is analogous to that expressed in Jobson v. Henne, 355 F.2d 129 (2d Cir. 1966), in which the court held that it would not violate the thirteenth amendment to force an inmate in a mental institution to work if that work were reasonably related to a therapeutic program or normal housekeeping.

    From this, the conclusion could be drawn that civil prisoners or those imprisoned for debt could be required to do work which is reasonably related to normal housekeeping. *See* Draper v. Rhay, 315 F.2d 193 (9th Cir.), *cert. denied,* 375 U.S. 915 (1963); Kent v. Prosse, 265 F. Supp. 673, 674 (W.D. Pa.), *aff'd,* 385 F.2d 406 (3d Cir. 1967); Note, *Supra* note 61.

D. *Equal Protection*

The equal protection clause[77] in the fourteenth amendment[78] did not have a definite meaning when it was written and its interpretation is ever changing today. Perhaps because of this, it has been relied on with increasing frequency to support individual rights in recent years. The generally accepted meaning of the clause is that all persons must be treated equally under the law.[79] Since everyone, rich and poor alike, seems to face the same consequence when in debt, that of paying the debt or going to jail, it might appear that no equal protection question is involved. In reality, however, a non-indigent rarely faces the same consequences as an indigent. The non-indigent has the same choice of paying or not paying, but he has the additional alternatives of posting bail to remain free[80] or paying a lawyer to keep him out of jail or at least to get him out quickly. The indigent, on the other hand, since he cannot pay and frequently lacks the funds to post bond, does not have these alternatives. He cannot afford a lawyer to advise him of his rights or to guide him through the complicated procedures necessary for his release. The case of *In re Harris*[81] illustrates what can happen to an indigent without aid of counsel. Because the petitioner did not have money to post bond or to hire a lawyer, he spent five weeks in jail before his case happened to come to the attention of the Public Defender.[82]

---

77. In this Comment the due process clause and the equal protection clause have been considered separately, mainly for the sake of convenience and clarity. The equal protection clause and the due process clause are often used interchangeably. Both have meanings so broad, general and closely related that it is often difficult to distinguish between the two in this context. In the District of Columbia and in federal courts where the fourteenth amendment does not apply, the equal protection clause is not applicable. The Supreme Court has expanded the due process clause of the fifth amendment in these jurisdictions to cover relatively the same area. *See, e.g.*, Schneider v. Rusk, 377 U.S. 163, 168-69 (1964); Bolling v. Sharpe, 347 U.S. 497, 498-99 (1954).

78. "No State shall . . . deprive any person of life, liberty, or property, without due process of law; nor deny to any person within its jurisdiction the *equal protection* of the law." U.S. CONST. amend. XIV, § 1 (emphasis added).

79. Loving v. Virginia, 388 U.S. 1 (1967) (antimiscegenation statute — good discussion of equal protection); Swain v. Alabama, 380 U.S. 202 (1965) (all white juries); Brown v. Board of Educ., 347 U.S. 483 (1954) (segregated schools); Strauder v. West Virginia, 100 U.S. 303 (1879) (all white juries, good history and discussion of fourteenth amendment and equal protection clause).

80. In the case of post judgment arrest the debtor can post bond to assure that he will show up for a hearing to determine whether his situation is included in the statutory exception allowing imprisonment for debt. Bond is generally set in the amount of the debt plus court costs or in some instances double the amount of the debt. If the debtor does not appear or is found to fall within the statute the posted bond can be used to pay the debt. Only if he is found to fall within an exception in the statute and still refuses to pay, will he be jailed.

81. 69 Cal. 2d 486, 446 P.2d 148, 72 Cal. Rptr. 340 (1968).

82. In this case the petitioner was arrested on mesne process because he had defaulted on payments for a truck. The repossessing agent had filed an affidavit to the effect that he had been unable to find the truck and that he had been told by the petitioner that the truck would be kept out of the agent's reach to prevent it from being repossessed. When arrested the petitioner was given a copy of the affidavit and allowed to call his employer and an attorney. An attorney, referred by his employer, visited

While the argument that the indigent and the wealthy defendant are not treated equally is a valid one, there is equal merit to the contention that creditors need a remedy against both the rich and the poor who are in their debt. If either fails to pay, for whatever reasons, the law ultimately provides for the same penalties,[83] although realistically the poor may not have the same alternatives.

It has been suggested that going into debt is a voluntary action and that people should be held responsible for any voluntary change they make in their own economic status. This reasoning has been used to hold that differences in the law's treatment of individual debtors have not violated the equal protection clause.[84] While going into debt may be an entirely voluntary action for those who have the ability to pay, it is all too often an involuntary action for the indigent. It would thus appear that laws permitting imprisonment for debt without first determining the debtor's ability to pay discriminate against the indigent.

One of the areas currently receiving a great deal of scrutiny under the equal protection clause is that of statutory classification schemes. There are many rules of construction for deciding whether different classification schemes violate the equal protection clause. Statutory classifications must have a natural and reasonable or fair basis and must not be arbitrary or capricious. They must be based on real, natural or substantial differences or distinctions, clearly differentiating between those to whom they apply and those to whom they do not apply. They must be based upon differences reasonably related to a legitimate legislative purpose, and the law must be so framed as to extend to and embrace equally all persons in like situations and circumstances.[85]

In states allowing imprisonment for debt, a distinction is made between contract debts and other debts. Most states forbid imprisonment for a debt on a contract, express or implied, but allow imprisonment for other debts, especially judgment debts or obligations arising from torts.[86] This distinction seems to have no natural, reasonable, or fair basis, nor does it appear to have a

---

him in jail but would do nothing toward his release unless the petitioner could pay $500.00. Petitioner could not pay $500.00 so he sat in jail for five weeks unaware of his right to appear in the superior court to seek release. He wrote to the Better Business Bureau stating that he would be held until the truck company obtained a date for his court appearance or arranged for his release. The bureau sent his letter to the Los Angeles County Public Defender who determined that he was indigent and obtained a bail reduction from $16,000 plus $4,000 penalty to $1,000 plus $250 penalty. Petitioner was able to obtain a bond for that amount and was released.

83. "[T]he law, in its majestic equality, forbids the rich as well as the poor to sleep under bridges, to beg in the streets, and to steal bread." J. Courners, A Modern Plutarch 27 (1928) (Quote from Anatole France).

84. St. Louis & Kansas City Land Co. v. Kansas City, 241 U.S. 419, 428 (1916).

85. *See* Loving v. Virginia, 388 U.S. 1 (1967); Schneider v. Rusk, 377 U.S. 163 (1964); Bolling v. Sharpe, 347 U.S. 497 (1954).

86. *See* p. 662 & note 29 *supra*.

legitimate legislative purpose. The only basis for the distinction could be the historical notion that debts, other than those on a contract, were the result of some wrong the debtor had committed and for which he must be punished. Debt is no longer considered a wrong punishable in itself, nor is there any rational basis for distinguishing between two debtors because one became indebted under a contract and the other as the result of a judgment on a tort. This distinction clearly seems to violate the equal protection clause.

Another argument that imprisonment for debt violates equal protection also has due process overtones. If the objective of the imprisonment is to force payment of debt, then to the extent that those who fail to pay their debts are indigent and unable to pay, imprisonment is not rationally related to the objectives of forcing payment. Because imprisonment cannot compel indigents to pay, it deprives them of their liberty and draws an arbitrary distinction between poor and nonpoor debtors, thus denying indigents due process and equal protection under the law. The Constitution prohibits the arbitrary selection of a class of individuals for imposition of special burdens.[87]

E. Due Process

The due process clause like the equal protection clause does not have a definite meaning. Expanded by courts in recent years, this clause basically guarantees the right to be heard by a fair and just tribunal before any action is taken against a person, his life, his liberty, or his property. The most basic of the due process requirements are the rights to proper notice and a fair hearing in both civil and criminal actions.[88] These safeguards should be required as a matter of right in imprisonment for debt actions.

A few statutes prescribing the procedure for civil arrests specifically require that these due process requirements be met. Indiana, for example, requires that after a creditor has filed an affidavit claiming that the judgment debtor is conveying, concealing, or removing property from the state for the purpose of delaying or fraudulently avoiding payment of a judgment debt, the clerk of the court must give notice to the defendant to appear and show cause why he should not be imprisoned. If he does not appear for the hearing, the court will decide whether to imprison the debtor on the basis of the

---

87. *E.g.*, Loving v. Virginia, 388 U.S. 1 (1967); Comment, *Fines, Imprisonment, and the Poor: "Thirty Dollars or Thirty Days,"* 57 CALIF. L. REV. 778, 796-97 (1969).

88. Armstrong v. Manzo, 380 U.S. 545, 550-52 (1965); Rochin v. California, 342 U.S. 165 (1952) (good discussion of due process); Snyder v. Massachusetts, 291 U.S. 97, 105 (1934). The Supreme Court has held that adequate notice must be given in civil cases. Schroeder v. City of New York, 371 U.S. 208 (1962); Mullane v. Central Hanover Bank & Trust Co., 339 U.S. 306 (1950); Milliken v. Meyer, 311 U.S. 457, 463 (1940). The Court has also insisted on a right to be heard in civil cases. Hansberry v. Lee, 311 U.S. 32, 40-41 (1940); Baldwin v. Iowa State Traveling Men's Ass'n, 283 U.S. 522, 525 (1931); Twining v. New Jersey, 211 U.S. 78, 110-11 (1908).

affidavit filed by the creditor. If the judgment debtor appears for the hearing, he may take issue with the contents of the affidavit, and the issue raised may be resolved by the court or by a jury. If the decision goes against the debtor, then he must pay the judgment or deliver the property to which the affidavit referred, or he will go to jail.[89]

Not all states have provisions for notice and a hearing before imprisonment, however. In Arkansas, if the judge finds that the affidavit filed by the plaintiff shows that the debtor is about to abscond, a warrant for the arrest of the debtor is issued, and the debtor is put in jail unless he posts bond.[90] No hearing is held, and there is no finding by the court that the debtor is able to pay. To be discharged, the debtor must petition the court, offer to deliver up any property he has, and ask permission to take the oath of insolvency. The court may then hold a hearing to determine whether to allow the debtor to take the oath of insolvency. This hearing is not a matter of right to the debtor, but is provided at the discretion of the court.[91]

California is another example of a state whose statutes do not provide for notice and a hearing as a matter of right to the debtor. In California, a debtor must give notice to his creditor that he intends to apply to the court for release from jail. At a hearing on the motion, the debtor must answer under oath all the questions of the court or creditor. If the court is satisfied as to the truth of the debtor's statements, the debtor will be allowed to take the oath of insolvency[92] and the court will issue an order for his release.

Several states do not have statutory provisions granting the debtor any type

---

89. IND. ANN. STAT. § 2-4301 to -4310 (1967). *See also* ILL. ANN. STAT. ch. 77, § 68 (Smith-Hurd 1966) (debtor given hearing before imprisoned); IOWA CODE ANN. § 630.3 - .11 (1946) (personal notice and hearing).

90. ARK. STAT. ANN. § 34-601 to -613 (1947).

91. ARK. STAT. ANN. § 34-623 (1962). The oath of insolvency or debtor's oath as it is called in some states is, in Arkansas and most other states, an oath whereby the debtor swears that he lacks the means to pay the debt, and that he has answered truthfully the questions concerning any property he owns.

If the court finds that the debtor has answered all questions truthfully and in fact lacks the means to pay the debt, the debtor will be allowed to swear to such as being truthful and will then be released from jail.

A good example of a poor debtor's oath is from Rhode Island:

> I do solemnly swear (or, affirm) that I have not any estate, real or personal, in possession, remainder or reversion over $10.00 (or, except what is exempt from attachment by law not herein enumerated) nor any debts secured by bills of exchange or negotiable promissory notes, and that I have not, since the commencement of this suit against me or any other time, directly or indirectly sold, leased or otherwise conveyed or disposed of to, or intrusted any person or persons whomsoever with, all or any part of the estate, real or personal, whereof I have been the lawful owner or possessor, with any intent or design to secure the same or to receive or to expect any profit or advantage therefrom for myself or for any of my children or family or any other person, or have caused or suffered to be done anything else whatsoever whereby any of my creditors may be defrauded, so help me God: (or, this affirmation I make and give upon peril of the penalty of perjury.)

R.I. GEN. LAWS. ANN. § 10-13-8 (1969).

92. CAL. CIV. PRO. CODE § 1148 (West 1967).

of a hearing before putting him in jail.[93] Furthermore, in some situations he may not even deny the claims in the plaintiff's affidavit until he petitions the court for a hearing and discharge. The most essential element of due process is the right to notice and a hearing before being deprived of one's liberty. In these states, however, a person's liberty is taken without these most essential due process safeguards. The California Supreme Court, in *In re Harris,*[94] held that imprisonment for debt on mesne process violated due process. The court felt that the statutory scheme for arrest by mesne process did not provide the defendant with notice of his various statutory rights, including the right to challenge the legality of his arrest. It should be noted that the California statutes involved had greater requirements for notice and a hearing than those of many other states.

Imprisonment for debt is a civil action and should therefore include the basic due process safeguards that the Constitution requires of any civil proceeding. It may be argued, however, that because this remedy is actually penal in nature, it should be subject to the more extensive due process requirements of criminal procedures. Although the statutory machinery is set in motion by a private plaintiff seeking to satisfy a civil claim, the deprivation of liberty is effected by the state.[95] It is the state that deprives the debtor of his liberty through its courts and law enforcement officers. It follows that the protections essential to due process in state prosecutions for crimes should be applied.

Courts have specified certain criminal due process protections that must be met in civil arrest actions,[96] but no court has required all of such protections. Courts have held that to make the debtor's right to a hearing effective, he must also have the right to counsel, including the right to court-appointed counsel if he is an indigent.[97] This is especially true where the debtor must petition the court for a hearing to obtain his discharge from jail. Unless he

---

93. In addition to Arkansas and California, notes 91 & 92 *supra,* see *e.g.,* DEL. CODE ANN. tit. 10, § 5053 (1953) (If debtor after being arrested makes a motion and notifies the creditor, the court will hold a hearing to investigate the specifications of fraud and may discharge the prisoner or remand him to trial on the issue of fraud); ME. REV. STAT. ANN. tit. 14, § 3707 (1964) (debtor must apply to the court for a hearing).

94. 69 Cal. 2d 486, 446 P.2d 148, 72 Cal. Rptr. 340 (1968).

95. *See* Peterson v. City of Greenville, 373 U.S. 244, 247-48 (1963); Shelley v. Kraemer, 334 U.S. 1, 13-14 (1948).

96. *In re* Harris, 69 Cal. 2d 486, 446 P.2d 148, 72 Cal. Rptr. 340 (1968). The facts of this case are outlined in note 82 *supra.* In this case the court stressed that due process requires that a person be informed of his rights. The court felt that any rights provided a defendant are meaningless unless he is informed of them and how to effect them. The debtor in this case had the right to apply to the court to vacate his arrest or reduce bail, but these rights were meaningless since he was not informed of them nor did he have counsel to aid him in perfecting them. The court said that "[a] defendant who is deprived of his liberty by civil process is as much entitled to due process of law as a defendant who is deprived of his liberty because he is charged with crime." 69 Cal. 2d at 491, 446 P.2d at 152, 72 Cal. Rptr. at 344.

97. 69 Cal. 2d at 491, 446 P.2d at 151-52, 72 Cal. Rptr. at 343-44; Wright v. Crawford, 401 S.W.2d 47 (Ky. Ct. App. 1966).

is informed of his rights and counsel is provided to perfect them, he may as well not have those rights at all. In the Kentucky case of *Wright v. Crawford*,[98] the court went even further, holding that it was unable to perceive any difference between imprisonment in a civil action or in a criminal action.[99] Therefore, the civil defendant faced with possible imprisonment has a right to counsel similar to that set forth in the various criminal law decisions.[100] It was also held in *Wright* that the defendant has the right to a hearing on his claimed indigence for the purpose of establishing whether counsel should be assigned to him.[101]

The United States Supreme Court has held that the right to be heard, in many cases, would be of little value if it did not include the right to be represented by counsel.[102] Although these were criminal cases, the punishment to be inflicted (imprisonment) was substantially the same as the remedy sought in cases of imprisonment for debt. The constitutional basis for supplying legal counsel to indigent persons is to afford due process and equal protection, and to place the indigent on equal footing with those who, from their own resources, can employ counsel and litigate their causes.[103] This constitutional basis should also support a requirement that legal counsel be supplied to defendants in civil actions who may lose their liberty.

Many states limit the time a person may be imprisoned under civil arrest statutes to six months or a year.[104] This would make the imprisonment comparable to that for misdemeanors. States are not required by the Constitution to provide court-appointed counsel for indigents accused of misdemeanors or crimes that entail imprisonment for less than one year.[105] In

---

98. 401 S.W.2d 47 (Ky. Ct. App. 1966).

99. *Id.* at 49. The court said that "the statutorily permitted imprisonment of Wright [the debtor] brings this case within the rationale of the rule applicable to appointment of counsel for indigents in criminal cases." *Id.*

Similarly in *In re* Harris, 69 Cal. 2d 486, 491, 446 P.2d 148, 151, 72 Cal. Rptr. 340, 343 (1968), the court pointed out that an indigent imprisoned under civil arrest statutes is confined in the same jail as the indigent felon undergoing trial who is entitled to appointed counsel.

100. *E.g.*, Gideon v. Wainwright, 372 U.S. 335 (1963) (right to counsel); Douglas v. California, 372 U.S. 353 (1963) (right to counsel on appeal); Griffin v. Illinois, 351 U.S. 12 (1956) (right to have transcripts furnished).

101. Wright v. Crawford, 401 S.W.2d 47, 49 (Ky. Ct. App. 1966).

102. *In re* Gault, 387 U.S. 1, 36 (1967); Specht v. Patterson, 386 U.S. 605, 608-10 (1967); Gideon v. Wainwright, 372 U.S. 335, 344 (1963); Powell v. Alabama, 287 U.S. 45, 68-69 (1932).

103. Westberry v. State, 254 A.2d 44, 45 (Me. 1969).

104. COLO. REV. STAT. ANN. § 77-9-4 (1963) (not more than a year); ILL. ANN. STAT. ch. 77, § 68 (Smith-Hurd 1966) (six months); R.I. GEN. LAWS ANN. § 10-13-27 (1969) (three months if debt is less than one thousand dollars, six months if more).

105. As a result, some states only appoint counsel for indigents accused of felonies or crimes with penalties of more than one year imprisonment. California is one of the states that also appoints counsel for indigents accused of misdemeanors. CAL. CONST. art. I, § 13; CAL. PENAL CODE § 859 (West 1970); *In re* Johnson, 62 Cal. 2d 325, 398 P.2d 420, 42 Cal. Rptr. 228 (1965); *In re* Newbern, 53 Cal. 2d 786, 350 P.2d 116, 3 Cal. Rptr. 364 (1960).

these situations, then, where imprisonment for debt is limited to less than one year and the state criminal practices do not require appointed counsel for misdemeanors, it would seem that due process would not require that counsel be appointed in civil arrest actions.

Many statutes prescribing civil imprisonment are, however, silent as to any limit in length. Some state statutes specifically provide that the debtor will be held until he pays or meets other specified requirements such as taking an oath of insolvency or delivering up all his property to his creditor.[106] Louisiana prohibits imprisoning the debtor for more than three years.[107] In these states the term of imprisonment is comparable to that for felonies, and it would seem that the due process clause of the United States Constitution would require counsel be provided for indigents.

Other differences between criminal and civil procedures may violate due process when criminal consequences, such as imprisonment, are imposed from a civil judgment. A civil judgment may be entered on default whereas in a criminal action the defendant must appear and must plead to the charges. In civil actions charges need be proved merely by a preponderance of the evidence. But generally where imprisonment is the result, as in criminal cases, the charges must be proved beyond all reasonable doubt.[108]

Imprisonment for debt presents a further anomaly. A finding by the jury that the defendant was not guilty of the acts required to bring him within the statute, such as fraud or malicious tort, is not final, unlike other cases in which a defendant is placed in jeopardy of his liberty. As such, the debtor's liberty may be placed in double jeopardy in the event of an appeal by the creditor.[109]

Regardless of the conclusion as to the degree of procedural protection that should be necessary in an action to imprison a debtor, most of the statutes today violate the due process clause. Even if only the basic safeguards of civil procedure are deemed sufficient, a *majority* of the state statutes violate the due process clause.[110] But if the further requirements of criminal due process are necessary, then *all* of the statutes as written and interpreted violate the due process clause of the fourteenth amendment.

---

106. *E.g.*, Iowa Code Ann. § 630.11 (1946) (debtor may be held until he answers all of the court's and the creditor's questions concerning his property to the satisfaction of the court); Ky. Rev. Stat. § 426.400 (1969) (debtor may be held until he delivers up a schedule of all his property which the court finds is not fraudulent — debtor must give creditor notice and petition the court for a hearing to determine this); Me. Rev. Stat. Ann. tit. 14, § 3154 (1964) (debtor may be held until he pays or the creditor consents to his release).

107. La. Rev. Stat. Ann. § 9:2664 (West 1965).

108. Parnass, *Imprisonment for Civil Obligations in Illinois*, 15 Ill. L. Rev. 559, 571 (1921).

109. *Id.*

110. All those that do not provide the debtor with notice and a hearing would violate the due process clause. *See* note 93 *supra*.

III. Conclusion

It is clear that the practice of imprisonment for debt is subject to Constitutional attack. The first and probably most important reason is that imprisonment for debt violates the fundamental values of justice and reasonableness held by contemporary American society. Imprisoning the indigent is no longer an acceptable solution to indebtedness and poverty.

The second idea supporting the contention that imprisonment for debt violates the Constitution is similar to the first. It may well be argued that the American concept of cruel and unusual punishment prohibited by the eighth amendment has advanced to include imprisonment for debt in its prohibition. It is also contended that imprisoning a man for debt violates the thirteenth amendment prohibiting involuntary servitude except as a punishment for a crime. Being in debt is no longer considered to be either a sin or a crime.

The equal protection clause is violated by the practice of imprisoning debtors because of the arbitrary and unreasonable classifications and distinctions made by state statutes. There is no rational basis for protecting contract debtors from imprisonment while allowing tort debtors to be imprisoned at the will of creditors. Moreover, the condition that the debtor must pay or go to jail brings about an arbitrary distinction between those who are able to pay and those who are not.

The procedures followed by most states, if the concept of imprisonment for debt is accepted, show that the requirements for due process are seldom met. A man may lose his liberty without prior notice and often without a hearing.

The proponents of the present system contend that imprisonment for debt statutes are not intended to affect the honest but poor debtor but to force payment by the solvent debtor who employs dilatory tactics to avoid payment. To this contention there are several answers. One is simply that the honest but poor debtors are in fact affected. Although most statutes allow those who are unable to pay to take a debtor's oath and be released from prison, the poor are still imprisoned and kept there until they find their way through the maze of legal procedure that leads to freedom. Generally, they are left to try to find the way without legal guidance.

A second answer is that if the function of imprisonment for debt statutes is to force payment, other means exist to accomplish this end that are more effective and less offensive to fundamental rights. The alternative methods — garnishment[111] and attachment[112] — are more reasonable and logical methods

---

111. Garnishment is a process where the creditor, by order of a court, receives part of the debtor's salary or paycheck directly from the debtor's employer. Garnishment laws have many detrimental aspects, however, and are often as harmful and discriminatory to the poor as is imprisonment. *See* Sniadach v. Family Finance Corp., 395 U.S. 337 (1969).

112. Attachment is achieved by writ ordering the sheriff to find specific property be-

of collection. Because of their wide availability, these other remedies probably suit the creditor's purpose better.

The method of handling contempt proceedings in divorce and child support cases should be more closely followed in imprisonment for debt cases. Most courts apply the principle that a person cannot be imprisoned for contempt for failure to pay alimony or child support unless there has been a finding by the court that the defendant has the ability to pay.[113] If courts were required to do the same for every case involving imprisonment for debt, the requirements of due process and equal protection would be more likely met. Before a court issues a writ ordering the debtor's arrest, there should be a hearing to determine whether the debtor has the present ability to pay.

Imprisonment for debt violates the fundamental values and beliefs of the American people, thus violating the spirit of the United States Constitution which represents these basic ideals. Moreover as prescribed by state statutes, it violates the procedural aspects of the due process clause of the Constitution. In this enlightened civilization, where freedom is at a premium, the archaic practice of imprisoning poor and indigent debtors has no place, and should be abolished.

---

longing to the debtor and to sell it to satisfy the debt. The main problem with this remedy is that indigent debtors seldom have sufficient property to attach and fraudulent debtors can easily conceal or transfer their property to avoid attachment.

113. An example is Meeks v. State, 80 Ark. 579, 98 S.W. 378 (1906). In an action to recover a debt the court found in favor of the creditor and also found that at the time of the final hearing the debtor had $287.00 in his possession from the sale of lumber for which the debt was owed. The court ordered the debtor to pay this amount to the creditor within ten days. The money was not paid and petitioner was adjudged to be in contempt of court and was jailed. The court said that this did not violate the constitutional prohibition against imprisonment for debt. This was imprisonment for contempt, not debt, even though the order relates to the debt evidenced by the judgment against the estate. Contempt does not consist of the neglect or refusal to pay the debt but in the petitioner's disobedience of the order directing him to hand over money found in his possession. A later case, Leonard v. State, 170 Ark. 41, 278 S.W. 654 (1926), presented a situation very similar to *Meeks*. The imprisonment of the defendant for contempt for failure to pay the sum ordered was held to violate the prohibition against imprisonment for debt because the lower court had not found that the defendant had the money in his possession at the time he was ordered to pay. *See* Freeman v. Heiman, 426 F.2d 1050 (10th Cir. 1970); *In re* Burrows, 33 Kan. 675, 7 P. 148 (1885) (court allowed contempt imprisonment where the lower court had determined that the judgment debtor had money with which he could pay the debt and terminate his imprisonment).

THE NATURE, SCOPE AND SIGNIFICANCE OF PRE-TRIAL DETENTION OF JUVENILES IN CALIFORNIA

By Ernest L. Aubry

I. Introduction

As is so in many other aspects of juvenile law, the central defect of the California juvenile detention statute[1] and practices thereunder, is that the law, on its face and as applied, is inherently discriminatory *vis-a-vis* treatment of adults and, specifically, affords juveniles less protection than the right of bail guaranteed under the Eighth and Fourteenth Amendments.

Although much contemporary discussion is devoted to preventive detention statutes,[2] few persons have pointed out that for juveniles, such statutes have always existed[3] but, under the theory of *parens patriae,* have gone unquestioned.

The California law governing juveniles raises substantial questions of a minor's

1. Calif. Welfare and Institutions Code ("WIC") §§625 (re temporary custody by peace officers); 626 (re alternative dispositions by peace officers after taking minor into custody); 628 (re alternative dispositions by probation officer once he acquires custody of a minor child, and criteria for determining detention prior to a detention hearing); 630, 631, 632 (re holding minor in custody for up to 72 hours, *excluding non-judicial days,* prior to a detention hearing); 635, 636 (criteria utilized at detention hearing to determine whether or not it is "necessary" to further detain the minor pending trial).
2. See, e.g., District of Columbia Court Reform and Criminal Procedure Act of 1970, Pub. L. No. 91-358, 84 Stat. 493 (July 29, 1970), §210, D.C. Code Ann. §§23-1321 to -1332,
3. *Compare* D.C. Code Ann. §§ 23-1321 to -1332, *supra,* n. 2, *with* WIC §§ 628, 635, 636, *supra,* n. 1.

THE BLACK LAW JOURNAL, 1971, Vol. 1, pp. 160-170.

right to bail, equal protection of the laws and due process of law: Does the Eighth Amendment provision against excessive bail apply to juveniles? Is absence of bail or release on one's own recognizance, a denial of equal protection of the laws? Does the use of detention criteria (such as "for the protection of the person or property of another"[4]), not now a state statutory standard for adults, constitute a denial of equal protection? Since the juvenile's right to a fair trial is impaired by pre-trial detention (by reason, *inter alia,* of restricted consultation with counsel, and limitations upon ability to contact and screen potential witnesses), does state law deny him due process? Is the limitation upon the juvenile's access to the courts to determine the validity of pre-trial detention, a denial of due process?[5]

Not all of these issues will be treated herein, only those having peculiar significance for the black community. (No reiteration other than the following statement is needed herein to establish the differential treatment accorded blacks in being arrested and then processed through the juvenile courts, for this is not a "study" to bring out what is already known and prolifically documented: ". . . Negroes, who live in disproportionate numbers in slum neighborhoods, account for a disproportionate number of [juvenile] arrests."[5a])

Under California law,[6] any peace officer may, without a warrant, take a minor into temporary custody[7] and deliver custody of the minor to the county probation officer.[8] The disposition (release or detention) of the minor then rests within the discretion of the probation officer.[9] The current position of juvenile court judges is that from the point a juvenile is delivered into the custody of the probation officer until the time of the detention hearing provided for in WIC §632, the juvenile court lacks jurisdiction to order the minor's release since the California statute (WIC) makes no such provision and the detention and incarceration of juveniles are matters solely in charge of the probation officer and his staff.

Thus deprived of access to the courts, juveniles, without being able to obtain release by posting money bail[10] can, and frequently are, detained for periods of at least 72 hours by the probation officer after having been taken into custody.

> "Whenever a minor . . . is taken into custody . . . [he] shall be released within 48 hours . . . *excluding nonjudicial days,* unless within said period of time a petition to declare him a ward or dependent child has been filed . . ."[11]

> "Unless sooner released, a minor taken into custody . . . shall be brought before a judge of referee of the juvenile court for a [detention] hearing . . . to determine whether the minor shall be further detained, as soon as possible but in any event before the expiration of the next judicial day after a petition . . . has been filed.[12]

Under this statutory scheme, a minor may be detained in excess of 72 hours (because of intervening holidays and

4. WIC §§ 628(d), 635, 636.
5. Other issues include the following: incarceration for unproved, anticipated crime, rather than actual criminal conduct; the offense of "dangerousness" is unconstitutionally vague; preventive detention infringes upon the presumption of innocence and is a finding based on a standard of proof falling short of "beyond reasonable doubt;" coercion to waive privilege against self-incrimination; detention is imposed on the basis of hearsay and other forms of "evidence" not admissible at trial under accepted rules of evidence.

5a. President's Commission on Law Enforcement and Administration of Justice, *The Challenge of Crime in a Free Society* 57 (U.S. Gov't. Printing Office, 1957).

6. Although the discussion herein is framed in terms of California law, the California statute is not atypical, and the issues are the same in many other states, for other jurisdictions also have juvenile preventive detention statutes. See, e.g., Ill. 1965 Rev. Stat. §§ 701-9, 703-4, 703-6; Ia. Laws, 1965, Ch. 215, § 17; Mich. Stat. § 712A.15; Minn. Laws 1959, Ch. 685, § 25 (260.171); Neb. Rev. Stat. §§ 43-205.03, 43-205.04; Ohio Stat. § 2151.314.

   Nor are recent recommendations by "child welfare agencies" and others ameliorative. See, e.g., National Council on Crime and Delinquency *Standard Juvenile Court Act* (6th ed. 1959) § 16; National Conference of Commissioners of Uniform State Laws *Uniform Juvenile Court Law* (1968) §§ 14, 17; Children's Bureau, *Standards for Juvenile and Family Courts,* pp. 15-17 (1966).

7. WIC § 625.
8. WIC § 626(c).
9. WIC § 628.
10. *In re Castro,* 242 Cal. App. 2d 402 (1966)
11. WIC § 631 (emphasis added).
12. WIC § 632.

weekends—i.e., "nonjudicial days") before he can gain access to a court.

THE ONLY FACTOR determining whether or not the minor is to be released or incarcerated for such periods of time is the discretion of the probation officer.

In exercising that discretion, the probation officer considers both statutory criteria and certain *non-legal* factors (e.g., the nature[13] or degree[14] of the alleged offense; other non-legal factors include such matters as a juvenile's characteristics (ethnic background; prior police or probation department contacts as well as previous delinquency adjudications; economic status, etc.) and the goals of detention as perceived by the decision-maker (e.g., to deter from further delinquency; to remove the child from the home environment; to provide opportunity for short-term rehabilitative efforts; etc.)).[15]

The preventive detention provisions of the California Juvenile Court Law are found in the following statutory language:

> "Upon delivery to the probation officer of a minor who has been taken into temporary custody under the provisions of this article, the probation officer shall immediately investigate the circumstances of the minor and the facts surrounding his being taken into custody and shall immediately release such minor to the custody of his parent, guardian, or responsible relative unless one or more of the following conditions exist:
>
> •
>
> "d) Continued detention of the minor is a matter of immediate and urgent necessity for the protection of the person or property of another.
>
> •
>
> "(f) The minor has violated an order of the juvenile court.
>
> "(g) The minor is physically dangerous to the public because of a mental or physical deficiency, disorder or abnormality."[16]

When the probation officer makes a decision to detain, there is no procedure available for the minor for setting bail or reversing the decision to detain.

California has long been recognized as having detention practices out of proportion with recommendations of specialists in the area of juvenile detention. For example, it has been noted that California "Rates [of detention] proportionately have for years far exceeded nationally recommended figures."[17] When compared with national standards for rate of detention, it should be noted that no county [in California] could be considered to have low detention rates,"[18] and "The overall range [of markedly varied detention rates among counties] was from 19 percent detained to 66 percent detained."[19]

Within that range of average detention rates, the *Summary*[20] contains the following detention rates on the basis of children's characteristics:

> *"Ethnic Background*
>
> *"The largest proportion of children detained were Negro children.* Children classified as white were less often detained. The proportions were a third of the white children compared to nearly one-half those of the Afro-American group."
>
> *"Prior Offense* (considered a crime if committed by an adult) and *Prior Delinquency* (not considered a crime if committed by an adult)
>
> *"Nearly one-half* of the children falling in each of these two categories were detained."
>
> *"Probation Status*
>
> "Seventy-one percent of all children referred had never been placed on probation. Among these children, the detention rate was 25 percent. For those presently on probation, the rate was 67 percent. Of

13. E.g., *In re William M.*, 3 Cal. 3d 16 (1970).
14. E.g., *In re Macidon*, 240 Cal. App. 2d 600 (1966).
15. See Sumner, *A Summary of Locking Them Up: A Study of Initial Juvenile Detention Decisions in Selected California Counties* (a project sponsored by the California Council of the National Council on Crime and Delinquency, 1968), pp. 8-15; hereinafter cited as "Summary."
16. WIC § 628. Also see WIC §§ 635, 636.
17. *Summary, supra*, n. 15, at p. 1.
18. *Ibid.*, p. 2.
19. *Ibid*, p. 10.
20. *Ibid*, pp. 8-11.

The data relating to the categories of prior offense, probation status, prior record and prior delinquency adjudications were chosen since blacks fall into those classes more frequently than is justified by their total numbers within the general population. Hence, use of such criteria in the detention decision bears significantly upon the black community.

those previously on probation, with probation revoked, 74 percent were detained."

"Prior Record

"This item was related to decision outcomes for both sets of counties. But *54 percent* of those children with a prior offense record were detained in high rate counties as against *23 percent* (less than one-half as many) in the low rate counties. Also, in low rate counties, considerably fewer children apprehended for alleged delinquency were detained with no history of past offense than was true for high rate counties.

"Prior Offense (considered a crime if committed by an adult) "Here again, there was association for both groups of counties between the item and the detention outcome. But *53 percent* were detained in high rate counties as against *32 percent* in low rate counties.

"Prior Delinquency Adjudication

"This item was closely associated with the detention decision in both sets of counties, but detention rates varied according to how many times a child had previously been found delinquent. Of those with a history of four or more prior offenses, high rate counties detained *87 percent.* For the same group, low rate counties detained *50 percent.* Where there was no history of past delinquency adjudication, high counties detained *32 percent* and the low *20 percent.*

Probation Status

On this item, although relationship was again established for both groups of counties, it was found that the number of children previously on probation was low for both groups, and the number of those with a history of revocation lower yet. *But* the high rate counties detained *91 percent* of such children as compared to *46 percent* for the low, or roughly almost twice as many."

IN 1960, the Governor's Special Study Commission on Juvenile Justice commented as follows on the rate of pre-adjudication detention in California:

"California has been severely criticized by national probation and child welfare organizations for excessive juvenile detention practices. The Commission's study, unfortunately, substantiates the validity of this criticism . . . [In 1958] almost three-fourths of the delinquent juveniles referred to probation departments by law enforcement agencies were detained in juvenile halls. In some communities, the ratio was even higher — virtually every juvenile referred by law enforcement officers to the probation department was detained, notwithstanding the fact that some minors were apprehended in error, many committed inconsequential offenses, and many others had responsible parents able to control the minor pending the juvenile court appearance."[21]

In spite of such criticism, California's record as regards pre-adjudication detention practices have worsened in the intervening years since 1961.[22] California's detention rate, as a percentage of arrests, averages three and one-half times the recognized norm,[23] and is currently *increasing* despite the recent emphasis on protection of the rights of minors, a trend which the California Bureau of Criminal Statistics characterizes as running "contrary to the tide of legal thought."[24]

Juvenile Hall Admissions of Minors Arrested for Delinquency and Delinquent Tendencies as Percentage of Arrests[25]

YEAR	ARRESTS	ADMISSIONS	PER CENT
1968	366,541	132,820	36.3
1967	323,427	115,100	35.6
1966	303,020	87,925	29.0
1965	277,649	78,669	28.3

In considering the foregoing statewide detention rates, it should be noted that the rates of detention as a percentage of minors referred to juvenile probation departments are even higher, since the police may admonish and dismiss a child

21. *Report,* Governor's Special Study Commission on Juvenile Justice, Part I, p. 41 (1960).
22. *Summary, supra,* p. 3.
23. "The number of children admitted to a detention facility should normally not exceed 10 percent of the total number of juvenile offenders apprehended by law enforcement officers, excluding traffic cases and cases outside the court's jurisdiction such as out-of-county runaways and federal court cases." National Council on Crime and Delinquency, *Standards and Guides for the Detention of Children and Youth* 18 (1961). More recently, NCCD has recommended detaining as little as two percent of juvenile arrestees. Letter from Central Office, NCCD, to San Francisco Bay Area Social Planning Council, 1/17/68, quoted in BASPC, *The San Francisco Juvenile Court, Background Information* 263 (1968).
24. Bureau of Criminal Statistics, *Crime and Delinquency in California — 1968,* 161.
25. Sources: 1968 figures: *Crime and Delinquency in California — 1968,* 126, 164; 1965-67 figures: BASPC, *supra,* note 23, 261-262, derived from *Crime and Delinquency in California — 1965, 1966, 1967.*

after arrest, or cite him to appear later before a probation officer. Thus in 1968, the detention figure of 132,820 equals *45.5 percent* of the 291,875 minors referred by police to probation.[26]

LOCKING UP CHILDREN charged with or suspected of offenses, prior to adjudication, is a self-defeating practice, for contrary to the avowed purpose of the Juvenile Court Law, to salvage young lives through rehabilitative efforts, the incarcerated child goes through a negative experience that is likely to contribute to future deliquent or criminal conduct.

Juvenile hall attendants have expressed surprise at the speed with which relative innocent youngsters succumb to the infectious miasma of "Juvy" and its practices, attitudes and language. But this is not surprising. The experience tells the youngster that he is "no good" and that society has rejected him. So he responds to society's expectation, sees himself as a delinquent, and acts like one. The President's Commission on Law Enforcement and Administration of Justice defined this psychological response:

> "Official action may actually help to fix and perpetuate delinquency in the child through a process in which the individual begins to think of himself as delinquent and organizes his behavior accordingly. The process itself is further reinforced by the effect of the labeling upon the child's family, neighbors, teachers, and peers, whose reactions communicate to the child in subtle ways a kind of expectation of delinquent conduct. The undesirable consequences of official treatment are maximized in programs that rely on institutionalizing the child."[27]

The California detention problem is that there is too much detention and that its imposition is inconsistent. A major reason for both aspects of the problem is widepsread detention for purposes which are not countenanced by the Federal Constitution, as much as it is due to utilization of subjective detention criteria, in a context where appellate review is as a practical matter unavailable.

Contrary to the espoused purpose of individualized treatment,[28] California pre-adjudicatory detention policies and practices on the whole result in processes in which persons are treated *en masse* and in a wholly undifferentiated manner."[29]

II. THE COSTS OF CALIFORNIA'S JUVENILE DETENTION STATUTE[30]

BECAUSE OF THE subjective nature of juvenile pre-trial detention criteria, the usual costs inhering in any system of pre-trial incarceration, assume peculiar importance for juveniles.

For blacks and other racial minority communities, the intangible human costs of pre-trial detention deserve specific mention at the "expense" of due process and equal protection discussions of general applicability.

A. PREJUDICE TO DETERMINATION OF GUILT

IT IS NO LONGER questionable that juveniles accused of acts of delinquency are entitled to the "essentials of due process and fair treatment" both in pre-jurisdictional adjudicatory proceedings[31] and

26. *Crime and Delinquency in California — 1968*, 126, 164. The figure for referrals is derived by adding the figures at p. 127 for "Total Delinquency" and "Delinquent Tendencies."

27. *The Challenge of Crime in a Free Society* 80 (U.S. Government Printing Office, 1967).

28. See *In re William M., supra*, 3 Cal. 3d 16, 31.

29. The problem in no small part is due to the refusal of the Juvenile Court to obey and implement appellate court decisions. See the description of the failure of this respect of the Los Angeles County Juvenile Court as described in *In re Larry W.*, 16 Cal. App. 3d 290, 292 (1971), a neglect of the courts which is borne out by this writer's own current experiences in Los Angeles County.

30. Discussion herein is limited to delinquency (WIC § 602) and "incorrigibility" (WIC § 601) cases, for dependency and neglect situations (WIC § 600) involve some entirely different considerations which warrant separate treatment not within the intent of this article.
Other matters also need not be treated herein, e.g., certain due process implications of preventive detention statutes, such as those mentioned *supra*, n. 5. The Eighth Amendment right to bail and violation of the Equal Protection clause by denying bail to minors have been accorded ample treatment elsewhere; see Foote, *The Coming Constitutional Crisis in Bail*, 113 U. Pa. L. Rev. 959 (1965); Note, *Preventive Detention: An Empirical Analysis*, 6 Harv. Civ. Rts./Civ. Lib. L. Rev. (No. 2, March, 1971) 300, 317-370; *Rivera v. Freeman*, Memorandum in Opposition to Motion to Dismiss (U.S. Dist. Ct., Central District of Calif., Civ. Action No. 70-2089-WPG), and Appellant's Opening Brief (C.A. 9th Cir., No. 71-1351).

31. *Kent v. United States*, 383 U.S. 541 (1966).

during the adjudicatory hearing.[32]

Yet, under the existing California law, pre-trial detention of a juvenile charged with commission of a crime denies the juvenile of due process of law by infringing upon the juvenile's right to a fair trial since pre-trial incarceration seriously impairs one's ability to prepare for trial.

The juvenile's right to the "essentials of due process and fair treatment" at the adjudicatory hearing would be meaningless if the right did not extend to include those fundamental rights which touch upon, and vitally affect, one's ability to receive due process and a fair trial. The mere statement that the right to counsel *prior to* trial and the right to compulsory process to obtain witnesses do not bear upon the final outcome, reveals its fallacy.[33] Yet, all of these rights are affected by whether or not the defendant is free on some form of pre-trial release.

The wrong done by denying pre-trial release is not limited to the denial of freedom alone. That denial will have other consequences, perhaps the most harmful of which is the adverse effect upon the preparation of the accused's defense, since he will have no opportunity to investigate his case, to cooperate with his counsel, to earn the money that is still necessary or maintain community, employment and school contacts necessary for a disposition other than incarceration after adjudication should he be found guilty. In a recent case the Ninth Circuit ordered the release of a minor to the custody of his parents after finding that "failure to permit appellant's release for the purpose of aiding the preparation of his defense unconstitutionally interfered with his due process right to a fair trial."[34] The Court made the additional observation:

> "The ability of an accused to prepare his defense by lining up witnesses is fundamental, in our adversary system, to his chances of obtaining a fair trial. Recognition of this fact of course underlies the bail system. *Stack v. Boyle,* 342, U.S. 1, ((1951). But it is equally implicit in the requirements that trial occur near in time, (citation), and place (citation) of the offense, and that the accused have compulsory process to obtain witnesses in his behalf (citation). Indeed, compulsory process as a practical matter would be of little value without an opportunity to contact and screen potential witnesses before trial."[53]

The substantial impairment of one's ability while incarcerated, to contact and confer with witnesses who can testify on his behalf at trial is exacerbated in the case of a juvenile whose witnesses most often are other juveniles whom he many times knows only by their first names and whose whereabouts only he can ascertain. Then there is the added factor of race. To the task of overcoming the reluctance of potential witnesses to testify, counsel must surmount the barriers of age *and race.* Such social realities cannot be overlooked. The necessary ingredient of trust toward the lawyer on the part of witnesses as well as other intermediary communication functions, compounded as they are by race, can often be performed only by the client, who knows the community, will feel less intimidated therein, and *be* less intimidating than an attorney, and generally perform the necessary interpretive, communicative role.

FURTHERMORE, the adverse consequences of pre-trial detention extend beyond trial. The effects of pre-trial detention upon the (increased) probability of conviction and of sentencing to an institution after conviction, as opposed to being placed on probation, have been amply documented. Studies continuously establish that the injury to an accused, detained pending trial, often is severe and carries over beyond the initial period of pre-trial detention, prejudicing his chances of acquittal or non-jail disposition.[36]

32. *Application of Gault,* 387 U.S. 1 (1967).
33. See, e.g., *Kinney v. Lenon* (9th Cir. 1970) 425 F.2d 209, 210.
34. *Kinney v. Lenon, supra,* n. 33, 425 F.2d at 210.
35. *Ibid.* See also *Stack v. Boyle,* 342 U.S. 1, 4, 8 (1951).
36. *Stack v. Boyle, supra,* 342 U.S. 1, 4; Atty. Gen. Comm. on Poverty and the Administration of Federal Criminal Justice, Report 26 (1963); Bratholm, Arrest and Detention in Norway, 108 U.Pa.L.Rev. 336, 340-341 (1960); Foote, Crisis in Bail, *supra,* at 1138-43; Freed and Wald, Bail in the United States at 45-48 (1964).

In addition to the other costs of pretrial detention,[37] the cost to the accused in terms of prejudice to the determination of guilt and dispositional alternatives has has been described as follows:[38]

"... One of the most serious costs of pre-trial detention is the possibility of prejudice to the outcome of the case. Several recent studies indicate that defendants incarcerated before trial are more likely to be found guilty and committed to prison than those released. This prejudice results from factors which discriminate solely on the basis of detention. The Boston data show that 74% of the comparison group were found guilty and 69% served prison sentences for the initial offense while the rates for those released were 53% found guilty and 26% incarcerated. Other studies corroborate these findings.

"While many factors could explain these differences, at least one study demonstrates that differences in findings and sentencing between detained and bailed defendants remain consistently large and are not affected when prior record, amount of bail (which often correlates, in practice, with the weight of the evidence), quality of counsel, family situation, or employment are held constant. These findings appear to support the conclusion that disposition and finding are to some extent related to incarceration itself.

"One factor which might explain differences in guilty findings is that the incarcerated defendant cannot consult with his lawyer as freely or as often as the person not detained. Neither is he free to prepare his case fully, to gather witnesses, or to establish an alibi . . .

"Because detention often results in loss of employment those not released are less likely to retain private counsel. A recent study of the Massachusetts lower court documents the extent to which court-appointed counsel makes a guilty finding more likely. Sixty-five precent of those with appointed counsel are found guilty compared to 49% of those who have private attorneys. Of those with an assigned attorney, 17% are found not guilty compared to 35% with a private lawyer. Detainees also are less able to afford the service of paid investigators, or the expense of witnesses. Incarcerated defendants are also more readily available to law enforcement officials for involuntary participation in line-ups and other police processes that may increase the likelihood of a finding of guilt. Finally, defendants who come into court in the custody of police officers, stripped of their self-confidence by detention, and wearing prison clothes or the clothes in which they were arrested, may be prejudiced in the eyes of the jury.

•

"The individual who is incarcerated is also prejudiced at sentencing. The defendant's loss of job and other economic and social dislocations resulting from pretrial incarceration reduce a judge's reason to suspend the sentence or place the defendant on probation. The granting of probation for example, depends upon the likelihood of successful reacclimatization to society, the difficulty of supervision, and the risk of criminal instability. Unemployed defendants or those with unstable or impoverished families are prejudiced in the probation determination. Pre-trial incarceration contributes to both factors."

Another not atypical survey revealed the following:[39]

"An examination was made of one hundred consecutive felony cases in a Kansas county . . . The objective of the survey was to gain some insight into the relationship between pre-trial detention and the probability of subsequent conviction and imprisonment. The following table summarizes the findings.

•

37. E.g., creation of a class of hardened criminals; economic disruption (loss of employment or of opportunity to pursue education, etc.); jail maintenance and administrative costs; erosion of community's sense of justice; imposition of punishment prior to determination of guilt; stigmatizing effect in the community resulting from the mere fact of detention.

38. Note, *Preventive Dententions: An Empirical Analysis,* 6 Harv. Civ. Rts./Civ. Liberties L.Rev. 289, 347-351 (No. 2, Mar. 1971) (footnotes omitted). The author cites numerous, extensive surveys to support his description, including the following: Foote, *Crisis in Bail, supra,* at 1137-1151; Wald, *Forward, Pretrial Detention and Ultimate Freedom,* 39 N.Y.U.L.Rev. 640 (1964); Freed & Wald, *supra,* note 36, at 45-48; Foote, *Compelling Appearance in Court,* 102 U.Pa.L.Rev. 1031, 1051-1053 (1954); Rankin, *The Effect of Pretrial Detention,* 39 N.Y.U.L.Rev. 641 (1964). Also see Skolnik, *The Politics of Protest,* Report to National Commission on the Causes and Prevention of Violence 300, 301-311 (Ballantine Books, 4th ed., 1970).

39. Wilson, New Approaches to Pre-Trial Detention, 39 Jo.Kan.BarAssn. 13 (1970), reprinted in 28 Legal Aid Briefcase 212, 213-214.

Disposition of Felony Cases

CASE DISPOSITION	Bailed Accused (67 Cases)	Jailed Accused (33 Cases)
Dismissed by Prosecutor	38%	18%
Plea of Guilty	41%	60%
Trial and Conviction	5%	12%
Trial and Acquittal	16%	10%
Granted Probation*	54%	26%
Sentenced to Penitentiary	46%	74%

* Includes 59 convicted
33 bailed
26 jailed

B. Fulfillment of Prophecy of Criminality

In their report to the National Conference on Bail and Criminal Justice, Freed and Wald stated that "the costs of pre-trial imprisonment . . . in terms of time, money, *human suffering and justice* are staggering."[40]

Deplorable as prison conditions are for the already convicted, [41] there is evidence that conditions in pre-trial detention facilities are even worse[42] and offer less chance for rehabilitation.[43] The inescapable and lasting impressions imprinted by the experience, the exposure to sophisticates and to the hopeless and those resigned to failure, leave many defendants hardened, embittered and more likely to recidivate after release than they were before incarceration.

The degrading and degenerative effects are no less so on minors,[44] who because of age, immaturity and vulnerability possibly occupy a precarious position between criminal activity and creative, productive conduct.

C. Economic Disruption

Pre-trial detention results in serious economic disruption to the defendant, his family and the community. Involuntary removal from the community leads, for the great majority of defendants, who are indigent and live but marginal economic existences, to serious economic dislocation.

Even if there is not immediate loss of present employment, foregoing current income during the detention period will cause severe depletion of any economic reserves possessed at the beginning of incarceration. This further decreases one's ability to perform investigations needed in trial preparation or to engage counsel of one's own choice.

In addition, even in cases of acquittal, the individual's credit ratings and potential for future employment are jeopardized. Regardless of guilt or innocence, the mere existence of arrest records prejudices employment opportunities.[45]

---

40. *Op. cit., supra,* n. 36, at 39.
41. They have been described as follows:
"Although prisons might become centers of rehabilitation in some ideal future, it is apparent that they are at present overcrowded, understaffed, poorly funded, oppressively regimented, often openly abusive of the fundamental human rights of prisoners, and woefully incapable of providing the job training and education necessary to rehabilitate their charges. Note, 6 Harv. Civ. Rts./Civ. Lib.L.Rev., *supra,* at 351-352.
42. Note, *The Constitutional Limitations on Conditions of Pretrial Detention,* 79 Yale L. J. 941, 942-943 (1970); A. Trebach, *The Rationing of Justices Constitutional Rights and the Criminal Process* 83, 264 (1964); *Wright v. McMann,* 387 F.2d 579 (2d Cir. 1967); *Sostre v. Rockefeller,* 312 F.Supp. 863 (S.D. N.Y. 1970); *Holt v. Sarver,* 309 F.Supp. 362 (E.D. Ark. 1970).
43. Intensive rehabilitative service is advanced by some in justification of pre-trial detention of juveniles. See *Summary, supra.* But not only are the jurisdictional facts necessary as a precondition to treatment, not yet adjudicated; in addition, treatment is not a super objective of pre-trial detention. See *Report,* Governor's Special Study Commission, *supra,* n. 21, Part I, p. 42. "Although it is difficult to delineate what does justify detention of a minor, it is relatively easy to set forth a number of factors that . . . are *not* relevant to detention . . . (4) the belief that detention would have a salutary effect on the minor (the juvenile court does not have the right to exercise its jurisdiction over a minor for this purpose, if at all, *until an adjudication of wardship or dependency has been made*) . . ." *In Re William M., supra,* 3 Cal.3d 16, 30, n. 24 (emphasis added).
44. See n. 27, *supra* and accompanying text. Although being jailed is obviously a traumatic experience for anyone, regardless of age, certainly it is likely to be much more so for a minor. In addition, the harm caused by missing one or more weeks of school — or of being suspended or expelled due to arrest and detention — can have lasting consequences. More importantly, a minor is likely to be thrown in contact — often for the first time — with experienced law breakers or confirmed juvenile delinquents. "Detention for juveniles has been repeatedly scorned as 'a disruptive experience' and should be used selectively; detention as therapy is semantic acrobatics. It often leads to identification as a confirmed law breaker; status as a bona fide delinquent or 'big shot' among his peers; and perhaps, even more dangerous, introduces him to the philosophies and actual *modus operandi* of more experienced and sophisticated offenders." Freed and Wald, *Bail in the United States,* 1964, page 95; *id.,* at 101. Finally the stigma attached to having been confined for a period of time may be felt more deeply by a minor, and may well have a more profound effect upon his relationship with others.
45. See, e.g., *Gregory v. Litton Systems, Inc.,* 316 F.Supp. 401 (C.D. Cal 1970).

These results are especially pronounced because of the pervasive lack of training and skills on the part of the indigent defendant.

Although present employment might to some extent be less among juveniles than adult defendants, the consequences in terms of lost educational opportunity are no less grave than loss of a job. Education under present conditions is the necessary precondition to economic viability; and present pursuit of education affects disposition.

D. Maintenance of Detention Facilities and Administrative Costs

Mention is made of these monetary outlays (such as increased expenditures for construction, operation and maintenance of physical plant; additional administrative personnel; more courts, referees, clerks, prosecutors, public defenders and probation officers by reason of the added procedural elements in juvenile detention hearings; food and clothing for inmates) only to make the point that such expenditures should be allocated to badly needed community services that can replace institutionalization as the standard mode for dealing with accused juveniles.[46]

E. Erosion of the Community's Sense of Justice

> ". . . it is costly for society when the law arouses . . . a sense of persecution and hopelessness before official power, and hostility to police and other authority that may tend to generate the very conditions of criminality society is seeking to extirpate."[47]

Yet, this is just the result very often induced: because of the experience of being punished without a trial and a finding of guilt, and the impairment of the presumption of innocence, legitimacy of the agencies responsible for such results is undermined, and conditions leading to criminal conduct gain added impetus.

The sense of injustice is heightened by preventive detention such as inheres in the juvenile court law of California, for by incarcerating a person on the basis of a prediction of future "dangerousness," principles of individual culpability and responsibility are abrogated. Also, it negates corrective action, for past acts are irrevocable. The individual is incapable of conforming to the law's demands.

The rehabilitation or treatment myth is no longer offered in justification for detention since preventive detention is for the "protection of society." Thus, one cannot even avail himself of the solace, whatever it might be, of a system espousing rehabilitation.

Rather than cure causes of criminality or protect society, preventive detention only adds to unrest and dissatisfaction in poor and ghetto communities (upon whose residents preventive detention is more often imposed than upon others), and by detracting from the concepts of bail reform and release on recognizance, which at least have the theoretical potential for aiding most in racial minority communities could only impair the desired result of societal protection.

Preventive detention of the kind by which juvenile court laws are characterized, is the worst variety, for it is an absolute denial of bail, which is not a universal quality of preventive detention statutes.

III. Conclusion and Recommendation: Alternatives to Juvenile Court Preventive Detention Statutes

Juvenile law, in terms of the rights of the person, can be considered only to be part of the general lag in the rights of youth *vis-a-vis* adult criminal (procedural and substantive) law. But there are omnious portents about in this society

46. See "Conclusion and Recommendations," *infra*.
47. President's Commission on Law Enforcement and Administration of Justice, *Task Force Report: The Courts* 104 U.S. Gov't. Printing Office 1967).

today. The juvenile law might be the precursor of things to come for adults—namely, an *officially sanctioned* system of preventive detention.

Before the adult law closes the gap (regresses) to the level of juvenile law, a strong effort must be made to eliminate the precedent of the juvenile court law.

One solution — the one most obvious and easiest to implement — is incorporation of money bail[48] into the law of juvenile courts. But this is only a partial solution, even if there is an "O.R." system, for (a) money bail is no bail for the indigent;[49] and (b) release on recognizance makes detention dependent upon such inherently discriminatory factors as family relations, monetary resources, employment and length of residence in the community.[50]

The better solution lies in a system of reform of juvenile preventive detention law, that will avoid the costs inhering in the present statutes and result in affirmative benefits for the individual and the community, by generally making the various alternatives for use of community-based services and resources, the norm rather than the extraordinary remedy.

This is based on the recognition that

> "Delinquency [as well as incorrigibility or neglect situations] is not so much an act of individual deviance as a multitude of pervasive societal influences . . ."[51]

This solution is offered not only in an effort to avoid the abuses inherent in

---

48. Though beyond the scope of this article, mention should be made of current discussions probing the meaning of "bail." The U.S. Supreme Court has not yet detailed the full significance of bail. When "bail" is mentioned, one most commonly envisions bail in the form of money or a surety. It is currently being contended, however, that implicit in the Eighth Amendment is the right that there be an adequate system of pre-trial release, and that the "excessive bail" clause, construed in light of our jurisprudential history and predicates, together with other provisions of the Constitution, establishes at least a system which provides for money bail *and* as an alternative thereto, release of the person from custody on his own (non-monetary) undertaking or that of someone else, that he will appear in court at the time and place appointed, but not a system of release predicated exclusively upon money or surety bail. See Foote, "The Coming Constitutional Crisis in Bail," 113 U. of Pa. L. Rev. 959 (1965).

    Although the word *bail* is often used to denote exclusively, and is equated solely with, money bail, to "bail" a person means nothing more than "To procure release of one charged with an offense by insuring his future attendance in court and compelling him to remain within [the] jurisdiction of [the] court," or "To procure the release of a person from legal custody, by undertaking that he shall appear at the time and place designated and submit himself to the jurisdiction of the court." Black's Law Dictionary, page 177 (4th Ed. 1051). And the "undertaking" may vary from release upon defendant's own recognizance to setting of money bail in varying amounts. Therefore, "bail" can be used to refer to the right to pre-trial release generally, rather than simply money bail.

49. But, that one's state of being able to post money bail — if "bail" is interpreted exclusively in the money or surety sense — places him in an advantageous position vis-a-vis persons unable to post the entire sum or to secure a surety and hence that such a system operates to the detriment of the indigent, may not be urged to negate the existence of such a constitutional right for juveniles, but rather punctuates the necessity for an alternative for protection of the rights of indigents. Because certain persons cannot afford money bail is no argument for abolition of the constitutional right; rather such a situation is persuasive that additional protective remedies should likewise be provided and made available for the poor. The present period of confinement is of no aid to either rich or poor but is detrimental to both classes.

    In re Antazo, 3 Cal.3d 100)1970), illustrates that where a right is predicated on one's economic status, adiitional protective remedies must be developed for safeguarding access of that right to the poor. The issue decided in *Antazo* was whether a convicted defendant upon being sentenced or otherwise ordered to pay a fine and a penalty assessment can be required to serve them out in jail at a specified rate per day because he is unable to pay them. Just as "such a defendant has no choice at all and in reality is being imprisoned for his poverty," *id.,* at 103, so also an indigent juvenile under a money bail system would be confined prior to trial simply because he is poor. Hence, if provision is made for money bail, alternative and less intrusive means whereby the state can further its interest — namely, to insure appearance at court — must be devised for the indigent. Also see *Williams v. Illinois,* ...... U.S. ......, 26 L.ed.2d 586, ...S.Ct. ...., 38 U.S.L.W. 4607 (1970).

    If "bail" is viewed only as a money or surety concept, that still does not preclude the existence of a constitutional alternative; but the two are not mutually exclusive or incompatible.

50. Lack of employment and economic resources makes a minor a "poor risk" under criteria for release of adults on recognizance. "Immaturity" might also be advanced as an argument against O.R. for a minor. But these very factors, plus a greater "fear" that might grip an adult, makes it less likely that a juvenile will not return to court as ordered, for he lacks both the financial and psychological independence and sophistication for existing apart from the home or his familiar community environment.

    Furthermore, juveniles are less likely to harm others. It should be noted that numerous cases allowing bail for adults involve persons who are suspected members of organized crime (see *Sica v. United States,* 82 S.Ct. 669 (1962)), suspected sexual psychopaths (see *Ex Parte Keddy,* 105 Cal.App.2d 215 (1951)), and the like. Although no statistics as such can be cited here, surely it is far more likely than not that persons who are in their teens — many or most of whom have been taken into custody for minor offenses — will upon release pose less real danger to the safety of others than will adults who, among other things, usually have more money and mobility and hence more power to inflict harm on others than do minors still living at home.

51. Task Force Report on *Juvenile Delinquency and Youth Crime* 423 (U.S. Gov't. Printing Office 1967).

present detention criteria, policies and practices, but also, since pre-trial detention prejudices one's possibility for a fair trial and disposition other than institutional confinement, as an aid in advancing one's interest in a fair trial and continued physical liberty after adjudication; and furthermore to lend greater acceptance to the concept that since the ultimate objective is return to the community, proper adjustment or reacclimatization to the community requires close, continuing contact with that community.

DEVELOPMENT and utilization of community agencies can be a method, not only of circumventing present deplorable detention practices, but also of *diverting from* or screening out of the court system many cases which by resort to the juvenile court result in detriment rather than benefit to the individual.[52]

Since the only legitimate criterion for denial of pre-trial release is lack of assurance that the person will appear in court when ordered,[53] and since money bail is neither presently guaranteed to minors nor would offer the best possible resolution of the detention dilemma,[54] organizations in the minor's home community can form the supervisory link between the individual and the court to minimize non-appearance at the appointed time. The community organization can constitute the "assurance' 'for appearance in court.

But use of resources in the minor's immediate community as an "O.R." device would not necessarily involve "incarceration" at a community facility (except when, in narrowly delineated situations, deemed desirable, or when voluntarily chosen) but would be for the purpose of supervising the minor's release and providing a reporting agency.[55]

Elimination of the prosecutorial function of the probation officer would greatly aid in the necessary process of increasing trust between the community and the probation department and enable the latter, through affirmative action programs and publicizing its availability as another comunity resource, to break present barriers and penetrate into the community and become part of it.

IN ADDITION to the function of community based organizations in reducing the incidence of pre-adjudication detention, and hence in preserving one's right to receive a fair trial, those agencies can bring to the community an increased awareness of probation department functions, thus resulting in enhanced credibility, which in turn betters the probability for rehabilitation or effective treatment as well as makes possible greater diversion from the court system and increased non-judicial disposition on the part of probation personnel.

Since the ultimate objective of juvenile rehabilitation is return to the community, the isolation from the community inherent in juvenile facilities ill prepares one to return; and in cases of probation or supervised release, the "treatment" fails to offer anything in the way of positive programs since it is a system of merely overseeing technical conditions of release.

But release under supervision of probation personnel acting conjunctively with community-based services offers a potentially ameliorative alternative not only to pre-trial preventive detention but also to automatic resort to judicial adjudication and to present post-adjudicative treatment methods.

52. WIC § 654 (although in need of revisions to eliminate certain coercive factors inducing infringement of the privilege against self-incrimination) does provide a basis for use by the probation department in making use of community resources to avoid detrimntal court processing.
53. *Stack v. Boyle, supra,* 342 U.S. 1.
54. See nn. 48 and 49, *supra,* and accompanying text.
55. It should be noted that these suggestions for use of community agencies are only for individuals who under present policy and with existing resources would be detained. Absence of community resources should not be seized as an excuse to increase present detention rates or exacerbate prevailing detention policies.

THE TRIAL COURT IN THE HIERARCHY OF JUDICIAL LAWMAKING: A THRESHOLD SCHEMA

Sherman L. Cohn & Joseph G. Baxter

Although broad questions surrounding the propriety of judicial activism have been extensively debated, the specific question of freedom to make law at the trial level has been largely overlooked. In this article, the authors attempt to identify and isolate those factors crucial to further analysis of this difficult issue.

> It is he who makes the law become a living teacher as he transmits it from the legislature and the appellate court to the citizen who stands before him. It is he who watches the impact of the formal rule, explains its purpose to laymen and seeks to make its application conform to the durable and reasonable expectations of his community. It is he who determines whether the processes of common law growth shall decay or flower with a new vigor.[1]

While dramatic assertions of judicial power mark our political age, the locus of this activity rarely extends below the higher appellate levels.[2] Although often functioning as the cutting edge of social reform initiated by these higher level courts, the trial court has not yet been accepted as a proper forum for active judicial lawmaking.[3] With few exceptions,[4] even the more ardent reformists relegate the trial judge to

---

[1] Wyzanski, *A Trial Judge's Freedom and Responsibility*, 65 Harv. L. Rev. 1281, 1304 (1952).

[2] For an example of this focus upon appellate courts, *see* Mason, *Judicial Activism: Old and New*, 55 Va. L. Rev. 385 (1969).

[3] Indeed, the unique problems of the trial judge in general have received little attention. Rutter, *The Trial and the Judicial Process*, 15 J. Legal Ed. 245 (1963).

[4] *E.g.*, Touchy, *The New Legality*, 53 A.B.A.J. 544, 546 (1967).

THE GEORGETOWN LAW JOURNAL, 1970, Vol. 59, No. 2, pp. 1-36.

a secondary or even tertiary role in the hierarchy of judicial activism. As Judge Charles Wyzanski has noted, in their wrestle with the substantive law trial judges "should not regard themselves as appellate judges writ small. Their freedom is inevitably more narrowly exercised." [5]

The trial judge usually is not considered free to ignore the ruling of a higher court, even where it clearly appears that the ruling is about to be reversed and his decision following it overruled. Thus, in *District of Columbia v. Ricks*,[6] Chief Judge Harold Greene of the District of Columbia Court of General Sessions employed the following logic in passing on the constitutionality of a local vagrancy statute:

> Everything that has been said points to the conclusion that the District of Columbia vagrancy statute is unconstitutional as violative of the due process clause of the Fifth Amendment. Were I free to do so, I would dismiss the indictment for that reason. But I am not free to do so. The appellate courts of this jurisdiction have several times upheld the constitutional validity of this law, and I am bound by their decision.
>
> It is only because I strongly believe in the duty of trial judges to follow the precedents established by higher courts that I shall find the defendant guilty; but I fully expect that eventually the D.C. vagrancy statute will be determined to be unconstitutional.[7]

Chief Judge Greene was correct in his prediction; in that very same case the statute was found unconstitutional by the Court of Appeals for the District of Columbia Circuit.[8]

The limited role occupied by trial judges is so well accepted that many assume it to be the only role available to them. Reasons justifying this role are often no more than inarticulate broadsides at all forms of judicial activism—for example, that too much judicial freedom will lead to chaos. Where the limited role is justified, the arguments are usually no more than conclusory. It is said that the principle of equality requires the trial court to apply mechanically the precedents decided by the courts above it. Similarly, the restrictions imposed upon the trial judge are said to follow from the need for uniformity and the need for respect for law. So commonly held are these conclusions that they are seen to be almost a priori.

---

[5] Wyzanski, *supra* note 1, at 1297-98.

[6] 94 WASH. L. RPTR. 1269 (D.C. Ct. Gen. Sess., June 16, 1966), *rev'd*, 134 U.S. App. D.C. 201, 414 F.2d 1097 (1968).

[7] *Id.* at 1274; B. BOTEIN, TRIAL JUDGE 141-43 (1952).

[8] Ricks v. District of Columbia, 134 U.S. App. D.C. 201, 414 F.2d 1097 (1968).

This article seeks to examine the role of the trial judge in the making of new law. Present day notions of what the trial judge's role ought to be are partly the result of what Morris Cohen calls the "normative function of the actual." [9] We begin to believe that because something is (the actual) it ought to be (the norm). For this reason alone, the secondary role of the trial judge deserves fresh examination.

Without attempting to define precisely a suggested role for trial judges, this study seeks to perceive and develop the considerations relevant to a determination of what that role ought to be. For conceptual simplicity, the many considerations involved have been broken down into five fundamental areas of inquiry:

1. What role comports with our general notions of justice?
2. What role is most conducive to respect for law?
3. How may justice be most ably and efficiently administered?
4. What is the need for uniformity and when is uniform law required?
5. What is the trial court's role in areas of legislative activity?

To a certain extent, some of these considerations embody or overlap each other. Each, however, is important enough in itself to deserve separate treatment since each provides a different perspective for an analysis of the problem. Often considerations may be competing. Conclusions drawn from one consideration may at times be at odds with conclusions drawn from another. Often they will reinforce one another. With the development of each of these considerations, it is hoped that a full view of the problem will be provided.

To better appreciate their role as it ought to be, trial judges in the District of Columbia of diverse attitudes were interviewed to obtain their views on what their role both is and should be. Each was asked to answer several uniform questions about his role. Wherever relevant, these views are referred to below.

General Notions of Justice

Any participation by the trial court in the making of new law necessarily should comport with generally established notions of justice. Three such notions of justice are: (1) equality before the law, (2) the full availability and dissemination of rules of law which may be ascertained and relied upon by citizens, and (3) the dispensing by a court of a "just" solution consonant with the basic equities of the litigation before it. Each is useful in analyzing the trial judge's role.

---

[9] M. Cohen, Law and the Social Order (1933).

The notion of equality may be expressed in many ways. Like cases should be treated in a like manner.[10] The judge should be impartial. The outcome of the case should not depend on the judge. These notions are peculiarly significant at the trial level. By the nature of our system of courts, there are many more trial courts than appellate courts. Within a given jurisdiction, the court which "makes" the most law will usually be the highest level appellate court; normally there is only one such court in a given jurisdiction. The appellate tribunal, moreover is usually composed of a number of judges; therefore, the individual, peculiarities of a given appellate judge are leveled by the smaller role he plays in the outcome of a case. Thus, other things being equal, it is more probable that one appellate body will treat like cases that come before it in a like manner than will different trial courts.

One study of the City Magistrate's Court in New York City during the years 1914-1916, for example, discloses radically inconsistent dispositions of the same type of cases by different judges.[11] Of 566 persons charged with intoxication brought before one judge, greater than 99 percent were found guilty; of 673 brought before another, 79 percent were found not guilty. One judge discharged 54 percent of his disorderly conduct cases, while another discharged only 18 percent. One judge discharged as few as 4.5 percent of all vagrancy charges brought before him; another judge discharged 79 percent.[12] Similar disparity was found in the sentences imposed. One judge granted suspended sentences to 59 percent of those found guilty, while another did so for only seven percent.[13]

Thus, the trial level clearly provides greater opportunity for disparate treatment and therefore may require the imposition of restrictions on the trial judge greater than those imposed on his appellate brother. General rules which bind a trial judge may serve a normative "leveling" function.[14] Imposing a body of binding precedent upon a trial judge, however, will not by itself guarantee equality of treatment. All too often the "letter" of the law is followed rather than the spirit, a technique highly developed among lower court judges attempting to avoid a rule of law created by an appellate court which a given judge personally finds distasteful.[15] Too tight a constraint upon a judge's

10 Dawson, *The Functions of the Judge*, in TALKS ON AMERICAN LAW 15, 21 (H. Berman ed. 1961).

11 Everson, *The Human Element in Justice*, 10 J. CRIM. L.C. & P.S. 90 (1919).

12 *Id.* at 96.

13 *Id.* at 97.

14 *See* Dawson, *supra* note 10, at 21-23.

15 *See* J. PELTASON, FEDERAL COURTS IN THE POLITICAL PROCESS 60-62 (1955).

freedom, moreover, may result in law being applied mechanically, with arbitrary distinctions being made on the basis of precedent which is all too often contradictory. Such mechanical application of precedent also offends our other notions of justice.

RELIANCE

A second notion of justice, that one ought to be able to ascertain the law and act in reliance thereon, follows from the notion of law itself. Lon Fuller derives such a rule from his description of law as "the enterprise of subjecting human conduct to the governance of rules." [16] If men are to guide their conduct by the law, it follows that laws must be promulgated and must not change too quickly to be grasped; similarly, law must be neither contradictory nor retroactive. Expressed as a notion of justice, it is deemed unfair to penalize a man for his conduct without giving him warning or notice.

To apply this notion in analyzing the actual judicial framework, the functions and characteristics of each level of our court system must be considered. The traditional distinction is that the appellate court makes law while the trial court applies it. This distinction hardly constitutes a dichotomy, for we certainly can conceive of the trial court making law, as it often does. A perhaps more basic distinction is that appellate courts instruct in the law while the trial court ordinarily cannot.[17] Trial judges ordinarily do not write opinions or meaningful conclusions as to the relevant law of the case.[18] Of the judges interviewed at the D.C. Court of General Sessions, the average judge wrote only five such opinions a year. Normally, trial judges do not even write "conclusions of law" unless requested to do so by the parties. Of the judges interviewed, the average judge wrote his conclusions on the law controlling a decision in less than five percent of the cases before him. Furthermore, even when opinions or conclusions on the relevant law are written, they provide little notice to anyone other than the review-

---

[16] L. Fuller, The Morality of Law 96 (1964).

[17] L. Clark & H. Shulman, A Study of Law Administration in Connecticut 42 (1937).

[18] Although trial courts are often required to state their "conclusions of law" where there is a trial to the court itself, a general, broad conclusion that a party is or is not entitled to relief is ordinarily held sufficient to satisfy that requirement. *E.g.*, Young v. Bunnell Cemetery Ass'n, 221 Ind. 173, 179, 46 N.E.2d 825, 827 (1943); Consolidated Placers, Inc. v. Grant, 48 N.M. 340, 351, 151 P.2d 48, 55 (1944); Jameson Cold Storage Door Co. v. Brown, 218 S.W.2d 883, 887 (Tex. Civ. App. 1949); 5 J. Moore, Federal Practice ¶ 52.06(1) (2d ed. 1951) and cases cited therein.

ing court since they ordinarily are not published[19] or are otherwise difficult to obtain.[20]

There are, moreover, many more trial courts and trial court judges than appellate courts and appellate court judges, making acquaintance with the philosophical development and propensities of a given trial judge difficult. The large number of trial judges within many court systems likewise makes a prediction as to which judge will preside over certain litigation virtually futile. Thus, if one is relying on the prediction of "the law" furnished by precedent to guide his conduct, precedent furnished by trial decisions will be all but useless unless by chance or guile one can obtain the judge who authored the decision relied upon.[21]

For these reasons, it follows that appellate courts are better equipped than trial courts to instruct in the law.[22] For the citizen and his lawyer,

---

19 *See, e.g.*, Dawson, *supra* note 10, at 22; N.Y. JUDICIARY CODE § 431 (McKinney 1968); PA. STAT. ANN. tit. 17, § 1731.1 (1962). Federal courts are somewhat exceptional in requiring judges to write "findings of fact and conclusions of law" where they act as triers of fact. FED. R. CIV. P. 52(a).

20 Rutter, *supra* note 3, at 246.

21 Increased trial court freedom would have the additional disadvantage of encouraging further jockeying for the more sympathetic judge. Consider the burden this might place on the attorney unfamiliar with the judges of a court. Where trial judges have assumed known and firm positions on a point of law, knowledgeable attorneys jockey to bring a case or motion concerning that point of law before a favorable judge. For example, in the Federal District Court for the District of Columbia prior to May 1, 1970, there was no firm rule concerning the plaintiff's right to discover the defendant's insurance coverage in a personal injury case. Furthermore, the court then had a master calendar system whereby judges would rotate assignments. Where an attorney seeking to obtain or defeat discovery of insurance coverage knew that the relevant motion was to come before a judge known to be certain to rule against his position, he would not uncommonly seek a postponement, hoping that when the motion was again ripe for consideration, a more favorably disposed judge would be sitting. This particular "skill" of advocacy has been rendered immaterial by the shifting of the district court to an individual calendar system, effective May 1, 1970, and by the firm rule concerning discovery of insurance contained in the 1970 amendments to the Federal Rules of Civil Procedure. FED. R. CIV. P. 26(b)(2).

Jockeying for judges more or less favorably disposed to defendants in criminal, particularly minor criminal, matters is well known. In prosecutions of businessmen for failure to pay taxes coming before the D.C. Court of General Sessions, one can easily imagine the attempts to obtain the judge who has been quoted as saying in such a case: "I will not penalize a businessman trying to make a living when there are felons out on the street." Judge Alfred Burka, *quoted in* Katz, *The White Collar Criminal*, THE WASHINGTONIAN, May 1970, at 40, 65. In so stating, that judge has made his own rule of law for the case.

These examples illustrate that the more a trial judge enjoys freedom to make law, the more intensified will be the jockeying for a favorable judge, well beyond the jockeying now common among many attorneys.

22 This is not to suggest that appellate courts are rendered necessary simply because they are better equipped to instruct in the law. Certainly there need be no appellate

it is easier to shape conduct in conformity with appellate court opinions than to seek out the more obscure holdings of one or more trial courts. Since appellate opinions are ordinarily published and thus are more broadly disseminated, a greater number of citizens may more easily predict a subsequent appellate decision or a decision by a trial court which follows appellate instructions. Although an appellate court may at times radically shift its view, usually some forewarning is provided.

This argument, however, too easily assumes that people consciously guide their conduct according to the law. If neither of two parties uses the law as a guide to his conduct, it would not appear unfair to make new law in determining a dispute between them. We may ask, therefore, how reasonable it is to assume that one or any litigant has acted in reliance on the law. Gray for one does not believe that the assumption is reasonable.

> Practically in its application to actual affairs, for most of the laity, the Law, except for a few crude notions of the equity involved in some of its general principles, is all *ex post facto.* When a man marries or enters into a partnership, or buys a piece of land, or engages in any other transaction, he has the vaguest possible idea of the law governing the situation, and with our complicated system of Jurisprudence, it is impossible it should be otherwise. If he delayed to make a contract or do an act until he understood exactly all the legal consequences it involved, the contract would never be made or the act done. *Now the Law of which a man has no knowledge is the same to him as if it did not exist.*[23]

It may be argued that Gray overstates his case, for does not the mere existence of a law create unconscious patterns of behavior and modes of thought? For example, the rigor of the laws of sales and of contracts has made many people inherently suspicious of any contract put before them and has spawned the maxim "let the buyer beware!" In the commercial world, moreover, it is common to be advised by counsel before acting, and patterns of action may result from his advice.

Gray, moreover, apparently fails to appreciate the extent to which reliance varies with the type of activity involved. Regarding the law of torts, people do not generally rely on the law per se before they

---

system and the legislature could be the sole instructor. However, that has not been the mode of our common-law system.

[23] J. Gray, The Nature and Sources of the Law § 225 (1909) (emphasis added).

act;[24] rather, they seem to guide their acts by community morals and customs. According to this notion of reliance, therefore, the best law would be that which best comports with the community standard, even if such law should disagree with an announced rule. Inasmuch as the trial judge is much closer to the facts and probably better able to appreciate the community standard, at least as it relates to the case before him, our second notion of justice suggests that new law covering most torts and similar primarily "human" activity should be made at the trial level. In the area of activity primarily commercial or economic, by contrast, where conduct is quite commonly guided by legal counsel and performed with particular law in mind, our second notion of justice dictates that trial courts ought to be more restrained when deciding cases in this area.[25]

The logic of this analysis and its distinctions, however, must not be carried too far. Certain parties, especially large commercial concerns, rely on the tort law when deciding whether or not to obtain liability insurance. There is thus a measure of injustice done when a court extends tort liability beyond where it had traditionally been found, as, for example, where the court overrules the "charitable immunity" doctrine.[26] Here, the "wrongness" of the doctrine and the damage it causes to the victim of the tort must be weighed against the damage done to the tortfeasor by suddenly making him liable where, in reliance upon nonliability, he had taken no steps to protect himself.

---

[24] Exceptions to this rule may be found where persons seek to protect themselves from future liability through insurance and indemnity agreements or through assessing the risk of libel judgments prior to publication; such situations should be differentiated from the usual negligence or intentional tort occurrences.

[25] Unfortunately, "human conduct" and "economic activity" do not always come in neat and separate bundles. *See* J. Frank, Law and the Modern Mind 211 (1930). In some instances, as when the court has before it two experienced businessmen each having been guided in his action in a contract context by the advice of counsel, the inappropriateness of the individualization of the law may be clear. All too often, however, this is not the case. Often the parties before the court do not have equal footing, one party being totally ignorant of the law, the other party relying upon the law's unfairness. For example, this occurs in the landlord-tenant area when the landlord intentionally fails to provide heat knowing that the rule of law is that such covenants in a lease are independent. In signing his lease, the tenant might reasonably have assumed the law would protect him. In such a case a more flexible application of the law would appear appropriate. Here the businessman's reliance on existing law should not be controlling, although he may have laid out large sums of money in purchasing the premises in reliance upon the law's permitting him to make a decent return by practicing what the law then permitted: legalized theft from disadvantaged tenants. In this context, in spite of his reliance a more flexible approach is called for. *See, e.g.*, Javins v. First Nat'l Realty Corp., — U.S. App. D.C. —, 428 F.2d 1071 (1970). *See generally* Williams v. Walker-Thomas Furn. Co., 121 U.S. App. D.C. 315, 350 F.2d 445 (1965).

[26] *E.g.*, President & Directors v. Hughes, 130 F.2d 810 (D.C. Cir. 1942).

In such a situation, an appellate court may mitigate the injustice through the device of prospective overrulings,[27] which protects the tortfeasor in the case at bar and gives him and others in his class an opportunity to obtain insurance protection. The victim must suffer, of course, but no more so than previous victims in similar situations. This "equality" does not remove the injustice of applying the "wrong" doctrine to the victim, but any solution here will work an injustice. It is significant that the device of prospective overruling, while useful in ameliorating unjust situations, does not work at the trial level because it involves instruction in the law, a function trial courts are not capable of adequately performing.[28]

Even where reliance exists, less weight may be given to it if accompanying circumstances provide some notice of the existence of an obligation. For example, community standards may recognize obligations which are not yet legally recognized. These standards nevertheless serve as some notice, and it may be argued that those who choose to ignore such standards must accept the risk that the standards will receive legal recognition. By similar logic, those who ignore legal obligations as a result of their knowledge of the inadequacy of recognized enforcing remedies do so at the risk that stronger and more effective remedies will receive legal recognition.[29]

Consider an example in the landlord-tenant area. Tenants in the District of Columbia have the right to have repairs made according to their lease if it contains such a provision,[30] but the traditional remedies to preserve this right were inadequate. A lessor's promise to make repairs is an independent covenant under traditional law, the breach of which does not excuse a tenant from his obligation to pay rent.[31] Until recently, only two remedies were generally available to the tenant: he could either abandon the premises within a reasonable time after they had become uninhabitable or file an action for damages. The first remedy, "constructive eviction," would require the tenant to find a new residence. In a city such as the District of Columbia where 41

---

27 For a discussion of prospective overruling, see Currier, *Time and Change in Judge-Made Law: Prospective Overruling*, 51 VA. L. REV. 201 (1965).

28 *See* notes 17-22 *supra* and accompanying text. More particularly, to be effective prospective overruling requires that everyone be aware of the decision. A trial court decision, however, is often known only by the parties involved. Moreover, as noted previously, awareness of a trial judge's decision is in no way a guarantee that the same judge will decide one's own case.

29 Morange v. States Marine Lines, 398 U.S. 375 (1970); Wyandotte Transp. Co. v. United States, 389 U.S. 191 (1967); J. I. Case v. Borak, 377 U.S. 426 (1964).

30 Paratino v. Gildenhorn, 55 U.S. App. D.C. 271, 272, 4 F.2d 938, 939 (1925).

31 Pinching v. Wurdeman, 56 U.S. App. D.C. 223, 224-25, 12 F.2d 164, 166 (1926).

percent of the residences available to low-income tenants are dilapidated and where the market is favorable to landlords, such a remedy is inadequate.[32] Alternatively, should he fail to pay his rent, a tenant may counterclaim for damages in a suit brought to evict him, but he still will be evicted for nonpayment.[33] If he maintains a separate suit for damages, the landlord will evict him as soon as he may legally do so, usually within thirty days.[34] There are numerous obstacles involved in proving damages,[35] moreover, and in most instances, the recoverable damages would not even pay for the services of an expert appraiser, much less those of an attorney.

In a real sense, the existence of the recognized right to a habitable premise puts the landlord on notice as to his legal obligation. The landlord would not be receiving unfair treatment if the trial court, contrary to the well-established rule, interpreted the covenants of the lease to be dependent and relieved the tenant of his obligation to pay rent until the premises were sufficiently repaired. Just such an equitable result was reached on the appellate level by a recent decision by the United States Court of Appeals for the District of Columbia implying warranties of habitability in all leases for urban dwellings in the District of Columbia.[36] Although the landlord could argue that it was unfair to force him to comply with a remedy which he had not anticipated, this same "unfairness" would have existed whether the new remedy was imposed by an appellate or a trial court. In either case it would seem more unjust to disappoint the tenant with the inadequate remedy which the traditional law had provided him.

If our society is to concern itself with the reliability of its legal system, perhaps it should first question the reliability of the fact-finding process before constraining the freedom of the trial judge.[37] Undoubtedly, the most unreliable aspect of our factfinding process is the jury system. Through their general verdicts, juries often ignore rules of law which do not comport with their sense of equity.[38] In the criminal area, for example, game laws, liquor laws, gambling laws, and laws prohibiting drunken driving often are viewed as unnecessarily severe

32 Comment, *Tenants' Remedies in the District of Columbia: New Hope for Reform*, 18 CATH. U. L. REV. 80, 83 (1968).

33 *Id.*

34 *Id.* at 83-84.

35 *Id.*

36 Javins v. First Nat'l Realty Corp., — U.S. App. D.C. —, 428 F.2d 1071 (1970).

37 *See generally* J. FRANK, *supra* note 25, at 170-85 (1930).

38 "[I]n its long history the jury has on occasion been a leavener of the strict law, a kind of critic and irregular reformer of the law, anticipating formal legal change." Kaplan, *Trial by Jury*, in TALKS ON AMERICAN LAW 45, 53 (H. Berman ed. 1961); *see* B. BOTEIN, *supra* note 7, at 178-95.

by the jury and thus are often avoided or ignored by them.[39] In the civil area, contributory negligence often is ignored as a jury seeks to work its sense of justice.[40] Described by Pound as "jury lawlessness," this process is called "the great corrective of law in its actual administration." [41] Jury lawlessness keeps the letter of the law in the books, while at the same time allowing the jury freedom to apply extra-legal considerations[42] in the actual decision of cases. "If," says Pound, "the ritual of charging the jury on the law with exactness is preserved, the record will show that the case was decided according to law, and the fact that the jury dealt with it according to extra-legal notions in conformity to the views of the community, is covered up." [43]

From the viewpoint of reliability, it is difficult to appreciate Pound's enthusiasm for the process of jury lawlessness. As Jerome Frank notes, "[I]f any legal rules are so inflexible that they work injustice, they should avowedly be made more flexible." [44] At least in those areas where the law is admittedly harsh, the trial judge ought to be allowed more freedom in making law, whether through alteration of a general rule or provision of a subcategory exception. Open change provides guidance for future conduct. Although this change can be worked in an individual case by the jury's disregard of law that has become harsh—and some may argue that this is a better process, the jury being more

---

39 H. KALVEN & H. ZEISEL, THE AMERICAN JURY 286-97 (1966).

40 *See* B. BOTEIN, *supra* note 7, at 178-80. *See generally id.* at 141-42.

41 Roscoe Pound, *quoted in* J. FRANK, COURTS ON TRIAL 127 (1949); *see* United States v. Moylan, 417 F.2d 1002, 1006 (4th Cir. 1969). As Judge Frank caveats, however, juries do not always react in such a rational manner or for such high motives: "Many juries in reaching their verdicts act on their emotional responses to the lawyers and witnesses; they like or dislike, not any legal rule, but they do like an artful lawyer for the plaintiff, the poor widow, the brunette with the soulful eyes, and they do dislike the big corporation, the Italian with a thick, foreign accent. We do not have uniform jury nullification of harsh rules; we have juries avoiding—often in ignorance that they are so doing—excellent as well as bad rules, and in capricious fashion." J. FRANK, *supra* note 25, at 130.

42 Roscoe Pound, *supra* note 41, at 127. The doctrine of jury nullification has received judicial recognition recently, in United States v. Spock, 416 F.2d 165 (1st Cir. 1969). It was referred to as a "basic reason" underlying the requirement that criminal verdicts be general. *Id.* at 181, *quoting* United States v. Ogull, 149 F. Supp. 272, 276 (S.D.N.Y. 1957), *aff'd on other grounds sub. nom.* United States v. Gernie, 252 F.2d 664 (2d Cir.), *cert. denied,* 356 U.S. 968 (1958). In the *Spock* case, the First Circuit also referred to the purpose of jury nullification in noting that, although "some defendants could be found to have exceeded the bounds of free speech, the issue was, in the jury's discretion, to be applied." *Id.* at 183. *See also* United States v. Sisson, 294 F. Supp. 520, 523-24 (D. Mass. 1968).

43 Roscoe Pound, *supra* note 41, at 127. The realization that juries will disregard the facts and instructions is institutionalized within our system by the techniques of directed verdict and judgments *non obstante veredicto.*

44 J. FRANK, *supra* note 41, at 132.

aware of community standards[45]—the harsh law still would remain on the books, counsel would have no opportunity to argue the advisability of change, the evolution of the law would be stifled, and persons seeking to temper their conduct by reliance on the law would have nowhere to turn for intelligent guidance.

In sum, our second notion of justice rests on the premise that people ought to be able to rely on the law.[46] This does not mean, however, that courts uniformly should assume that a given party has acted in

---

[45] The nullification of oppressive laws through "jury lawlessness" may at least be preferable to the enforcement of such laws. In our country's earlier days, the appropriateness of this alternative was commonly accepted. Thus, in the famous trial of John Peter Zenger, Alexander Hamilton successfully argued that the jury had "the right beyond all dispute to determine both the law and the facts" and to ignore the law if it offended their conscience. J. ALEXANDER, A BRIEF NARRATIVE OF THE CASE AND TRIAL OF JOHN PETER ZENGER 78, 93-94 (1963). In 1794 Chief Justice Jay expressed a similar viewpoint in Georgia v. Brailsford, 3 U.S. (3 Dall.) 1, 4 (1794). The Court, nevertheless, rejected this viewpoint in *Sparf v. Hansen,* arguing that such an approach, if fully followed, would also permit juries to create its own crimes or render stiffer punishment than the law allows. 156 U.S. 51, 101 (1895). This argument, however, ignores the limited function of jury nullification—protection against oppressive law.

Since the decision in *Sparf,* few courts have reviewed the basis for the decision. In a recent case involving the trial of political protestors, the "Catonsville Nine," the court faithfully followed *Sparf.* United States v. Moylan, 417 F.2d 1002, 1009 (4th Cir. 1969). Several recent cases which suggest a consciousness of the jury's political role, however, weaken the value of *Sparf* as a precedent. Witherspoon v. Illinois, 391 U.S. 510, 519 n.15 (1968); Duncan v. Louisiana, 391 U.S. 145 (1968); United States v. Spock, 416 F.2d 165, 181-83 (1st Cir. 1969). Professor Jon M. Van Dyke has argued that the only real rationale for the Court's decision in *Witherspoon v. Illinois* that Illinois could not, consistent with due process, allow jurors opposed to capital punishment to be excluded from murder juries, is one of jury nullification. Van Dyke, *The Jury as a Political Institution,* THE CENTER MAGAZINE, March 1970, at 23. *See also* Cox, *Conscience and Anarchy: The Prosecution of War Resistors,* 57 YALE L.J. 481 (1968); Farley, *Instructions to Juries—Their Role in the Judicial Process,* 42 YALE L.J. 194 (1932); Howe, *Juries as Judges of Criminal Law,* 52 HARV. L. REV. 582 (1939); Thayer, *The Jury and Its Development,* 5 HARV. L. REV. 249 (1892).

[46] Reliance could possibly be used as a defense to the making of new law. At the trial court level, however, such a defense might be unmanageable, inasmuch as everyone would raise it, and unfair, inasmuch as many who may have relied might be unable to prove reliance. It would require the court to distinguish between different levels of reliance and to determine which provided a satisfactory defense. The highest level of reliance would be the earliest, where a man relied on a judicially announced rule before he committed his allegedly tortious act or signed the contract in question. Such reliance indeed would be difficult to prove unless one had an attorney prepare a memorandum before acting. The next level of reliance might occur after a man has acted but before he is sued or brings suit. He might, for example, have offered to settle or refused to settle based upon the existing law. Beyond this point, however, decisions as to the validity of reliance become virtually impossible. For example, how important would an "act of reliance" be during the litigation itself? Questions such as this crystallize the difficulties which such a defense could create. *See generally* J. FRANK, *supra* note 25, at 269-70; Cohn, *Ex Injuria Jus Non Oritur: A Principle Misapplied,* 3 SANTA CLARA LAWYER 23 (1962).

reliance unless such an assumption reasonably comports with reality. In much tort litigation, the assumption is not deserved inasmuch as tortfeasors often act in total ignorance of the law. In commercial litigation, however, reliance more readily should be assumed. Even where reliance exists, less weight may be given to that factor when the reliance is upon a rule inconsistent with community standards or upon knowledge of the inadequacy of recognized remedies. Further consideration, moreover, suggests the advantages of bypassing unreliable jury lawlessness through the open alteration and individualization of the law. Thus, beyond being merely consistent with our second notion of justice, a limited lawmaking power at the trial level may also serve to further it.

AN EQUITABLE SOLUTION OF THE CASE

A "just" determination of each individual case is the goal to which any notion of justice ultimately aspires. Such a determination must be reached at the earliest stage possible; when the injustice or harshness of a rule is evident, no reason is sufficient to require a party to wait and suffer the injustice of a decision according to it. To the extent that a party's reliance on past law is relevant to the justice of any decision, the notion of a "just solution" encompasses the second notion of justice. The notion of equality differs, however, in that it is "macroscopic," requiring an awareness of all similar cases, while the notion of a just solution between the parties is "microscopic," requiring only a knowledge of the facts and circumstances of the specific case. It is this latter task, the analysis of the facts and circumstances of the case before it, which is most suited to the abilities of a trial court. A trial judge may not have the overview to apply a principle of equality broader than the notion of impartiality. Therefore, the notion of just individual determinations arguably ought to take priority at the trial level over any other notion of justice.

In a utilitarian sense, the similar notion of equality is much less an absolute ideal. Certainly, the handling of cases should be equally just in the sense that *all* cases should be handled justly. The notion of equality, however, should not lead to the rigid conclusion that one man should be treated unfairly simply because others in his situation have been treated unfairly. Thus, it does not follow that because other tenants have been denied a remedy for the landlord's failure to repair, the tenant presently before the court must be denied a remedy. Nor should a victim of a tort committed by a charitable institution be denied recovery merely to give him equality with all such previous victims and the charity equality with all such previous institutions, especially where the charitable immunity doctrine is recognized to be wrong. The notion of treating like cases similarly is designed to guarantee impartiality but ought not to be followed to produce unfairness.

Practical application of the third notion of justice is not without difficulty. It assumes the availability of an objective standard for determining when a rule of law is unfair or would produce an unjust solution if applied. One man's notion of justice may not be that of another, and judges are no exception. May trial judges be trusted to decide when a rule is unfair? Assuming they are competent to do this, may we further trust them to choose a new rule which is better?[47] Fortunately, there are many issues of law for which an objective standard does exist. Property law provides several good examples. Such rules as the Doctrine of Worthier Title, the destructibility of contingent remainders, and the Rule in Shelley's Case are widely decried;[48] yet they persist in many jurisdictions. Landlord-tenant law similarly is burdened by the concept of independent covenants and the rule that a lessor is not required to mitigate damages when the lessee abandons the leasehold.[49] Where a judge is faced with rules such as these which are rejected as unjust or arbitrary by consensus of the legal community, he acts according to a standard of justice more objective than merely his own subjective predelictions when he refuses to follow the rule.

The priorities which we assign our notions of justice might best be summarized in terms of the functions which we assign our courts at each level. The trial court judge must decide the case before him correctly in light of the law and the facts; a correct decision is expected to be consistent with each of our notions of justice, producing a just resolution of the equities of the case, taking reliance into consideration, and reaching a result similar to that in another case containing similar facts. A trial judge's discretion should be limited only to insure impartiality, not to produce an unbending and senseless uniformity of application for its own sake. Thus, two goals for the trial court judge may be posited: (1) of primary importance, to reach a just solution of the case; (2) secondarily, to reach this solution through impartial application of precedent. These priorities, however, are not inconsistent

---

[47] Each of the judges interviewed was asked whether or not his decisions would be more just if he were allowed the freedom to ignore precedent and decide cases so as to most fairly treat the parties. None of the judges were of the opinion that such freedom would result in more fairness. One judge said that in only a few cases would such freedom prove worthwhile and these few cases would not justify the chaos that would be produced. Another judge replied that "trial judges don't behave well ungoverned and most cases turn on the facts anyway."

[48] *See, e.g.*, J. Cribbet, Principles of the Law of Property 57-65 (1962).

[49] *See, e.g.*, *id.* at 181-82.

with a power in the trial judge to change harsh law where necessary, at least where there is a consensus that the then prevailing rule is inequitable. There is no basis for assuming that all such changes will be wrong, and errors or partiality are, of course, correctable on appeal, a prime function of the appellate level.

Respect for Law

Respect for law and the habit of obedience to decisions made according to its process are vital to the orderly operation of our society. As Professors Mishkin and Morris note, society "asks for and must receive obedience to decisions which individuals consider wrong; the use of force in the manner sanctioned by courts must be viewed as legitimate even by those who disagree with the particular decision." [50] Such obedience, according to Mishkin and Morris, is not "purely the product of rational decision." [51] Much more strongly operative in producing the emotional strength which is the foundation of the habit of obedience is "the symbol of the law as a fixed, certain body of authoritative rules which courts mechanically (and thus impartially) 'apply' or 'find' " [52]—the symbol of a government of laws and not of men.

Judicial lawmaking at any level necessarily involves change. Change weakens this symbolism. It lessens the certainty and shows the human element in the law. Nevertheless, change in the law is absolutely necessary; without it once just rules work injustices when societal facts upon which they were based have changed. Assuming the necessity of change, therefore, at what level would it encourage less respect?

Appellate courts, especially the higher level appellate courts which do most of our "judicial legislation," are removed from the everyday workings of society and from the parties themselves. The average man has little feeling for what goes on in an appellate proceeding. The proceedings themselves are rarely covered by the press; only the decisions emerging from them receive coverage. By contrast, trials receive extensive dramatic treatment through press, stage, television, and movies;

---

[50] P. Mishkin & C. Morris, On Law in Courts 80 (1965).

[51] Based upon an examination of courts' operations, individuals might come to the conclusion that law generally is sufficiently stable to be relied upon. They might similarly conclude that courts are normally impartial enough so that their franchise to authorize the use of society's force should be deemed legitimate. Or an analysis of the needs of an organized society and a lack of alternatives might lead to the same conclusion. But in fact, the general habits of reliance on the law and obedience to judicial decision rests in small part on such ratiocination.

Id. at 81.

[52] *Id.*

it is the trial court with which men have most contact. There are many more trials than appeals, and in most instances the parties themselves attend the trial. Thus, the parties have a better understanding of the trial court's mode of functioning and its activities. Activism on this "grass roots" level is more difficult to conceal; the human element of the law is more evident. At the same time, trial court decisions do not carry the same order of prestige and authority which ordinarily attaches to appellate decisions. In part this respect stems from the appellate court's special instructive position, its ability to effect more than the parties before the court, and its authority to reverse the decisions of lower courts.

Further respect is generated for an appellate decision because it is the reasoned opinion of a body of men rather than of one man. For this reason, an appellate court can practice safely "judicial legislation" in instances where a trial court cannot. Consider this point in the context of the overruling of *Plessy v. Ferguson*.[53]

> Quite apart from the general duty of puisne judges to follow rather than lead their appellate masters, there were special judico-political reasons for refusing to give *Plessy* its quietus at the lower level. For all its attenuation, *Plessy* continued into the 1950's to cloak the entire system of segregation in the mantle of legitimacy. To remove it all at once was a just, overdue, yet bold and historic act demanding the peculiar authority of the one Court which speaks with a national voice. Indeed the Justices themselves may have believed in 1953-1955 that nothing short of unanimity within the Court would turn the trick.[54]

Further consideration of the theory of Professors Mishkin and Morris, however, suggests certain distinct advantages in making law at the trial level. For the same reason that trial-court law provides little guidance for one seeking to act according to the law,[55] it also conceals its own activism. Very few trial decisions result in the writing of opinions or explicit conclusions as to the law of the case. Even where such opinions or conclusions of law are written, they are generally not published. The transcript of the trial itself is usually difficult and expensive to obtain.[56] Thus, law made at the trial level may be invisible to all save in those rare instances where a decision receives wide publicity in the

---

53 163 U.S. 537 (1869).

54 Kelman, *The Force of Precedent in Lower Courts*, 14 WAYNE L. REV. 3, 8 n.26 (1967).

55 *See* notes 17-22 *supra* and accompanying text.

56 *See* notes 18-20 *supra* and accompanying text.

popular press.[57] On appeal, a reviewing court may be unable to divine the basis for a decision, especially in a nonjury case where no meaningful conclusions of law are made.[58] Normally such a court will presume the decision to be correct and look to the transcript to find a basis, either in law or in fact, upon which the trial judge *could* have supported his decision.

Some challenge the Mishkin and Morris theory by disputing the premise that the facade of law as certain and unchanging is significantly related to respect for law.[59] If that relation does not exist, even the most overt making of law at the trial level would not undermine respect for law, at least not in the manner posited by Mishkin and Morris. Jerome Frank is one who criticizes the legal craving for sureness and certainty, contending that it ultimately hinders the development of a mature legal system. According to Frank, the craving for unrealizable certainty is but a symptom of an unrelinquished childhood need for an authoritative father and the unconscious attempt "to find in the law a substitute for those attributes of firmness, sureness, certainty, and infallibility ascribed in childhood to the father." [60] By maintaining this "symbol of the law as a fixed, certain body of authoritative rules which courts mechanically and thus impartially 'apply' or 'find' " [61] we inhibit a mature legal and social system and mature analysis of how law can best serve society.

Beyond theoretical considerations, there is little hard evidence to suggest that the habit of obedience is related to mechanical (as opposed to the human) application of rules. Followed rigidly, the theory would dictate the doubtful conclusion that courts of equity are less respected or less obeyed than courts governed by more mechanical rules of law. A French example suggests the contrary. Gény tells of a certain Judge Magnaud who served on the trial court of Château-Thiery between 1889 and 1904 and who, "acting under the influence of his shifting humanitarianism," [62] decided each case according to his own sense of the equities involved, often ignoring clear statutory mandates. His record on the bench is replete with revolutionary decisions; for example, he acquitted a woman who stole bread under an irresistible hunger, held a vagrant completely irresponsible for his poverty, and

57 *See, e.g.*, Washington Post, Nov. 11, 1969, at 1, col. 7.

58 *See* note 18 *supra* and accompanying text.

59 *See, e.g.*, Miller & Scheflin, *The Power of the Supreme Court in the Age of the Positive State*, 1967 DUKE L.J. 273, 278-79.

60 J. FRANK, *supra* note 25, at 21.

61 P. MISHKIN & C. MORRIS, *supra* note 50, at 81.

62 F. GÉNY, METHODE D'INTERPRÉTATION ET SOURCES EN DROIT PRIVE POSITIF 503 (La. St. L. Ins. transl. 1954).

admitted into the criminal law a defense of moral provocation against a charge of public offense.[63] In interpreting a statute, he chose to do so "penetrated by the idea that the legislator . . . did not intend that the statute result in any inequality or any inequity." [64] Gény entirely disapproves of Magnaud, and yet he notes the "favorable reaction of the public opinion toward the Magnaud decisions," [65] reaction broad enough to earn him the name "le bon juge" (the good judge).[66]

It may be argued further that the theory of Mishkin and Morris once was relevant but has now outlived its usefulness; perhaps it suited an earlier age when law was more irrational and chose not to look to contemporary notions of justice for support. Consider in this respect Pound's view that in time the ends of law have changed.[67] In earlier times, its function was to preserve peace and, later, to keep the status quo.[68] In such a static society, the symbol of law as certain and unchanging was appropriate to its function. Pound suggests that the law today is more concerned with the maximum satisfaction of wants.[69] Such a notion requires a changing, growing law and is poorly served by a symbol of the law that is neither.[70]

Today, moreover, people are more educated and are becoming increasingly aware of the subjective element in the law;[71] they more easily question laws not based on reason and justice. Perhaps it is the symbol of *justice* which is more important today in creating respect for law and in developing the habit of obedience. It would appear that such a symbol would carry more emotional strength than the symbol of law as a body of fixed rules which courts mechanically apply.

---

63 *Id.* at 499.

64 *Id. at* 501.

65 *Id.* at 500.

66 *Id.* at 497. Not all trial judges fit this appellation, however. *See* Katz, *Some Call It Justice,* THE WASHINGTONIAN, Sept. 1970, at 46.

67 R. POUND, INTRODUCTION TO THE PHILOSOPHY OF LAW 24-30 (1954).

68 *Id.* at 33-35.

69 *Id.* at 42.

70 *Cf.* J. FRANK, *supra* note 25, at 19-21. *See also* National Presto Industries, Inc. v. United States, 338 F.2d 99 (Ct. Cl. 1964). In *National Presto,* the court "recognized" a new right of recovery and a new remedy of reformation for mutual-mistake-of-fact and sharing of damage: "The courts have thus far chosen, in passing upon claims of the latter type, to hug closely the notched coastlines of the particular litigations, rather than to chart straight paths across the troubled sea. . . . [I]t is difficult to find general principles or a developed body of law. This caution, which we accept, follows the wisdom of the common law; premature generalization can bear strange fruit. Nevertheless, there are some existing guidelines which we can usefully follow." *Id.* at 108. *See also* Deems v. Western Md. Ry., 247 Md. 95, 112-13, 231 A.2d 514, 524 (1967); B. CARDOZO, THE NATURE OF THE JUDICIAL PROCESS 113 (1921).

71 *Cf.* Hess, *Political Attitudes in Children,* PSYCHOLOGY TODAY, Jan. 1969, at 24.

"Free men," as Whitehead notes, "obey the rules which they themselves have made." [72] Laws which comport with a community's standards and sense of justice are obeyed because, though judicially created, they are at least adoptively a product of the community. Thus if we are to preserve respect for law, change must occur at that level which is most responsive to the standards of the community. Just which level meets this requirement will be determined in the context of our next consideration.

Practical Administrative Considerations: Competency and Efficiency

Courts must provide a just solution for each case before them, do so in an impartial manner, and employ means and procedures which do not undermine respect for their decisions. Justice which consumes many years of the parties' time, however, perhaps is not justice at all. Courts must render justice efficiently, with the most competent person rendering a final decision at the earliest possible time. Let us therefore examine trial-court lawmaking in the context of the practical administrative considerations of competency and efficiency.

COMPETENCY

Questions of competence are best considered comparatively. Consideration must be given to the functions of both trial and appellate courts in order to evaluate their comparative ability to make new law within the scope of their traditional functions. Simply stated, the trial court's function is to decide correctly the case before it. Traditionally, this function has been viewed as involving little more than deciding cases through the application of the law made by higher courts and by the legislature. Whatever the method through which the trial court reaches its decision, whether it be this traditional method or a less restrictive one, it only serves to define the term "correctly"; it neither expands nor contracts the essential trial function.

The appellate tribunal, especially the higher level appellate court, has two functions. The first of these is the correction of error.[73] The appellate court need not correct all errors; its jurisdiction may be limited to particular types of questions. Even when jurisdiction is shown, the appellate court may choose to correct only those errors of the most flagrant type or only error which is prejudicial.[74] The second appellate

72 A. Whitehead, Symbolism: Its Meaning and Effect 88 (1927).

73 L. Clark & H. Shulman, *supra* note 17, at 42.

74 One might wish to argue that the function of correcting errors is the same as the

function is instruction in the law.[75] Such instruction may be binding on later courts, but this will depend on whether later courts consider appellate wisdom "holdings" or merely "teachings" or dicta. Appellate opinions outlining the rationale behind decisions are usually published; these may therefore become "general law," law which applies not only to the case at bar but to all future cases on the point at issue. To this extent, appellate courts are quasi-legislative in that in deciding cases they create norms.

The quasi-legislative role assumed by an appellate court does pose problems, the most serious being the limited perspective through which the court views the problems it handles. Inasmuch as higher level courts make general law, they are often required to make policy determinations for which a court may not be best suited. Courts do not have the fact-finding machinery often necessary to arrive at intelligent social-action decisions. Unlike the legislature, they generally are limited to the information presented to them by the adversaries and, to a limited extent, that provided by friends of the court and that which is judicially noticeable. They cannot hold hearings or create committees to study problems.[76]

Courts, moreover, operate upon a level of morality which Hyneman calls a "morality of distant contemplation;" conversely, the legislature operates on a level of "direct confrontation."[77] "[I]t is Congress that

---

function of correctly deciding cases, in that the correction of error resolves incorrectly decided cases. At the very least, however, these functions involve a difference in focus. Only single issues of a case may be before the appellate court and presumptions normally operate in favor of the decisions below. Moreover, as the appellate court may only reverse decisions in which there are prejudicial errors or which are clearly erroneous, the decisions it upholds may not be "correct" in the trial-court sense.

75 L. Clark & H. Shulman, *supra* note 17; see B. Cardozo, *supra* note 70, at 135; Keeton, *Judicial Law Reform—A Perspective on the Performance of Appellate Courts*, 44 Texas L. Rev. 1254, 1260-61 (1966); Tate, *The Lawmaking Function of the Judge*, 28 La. L. Rev. 211, 212 (1968).

76 *Cf.* S. Hyneman, The Supreme Court on Trial 240-43, 250-51 (1963).

77 *Id.* at 272. Hyneman describes these moralities in terms of the attitudes of most white men towards blacks. "Contemplating relations between races as a problem enduring over time . . . as a source of indignity and pain in places far away . . . no doubt most white American citizens would come out against it. They would feel better if it did not exist." *Id.* This is the morality of distant contemplation. Immediate confrontation, however, such as a black invasion of his residential area or black demands for admission to his union, will produce different responses. This is the morality of immediate confrontation.

Judicial opinions reveal the theoretical nature of a court's deliberations. Note the strangeness one feels in Mr. Justice Clark's references to his personal experiences in Abbott Laboratories v. Gardner, 387 U.S. 136, 201 (1967) (Clark, J., dissenting).

The moral level of the Supreme Court may be due in part to the type of men selected for that court. Typically, Supreme Court nominees were chosen from among

hears most about the sacrifices necessary for achievement, least about the delights of vision and the rewards of magnanimity."[78] Congressmen do not dare to do more than their constituents will tolerate.[79] By contrast, the judiciary is more independent and detached. Hyneman notes that the Supreme Court Justices "are not confronted by the people who make the sacrifices necessary for achieving ideals."[80] They are not "visited by a delegation of bakers demanding relief after ten hours in front of an oven."[81]

This detachment and independence among our judges does provide one distinct advantage; fundamental liberties should be beyond the reach of any majority, and only independent judges may be trusted to guard steadfastly these liberties against irresponsible waves of popular sentiment. In protecting the majority from its own excesses, courts preserve freedoms fundamental to our notion of a pluralist democracy.[82] Nevertheless, due to the court's "moral" distance from the problems before them, judicial experimentation in legislation may be unrealistic and, where many are affected, difficult to enforce.

Certain critics find the quasi-legislative role of appellate courts offensive to the doctrine of separation of powers. According to one doctrinal interpretation, the need for a distribution of powers requires a clear line of demarcation between the judicial and legislative functions. The "proper task of the judge is to decide the case before him correctly," while the "proper task of the legislature" (various exceptional and ceremonial bills not withstanding) is to "formulate and promulgate general norms."[83] Such a definition of judicial function would mean that the creation of binding precedent by a court is a usurpation of the legislative function to whatever degree it goes beyond the case and creates a general norm.[84] Such a concept does not

---

the socially advantaged families. "The typical Supreme Court Justice has invariably been white, generally Protestant with a penchant for high social status denomination, usually of ethnic stock originating in the British Isles, and born in comfortable circumstances in an urban or small town environment." J. SCHMIDHAUSER, THE SUPREME COURT: ITS POLITICS, PERSONALITIES, AND PROCEDURES 58-59 (1960). If the Supreme Court is the keeper of the American conscience, "it is essentially the conscience of the American upper-middle class sharpened by the imperative of individual social responsibility and political activism, and conditioned by the conservative impact of legal training and professional legal attitudes and associations." *Id.* at 62.

[78] S. HYNEMAN, *supra* note 76, at 273.

[79] Dawson, *supra* note 10, at 25.

[80] S. HYNEMAN, *supra* note 76, at 273.

[81] *Id.*

[82] Rostow, *The Democratic Character of Judicial Review*, 66 HARV. L. REV. 193, 194-97 (1952).

[83] Mayda, *Gény's Méthode After 60 Years*, in F. GÉNY, *supra* note 62, at LIX.

[84] As this view applies to French law, see F. GÉNY, *supra* note 62, at 326.

mean that case law is irrelevant. Judicial decisions may have "force beyond the particular case only *rationis imperio*, not *ratione imperii*—because of the force of their reason, not because of their formal authority." [85]

Greater freedom at the trial level sidesteps many of these issues. Trial-court law is personal, not general; it is usually known by and applied to only the parties; the impact of the decision is limited mostly to the parties. Therefore, broad policy considerations regarding the impact of the decision are usually not necessary; generally, the only "policy" considerations need be "microscopic" ones. What decision by the court will do the most equity between the parties? What remedy is most suitable? Being in close contact with the parties and their problems, the trial judge is the obvious person to reach such decisions. For the same reasons, he is more realistic and operates more on the level of direct confrontation than his appellate brother.[86] Moreover, as one of the trial judges interviewed said, all trial judges see the "results" of their decisions—the "smirk on the face of the dope peddler when the narcotics he possessed are suppressed," the "frustrated look on policemen when the peddler is released on a technicality," the repeated appearance of certain criminals before him.[87] In a sense, this constitutes "impact analysis," however limited, which is denied the appellate court.

The perspective of the trial court, nevertheless, is limited in its own way. As Judge Wyzanski noted, trial judges usually "do not even see the points of difficulty too clearly. With them the pace is quicker, the troublesome issues have not been sorted from those which go by rote, the briefs of counsel have not reached their ultimate perfection." [88] Although the trial judge is able to weigh the equities of the situation better than the appellate judge, he is often enmeshed in the intimacies of the case and lacks appreciation of the broad policy considerations which ultimately may control the decision of the appellate court. In the revealing words of one judge interviewed, "the trial judge is too busy with the facts to get the big picture." [89]

The trial judge, moreover, is ordinarily limited to the facts and argu-

---

85 Mayda, *supra* note 62, at LXV.

86 *See* Wall Street Journal, Jan. 29, 1969, at 16, col. 1. That trial judges are more "realistic" is difficult to prove; of the trial judges interviewed, however, all were in agreement that trial judges are so.

87 The same judge, however, would not entrust the trial court with more freedom inasmuch as "too many trial judges are abusive and arrogant."

88 Wyzanski, *supra* note 1, at 1298.

89 For an interesting and most unusual exception to this rule, see General Order on Judicial Standards of Procedure and Substance in Review of Student Discipline in Tax Supported Institutions of Higher Education, 45 F.R.D. 133 (W.D. Mo. 1968).

ments presented by the parties. At the appellate level, the court may have the benefit of amicus briefs, when the issues before the court are of significant interest to others, thereby at least partially overcoming one of the disadvantages of the adversary system. This is less likely to occur at the trial level. Such third parties would very probably not be aware of the trial and, even if aware, would neither desire to nor be permitted to participate in the sorting out of the many issues, both factual and legal, central to the case without directly involving the specific policy issue concerning them. Given these limitations upon perspective, trial-court experimentation is less desirable when intelligent judgment requires consideration of facts and arguments beyond the equities of the case.

EFFICIENCY

Efficiency is an objective consideration which transcends cultural and legal ideology. It is practical, concerned not with what justice is but with how justice may be achieved in the least possible time with the least possible expense. Employing efficiency criteria, the question becomes which judicial attitude is most time and money saving. There are many possible attitudes which a trial judge may adopt toward precedent. At the risk of oversimplifying, six are described below. By degree they are:

(1) The trial judge must follow a precedent until it has been expressly overruled. As one court of this opinion said, "[W]e would prefer to see the death certificate." [90]

(2) The trial judge must follow a precedent unless it at least has been impliedly overruled. Possibly to preserve the facade of unchanging law, an appellate court often will overrule sub silentio. Moreover, it is altogether possible that an appellate court failed to overrule a precedent simply because it was not brought to the court's attention.[91]

(3) The trial judge is bound by a precedent unless it has been at least substantially impaired. A judge with this attitude not only will not follow a precedent which has been impliedly overruled but also will not follow a precedent whose factual or legal foundation has been substantially undermined. Such may occur where a case is continually distinguished on unconvincing grounds; adherence to the older case would be against the logic of the more recent ones. Such a situation

---

[90] Opinion of the Justices, 328 Mass. 679, 683, 106 N.E.2d 259, 262 (1952).

[91] Kelman, *supra* note 54, at 24.

also would exist where a significant change in conditions had occurred since the time of the original decision.[92]

(4) The trial judge must do his duty to divine, as best he can, what would be the result of an appeal in the case before him. If fully followed, such an approach would consider all possible factors which might determine the outcome of the case before the reviewing court. For the trial judge the test would be: Will the appellate court overrule me? In divining what the appellate court will do, the trial court may consider that court's past decisions, its recent trends, and changes in membership.

(5) The trial judge is not bound by the authority of any court, although he ought to pay great respect to the reasoning of appellate decisions.

(6) The trial judge ought to decide only upon the equities of the case at bar, looking to other decisions only as a source of wisdom.

Other things being equal, the trial-court attitude most efficient from the parties' standpoint would appear to be the predictive (fourth) approach. Where it is clear that an appellate court will overrule a precedent, efficiency suggests that parties ought not be required to travel the expensive and time consuming appellate route. Justice should be done in the first instance. This is especially, though not uniquely, true where it appears that the party who would be benefited by an appeal is incapable of financing one.[93]

Few trial judges will accept such an approach. Like Judge Greene in the earlier mentioned *Ricks* case,[94] most will pay their respects to

---

[92] *See, e.g.,* Gardella v. Chandler, 172 F.2d 402 (2d Cir. 1949). In this case, it was successfully argued that a 27 year old decision, Federal Baseball Club v. National League, 259 U.S. 200 (1922), holding that professional baseball teams were not engaged in "interstate commerce" within the antitrust acts, was not controlling for present day baseball since not only had the precedents upon which the decision had been based been overruled, but the interstate activities of baseball had expanded so extensively as to make the original case factually dissimilar from those of the present case. *Id.* at 407-08, 413-15. Similarly, the Court of Appeals for the District of Columbia refused to follow a 1914 precedent of the Supreme Court, stating that a principle adopted "in an age still largely in thrall to the rigors of common-law pleadings . . . appears differently in a light refracted by the supervening Federal Rules of Civil Procedure." Aetna Cas. & Sur. Co. v. Circle Equip. Co., 126 U.S. App. D.C. 275, 278, 377 F.2d 160, 163 (1967).

[93] One commentator suggests as an alternative to the "dangerous" proposal of relieving lower courts of their duty to adhere to precedent the "provision of adequate legal services to all persons needing them," thus enabling all to appeal. Kelman, *supra* note 54, at 5 n.12. This would not, however, eliminate the very substantial social cost. Nor would it alone justify shackling those of some means with otherwise needless expense.

[94] *See* notes 6-8 *supra* and accompanying text.

the doctrine of stare decisis and stand uninfluenced by predictions as to the ultimate outcome of a case.[95] For many, the reasons for adherence to this doctrine remain unexamined and unchallenged. Some justify their position in terms of other of our considerations, namely, respect for law, the need for stability, and uniformity. Still others argue that trial judges are not fit to do such guesswork, having neither the time nor the experience to engage in armchair analysis of how a higher court might rule. They would question the availability of truly valid criteria with which to work. For example, changes in appellate court membership may be misleading inasmuch as the responsibilities of high judicial office have a way of changing men and their modes of thinking.[96]

---

[95] None of the judges interviewed would accept the predictive approach as a general trial-court technique. Each was presented with the following hypothetical:

> It is October 1970, you are sitting in the Criminal Division, and the accused moves to suppress a confession which the prosecutor admits was obtained without *Miranda* warnings. It appears, however, that the confession, even though obtained after hours of custodial interrogation, was voluntary and, before *Miranda*, would have been admissible. The prosecutor argues that, although the Supreme Court has not even undermined *Miranda* by implication, since June 1969, the membership of the Court has changed and that it clearly appears that *Miranda* will be overruled. *Miranda*, you remember, was a 5-4 decision, the majority composed of Warren, Brennan, Douglas, Black, and Fortas. Warren, Douglas and Fortas have retired from the High Bench. President Nixon has appointed Judge Friendly, Thomas Dewey and Strom Thurmond to replace them. (The survey was taken prior to the appointment of Mr. Chief Justice Burger and Mr. Justice Blackmun.) All have on occasion strongly denounced the Supreme Court's holding in *Miranda*. You conclude that as soon as the Court has the opportunity it will overrule *Miranda* or at least distinguish it to its grave. How do you rule?

Although none were sympathetic with the rule of *Miranda*, all except one would uphold it. The "dissenting" judge would ignore *Miranda*, but only because of the common rule peculiar to criminal law that the government cannot appeal from an adverse trial court decision. This judge saw law as an "evolving concept" requiring the challenge of accepted notions, and believed that, since the government could not challenge *Miranda* by way of appeal, the courts must provide some other route to do so. *See also* Mr. Chief Justice Burger's views in *Coleman v. Alabama*, 38 U.S.L.W. 4535, 4540-41 (U.S. June 22, 1970) (Burger, C. J., concurring in part and dissenting in part):

> I do not acquiesce in prior holdings which purportedly, but nonetheless erroneously, are based on the Constitution. That approach simply is an acknowledgment that the Court, having previously amended the Sixth Amendment, now feels bound by its action . . . .
>
> With deference, then, I am bound to reject categorically . . . [the] thesis that what the Court said lately controls over the Constitution. While our holdings are entitled to deference I will not join in employing recent cases rather than the Constitution, to bootstrap ourselves into a result . . . .

[96] "[M]ost chief executives tend to appoint justices who share their *general* political and social views. But this is certainly not a guaranty of future judicial expression.

The problem of prediction is complicated by the number of courts above a trial court judge. At the writing of this paper,[97] a judge of the Court of General Sessions in the District of Columbia is subject to review by the District of Columbia Court of Appeals, the United States Circuit Court of Appeals for the District of Columbia, and the United States Supreme Court. Which court should the trial judge predict? To attempt to anticipate all would be unmanageable, especially where it appears that the lower appellate court will overrule the trial court, only to be overruled by a higher appellate court. The rule of efficiency which requires that justice be done as soon as possible would suggest that the decision which will *finally* be upheld should be made in the first instance. Such an approach, nevertheless, would be difficult to administer.

One further aspect of efficiency deserves mentioning. So far our discussion of efficiency has been oriented primarily towards the question of what is most time and money saving for parties before a court. What is most efficient for litigants, however, need not be that which is most efficient for our courts. It is more timesaving for courts to apply mechanically the law of another court than independently to develop just law for the parties.[98] Present day problems of docket backlog might suggest the desirability of such a course. When parties argue for new law, however, such an approach may involve no less than an abdication of judicial responsibility. The criticism that trial judges are too busy to involve themselves actively in the making of new law thus becomes less a criticism of trial-court lawmaking than an indictment against our judicial system. Our third notion of justice suggests that trial judges ought to have enough time to reach a "just solution" in each case before them. How far can this notion be compromised?

President Roosevelt could never have predicted so conservative a Frankfurter; President Eisenhower must [have been] surprised at so liberal a Warren. And President Truman was actually outraged when two of his four appointees—Burton and Clark voted against the Government in the *Steel Seizure Case*." Blaustein & Field, *"Overruling" Opinions in the Supreme Court,* 57 MICH. L. REV. 151, 182 (1958).

[97] By reason of P.L. 91-358, enacted July 29, 1970, this court structure will be changed so that cases emanating in the Court of General Sessions (to be renamed the Superior Court) will no longer be subject to review both by the District of Columbia Court of Appeals and the United States Court of Appeals. With one exception, the latter route of appeal will be eliminated with ultimate review going from the District of Columbia Court of Appeals to the United States Supreme Court, on the same basis as review of a decision of a state supreme court. District of Columbia Court Reform and Criminal Procedure Act of 1970, tit. I, § 111, 84 Stat. 476, *to be codified as* D.C. CODE ANN. §§ 11-301, -901.

[98] Mishkin and Morris refer to this approach as taking advantage of the "inherited wisdom" of the past. P. MISHKIN & C. MORRIS, *supra* note 50, at 79.

The Need For Uniformity

More than any other reason, the limitations imposed on the trial judge are justified in terms of a need for uniformity.[99] Uniformity occurs where different courts faced by similar problems arrive at similar conclusions. Traditionally, uniformity at the trial level has been achieved by the application of the doctrine of stare decisis. Thus, the case for uniformity clearly may be at odds with any significant expansion of trial court freedom.

To a large extent the need for uniformity is a corollary of several more basic notions, some of which have already been discussed at length. Uniform application of law comports with our notion of equality. A uniform rule is easier to ascertain and is therefore more productive of law by which people may guide their activities; thus, it comports with our second notion of justice. Respect for law is enhanced by uniform law inasmuch as the general recognition of a rule lends force to the authority of a decision which embodies it. For example, no one would question the contractual doctrine of consideration before a court of law, though they might question the authority of a decision which declared that doctrine to be a bit of historical nonsense. Uniformity, moreover, breeds efficiency inasmuch as it is more predictable and encourages settlements without trial.[100] Furthermore, as one commentator argues, "the habit of lower court adherence to precedent . . . gives us hope that a change, once announced, will be accepted by all judges." [101]

The most convincing justification for uniformity of application, however, is that it most closely corresponds to the needs of a growing yet stable economy. Pound observes that:

> [O]ur economically organized society postulates certainty and predictability as to the incidents and consequences of industrial undertaking and commercial transactions extending over long periods. *Individualization* . . . [is] *out of place here*. . . . One fee simple is like another. Every promissory note is like every other. *Mechanical application of rules as a mere repetition precludes the*

---

[99] *See* Comment, *Stare Decisis and the Lower Courts: Two Recent Decisions*, 59 Colum. L. Rev. 504, 508 (1962).

[100] The role of settlements in our judicial system cannot be underestimated. Most cases are settled before they go to trial. It is estimated, for example, that only two to three percent of all personal injury cases are actually tried. Keeton, *Creative Continuity in the Law of Torts*, 75 Harv. L. Rev. 463, 469 (1962).

In many courts, according to another estimate, "if all cases were tried to a conclusion, they could not be reached for trial in less than fifteen years." B. Botein, supra note 7, at 251. Such a result would defeat justice. *See generally*, *id.* at 226-52.

[101] Kelman, *supra* note 54, at 5-6.

tendency to individualization which would threaten the security of acquisitions and the security of transactions.[102]

Uniformity increases certainty and predictability, thus encouraging economic stability. Similarly, uniform law is productive of vigorous business exchange which over and above security requires that business practices in one community be on the same legal footing as those in other communities; business can then operate more efficiently, less burdened by the confusion of the legal jungle. Within the boundaries of the given jurisdiction and with respect to that issue litigated, a company need not tailor its activity to meet the vagaries of each jurisdictional subdivision. The binding effect of appellate precedent thus is beneficial to our economy insofar as it creates uniform law.[103]

The case for uniformity is exaggerated, however, and its application is extended beyond the logic of its rationale. The argument that general recognition of a rule lends force to a decision embodying it assumes that the person who is affected by a decision has knowledge of whether or not the rule is generally recognized. The average person has but a nebulous notion of the law and acts largely in ignorance of it.[104] At the very most, the general recognition of a rule affects only the lawyer representing a party and is only one factor influencing the attorney's choice of advice.

The logic of uniformity does not by itself require uniformity in all areas of the law and with respect to remedies as well as rights. By their very nature, remedies should be personal and unique to the situation of the parties. Like court procedures, they must be flexible to be effective. While rights may be established by general norms, the remedy most effective to preserve a given right requires an intimate knowledge of the facts of the case; to this extent, effective remedies may not be uniform. Moreover, to the extent that rights hold more emotional significance for the average person than remedies, the use

---

102 R. Pound, Interpretations of Legal History 154 (1923) (emphasis added). Judge Wyzanski expresses a somewhat similar view, suggesting that courts should distinguish between tort cases and commercial litigation. "[S]trong mercantile interests favoring certainty . . . sometimes warrant giving juries written instructions or summaries and often warrant the use of special verdicts" in commercial cases, while such techniques are inappropriate in other areas of the law. Wyzanski, *supra* note 1, at 1289.

103 But see Dean Pound's caveat that one of the most important and most constant causes of dissatisfaction with all law at all times is to be found in the necessary mechanical operation of legal rules. This, he feels, is one of the penalties of uniformity. Address by Dean Roscoe Pound before the American Bar Association, *The Causes of Popular Dissatisfaction with the Administration of Justice*, 1906, *reprinted in* 46 J. Am. Jud. Soc'y 55, 56 (1962).

104 *See* note 23 *supra* and accompanying text.

of a novel remedy to preserve a generally recognized right does not undermine the authority of the decision.

The ideal of uniformity is hardly an absolute one. One would not want a bad rule of law to be applied uniformly. A certain healthy suspicion of precedent should attend trial court deliberations; for example, a court should hesitate to accept without question a 30 year old appellate precedent which has not since been reviewed by the higher level appellate courts. Experimentation and variety in the law is valuable. Its value to an extent accounts for our political structure which allows for much nonuniformity across 50 diverse states within whose boundaries further variety in the law occurs from county to county, municipality to municipality. Mr. Justice Brandeis once observed that "[i]t is one of the happy incidents of the federal system that a single courageous State may, if its citizens choose, serve as a laboratory; and try novel social and economic experiments without risk to the rest of the country." [105] As a result of this nonuniformity, one jurisdiction may look to others for lessons in what the law ought to be.[106]

By similar logic, some experimentation is desirable at the trial level. Experimentation at this level is not accompanied by the large scale displacements which may result from changes in the law on the appellate level.[107] Inasmuch as they create general law, precedent shattering appellate courts may force a whole jurisdiction to live with untried or experimental theories; in contrast, activist trial courts create law which is binding only on the parties. Where a precedent is old and under attack, trial courts can serve a valuable function in creating new law, for they may supply the appellate courts not only with new ideas but also with the conclusions of experienced men who have been working with the older law on a day to day basis and have found it unworkable or unjust.

In determining the need for uniformity in any area of the law, complex policy decisions requiring fact-finding machinery available only to the legislature are necessitated. Since all courts are generally less competent in making complex determinations of public policy, the ideal governmental system would have all such decisions made by the

---

[105] New State Ice Co. v. Liebmann, 285 U.S. 262, 311 (1931) (Brandeis, J., dissenting).

[106] Recent developments in the field of conflict of laws exemplify this process. The hoary, almost universally recognized doctrine of *les loci delicti* was first discarded by New York in Kilberg v. Northeast Airlines, 9 N.Y.2d 34, 172 N.E.2d 526 (1961), and many other states soon followed this experiment. *See* RESTATEMENT (SECOND) OF CONFLICT OF LAWS §§ 379, 379a.

[107] It might be argued that large scale displacement is advantageous in that it may stir the legislature to action. Unless a bad rule is universally applied it is difficult to get legislative action since few people would be affected.

legislature. Drawing an example from the area of commercial law, in enacting the *Uniform Commercial Code* state legislatures have determined the need for such uniform commercial law by the business community. But uniformity, as we have seen, is not always justified, and the need for uniformity being a legislative determination, courts should not quickly assume that uniformity is required. In the absence of constitutional or legislative norms, appellate courts, therefore, ought to avoid creating inflexible rules binding on the trial court where the need for them is not convincing and clear. Similarly, absent constitutional or legislative guidance, appellate courts ought to avoid binding lower courts by their decisions where complex policy itself is unclear. In such cases, trial courts should be left to decide according to the equities, subject to correction only for partiality or flagrant error.[108]

The Boundaries of Trial-Court Freedom as a Function of Legislative Activity

In the earlier discussion of the distribution of functions in government, the legislative function was conceived as that of formulating and promulgating general norms, while the judicial function was described as that of correctly deciding the cases before it. In addition to exemplifying the doctrine of the separation of powers, these distinct functions delimit the area of maximum competence of each of the branches. The legislature is most competent in creating law which applies generally. With its superior fact-finding machinery, it is most able to determine questions of policy and the possible broad effects of a change in the law. The judiciary is at its best when it limits its scope to the problems of the parties before it; the trial judge is best able to know the facts of the particular case, the equities between the parties, and the remedy which would best settle the dispute. Our notions of efficiency suggest that each branch generally ought to defer to the other's expertise and avoid overstepping the line demarcating their respective functions. We have noted already that such considerations suggest greater trial-court

108 Such a governmental system might be criticized as unrealistic since the legislatures cannot be relied upon to make all complex policy decisions. We are often spoiled by the example of the United States Congress, and tend to overlook that many state legislatures meet only for a month or two a year. *See* Tate, *The Law-Making Function of the Judge*, 28 La. L. Rev. 211, 232 (1968). Furthermore, these bodies are ill-equipped to make all such policy determinations in such a short time, and have little fact-finding capabilities. However, even the collected private experiences of many legislators is a rudimentary fact-finding device superior to that often available to an appellate court. *But see* R. Pound, Justice According to Law 87-88 (1951) (private law receives little legislative attention inasmuch as it is neither politically valuable nor ordinarily the subject of much lobbying).

freedom in the absence of legislation. In those areas of the law in which a constitutional or legislative norm has been erected, the appropriateness of trial-court lawmaking is necessarily a function of the scope of the norm, the completeness of its detail, and the type of issues before the court.

Where the legislature has explicitly provided a norm determination of the outcome of a case, considerations of competence suggest that trial-court freedom be more restricted. Thus, activism is ordinarily less appropriate when legislation has completely preempted an area of law. The *Uniform Commercial Code* and the Patent Act of 1952[109] are examples of such preemption. Similar principles would apply in areas of the law wherein the legislature, although not completely preempting common law, has created certain minimum rights which all courts ought to respect. For example, it may not be necessary for the legislating body to detail elaborate rules of negligence, yet it may wish to declare that negligence is an actionable tort. Similarly, all courts should be strictly bound to respect individual rights and liberties, whether defined constitutionally or legislatively.[110] In such a way a representative body guarantees rights which are considered too precious to be subject to judicial experimentation.

Even in the aforementioned areas of law, judicial freedom is not completely foreign. Statutes require interpretation and application to concrete factual situations. One might argue, for example, that the legislature speaks generally and may not envision all the particular results of the application of its norms. If this argument is plausible, one should assume that the legislature can only be highly motivated and did not intend a statute to result in any inequity or inequality.[111] Where a statute clearly is inequitable as applied in a particular instance, the trial judge should ignore it.[112] The freedom of the trial judge, moreover,

---

[109] 35 U.S.C. §§ 1-293 (1964), *as amended*, (Supp. V, 1970).

[110] This conclusion may override the earlier mentioned notion that the best laws are those which most comport with the standards of a community. *See* notes 29-36 *supra* and accompanying text. Concepts such as free speech and equal protection, for example, may often serve to protect those who offend or outrage the established community standards. In Mr. Justice Jackson's phrase: "One's right to life, liberty and property, to free speech, a free press, freedom of worship and assembly, and other fundamental rights may not be submitted to vote; they depend on the outcome of no elections." West Virginia State Bd. of Educ. v. Barnette, 319 U.S. 624, 638 (1943).

[111] This, it will be remembered, is a notion expressed by the notorious Judge Magnaud. F. GÉNY, *supra* note 62, at 501.

[112] The classic example offered by Puffendorf, and repeated by Blackstone, was the statute of Bologna which stated anyone who drew blood in the streets would be punished with the utmost severity. This statute was held not to apply to a surgeon who opened the vein of a person who fell down in the street with a fit. 1 W. BLACKSTONE, COMMENTARIES *60. *See also* Sackett v. Andross, 5 N.Y. 326, 364 (1843).

should also depend on whether he is dealing with rights or remedies. Where the legislature has created a right, courts ought to create whatever remedy is necessary to preserve and protect the right.[113]

It is arguable, however, that the remedy is itself the right, that in creating new remedies a court creates new rights which the legislature did not see fit to create. Whether or not semantically appealing, this argument ignores the functional differences between the verbal statement of a right and its actual enforcement, between the concept of rights and the concept of remedies. As is so often noted, the function and competence of the legislature lies in the creation of norms; the legislature most clearly perceives the universal aspects of a problem, while being less capable of envisioning its individual application. Rights lend themselves to such general definition and declaration, while remedies only take shape in the context of particular problems. Above all others, the trial judge senses the individual aspects of a case and therefore ought to be granted more freedom in fixing remedies for the infringement of legislatively declared rights.

Where the legislature has explicitly provided a norm determinative of the outcome of a case, the trial judge at times may find himself torn between conflicting loyalties, between his judicial obligation to apply faithfully the legislative norm and his obligation to follow the precedents of the court above him. When it clearly appears that the appellate court has deviated from the norm established by the legislature, the trial judge, arguably, should consider himself free from the higher-court decision.[114] Such a course, in addition to paying respect to the legislature's greater policy-making ability, would seem to follow from

---

113 Moragne v. States Marine Lines, 398 U.S. 375, 402-09 (1970); Allen v. State Bd. of Elections, 393 U.S. 544, 557 (1969); Wyandotte Transp. v. United States, 389 U.S. 191, 202 (1967); J. I. Case Co. v. Borak, 377 U.S. 426, 433-35 (1965); Bell v. Hood, 327 U.S. 678, 684 (1946).

114 This hypothetical was posed for the judges interviewed:

> Congress has passed a statute to create new remedies for the tenant whose landlord has allowed the premises to lapse into disrepair. The appellate court above you has decided that the statute does not relieve tenants whose apartment houses fail to meet the Housing Code from the duty to pay their rent in full and on time. In a later case before you the point is argued that the statute did relieve the tenant of just such a duty. Your study of the matter clearly shows this to be true. It appears that the issue was poorly argued by counsel at the appellate court and that certain committee hearings and draftsman's notes which clearly indicate Congress' intent were not brought to the appellate court's attention. You are convinced, moreover, that with this material before it the court above you will change its mind. How do you decide?

All the judges said they would follow the appellate precedent. One indicated he might rule otherwise if it appeared the tenant could not finance an appeal.

the doctrine of the separation of powers. That doctrine, if rigidly followed, suggests that the judicial function should at no time infringe upon the legislative function of creating general norms. Where the legislature has not acted, arguably it has abdicated its authority to create norms in favor of the judiciary. Such is not the case where the legislature has acted. By enabling appellate courts to bind in such cases, one thereby empowers them to create deviant norms which infringe upon the legislative function.

Trial judge freedom from even deviant precedent, however, may be inconsistent with the rule of efficiency that trial-court decisions should be the same as the ultimate decisions rendered. Therefore, a trial judge should not ignore precedent when by doing so he will be ultimately overruled. To ignore precedent in such a case only delays the ultimate decision and renders it more costly. These considerations do not obtain where the parties will not appeal or where it appears that the upper court may be convinced of its mistake. In such a situation, a strong case is made for the trial judge to ignore the precedent.[115]

Where the legislature, although not explicitly providing a norm determinative of a case, has made policy statements applicable to it, trial-court freedom is highly appropriate. In such instances, the courts may use these legislative declarations as a basis for making new law, thereby compensating for their inadequate fact-finding and policy-determining machinery. The Housing Regulations for the District of Columbia thus may be seen as a declaration by the D.C. Commissioners of public policy on slum housing. In their preamble to the Housing Regulations, the Commissioners stated that slums and otherwise blighted areas "are due to . . . delapidation, inadequate maintenance . . . toilet facilities . . . heating, insufficient protection against fire hazards, inadequate lighting and ventilation, and other unsanitary or unsafe conditions." [116] The Commissioners went on to require that "no owner, licensee, or tenant shall occupy or permit the occupancy of any habitation in violation of these regulations." [117] Congress has made an equally forceful declaration of housing for the District of Columbia.[118] In view of these policy statements, Judge Edgerton of the Court of General Sessions held in *Adams v. Lancaster*[119] that a contract to rent premises

---

[115] *See, e.g.*, Aetna Cas. & Sur. Co. v. Circle Equip. Co., 126 U.S. App. D.C. 275, 278, 377 F.2d 160, 163 (1967).

[116] Washington, D.C., Housing Regulations § 2101 (1967).

[117] *Id.* § 2301.

[118] *See* D.C. Code Ann. § 5-701 (1966).

[119] Small Claims No. C 12912-67 (D.C. Ct. Gen. Sess., Oct. 25, 1967), *reported in* Note, *Cases Decided in the District of Columbia Court of General Sessions*, 17 Cath. U.L. Rev. 510, 537 (1968).

in violation of the Housing Regulations was void as against public policy. Against the backdrop of legislative declarations, the holding seems perfectly reasonable.

Is it the trial or appellate court which is best able to analyze the evidence of legislative policy and recognize new private rights or remedies which implement that policy? Where as in *Adams* the policy is clear, there is no reason why the trial court should restrain itself. Where the policy is less clear or where conflicting legislative policy statements have been issued, appellate courts may be better equipped to handle the task. Among other considerations, trial courts have less experience in operating on this level; appellate courts not only are more experienced in interpreting legislative evidence and are less rushed, but they also benefit from the better prepared argumentation and briefing of the counsel before them.

Where the trial judge is presented with a claim that a statute is unconstitutional, further considerations may obtain. In such a case, Judge Wyzanski suggests that the trial court ought to occupy a minor role.

> [The trial judge] ought to remind himself not only of the universal maxim that every possible presumption is in favor of the validity of the legislation but also of the policy represented by those statutes providing that in certain constitutional controversies a district judge has no jurisdiction to act unless he is sitting with two other trial judges. Though in a constitutional case or any other case he must not surrender deliberate judgment and automatically accept the views of others, he can ordinarily best fulfill his duty in a constitutional case by explicitly stating for the benefit of the appellate court any doubts he has, without going so far as to enter a decree against a statute which has commanded the assent of the majority of the legislature and generally, of the executive.[120]

The theoretical underpinnings of this position are the deference which the trial judge ought to pay to the legislature in the areas of their competence and the fact that, in the constitutional area, the trial judge acts without many of the advantages he otherwise may possess over the appellate court. In nonconstitutional litigation, the trial judge operates with a wealth of firsthand experience in other similar cases. His decisions in such cases therefore may be well reasoned. In the constitutional area, however, the trial judge brings little experience to his task. Considerations of competence therefore suggest that a higher level appellate court with greater acumen in constitutional law is the preferable forum for such determinations and that appellate decisions in this

---

120 Wyzanski, *supra* note 1, at 1298.

area be given a higher degree of respect. Furthermore, the trial judge ordinarily acts without the fear that his decisions will have a widespread impact. The effect of his decisions usually reaches no further than the parties themselves. This offers the trial judge room for experimentation. When a trial judge is asked to declare a statute unconstitutional, however, the potential impact is far-reaching. Although no other court may be bound by the trial judge's decision, a declaration that a statute is unconstitutional cannot help but have an unsettling effect upon the statute and impede its effective enforcement.[121]

Conclusion

The trial judge has traditionally occupied a minor place in the hierarchy of judicial lawmaking. The accepted role of the trial judge in the process of developing new law rarely exceeds that of an intermediary who transmits and applies the message of his appellate brethren. The appropriateness of this secondary role and the development of an analytical structure with which to evaluate it have been the subjects of this paper.

The analytical structure developed comprises a set of five, often competing, considerations with which the comparative advantages of lawmaking at any judicial level may be evaluated. The schema includes notions of justice, efficiency and competency, the problem of respect for law, the commercial need for uniformity, and the interrelation of the judicial and legislative functions.

Evaluated with the help of this schema, the appropriateness of active lawmaking at the trial level is seen to be a function of many variables, some of which are appellate history, the scope of legislative activity, the availability of an objective standard regarding a contested rule, the area of legal activity, the degree of reliance, and whether rights or remedies are at issue. Thus, where there is little recent appellate history or where there is a consensus within the legal community that a rule deserves to be overturned or the creation of remedies rather than rights are involved, greater trial judge freedom seems appropriate. Similarly, lawmaking is more appropriate at the trial level in cases involving primarily

---

[121] The position of the Supreme Court in interpreting the Constitution is somewhat unique. Stare decisis is less appropriate here, according to Mr. Justice Brandeis, since "correction through legislative action is practically impossible." Burnet v. Colorado Oil & Gas Co., 285 U.S. 393, 406-10 (1932) (Brandeis, J., dissenting). In Mr. Justice Douglas' words, a judge should remember "that it is the Constitution which he swore to support and defend, not the gloss which his predecessors may have put on it." Douglas, *Stare Decisis*, 49 Colum. L. Rev. 735, 736 (1949). It is of note that Mr. Chief Justice Burger has expressed himself to the same effect. *See* note 92 *supra.*

human activity than in cases involving primarily commercial activity, to the extent that these terms are capable of adequate definition. Notions of efficiency suggest, however, that a trial judge should not exercise such freedom when his ruling would ultimately be reversed. Within such boundaries the trial court can be a suitable forum for change.

Greater judicial freedom at the trial level need not impair the symbolic strength of our notion of "government of laws and not of men" any more than lawmaking at other judicial levels. Some, moreover, consider such a notion to be inappropriate to the mood and needs of our age and believe that, in a free society, the habit of obedience should issue not from such symbolism but from the fairness of that community's laws. They perceive an increasing impatience with laws that have outlived their usefulness and with judicial rulings upholding such laws because of the court's claimed lack of power or because of the need for legal stability. If their assessment of our age is correct, we can hardly afford to ignore the vast resource of practical experience which our trial judges can contribute to the cause of relating law to justice.

WAYNE R. LAFAVE

The Prosecutor's Discretion in The United States

I. INTRODUCTION

One of the most striking features of the American system of criminal justice is the broad range of largely uncontrolled discretion [1] exercised by the prosecutor.[2] Particularly noteworthy are these kinds of discretionary decisions: (1) the decision not to prosecute an individual notwithstanding sufficient evidence to meet the legal requirements for commencing a prosecution; and (2) the decision to tender concessions to a charged individual on the condition that he plead guilty rather than stand trial.[3]

Much has been written, particularly in recent years, about the exercise of such discretion by prosecutors in this country.[4] The subject obviously cannot be exhaustively treated in a single article. This paper is directed toward a more modest goal—that of bringing out the main

---

[1] The word "discretion" may be defined in several ways. Narrowly conceived, discretion is said to be "an authority conferred by law to act" one way or another according to one's "own considered judgment and conscience." Pound, "Discretion, Dispensation and Mitigation: The Problem of the Individual Special Case," 35 *N.Y.U.L. Rev.* 925, 926 (1960). But in discussing the prosecutor's discretion, I find more helpful the notion that "a public officer has discretion whenever the *effective limits* on his power leave him free to make a choice among possible courses of action *or inaction.*" (Emphasis added). K. Davis, *Discretionary Justice* p. 4 (1969). Under this definition, discretion may be exercised by doing nothing and may exist without express recognition in law.

[2] Discretion in criminal law enforcement is usually thought of as being vested solely in the prosecutor, perhaps because this official is recognized by law as possessing considerable discretion. But, as recent empirical studies have emphasized, discretion is also frequently exercised elsewhere in the criminal process, as with the police decision not to arrest certain individuals who could be lawfully arrested (see W. LaFave, *Arrest: The Decision to Take a Suspect Into Custody,* chs. 3-8 (1965); the decision of trial judges not to convict certain persons who have been proven guilty (see D. Newman, *Conviction: The Determination of Guilt or Innocence Without Trial* chs. 9-12, 14, 1966); and the decision of juries to find not guilty certain individuals who have been proven guilty (see H. Kalven & H. Zeisel, *The American Jury* chs. 15-27, 1966). In some respects, the discretion exercised by the police may be most important, for the prosecutor seldom has occasion to consider a case unless it is first brought to his attention by the police.

[3] There are, of course, other important facets of the American prosecutor's discretion, such as the decision to prosecute, but not to the extent possible, by charging a lesser offense than could lawfuly be charged or by charging fewer than the total number of offenses which could lawfully be charged. See notes 45 and 46 infra. Such uncontrolled discretion to undercharge raises significant issues not unlike those discussed in this paper.

[4] See, in particular, the sources cited in notes 5 and 42 infra.

AMERICAN JOURNAL OF COMPARATIVE LAW, 1970, Vol. 18, pp. 532-548.

lines of American law and practice relevant to a comparison with the foreign procedures described in the other articles in this symposium.

II. The Decision Not to Prosecute

A. The Current Practice [5]

The American prosecutor has traditionally exercised considerable discretion in deciding whether or not to prosecute, that is, in determining whether prosecution is called for in a given case as a matter of enforcement policy. Insufficient attention has been given to the question of precisely why this is so, but the most common explanations are these:

(1) Because of legislative "overcriminalization." As one commentator has said, "The criminal code of any jurisdiction tends to make a crime of everything that people are against, without regard to enforceability, changing social concepts, etc. The result is that the criminal code becomes society's trash bin." [6] Examination of the typical state code of criminal law supports this judgment. Included therein are likely to be crimes which are over-defined for administrative convenience (e.g., the gambling statute which bars *all* forms of gambling so as "to confront the professional gambler with a statutory facade that is wholly devoid of loopholes" [7]); crimes which merely constitute "state-declared ideals" [8] (e.g., the crime of adultery, which is "unenforced because we want to continue our conduct, and unrepealed because we want to preserve our morals" [9]); and now outdated crimes which found their way into the law because of "the mood that dominated a tribunal or legislature at strategic moments in the past, a flurry of public excitement on some single matter." [10]

(2) Because of limitations in available enforcement resources. No prosecutor has available sufficient resources to prosecute all of the

[5] Among the most useful descriptions of current practices concerning the decision not to charge are those found in F. Miller, *Prosecution: The Decision to Charge a Suspect With a Crime* (1970); Brezner, "How the Prosecuting Attorney's Office Processes Complaints," 27 *Det. Law.* 3 (1959); Kaplan, "The Prosecutorial Discretion —A Comment," 60 *Nw. U.L. Rev.* 174 (1965); Klein, "District Attorney's Discretion Not to Prosecute," 32 *L.A.B. Bull.* 323 (1957); Schwartz, "Federal Criminal Jurisdiction and Prosecutor's Discretion," 13 *Law & Contemp. Prob.* 64 (1948); Seymour, "Why Prosecutors Act Like Prosecutors," 11 *Record of N.Y.C.B.A.* 302 (1956); Worgan and Paulsen, "The Position of a Prosecutor in a Criminal Case—A Conversation with a Prosecuting Attorney," 7 *Prac. Law.* 44 (Nov. 1961); Comment, 42 *S. Cal. L. Rev.* 519 (1969).

[6] Statement by a representative of the Federal Bureau of Investigation, quoted in The President's Commission on Law Enforcement and Administration of Justice, *Task Force Report: The Courts* 107 (1967).

[7] 2 A.B.A. Commission on Organized Crime, *Organized Crime and Law Enforcement* 75 (1952).

[8] R. Pound, *Criminal Justice in America* 67 (1930).

[9] T. Arnold, *The Symbols of Government* 160 (1935).

[10] Wechsler, "The Challenge of a Model Penal Code," 65 *Harv. L. Rev.* 1097, 1101 (1952).

offenses which come to his attention. To deny the authority to exercise discretion under these circumstances, it is said, is "like directing a general to attack the enemy on all fronts at once." [11] Thus, so the argument goes, the prosecutor must remain free to exercise his judgment in determining what prosecutions will best serve the public interest.

(3) Because of a need to individualize justice. A criminal code can only deal in general categories of conduct. As Roscoe Pound observed:

> "No lawmaker has been able to foresee more than the broad outlines of the clash of interests or more than the main lines of the courses of conduct to which the law even of his own time must be applied. Moreover, a legal system which seeks to cover everything by a special provision becomes cumbrous and unworkable." [12]

Individualized treatment of offenders, based upon the circumstances of the particular case, has long been recognized in sentencing, and it is argued that such individualized treatment is equally appropriate at the charging stage so as to relieve deserving defendants of even the stigma of prosecution. Were it otherwise, so that the prosecutor acted "in strict accordance with rules of law, precisely and narrowly laid down, the criminal law would be ordered but intolerable." [13]

The current practice, as set forth in a recently-published empirical study of the charging decision,[14] clearly reflects these three considerations. But of the most common situations in which prosecutors typically decline to prosecute, the following are deserving of particular mention:

(a) When the victim has expressed a desire that the offender not be prosecuted.[15] Particularly in assault cases involving a dispute between spouses or prior acquaintances, the victim's disinterest in prosecution usually is determinative. The assumption apparently is that uncoerced forgiveness reflects a lack of importance attached to the incident by the victim (and, perhaps, by the aggressor), so that nonprosecution is not contrary to the statutory policy of discouraging the settlement of disputes by force.

(b) When the costs of prosecution would be excessive, considering the nature of the violation.[16] Most significant here are those cases which would involve unusual costs, as where the offender is now known to be in a distant state and could be extradited and returned only at considerable expense. Prosecution of certain offenders who would be prosecuted if they were in custody within the jurisdiction (e.g., professional bad check passers), is abandoned under these circumstances.

---

[11] T. Arnold, supra note 9, at 153.
[12] R. Pound, supra note 8, at 40-41.
[13] Breitel, "Controls in Criminal Law Enforcement," 27 *U. Chi. L. Rev.* 427 (1960).
[14] F. Miller, supra note 5, at chs. 8-20.
[15] Id. at ch. 9.
[16] Id. at ch. 10.

(c) When the mere fact of prosecution would, in the prosecutor's judgment, cause undue harm to the offender.[17] For example, when it was learned that a married woman had filed a false report of rape with the police and that she had done so to conceal her indiscretions from her husband, it was decided that prosecution for filing a false crime report would be unwise because it would jeopardize her marriage.

(d) When the offender, if not prosecuted, will likely aid in achieving other enforcement goals.[18] Nonprosecution is used as an inducement to make informants out of offenders, and also as an inducement for present informers to take on additional duties. This occurs most frequently when the individual is in a position to aid in vice enforcement, particularly against the sale of narcotics.

(e) When the "harm" done by the offender can be corrected without prosecution.[19] The best example is the frequent decision not to prosecute persons who have committed minor property crimes, such as writing bad checks, if full restitution to the victim is made.

A full appreciation of the extent of the prosecutor's power, however, requires consideration of the fact that his discretion may be exercised in the other direction; a particular individual may be selected out for prosecution notwithstanding the fact that the case is one which ordinarily would not result in an affirmative charging decision. Sometimes the purpose is to benefit the offender in some way,[20] but usually it is not. Such selection may occur in response to press and public pressure for "law and order," to rid society of certain "bad actors" who are thought to have committed more serious crimes, and for similar reasons.[21]

B. Some Major Problems

Should this aspect of the prosecutor's discretion be a matter of concern? Some would undoubtedly say no, on the ground that only acts of leniency are involved, but there are two answers to this. For one thing, not all leniency is consistent with the public interest in effective law enforcement.[22] Moreover, as Professor Kenneth Davis has aptly pointed out:

"A fundamental fact about the discretionary power to be lenient is extremely simple and entirely clear and yet is usually overlooked: *The*

[17] Id. at ch. 11.

[18] Id. at ch. 17.

[19] Id. at ch. 18.

[20] See, e.g., F. Allen, *The Borderland of Criminal Justice* 5-6 (1964), describing the practice of prosecution and conviction of prospective mothers for some offense relating to extramarital sexual relations when they are without the financial resources to pay for the medical expenses of childbirth or the subsequent care of their offspring.

[21] F. Miller, supra note 5, at ch. 19.

[22] On underenforcement in the ghetto, see The National Advisory Commission on Civil Disorders, *Report* 161-62 (1968).

discretionary power to be lenient is an impossibility without a concomitant discretionary power not to be lenient, and injustice from the discretionary power not to be lenient is especially frequent; the power to be lenient is the power to discriminate." [23]

The discretion of the American prosecutor to decide, as a matter of policy, when to prosecute and when not to prosecute is clearly recognized in the case law.[24] It is said, for example, that the prosecutor must be allowed to consider whether "a prosecution will promote the ends of justice, instill a respect for law, and advance the cause of ordered liberty," and to take into account "the degree of criminality, the weight of the evidence, the credibility of witnesses, precedent, policy, the climate of public opinion, timing, and the relative gravity of the offense." [25] Indeed, it would hardly make sense to contend that the prosecutor should have *no* discretion; full enforcement would be neither possible nor tolerable. The issue is not discretion versus no discretion, but rather how discretion should be confined, structured, and checked. As Davis notes: "Half the problem is to cut back *unnecessary* discretionary power. The other half is to find effective ways to control *necessary* discretionary power." [26]

1. Confining the prosecutor's discretion to decide when to prosecute

A significant part of the discretion currently exercised by American prosecutors is "unnecessary," in the sense that adequate reform of the substantive criminal law would eliminate, as a matter of law, many cases now screened out only at the option of the prosecutor. Clearly, "one of the major consequences of the state of penal law today is that administration has so largely come to dominate the field without effective guidance from the law." [27]

No one would seriously contend that the prosecutor's discretion could be eliminated by penal law reform. It is clear, however, from even the most casual inspection of the typical state criminal code, that some significant portion of that discretion would be unnecessary if many obsolete or largely unenforceable statutes were repealed [28] and if other statutes were more narrowly drawn.[29] The principal benefit

[23] K. Davis, supra note 1, at 170.

[24] E.g., United States v. Cox, 342 *F.2d* 167 (5th Cir. 1965); Moses v. Kennedy, 219 *F. Supp.* 762 (D.D.C. 1963); Howell v. Brown, 85 *F. Supp.* 537 (D. Neb. 1949); Taliaferro v. Locke, 182 *Cal. App.* 2d 752, 6 *Cal. Rptr.* 813 (1966); Hassan v. Magistrates' Court, 20 *Misc. 2d* 509, 191 *N.Y.S.2d* 238 (Sup. Ct. 1959).

[25] Pugach v. Klein, 193 *F. Supp.* 630, 634-35 (D.D.C. 1961).

[26] K. Davis, supra note 1, at 51. The Davis book presents a most helpful analysis of the ways in which these objectives might be met.

[27] Wechsler, supra note 10, at 1102.

[28] See *Task Force Report,* supra note 6, at ch. 8.

[29] For example, if the attitude of the victim is in fact an appropriate consideration as to ceretain crimes, this could be reflected in the substantive law. See Model Penal Code §§ 206.13(4), 207.1 (Tent. Draft No. 4, 1955).

of such reform would be that it would eliminate that part of the prosecutor's discretion which carries with it the greatest potential for misuse:

> "The worst abuses of discretion in enforcement occur in connection with those offenses that are just barely taken seriously, like most consensual sex offenses. Here, especially in the case of fornication and adultery, enforcement is so sporadic as to be just one step short of complete cessation. And it is here that the greatest danger exists of using enforcement discretion in an abusive way: to pay off a score, to provide a basis for extortion, to stigmatize an otherwise deviant or unpopular figure." [30]

2. Structuring the prosecutor's discretion to decide when to prosecute

Nearly forty years ago, Thurman Arnold noted that "the idea that a prosecuting attorney should be permitted to use his discretion concerning the laws which he will enforce and those which he will disregard appears to the ordinary citizen to border on anarchy." [31] This may be the reason why this particular aspect of the prosecutor's discretion has traditionally been exercised sub rosa and on an ad hoc basis, and has thus remained largely unstructured.

The President's Commission on Law Enforcement and Administration of Justice identified three basic needs which must be met before the prosecutor's charging discretion may become more structured and thus more rational.[32] They are:

(a) The need for more information. More detailed background information about the offender is needed so that it may be determined whether he is a dangerous or only marginal offender. (In the absence of any information, or only the limited information provided by a brief police report, the temptation is great to resort to rule-of-thumb policies based only upon the nature of the crime.) In addition, most prosecutors lack sufficient information about alternative treatment facilities and programs in the community to be able to make a rational determination of whether there exists some better course than prosecution.

(b) The need for established standards. "Standards should pertain to such matters as the circumstances that properly can be considered mitigating or aggravating, or the kinds of offenses that should be most vigorously prosecuted in view of the community's law enforcement needs." [33] In large offices, the absence of such standards often results in a lack of uniformity in decision-making by the several assistant prose-

[30] H. Packer, *The Limits of the Criminal Sanction* 291 (1968).

[31] Arnold, "Law Enforcement—An Attempt at Social Dissection," 42 *Yale L.J.* 1, 7 (1932).

[32] The President's Commission on Law Enforcement and Administration of Justice, *The Challenge of Crime in a Free Society* 133-34 (1967).

[33] Id. at 133.

cutors. But even in a one-man office, consistency would seem more likely if the prosecutor had beforehand attempted to articulate general enforcement standards.

(c) The need for established procedures. These procedures might include a "precharge conference" at which the prosecutor and defense counsel could discuss the appropriateness of a noncriminal disposition. At least in serious cases, a decision not to prosecute should be supported by a written statement of the underlying reasons, and this statement should become a public record.

3. Checking the prosecutor's discretion to decide when to prosecute

Although the American criminal justice system has reasonably effective controls to ensure that the prosecutor does not abuse his power by prosecuting upon less than sufficient evidence, there are—as a practical matter—no comparable checks upon his discretionary judgment of whether or not to prosecute one against whom sufficient evidence exists. The prosecution function has traditionally been decentralized, so that state attorneys-general exercise no effective control over local prosecutors.[34] Actions such as impeachment and quo warranto have only served to reach extreme cases of continued and flagrant abuse.[35] If a specific instance of nonenforcement is challenged in the courts by way of a mandamus action, the usual response is that the matter rests with the executive rather than the judicial branch of government.[36] Or, if a specific instance of enforcement is called into question as an arbitrary deviation from a general pattern of nonenforcement, the complaining prospective defendant can seldom overcome the several hurdles to establishing his denial-of-equal-protection claim.[37] And while the local prosecutor is in theory responsible to the electorate, the public can hardly assess prosecution policies which are kept secret. "The plain fact is that more than nine-tenths of local prosecutors' decisions are supervised or reviewed by no one."[38]

While it may be apparent that this is an unfortunate state of affairs, it is not so apparent how the situation might be best remedied. A system

[34] Note, 103 *U. Pa. L. Rev.* 1057, 1077-80 (1955).

[35] See Dession, "Private Prosecution: A Remedy for District Attorney's Unwarranted Inaction," 65 *Yale L.J.* 209 (1955).

[36] "Such actions [as the initiation of criminal prosecutions] are clearly discretionary, and decisions respecting such actions are committed to the executive branch of the government, not to the courts." Moses v. Kennedy, 219 *F. Supp.* 763 (D.D.C. 1963).

[37] He may be unable to establish the fact of nonenforcement against others or that his selection was intentional or purposeful. Moreover, he may be confronted with narrow interpretations of the reach of the equal protection guarantee, such as that a criminal has no right to demand equal protection of the law, that he must show that he alone has been prosecuted under the statute, or that he must establish that he would be in a better position if other violators were also prosecuted. See Comment, 61 *Colum. L. Rev.* 1103 (1961); Note, 59 *Yale L.J.* 354 (1950).

[38] K. Davis, supra note 1, at 208.

of close administrative review, perhaps modeled after the practice in West Germany,[39] would seem to require a hierarchical arrangement quite different from the present structure of most state governments. Whether such a significant change in structure would be an improvement is not readily apparent. As for judicial review, it is probably true that courts have exercised undue restraint in responding to challenges of prosecutorial discretion.[40] Yet, there may be something to the contention that courts are ill-equipped to make enforcement policy. Finally, greater control by the electorate could readily be achieved by exposing the prosecutor's nonenforcement decisions to the public, but it is by no means clear that the soundest enforcement policies are those which would draw approval from the "silent majority." [41]

III. The "Negotiated Plea"

A. The Current Practice [42]

In the United States, only a small portion of all criminal cases involve a trial on the merits. Although precise statistics are unavailable, it has been estimated that guilty pleas account for approximately ninety percent of all criminal convictions.[43] A significant but undetermined number of these pleas are "negotiated pleas," in that the defendant decided to plead guilty because the prosecutor expressly promised to obtain, to seek, or not oppose certain concessions in exchange for the pleas.[44]

One common form of plea bargaining consists of an arrangement whereby the defendant and prosecutor agree that the defendant should be permitted to plead guilty to a charge less serious than is supported by the evidence. There are several reasons why this kind of "deal" may seem advantageous to the defendant. For one, the less serious offense is likely to carry a lower statutory maximum penalty than the

---

[39] See id. at 191-95.

[40] Professor Davis has pointed out that the reason most often given for this restraint, namely, that it is not the function of the courts to review the exercise of executive discretion, is contrary to "more than a hundred Supreme Court decisions spread over a century and three-quarters." Id. at 210.

[41] On the disadvantages of public accountability, see R. Pound, supra note 8, at 185-87; Note, 34 *Ind. L.J.* 477 (1959); Note, 48 *J. Crim. L. C. & P.S.* 516 (1958).

[42] Among the most useful descriptions of current plea bargaining practices are those found in D. Newman, supra note 2; Alschuler, "The Prosecutor's Role in Plea Bargaining," 36 *U. Chi. L. Rev.* 50 (1968); Enker, "Perspectives on Plea Bargaining," in *Task Force Report,* supra note 6, at 108; Kuh, "Plea Copping," 24 *N.Y. Co. Bar Bull.* 160 (1966-67); Rosett, "The Negotiated Guilty Plea," 374 *Ann. Am. Pol. & Soc. Sci.* 70 (1967); Note, 112 *U. Pa. L. Rev.* 865 (1964); Comment, 66 *Yale L.J.* 204 (1956).

[43] D. Newman, supra note 2, at 3 n.1.; *Task Force Report,* supra note 6, at 9.

[44] Many other pleas are the result of what has been characterized a "tacit bargain," where there are no formal negotiations but the defendant pleads guilty because he is aware of the established practice in the court to show leniency to defendants who plead guilty. See Enker, supra note 42, at 111-12.

offense actually committed, so that the defendant has an assurance at the time of his plea that the judge's sentencing discretion will be limited. Or, the plea to the lesser offense may instead maximize the judge's sentencing discretion; by his plea, the defendant may avoid a high statutory minimum sentence or a statutory bar to probation. A third reason why defendants bargain as to the charge is to avoid a record of conviction on the offense actually committed. Sometimes the desire is to avoid a repugnant conviction label, as where a defendant charged with a sex offense is permitted to plead to the nondescript charge of disorderly conduct. On other occasions, the purpose is to avoid conviction on a felony charge, which would carry with it certain undesirable collateral consequences (e.g., loss of certain civil rights, loss of eligibility for certain types of employment).

When such an agreement is reached before any formal charge has been filed, the prosecutor's discretion in filing a lesser charge is not even in theory subject to any formal judicial control. If, as is often the case, the charge-bargaining occurs after the higher charge has been formally entered, the trial judge in theory can exercise some supervision. Many jurisdictions require concurrence by the trial judge in charge reduction, and some states also require the prosecutor to file a statement with the court indicating the reasons for the reduction. In practice, however, judicial control is usually minimal; the judge typically accepts the lesser plea without question, and the prosecutor's explanation (if required by law or practice) is usually no more explicit than "in the interests of justice."[45]

A second form of plea bargaining involves an agreement whereby the defendant pleads "on the nose," that is, to the original charge, in exchange for some kind of promise from the prosecutor concerning the sentence to be imposed. The prosecutor may agree in a general way to seek leniency, or he may promise to ask for some specific disposition, such as probation. On occasion, the prosecutor may do no more than promise that he will refrain from making any recommendation to the judge, or that he will not oppose a request for leniency put to the judge by the defendant. Or, the prosecutor may be so bold as to promise a certain sentence upon a guilty plea, a promise he may know he can

---

[45] The same may be said for another significant aspect of the American prosecutor's discretion: charge reduction without plea bargaining. While there are cases holding that the legislature may not expressly grant the prosecutor power to choose under which statute he will proceed, e.g., State v. Twitchell, 8 *Utah 2d* 314, 333 *P.2d* 1075 (1959), the prosecutor is free to ignore certain aggravating circumstances of the crime and thus charge a lesser offense. For the charging possibilities open to the prosecutor against a person accused of committing robbery in New York, see Polstein, "How to Settle a Criminal Case," 8 *Prac. Law.* 35 (Jan. 1962). The uncontrolled discretion of the prosecutor in selecting the charge has sometimes been criticized; see Judge Bazelon's dissenting opinions in Hutcherson v. United States, 345 *F.2d* 964 (D.C. Cir. 1965); and Henderson v. United States, 349 *F.2d* 712 (D.C. Cir. 1965).

fulfill because of the trial judge's practice of following the prosecutor's recommendations.

Sentence-bargaining carries with it a somewhat greater risk than charge-bargaining. When a defendant bargains for a plea to a lesser offense, he receives his bargain the instant he enters his guilty plea, but when he pleads guilty in exchange for the prosecutor's promise to seek a certain sentence there remains some possibility that in this case the trial judge will not follow the prosecutor's recommendations. However, a great many defendants, often on advice of counsel, enter into these kinds of agreements, which attests to the fact that the risk is slight and that the judge will most likely act in conformance with the parties' expectations. Because this is so, it is apparent that the prosecutor's discretion in sentence-bargaining is not effectively controlled by the trial judge.

One final form of plea negotiation deserves mention: the on-the-nose plea of guilty to one charge in exchange for the prosecutor's promise to drop or not to file other charges. Multiple charges, either actual or potential, against a single defendant are not uncommon; a single criminal episode may involve violation of several separate provisions of the applicable criminal code, or investigation of the defendant may show that he was responsible for several unrelated crimes (e.g., several burglaries committed in the course of many months). This kind of bargain is most likely to be illusory, in that multiple charges are seldom brought against the defendant who does not plead guilty,[46] and, if brought, often result in concurrent sentencing.

As with other kinds of plea bargaining, the prosecutor's exercise of discretion in abandoning other charges in exchange for the plea is not subject to any effective control. If the other charges have not yet been filed, the prosecutor is free to decide on his own not to file them. If the charges to be abandoned have been filed, many jurisdictions require the prosecutor to obtain the approval of the court to a *nolle prosequi,* but such approval is usually granted as a matter of course.

What accounts for the pervasive practice of plea bargaining in the United States? To some extent, "the negotiated plea is motivated by a desire to individualize the consequences of conviction for deserving defendants"[47]; as noted above, charge-bargaining may be an effective way for avoiding the undesirable consequences of a harsh and rigid sentencing structure. But, "the most commonly asserted justification of plea bargaining is its utility in disposing of large numbers of cases

---

[46] Thus, another significant aspect of the American prosecutor's discretion is the power to decide, in many cases, how many different charges will be accumulated against the defendant. See F. Miller, supra note 5, at 197-202.

[47] D. Newman, supra note 2, at 77.

in a quick and simple way."[48] As to the situation on the state level, one state judge has written;

> "If all the defendants should combine to refuse to plead guilty, and should dare to hold out, they could break down the administration of criminal justice in any state in the Union. . . . The truth is, that a criminal court can operate only by inducing the great mass of actually guilty defendants to plead guilty, paying in leniency the price for the pleas."[49]

A federal judge has made essentially the same observation as to the federal system, where, as he pointed out, in a recent year 248 district judges had to dispose of cases involving 35,517 criminal defendants.[50]

B. Some Major Problems

Plea negotiation, as it is practiced in the United States, raises a host of significant problems. For example, one aspect of the practice is its low visibility; promises are made and agreements are reached in private, but when the defendant is called upon to plead in open court he is expected to "follow the rubric of telling the court no promise has induced the plea, and while this game is played the prosecutor and defense counsel mutely corroborate the defendant's false statement."[51] Whatever might be said in favor of plea bargaining, it is apparent that something is wrong with a system which requires such misrepresentations by defendants and counsel.[52] There are, however, two major problems which go to the heart of this aspect of the American prosecutor's discretion: (1) whether the prosecutor's inducements are unfair to pleading defendants, in the sense that their constitutional rights are "chilled"; and (2) whether the prosecution-induced disparity in disposition between guilty plea defendants and those defendants who go to trial is inconsistent with a rational sentencing system.

1. Plea negotiation as a "chilling" of constitutional rights

If a defendant pleads guilty in exchange for a prosecutor's promise to obtain certain concessions, it is clear that the plea cannot stand if the prosecutor thereafter reneges on his promise.[53] But, what if the prosecutor keeps his promise? Should the guilty plea be characterized as

---

[48] Enker, supra note 42, at 112.

[49] H. Lummus, *The Trial Judge* 46 (1937).

[50] United States v. Wiley, 184 *F. Supp.* 679 (N.D. Ill. 1960).

[51] United States v. Jackson, 390 *F.2d* 130, 138 (7th Cir. 1968) (Kiley, J., dissenting).

[52] For recommendations that plea bargaining should be brought out into the open by having the terms of each agreement stated in court at the time the guilty plea is received, see *Task Force Report,* supra note 6, at 12; American Bar Association Project on Minimum Standards for Criminal Justice, *Standards Relating to Pleas of Guilty* § 1.5 (Approved Draft, 1968).

[53] See, e.g., State v. Wolske, 280 *Minn.* 465, 160 *N.W.2d* 146 (1968).

"involuntary" on the ground that it was induced by the prosecutor's promises? Although there is some authority to that effect,[54] the prevailing view has been that the defendant may be held to his bargain. As one court noted:

> "In a sense, it can be said that most guilty pleas are the result of a 'bargain' with the prosecutor. But this, standing alone, does not vitiate such pleas. A guilty defendant must always weigh the possibility of his conviction on all counts, and the possibility of his getting the maximum sentence, against the possibility that he can plead to fewer, or lesser, offenses, and perhaps receive a lighter sentence. . . . The important thing is not that there shall be no 'deal' or 'bargain,' but that the plea shall be a genuine one, by a defendant who is guilty; one who understands his situation, his rights, and the consequences of the plea, and is neither deceived nor coerced."[55]

Even accepting that analysis, the prosecutor's conduct in inducing guilty pleas may now be open to serious question as a result of the recent Supreme Court decision in *United States v. Jackson*.[56] The *Jackson* case involved the Federal Kidnapping Act, under which a defendant could obtain the death penalty only if the jury so recommended; by either waiving jury trial or pleading guilty, a defendant charged under this statute could avoid the risk of the death penalty. The Court struck down the death penalty clause of the statute on the ground that it unnecessarily chilled the Fifth Amendment right to plead not guilty and the Sixth Amendment right to jury trial:

> "It is no answer to urge, as does the Government, that federal trial judges may be relied upon to reject coerced pleas of guilty and involuntary waivers of jury trial. For the evil in the federal statute is not that it necessarily *coerces* guilty pleas and jury waivers but simply that it needlessly *encourages* them. A procedure need not be inherently coercive in order that it be held to impose an impermissible burden upon the assertion of a constitutional right. Thus the fact that the Federal Kidnapping Act tends to discourage defendants from insisting upon their innocence and demanding trial by jury hardly implies that every defendant who enters a guilty plea to a charge under the Act does so involuntarily. The power to reject coerced guilty pleas and involuntary jury waivers might alleviate, but it cannot totally eliminate, the constitutional infirmity in the capital punishment provision of the Federal Kidnapping Act."[57]

[54] E.g., Bailey v. MacDougall, 392 *F.2d* 155 (4th Cir. 1968).
[55] Cortez v. United States, 337 *F.2d* 699, 701 (9th Cir. 1964).
[56] 390 *U.S.* 570, 88 *S. Ct.* 1209, 20 *L.Ed.2d* 138 (1968).
[57] 390 *U.S.* at 583, 88 *S. Ct.* at 1217, *L.Ed.2d* at 148.

What then is the status of a guilty plea prompted by the prosecutor's discretionary act of tendering to the defendant some concession, such as a sentence several years shorter than he might receive if he were to stand trial? Does such action by the prosecutor "needlessly chill" the defendant's constitutional right to plead not guilty? It has been suggested that *Jackson* is not applicable to the typical plea bargaining situation because the case only reflects a "growing judicial distaste for capital punishment," [58] although it would seem difficult to distinguish *Jackson* on that basis. Somewhat more credible is the suggestion that *Jackson* concerned "legislative coercion," [59] whereby every defendant charged under the statute was confronted with the hard choice, while plea negotiations based upon the facts of the individual case may not be coercive. Thus, it has been suggested that a defendant's rights are not chilled when he and the prosecutor have reached an agreement based upon a "substantial uncertainty concerning the likely outcome" at trial, as the defendant pays no price by opting for a certain but low sentence instead of the all-or-nothing outcome of the trial.[60]

Finally, it is important to note that the Court in *Jackson* found the chilling of the right to stand trial to be "unnecessary and therefore excessive" because the goal of mitigating the severity of capital punishment could have been achieved in other ways. It might thus be argued that the "chilling effect" of plea bargaining is permissible if this aspect of the prosecutor's discretion serves some legitimate goal which cannot otherwise be realized. Whether the latter is true is a matter which is bound to evoke strong differences of opinion. On the one hand, it might be contended that plea bargaining practice is primarily attributable to a lack of prosecutorial and judicial resources, a problem which is best solved by committing the needed resources to the criminal process. Others question the more-resources solution, noting that the funds and personnel might be diverted from other segments of the criminal process where they are more needed, and that competent personnel (prosecutors and judges) in sufficient numbers might not be available.[61] Moreover, it must also be considered whether maximiza-

---

[58] Note, "The Supreme Court, 1967 Term," 82 *Harv. L. Rev.* 63, 162 (1968).

[59] Ibid.

[60] Scott v. United States, 419 *F.2d* 264 (D.C. Cir. 1969). "The argument that the defendant who receives a heavier sentence after trial has 'paid a price' because he receives a heavier sentence than the defendant who is acquitted (and goes free) or pleads guilty (and receives a shorter sentence on the same or a reduced charge) errs on two counts: (1) the comparison is made at the wrong time—after trial, when the uncertainty of litigation has passed, rather than before trial—and (2) the comparison is made between the wrong categories of defendants—the class of defendants convicted after trial versus the class of defendants who plead guilty or are acquitted rather than the class of defendants who exercise their right to trial versus the class of defendants who do not." Id. at 277.

[61] Enker, supra note 42, at 112.

tion of adjudication by trial would not have the unfortunate consequence of more inaccurate verdicts.[62]

2. Plea negotiation and rational sentencing

Assume that two defendants, *A* and *B,* have been jointly charged with having committed the same offense together; assume also that the usual presentence information gathered as to *A* and *B* does not differ in any material respect. *A* goes to trial, is convicted, and receives a sentence of 5 years, but *B* pleads guilty and, as promised by the prosecutor, receives a sentence of 4 years. Is not this exercise of the prosecutor's discretion improper in that, from the standpoint of sound sentencing policy, either *A's* sentence or *B's* sentence is "wrong"?

Not necessarily, is the view taken in the American Bar Association's Minimum Standards on Pleas of Guilty. Under the Standards, the routine granting of concessions to all guilty plea defendants is considered improper, yet it is deemed appropriate for the prosecutor to tender concessions [63] and "for the court to grant charge and sentence concessions to defendants who enter a plea of guilty . . . when the interest of the public in the effective administration of criminal justice would thereby be served." [64] Relevant considerations are listed in the standards:

> "(i) that the defendant by his plea has aided in ensuring the prompt and certain application of correctional measures to him;
>
> "(ii) that the defendant has acknowledged his guilt and shown a willingness to assume responsibility for his conduct;
>
> "(iii) that the concessions will make possible alternative correctional measures which are better adapted to achieving rehabilitative, protective, deterrent or other purposes of correctional treatment, or will prevent undue harm to the defendant from the form of conviction;
>
> "(iv) that the defendant has made public trial unnecessary when there are good reasons for not having the case dealt with in a public trial;
>
> "(v) that the defendant has given or offered cooperation when such cooperation has resulted or may result in the successful prosecution of other offenders engaged in equally serious or more serious criminal conduct;

---

[62] "So long as trials are the exception rather than the rule and are limited, by and large, to cases in which the defense offers a substantial basis for contesting the prosecutor's allegations, the defendant's presumption of innocence and the requirement of proof beyond a reasonable doubt are likely to remain meaningful to a jury. . . . If contest becomes routine, jurors may likely direct their skepticism at the defense." Id. at 112.

[63] ABA *Standards* supra note 52, at § 3.1(a).

[64] Id. at § 1.8(a).

"(vi) that the defendant by his plea has aided in avoiding delay (including delay due to crowded dockets) in the disposition of other cases and thereby has increased the probability of prompt and certain application of correctional measures to other offenders." [65]

The Standards also assert that a defendant who does *not* plead guilty should not receive a sentence "in excess of that which would be justified by any of the rehabilitative, protective, deterrent or other purposes of the criminal law." [66] In the commentary, it is argued that this scheme is "in no sense unfair or inconsistent with the goal of uniformity in sentencing," [67] in that the disparity in treatment between guilty plea defendants (as class) and trial defendants (as a class) results not merely from the plea but from circumstances surrounding the plea which have traditionally been considered relevant on the issue of sentencing.

This theory has not gone unchallenged. For one thing, it has been questioned whether the six "considerations" listed in the Standards are in fact relevant to the sentencing decision.[68] For another, it is argued that plea bargaining must inevitably result in improper sentencing for one class of defendants or the other:

"The temptation is strong in the area of plea bargaining to assume that defendants convicted after trial receive a 'normal' sentence while those who plead guilty and save the Government the cost of a trial receive special 'leniency' in exchange. If this analysis were valid, some defendants would win and none would lose. But in reality there are winners and losers. The 'normal' sentence is the average sentence for all defendants, those who plead guilty and those who plead innocent. If we are 'lenient' toward the former, we are by precisely the same token 'more severe' toward the latter." [69]

But even if the Minimum Standards theory does make some sense, it is clear that not all current plea bargaining practices produce results consistent with a rational scheme of sentencing. In contrast to the approach in the Standards, much plea bargaining is a matter of routine, and thus in a given case "the sentence may bear no relation at all to the specific facts of the case, the correctional needs of the defendant, or the social interest in vigorous prosecution." [70] The most likely

---

[65] Ibid.
[66] Id. at § 1.8(b).
[67] Id. at p. 51.
[68] See People v. Earegood, 12 *Mich. App.* 256, 162 *N.W.2d* 802 (1968).
[69] Scott v. United States, 419 *F.2d* 264, 278 (D.C. Cir. 1969).
[70] Rosett, supra note 42, at 71.

result is undue leniency,[71] but it may also happen that a given defendant will be denied (perhaps arbitrarily) any opportunity to plea bargain, only to learn that "no court has any jurisdiction to inquire into or review [the prosecutor's] decision."[72]

IV. Conclusion

This brief glimpse at two major facets of the prosecutor's discretion in the United States would seem to justify certain general conclusions. For one, discretion in law enforcement is not inherently bad; it can (and often does) serve the public interest in more effective enforcement and the concern of those who have violated the law for compassionate and understanding treatment. Secondly, discretion which is largely unrestricted and uncontrolled carries with it an enormous potential for abuse. Individual defendants may be dealt with too harshly or unfairly, and the interests of society may on occasion be poorly served.

It is not easy to determine precisely how we might best maximize the benefits and minimize the risks flowing from the prosecutor's discretion. With a problem of this complexity, it is tempting to accept the familiar and conclude that the system is beyond meaningful improvement. Such a conclusion should not be reached without hesitation, however, and certainly not without taking into account different approaches to be found in other criminal justice systems. One meaningful way of appraising the procedures described in this paper, then, is through comparison with the law and practice in the other countries covered in this symposium.

Addendum

After this article was in galleys, the United States Supreme Court decided the case of *Brady v. United States,*[73] which bears directly upon the discussion in section III.B.1. of the article because it clarifies the scope of *Jackson v. United States.* Prior to the decision in *Jackson,* the defendant in *Brady* pleaded guilty to a federal kidnapping charge which could have resulted in the death penalty following jury trial. Concluding that "*Jackson* ruled neither that all pleas of guilty encouraged by the fear of a possible death sentence are involuntary pleas nor that such encouraged pleas are invalid whether involuntary or not,"[74] the Court upheld Brady's guilty plea because it was

[71] See Kuh, supra note 42.

[72] Newman v. United States, 382 *F.2d* 479, 482 (D.C. Cir. 1967). The assumption in *Newman,* that this is simply another aspect of the prosecutor's discretion and thus no more subject to judicial review than a decision not to prosecute, has been questioned. See Alschuler, supra note 42, at 105.

[73] 397 U.S. 742, 90 S.Ct. 1463, 25 L.Ed. 2d 747 (1970).

[74] 397 U.S. at 747, 90 S.Ct. at 1468, 25 L.Ed. 2d at 756.

tendered upon advice of competent counsel and after his codefendant had decided to testify against him.

More important, for present purposes, is the fact that the Court rather clearly indicated that *Jackson* does not render unconstitutional plea bargaining between the defendant and the prosecutor:

> "We decline to hold, however, that a guilty plea is compelled and invalid under the Fifth Amendment whenever motivated by the defendant's desire to accept the certainty or probability of a lesser penalty rather than face a wider range of possibilities extending from acquittal to conviction and a higher penalty authorized by law for the crime charged.
>
> "[W]e cannot hold that it is unconstitutional for the State to extend a benefit to a defendant who in turn extends a substantial benefit to the State and who demonstrates by his plea that he is ready and willing to admit his crime and to enter the correctional system in a frame of mind which affords hope for success in rehabilitation over a shorter period of time than might otherwise be necessary." [75]

[75] 397 U.S. at 751, 90 St.Ct. at 1470-71, 25 L.Ed.2d at 758. Justice Brennan, joined in dissent by Justices Douglas and Marshall, observed: "The principal flaw in the Court's discourse on plea bargaining, however, is that it is, at best, only marginally relevant to the precise issues before us. There are critical distinctions between plea bargaining as commonly practiced and the situation presently under consideration—distinctions which in constitutional terms, make a difference. Thus, whatever the merit, if any, of the constitutional objections to plea bargaining generally, those issues are not presently before us." 397 U.S. at 808, 90 S.Ct. at 1479, 25 L.Ed.2d at 798.

ROBERT W. MCCLURE

Plea Bargaining: The Judicial Merry-Go-Round

INTRODUCTION

The last decade has brought to our courts the increasing awareness that the criminal is winning the war against crime. He is not winning through cunning or guile, nor even with the aid of modern technology. He is winning because the sheer number of his comrades-in-arms is beginning to buckle our cumbersome system of justice. Realizing the need to relieve its congested dockets, the courts have resorted to various methods to expedite the legal process. One of these methods, plea bargaining, is not designed to accelerate the trial level but instead eliminate it. It has done just that with remarkable efficiency. Unfortunately the price for a more efficient system of justice is high, and too often paid by the very individuals who need its protection most. The purpose of this article is to examine plea bargaining in our courts and assess its impact upon the judicial system. The analysis will include the role of the trial judge in the bargaining process, problems involved in withdrawing a guilty plea, and reasons why the process is used so extensively today. The dangers of plea bargaining will also be examined in conjunction with recent Pennsylvania Supreme Court decisions.

The rise of plea bargaining to its present status has not been without controversy.[1] Its foes have wielded such verbal weapons as "denial of due process," and "unethical," which have been successfully countered by retorts of "necessary" and "efficient." Whatever the future of plea bargaining may be, one thing must be made absolutely clear—it is dangerously susceptible to abuse.

PLEA BARGAINING DEFINED

Plea bargaining is a process by which a defendant is induced to plead guilty for a consideration, and forgo his or her right to trial. Several questions are raised by this definition. First, what type of inducements are used? One method is to plead guilty to a lesser offense. For example,

1. *See generally*, Arnold, *Law Enforcement—An Attempt At Social Dissection*, 42 YALE L.J. 1 (1932); Dash, *Cracks in the Foundation of Criminal Justice*, 46 ILL. L. REV. 385 (1951); Newman, *Pleading Guilty for Consideration: A Study of Bargain Justice*, 46 J. CRIM. L.C. & P.S. 780 (1956); Weintraub and Tough, *Lesser Pleas Considered*, 32 J. CRIM. L.C. & P.S. 506 (1941); Comment, *The Influence of the Defendant's Plea on the Judicial Determination of Sentence*, 66 YALE L.J. 204 (1956); Note, *Guilty Plea Bargaining: Compromise By Prosecutors To Secure Guilty Pleas*, 112 U. PA. L. REV. 865 (1964).

DUQUESNE LAW REVIEW, 1971, Vol. 10, pp. 253-269.

a person in Pennsylvania charged with assault with intent to maim[2] faces a possible $2,000 fine, five years in solitary confinement, or both. The accused will be offered a reduced charge of aggravated assault and battery,[3] carrying a $2,000 fine and/or three years imprisonment, or even simple assault and battery[4] consisting of a $1,000 fine and/or two years imprisonment in return for a plea of guilty. The defendant is not only assured of receiving a lighter punishment (and a greater probability of suspended sentence or probation) but also is spared the stigma of a felony conviction.[5] The penal codes of most states are conducive to this type of bargaining.[6] This amicable arrangement is based on one fundamental premise—that the defendant is initially guilty, or from all indications would have been found guilty, on all charges. This suggests one of the abuses to which plea bargaining may be subject. If a prosecutor desires a conviction, but does not feel the evidence will sustain one, he merely adds several unwarranted charges to the original ones in order to give himself some bargaining leverage for a guilty plea. If this method is used in good faith by the prosecutor, it is most advantageous to the accused. He is assured of a reduced sentence since the bargain is actually consummated at the arraignment. The problem of whether the judge will accept a recommendation is not present, and if the prosecutor does not uphold his end of the bargain, the defendant will be aware of it *before* he makes his plea. Any abuses by the prosecutor can in most cases be foreseen by the defendant's attorney.

Another inducement is that of recommending to the judge that the defendant be given a lighter sentence.[7] This method is not without its drawbacks. The accused runs the risk that the prosecutor will neglect to make the recommendation.[8] Even if it is made there is always the

---

2. PA. STAT. ANN. tit. 18, § 4712 (1963).
3. *Id.* § 4709.
4. *Id.* § 4708.
5. A felony conviction is a considerable threat to the recidivist since sentences may be doubled and even tripled with second and third offenses. *See* Ohlin & Remington, *Sentencing Structures: Its Effect Upon Systems for the Administration of Criminal Justice*, 23 LAW & CONTEMP. PROB. 495 (1958).
6. In New York there are three types of assault: Assault in the third degree (max. 1 year); Assault in the second degree (max. 3 to 7 years); Assault in the first degree (max. 3 to 15 years). N.Y. CONSUL. LAWS ANN. tit. 39, §§ 120.00, 120.05, 120.10 (McKinney 1967). In Illinois the crime of kidnapping is divided into three categories: Kidnapping (max. 1 to 5 years); Aggravated Kidnapping (max.-death); Unlawful Restraint (max. $500 fine, 1 year or both). ILL. STAT. ANN. ch. 38 §§ 10-1, 10-2, 10-3 (1964).
7. Newman, *Pleading Guilty for Consideration: A Study of Bargain Justice*, 46 J. CRIM. L.C. & P.S. 780, 787 (1956):

> This ordinarily occured in cases where the offense in question carried statutory degrees of severity such as homicide, assault, and sex offenses.

8. Commonwealth v. Alvarado, 442 Pa. 516, 276 A.2d 526 (1971). The prosecutor failed

possibility that the court may not heed the appeal.[9] Studies have shown, however, that generally the judges do heed these recommendations. One finding showed that of a group of federal district court judges who believed the plea relevant in sentencing procedures, 84% indicated that a defendant pleading guilty would be given a lighter sentence.[10] The reason for this attitude among judges is the belief that a defendant pleading guilty is attempting to atone for his wrong, and is thus less culpable than the accused who flaunts his innocence till the end.[11] Another theory is that the judge is not prejudiced by the inflamatory details of the crime given by the prosecutor.[12]

It is this latter method which has caused the greatest concern to liberal legal scholars. Upon initial reflection one envisions the courtroom scene of a soap opera where the assistant district attorney approaches the hardened criminal and in a tough but compassionate voice says, "Throw yourself on the mercy of the court and I'll do everything I can to see the judge goes easy on you." This may have been the birth of the modern day plea bargain but since then it has developed ramifications far beyond what was initially intended.

Another problem of importance in relation to plea bargaining is by whom is it done, and for what reasons? These two questions have been a source of some consternation within the courts themselves.

In answer to the former question, there is little doubt that the main ingredient to any bargaining venture is the prosecutor. It is he who sets the legal machine in motion, and it is he who can put a stop to it or at least shorten its duration. Due process and the judicially inherent sense of fair play require that the defense counsel also be present in the bargain.[13]

Role Of The Judge

The serious issue revolves around the role of the trial judge. The Pennsylvania Supreme Court has stated that "for a judge to make a bargain, engagement or promise in advance of the hearing of the case

---

to recommend to the judge as promised that defendant receive life imprisonment instead of death.

9. Commonwealth v. Banmiller, 193 Pa. Super. 411, 165 A.2d 121 (1960).

10. Comment, *The Influence of the Defendant's Plea on the Judicial Determination of Sentence*, 66 Yale L.J. 204 (1956).

11. *Id.* at 209.

12. *Id.* at 218.

13. Cases have arisen involving instances where bargains have been made to defendants without their being represented by counsel. *See* Shelton v. United States, 242 F.2d 101 (5th Cir. 1957).

irrespective of what the evidence might thereafter show the facts to be and as to what judgment he should render therein, would be judicial misconduct."[14] The opinion goes on, however, to note by way of dictum that in the future, should a judge happen to discuss the disposition of a case with counsel for one side, he had better be sure the counsel for the opposing side is present.[15]

In 1966, the court gave its unofficial seal of approval to plea bargaining in *Commonwealth ex. rel. Kerekes v. Maroney*.[16] Citing *United States ex. rel. McGrath v. LaVallee*,[17] however, it qualified that approach with a veil of judicial rhetoric giving the concession an air of constitutional respectability.

> Our concept of due process must draw a distinct line between, on the one hand, advice and "bargaining" between defense and prosecuting attorneys and, on the other hand, discussions by judges who are ultimately to determine the length of the sentence imposed.[18]

More recently the case of *Commonwealth v. Evans*[19] came before the Pennsylvania Supreme Court. Citing *Kerekes*,[20] the majority again announced that any participation by the trial judge in a plea bargain is forbidden.[21] The reasons given by the court were first, that defendant will get the impression that he would not receive a fair trial if in fact he chose to have one. Secondly, the judge will not be able to objectively consider the voluntariness of the guilty plea. Thirdly, the defendant, not wanting to raise the ire of the judge, may plead guilty despite his alternative desires.[22] One federal court stated the problems in these terms:

---

14. Commonwealth v. Senauskas, 326 Pa. 69, 71, 191 A. 167, 168 (1937). *See also* Commonwealth v. Scoleri, 415 Pa. 218, 202 A.2d 521 (1964) where the court held that defendant was entitled to withdraw his plea where defense counsel claimed one judge of a three-judge court had made a commitment against the death penalty which defendant had relied upon.

15. Commonwealth v. Senauskas, 326 Pa. 69, 71, 191 A.2d 167, 168 (1937).

16. 423 Pa. 337, 349, 223 A.2d 699, 705 (1966):

While we are not willing to completely proscribe plea bargaining, we do recognize that the awesome effect of a guilty plea and the sensitive nature of the bargaining process makes certain safeguards essential.

17. 319 F.2d 308 (2d Cir. 1963) (dissenting opinion).

18. 423 Pa. 337, 349, 223 A.2d 699, 705 (1966).

19. 434 Pa. 52, 252 A.2d 689 (1969).

20. *Id.* at 54, 252 A.2d at 690.

21. The court cites Informal Opinion No. 779, A.B.A., Professional Ethics Committee: A judge should not be a party to advance arrangements for the deterimination of sentence, whether as a result of a guilty plea or a finding of guilty based on proof. A.B.A. MINIMUM STANDARDS FOR CRIMINAL JUSTICE, *Pleas of Guilty*, § 3.3 (Tent. Draft, February, 1967).

22. Commonwealth v. Evans, 434 Pa. 52, 54, 252 A.2d 689, 690 (1969). *See* 8 DUQ. L. REV. 461 (1970).

> The unequal positions of the judge and the accused, one with the power to commit to prison and the other deeply concerned to avoid prison, at once raise a question of fundamental fairness. When a judge becomes a participant in plea bargaining he brings to bear the full force and majesty of his office. His awesome power to impose a substantially longer or even maximum sentence in excess of that proposed is present whether referred to or not. A defendant needs no reminder that if he rejects the proposal, stands upon his rights to trial and is convicted, he faces a significantly longer sentence.[23]

Dissenting in the *Evans* case, Justice Bell takes a more pragmatic view.[24] Since the judge is going to hear the recommendations from the district attorney in any event, he should be a party to the conference from its inception. Not only would the process be brought into the open, away from "chicanery, partiality, politics or compulsion,"[25] but it also would expedite litigation and help to relieve the great backlog of criminal cases.[26] Perhaps realizing what he has suggested in his dissent is not totally in line with a system of justice based upon due process of law, Bell states "parenthetically" in a footnote that "the law is well settled that a trial Judge is not bound by any agreement between the defense counsel and the district attorney that if a guilty plea is entered, the district attorney will agree to or will recommend a specific sentence, nor would he be bound even if he had participated in the conference."[27] What the Justice is objecting to is the abolition of the long standing practice in Pennsylvania for the trial judge to be present but not actively participate in a plea bargain. He fails to recognize that the judge's participation in the bargaining process has a dramatic impact upon the defendant. Whether the defendant believes that the judge is participating in the actual decision or not is irrelevant, since he does believe that the judge must have acquiesced in the final determination. The fact the judge makes a special point, before the plea is given, to inform the accused that he, as judge, is in no way bound by the recommendations is also of little importance. It appears to the defendant that this is done purely for the sake of judicial propriety.

---

23. United States *ex. rel.* Elksnis v. Gilligan, 256 F. Supp. 244, 254 (S.D. N.Y. 1966).
24. Commonwealth v. Evans, 434 Pa. 52, 57, 252 A.2d 689, 692 (1969).
25. *Id.* at 57, 252 A.2d at 692.
26. Justice Bell pointed out that as of April 1, 1969, the criminal courts of Philadelphia County had a backlog of 284 untried homicide cases, at least 50% of which should be disposed of by plea bargaining. *Id.* at 58, 252 A.2d at 692.
27. *Id.* at 58 n.*, 252 A.2d at 692 n.*.

In analyzing the court's position, it can be seen that the Justices are divided between their duty to insure every defendant his constitutional right to a trial by jury,[28] in accordance with due process,[29] and recognition that something must be done to relieve the great congestion of pending criminal cases. The solution offered is that under no circumstances may a judge participate or be bound by a plea bargain, however, in the interest of expediency he should consider any such agreements made between the prosecution and the defense. It is submitted that although this may be a laudable compromise, it may in fact handicap both interests. This amicable agreement between the two attorneys and the defendant, coupled with a judicial wink from the court, may be subject to some very fundamental abuses of judicial propriety and fair play.

COMMONWEALTH V. WILKINS

In some instances the plea bargain attempt may serve to even further delay the system it was meant to expedite. The case of *Commonwealth v. Wilkins*[30] displayed both the confusion and failure of purpose to which plea bargaining is susceptible. The defendant in this instance was indicted in a purse snatching case, for assault and battery, assault with intent to rob, and robbery.[31] There seemed little doubt that Wilkins was the one involved since he was identified both by the victim, and by a card with his name on it found in the victim's hand bag when it was returned. This in itself says something about the defendant's ability to make a rational judgment as to the significance of a plea bargain.[32] These factors coupled with the defendant's prior juvenile record led the defense counsel and prosecutor to the conclusion that there was little chance for acquittal. They suggested to Wilkins that if he pleaded guilty, the Commonwealth would recommend a sentence of from eleven and one-half to twenty-three months on the robbery bill, and a year's probation on the assault and battery bill. Apparently, Wilkins facing a possible term of twelve years imprisonment,[33] decided

---

28. U.S. CONST. amend. VI & VII.
29. *Id.* amend. XIV.
30. 442 Pa. 524, 277 A.2d 341 (1971).
31. In Pennsylvania, the charges of assault with intent to rob, and robbery, should be combined under the heading *Robbery and Robbery by Assault and Force*, PA. STAT. ANN. tit. 18, § 4704 (1963).
32. The possibility that the victim was mistaken in her identification and that Wilkins had been framed by the real assailant was not pursued.
33. PA. STAT. ANN. tit. 18, § 4704 (1963), *Robbery and Robbery by Assault and Force*

under the circumstances to accept the bargain. Before making his plea, defendant made a statement to the court that he was promised nothing and that he fully understood the nature of the offense against him, and that he "could be sent away . . . for a long time."[34] At that time the prosecuting attorney made his recommendation at a side bar conference but no such recommendation ever appeared on the record. Due to the preparation of the pre-sentence report, a sentence was not actually handed down till four months later. A different prosecuting attorney was assigned to the sentence hearing who had only a vague notion of a recommendation which had been made in behalf of defendant. The judge also had forgotten the recommendation which was never again brought to his attention. Wilkins was then sentenced to eighteen months to fifteen years on the robbery charge.[35] Suggestions of shorter minimum sentences were offered by both the defense counsel and the prosecution, but never was the specific recommendation made as promised. Upon appeal, it was discovered that defendant had been "coached" by the two attorneys into telling the judge that he had been promised nothing and that his plea was voluntarily made.[36]

The Supreme Court of Pennsylvania, in accordance with the majority of states,[37] held that a defendant may withdraw[38] a plea of guilty when a promise to recommend a lenient sentence is not kept by the prosecutor.[39] For a trial judge to rule any other way would be an abuse

---

carries a ten year maximum sentence; *Id.* § 4708 (1971), *Assault and Battery* carries a two year maximum sentence.

34. Commonwealth v. Wilkins, 442 Pa. 524, 526, 277 A.2d 341, 342 (1971).

35. The fifteen year maximum is five years longer than is allowed by state law. PA. STAT. ANN. tit. 18, § 4704 (1963), *Robbery and Robbery by Assault and Force* carries a ten year maximum sentence.

36. Commonwealth v. Wilkins, 442 Pa. 524, 529-30, 277 A.2d 341, 343-44 (1971). Upon post-conviction hearing, defendant, upon interrogation by his own counsel, stated:

Q. Did they tell you anything about how you should respond to the question the judge would present before the court? Now, specifically, when the judge said, 'Are you doing this voluntarily or have any promises been made to you' did they tell you how to answer those questions?

A. Yes.

Q. What did they tell you to say?

A. They told me I was being asked, and when asked was there any deal or bargaining made I was to say, no.

37. Commonwealth v. Alvarado, 442 Pa. 516, 522, 276 A.2d 526, 529 (1971). Decisions among the majority which allow a change of plea for a broken promise: White v. Gaffney, 435 F.2d 1241 (10th Cir. 1970); People v. Fratianno, 6 Cal. App. 3d 211, 85 Cal. Rptr. 755 (1970); State v. Wolske, 280 Minn. 465, 160, N.W.2d 146 (1968); People v. Sigafus, 39 Ill. 2d 68, 233 N.E.2d 386 (1968); State v. Reppin, 35 Wis. 2d 377, 151 N.W.2d 9 (1967).

Decisions among the minority which do not allow a change of plea for a broken promise: People v. Chadwick, 33 App. Div. 2d 687, 306 N.Y.S.2d 182 (1969); Courtney v. State, 341 P.2d 610 (Okla. Ct. App. 1959).

38. *See* Commonwealth v. Scoleri, 415 Pa. 218, 247-48, 202 A.2d 521, 536 (1964) for general propositions as to when withdrawal is or is not legally justifiable.

39. Commonwealth v. Wilkins, 442 Pa. 524, 529, 277 A.2d 341, 343 (1971); *See also*

of discretion. More importantly the court stated that a shy recommendation to the trial judge at side bar would not be sufficient in upholding the Commonwealth's end of the bargain. Any recommendation must be made audibly to the court and placed on record.[40] The court went on to note:

> In the future, if a defendant or his counsel wish to protect a bargain they received for a plea, when the court asks the defendant if any promises were made to him, the defendant should answer in the affirmative, stating that the district attorney's office promised that they would make the specific recommendation which had, in fact, been promised. The court should then make it clear to the defendant that he is not bound by the district attorney's recommendation and at that time allow that defendant to plead guilty or go to trial.[41]

Justice Jones wrote a dissenting opinion[42] in which he attempted to correct the court on one important point. When a defendant pleads guilty, whether he has been promised anything or not, he presumably is admitting his complicity in the crime he has been charged with. It is anomolous to later allow him to withdraw that plea. After all, a man is either guilty or he is not. The only change that should be made according to the Justice is to allow the recommendation (eleven and one-half to twenty-three months) to to take the place of the actual sentence of eighteen months to fifteen years. He also concurs with the majority but adds:

> Whenever a trial judge is informed by the accused of a desire to plead guilty, any proposed bargains should be brought to light before a guilty plea is entered. At that juncture, the judge may take evidence if he believes that concessions are unwarranted. If the judge then concludes he will not follow the agreement he should then so inform the accused before receiving any guilty plea.[43]

From August, 1967 when Wilkins was indicted to May 14, 1971 when the Supreme Court of Pennsylvania decided the case, was a period of almost four years which Wilkins spent in prison. He went

---

Commonwealth v. Alvarado, 442 Pa. 516, 276 A.2d 526 (1971); Commonwealth v. Scoleri, 415 Pa. 218, 202 A.2d 521 (1964); Commonwealth v. Todd, 186 Pa. Super. 272, 142 A.2d 174 (1958).

40. *Id.*
41. *Id.* at 532, 277 A.2d at 345.
42. *Id.*
43. *Id.* at 535, 277 A.2d at 346-47.

through an indictment, trail court, sentence hearing, post-conviction hearing, an appeal to the Superior Court and one to the Supreme Court of Pennsylvania only to find out that he must start all over at the trial level. He has cost himself and the state taxpayers hundreds of dollars for a crime amounting to a few dollars. All of this because of a desire to expedite litigation.

If the theory of the dissenting Justice in the *Wilkins* case is followed, the trial judge must inform the defendant whether or not he intends to follow the recommendation *before* the guilty plea is entered.[44] Although this eliminates the "casino-like game of chance,"[45] it brings about a most unconscionable situation. If the bargain is rejected, the guilty defendant will plead innocent, thus frustrating the purpose of the entire process. And if the bargain is accepted, it is submitted that the innocent defendant will be as coerced into pleading guilty as if he had been rubberhosed at the station house. This is especially true where the accused is offered probation or a suspended sentence. Even an innocent man will plead guilty and insure his freedom, rather than chance imprisonment after a conviction based on circumstantial evidence.[46] Although he has retained his freedom, he will be plagued for the rest of his life by the black mark of a felony conviction.

Reasons For Its Use

In order to scrutinize the process of plea bargaining, the reasons why it is done must be further explored. This entails two points of view, one from the side of the accusor (*i.e.*, prosecuting attorney, judge and society), and the other from the accused. Both can be summarized by one word—expediency.

The accusor is interested in plea bargaining primarily because of the circumstances first mentioned in the comment—the fact that it is becoming more and more difficult for a system of justice based upon due process for all to stem the tide of an ever increasing crime rate. One author wrote:

---

44. *Id.* at 529, 277 A.2d at 343.
45. *Id.* at 533, 277 A.2d at 346.
46. Justice Roberts in defending plea bargaining made this statement:

> Even when the evidence, although not overwhelming, is more than sufficient to sustain a conviction, it may well be in the defendant's best interest to plead guilty rather than to gamble and lose, when losing may result in the deprivation of liberty for an extended period of time or the death sentence.

Commonwealth v. Maroney, 423 Pa. 337, 348, 223 A.2d 699, 705 (1966).

When a system is threatened by offenders demanding full, formal adjudication of their cases, it faces the alternatives of either not adjudicating many serious offenders or requiring greatly increased staff and other facilities. The former is not possible; the latter probably unrealistic. Particularly is this so when there is a known way of conforming to currently-acceptable objectives, with a relatively modest expenditure of time and money. This can be done by operating the system in a way that will encourage a large number of pleas of guilty.[47]

To be more specific, a number of reasons are given for the use and encouragement of plea bargaining by the accusor. For example, it is suggested as an aid in decreasing the number of trials.[48] This in turn will relieve the long term incarceration of some persons waiting trial.[49] Less facilities will be needed and thus fewer state employees to absorb taxes.[50] Also, defense counsels will not be spread so thin, and thus be better able to prepare for their client's cases.[51] When confronted with the constitutional perils of plea bargaining, its supporters will state that if the proper safeguards are maintained, the right of the accused will never be threatened. The most important safeguard is to insure that the plea is voluntarily and understandingly made by the defendant. The trial judge, before accepting the plea, should hear the evidence against the accused and determine how likely a conviction will be. If the prosecutor is likely to sustain his case, the judge should then make absolutely certain that the defendant fully understands the nature of the charge against him, the consequences that may follow and, most importantly, the fact that the recommendation of the prosecutor has no binding effect upon the judge.[52] As will later be developed, these safeguards may not be as effective as would first appear.

The reasons why the accused will accept a plea bargain are also varied. In some instances, the defendant will be afraid of antagonizing the sentencing officials or possibly that his record will be held against him by the jury.[53] He may believe that the judge will be more severe if subjected to a full scale trial.[54] Or the defendant may simply wish to

47. Ohlin & Remington, *Sentencing Structures: Its Effect Upon Systems for the Administration of Criminal Justice*, 23 LAW & CONTEMP. PROB. 495, 500 (1958).

48. Note, *Guilty Plea Bargaining: Compromises By Prosecutors To Secure Guilty Pleas*, 112 U. PA. L. REV. 965, 881 (1964).

49. *Id.* at 882.

50. *Id.*

51. *Id.*

52. *Id.* at 884.

53. Newman, *Pleading Guilty for Consideration: A Study of Bargain Justice*, 46 J. CRIM. L.C. & P.S. 780, 783 (1956).

54. *Id.*

forgo all the embarrassment and inconvenience of a protracted trial. As uncontroversial as these reasons would seem, it must be noted that they all would provide a similar inducement even if recommendations had not been promised.

The Dangers Of Plea Bargaining

In reference to the above mentioned reasons it would appear that plea bargaining will continue to be a powerful tool in alleviating our over burdened courts. The process has been shown to be most effective, and in the majority of cases will produce results that are both efficient and justifiable. However, its limitations and dangers must be realized.[55] One major danger associated with plea bargaining is the irreconcilable results it sometimes gives. As was stated by one author:

> Modern penal theory holds that the interests of both society and the defendant are served by adjusting the sentence to reflect the individual's prospects for rehabilitation. But when defendants guilty of the same crime are awarded different sentences for administrative reasons, such a discrimination cannot be justified in terms of individual culpability.[56]

This raises a critical question—who is receiving the benefits of plea bargaining? It has been suggested that it is the recidivist because he is better able to use his past experience to obtain a lighter sentence.[57] In defense of this conclusion it could be argued that if anyone is entitled to the time and expense of a full trial, it must be the first offender. For the experienced criminal this can often foster disrespect for the effectiveness of the law.[58]

> A principal purpose for long sentences in felony cases is to deter persons from committing felonies. But when the seasoned criminal knows that he will be permitted to plead to a lesser charge and get a few months in the county jail, he may well conclude that it is worth his while to commit the crime in face of such light punishment.[59]

Even though some may argue that a criminal is rarely deterred by the

---

55. *Id.* at 789.
56. Comment, *The Influence of the Defendant's Plea on the Judicial Determination of Sentence*, 66 Yale L.J. 204, 219-20 (1956).
57. Newman, *supra* note 53 at 790.
58. *Id.*
59. Dash, *Cracks in the Foundation of Criminal Justice*, 46 Ill. L. Rev. 385, 395 (1951).

possible consequences of his actions, the incongruity of a repeated offender receiving a lighter sentence than the one or two time loser still remains.

As with any process which can affect the destiny of another individual, it is subject to misuse and exploitation. One such misuse which has sprung from plea bargaining is the securing of a plea of guilty when the State has a weak case,[60] *i.e.*, where it is not likely that the evidence will sustain a conviction. A number of situations may give rise to a weak case. Crimes involving small or uncertain pecuniary amounts such as larceny of second-hand items, lack of credibility of the state's witnesses,[61] or inability to prove intent or premeditation in a homicide are a few examples.[62] Realizing that a conviction would not be sustained, the prosecutor might conceal his dilemma from the defendant and persuade him to plead guilty.[63] These procedures might, in many instances, be used to place the criminal behind bars who because of a procedural defect, or insufficient evidence, would otherwise be free. They may also be used to incarcerate one who under the eyes of the law is innocent. It is not suggested that these irreprehensible practices cannot be stopped by the careful scrutiny of the trial and appellate judges. It is submitted, however, that real danger lies in overlooking these unethical procedures in the name of a more efficient system of justice.

There is another danger inherent in plea bargaining which the most elaborate and conscientious safeguarding may not prevent.[64]

---

60. Weintraub and Tough, *Lesser Pleas Considered*, 32 J. CRIM. L.C. & P.S. 506, 513 (1941).

61. *Id.* at 513:

> Since society brands drug addicts, prostitutes and persons with prior felony convictions as notorious or immoral, they are considered poor risks as witnesses. [A]lso the complainant who is reluctant to give testimony is of little value to the prosecution. This type of complainant is likely to be so involved himself, that, on second thought, he is anxious to have the indictment quashed; for example, a victim of a hold-up in a house of prostitution.

62. *See* PERKINS, CRIMINAL LAW 30-40 (1957).

63. Again, this may be accomplished by the prosecutor promising to make a recommendation of leniency, or by intentionally drawing up more charges than the facts call for and then offering to drop the unwarranted ones. Note that this latter tactic of the prosecutor is specifically prohibited by the ABA CODE OF PROFESSIONAL RESPONSIBILITY:

> DR 7-103 Performing the Duty of Public Prosecutor or Other Government Lawyer.
> (A) A public prosecutor or other governmental lawyer shall not institute or cause to be instituted criminal charges when he knows or it is obvious that the charges are not supported by probable cause.
> (B) A public prosecutor or other government lawyer in criminal litigation shall make timely disclosure to counsel for the defendant, or to the defendant if he has no counsel, of the existence of evidence, known to the prosecutor or other government lawyer, that tends to negate the guilt of the accused, mitigate the degree of the offense, or reduce the punishment.

64. This same danger is being confronted today in the area of confession of judgments.

> The concept of fairness and justice embodied in the fourteenth amendment to the Constitution of the United States is incompatible with the practice of permitting convictions based upon guilty pleas not made voluntarily and no plea can be viewed as voluntary that is produced of ignorance.[65]

The United States Supreme Court has stated, as far back as 1897, that a confession must be "free and voluntary; that is, it must not be extracted by any sort of threats or violence, nor obtained by any direct or implied promises, however slight, nor by the exertion of any improper influence."[66] More recently the Court has stated that the *Bram* decision "did not hold that the possibly coercive impact of a promise of leniency could not be dissipated by the presence and advice of counsel."[67] Both the Supreme Courts of the United States and Pennsylvania have made it clear that the two elements of understanding and voluntariness are requisite before a guilty plea may be accepted.[68] It is submitted that even with these safeguards being applied in good faith, a certain element of unconscionability still exists.

The problem was first recognized in Pennsylvania in the 1930 case of *Commonwealth v. Patch*.[69] On an appeal before the Superior Court, the defendant, charged with forgery, was induced to plead guilty by the assurance of his attorney that sentence would be suspended and probation given. The accused at the time was painfully sick with duodenal ulcers and hemorrhages, and as a result was interested in the quickest solution available. Upon acceptance of his guilty plea, defendant was sentenced to four to eight years in the Eastern Penitentiary. On appeal, the plea was permitted to be withdrawn, "if it fairly appears that the defendant was in ignorance of his rights and of the consequences of his act, or was influenced unduly and improperly either by hope or fear in the making of it, or if it appears that the plea was entered under some mistake or misapprehension."[70] The Pennsylvania Supreme Court later renounced the "broad enunciation"[71] of the *Patch* case but did

---

See Swarb v. Lenox, 314 F. Supp. 1091 (E.D. Pa. 1970), *prob. juris. noted*, 401 U.S. 991 (1971).

65. Commonwealth v. Myers, 423 Pa. 1, 5-6, 222 A.2d 918, 921 (1966). *See also* Machibroda v. United States, 368 U.S. 487 (1962).

66. Bram v. United States, 168 U.S. 532, 542-43 (1897); Malloy v. Hogan, 378 U.S. 1 (1964).

67. Brady v. United States, 397 U.S. 742 (1970).

68. Commonwealth v. Rundel, 428 Pa. 102, 237 A.2d 196 (1968); Machibroda v. United States, 368 U.S. 487 (1962); Brady v. United States, 397 U.S. 742 (1970).

69. 98 Pa. Super. 464 (1930).

70. *Id.* at 469.

71. Commonwealth v. Kirkland, 413 Pa. 48, 55, 195 A.2d 338, 341 (1963).

state that "the withdrawal of the plea of guilty should not be denied in any case where it is apparent that the ends of Justice will be served by permitting not guilty to be pleaded in its place."[72] In that case, the defendant, Catherine Kirkland, pleaded guilty to murder on the assurance of the assistant district attorney that a recommendation would be made to the court at the conclusion of the Commonwealth's evidence that a sentence only be imposed for voluntary manslaughter.[73] She was also advised by her counsel that although the judge was not bound to follow the recommendation, "leniency was ordinarily extended to individuals of her age, extreme poor physical condition, and previous good character and reputation."[74] Despite the recommendation, the judge, after hearing the evidence against her, found her guilty of second degree murder and sentenced her to imprisonment from four to eight years. On appeal, the Supreme Court noted that the trial judge "catechized" the accused in order to make certain she understood the nature and effect of her plea.[75] It then held that withdrawal of a plea of guilty based upon misapprehension of material facts or of the law was not justifiable where the defendant wished to change her plea merely because her expectations as to the sentence were not realized.[76] Although *Kirkland* indicated a new hardline approach on the withdrawal of guilty pleas after a bargain had been made, the case was distinguishable in that the motion to withdraw was not made until after the sentence had been given. Traditionally, the federal government has been less likely to allow a post-sentence withdrawal than a pre-sentence withdrawal.[77]

In *Commonwealth v. Scoleri*,[78] the court held that although withdrawal of a guilty plea was proper when "not made freely and voluntarily" or "where the plea was entered by mistake,"[79] it was not legally justifiable where it is entered "(a) under the belief that as a result of

72. *Id.*

73. *Id.* at 51, 195 A.2d at 339. Prosecutor admitted to defense counsel that there was not sufficient evidence in his opinion to sustain a conviction for murder.

74. *Id.* at 53, 195 A.2d at 340.

75. *Id.* at 51, 195 A.2d at 339.

76. *Id.* at 56-57, 195 A.2d at 341-342. *Accord,* Commonwealth v. Green, 396 Pa. 137, 151 A.2d 241 (1959); Commonwealth v. Banmiller, 193 Pa. Super. 411, 165 A.2d 121 (1960).

77. A.B.A. Project on Minimum Standards for Criminal Justice, *Pleas of Guilty:*

§ 2.1(a)—The court should allow the defendant to withdraw his plea of guilty . . . whenever the defendant, upon timely motion for withdrawal, proves that withdrawal is necessary to correct a manifest injustice.

§ 2.1(b)—Before sentence, the court in its discretion may allow the defendant to withdraw his plea for any fair and just reason unless the prosecution has been substantially prejudiced by reliance upon the defendant's plea.

78. 415 Pa. 218, 202 A.2d 521 (1964).

79. *Id.* at 247, 202 A.2d at 536.

such plea he will receive life imprisonment or lenient treatment, or (b) where he and his lawyer had erroneously drawn the conclusion that he will not receive a penalty of death or a severe penalty, or (c) where his lawyer and the district attorney have agreed upon the exact crime which he has committed and the penalty to be imposed. . . ."[80] Two years later it was decided that a defendant was entitled to a post-conviction hearing on the voluntariness of his plea where his counsel had urged him to plead guilty, but never explained the consequences of such a plea.[81]

In 1970, the Pennsylvania Supreme Court laid to rest any ambiguity about whether or not a court could deny a pre-sentence motion for withdrawal. In *Commonwealth v. Culbreath*,[82] defendant pleaded guilty to murder. Before sentencing Culbreath petitioned for leave to withdraw his plea of guilty on the grounds that he was under a misapprehension as to the sentence which was to be imposed. Defendant pleaded not guilty at his arraignment, but before trial, defense counsel, the prosecutor and the judge all met in chambers to discuss the fate of Culbreath. He was later told by his counsel that if he pleaded guilty, the assistant district attorney would recommend that he receive a maximum sentence of two years and that "the probabilities" were good that the judge would follow it.[83] The judge did not accept the recommendation and sentenced him to from six to twelve years. The Supreme Court upheld the decision for much the same reasons as in *Kirkland.*

> We are convinced from the record that the defendant fully understood the nature of the crime with which he was charged and his rights, and the possible sentences which could be imposed and the consequences of his guilty plea, and that his sole reason for attempting to have it withdrawn is his disappointment in the length of sentence imposed.[84]

Justice Roberts dissented, expressing the federal philosophy that a defendant should be permitted to withdraw his plea of guilty before sentencing if a fair and just reason is given for withdrawal.[85]

It is submitted that Pennsylvania is leading its defendants down a dangerous road. Culbreath did what perhaps most people would do

---

80. *Id.* at 248.
81. Commonwealth v. Myers, 423 Pa. 1, 222 A.2d 918 (1966). *See also* Commonwealth v. Metz, 425 Pa. 188, 228 A.2d 229 (1967).
82. 439 Pa. 21, 264 A.2d 643 (1970).
83. *Id.* at 27, 264 A.2d at 645.
84. *Id.* at 28, 264 A.2d at 646.
85. *Id.* at 29, 264 A.2d at 647.

in his position. First, he was asked whether or not he desired to plead guilty to murder. He was told that the penalty for first degree murder was death or life imprisonment. The penalty for the more likely finding in his case, second degree murder, was imprisonment in solitary confinement for a term not to exceed twenty years. For manslaughter, the term can run from three to twelve years. On the advice of his counsel, and what he had seen transpire between his attorney, the prosecutor and the judge, defendant pleaded guilty to murder. He pleaded guilty not because he realized he had killed his victim with malice rather than in the heat of passion, but because he was taking the best possible alternative—a maximum of two years imprisonment. And yet the Supreme Court of Pennsylvania has stated that he made his decision voluntarily, and with no misapprehension. Would he have made this decision so "voluntarily" if he had known what the outcome was to be? The answer is obvious, but the court will not let him make his choice from hindsight. It is difficult to believe that this is the same court which in *Commonwealth v. Evans*[86] recognized the danger of a judge being present during the discussion of a plea bargain, whether he participates in the actual bargain or not. The conclusion of Justice Roberts aptly states the pitfalls of not only the *Culbreath* decision, but the entire process of plea bargaining.

> Appellant was merely the victim of an admitted plea bargain which he thought would bind the judge. Certainly it cannot matter that the judge, unbeknownst to appellant, was not aware of the plea bargain and was not in any way bound by the agreement. Such a misunderstanding can occur easily and we should not penalize appellant for it.[87]

Conclusion

It must again be stressed that plea bargaining is not a totally onerous procedure. It is an effective answer to relieving our crowded courts. The problems lie with the means to that end. It is this author's contention that the most formidable problem is the failure to recognize that dangers do exist. The courts must recognize that even though a trial judge may not actually participate in the bargaining process, his mere awareness of it may indicate to the defendant that he has acquiesced. This belief can remain despite any instructions to the contrary.

86. 434 Pa. 52, 252 A.2d 689 (1969).
87. Commonwealth v. Culbreath, 439 Pa. 21, 33-34, 264 A.2d 643, 649 (1970).

They must be cognizant of dangers such as the irreconcilable results and misuse to which plea bargaining is subject.

Most importantly, the courts must be honest with themselves in assessing the true impact of plea bargaining in the voluntariness and understanding of a guilty plea. As mentioned previously, the basic premise of plea bargaining is that the defendant is guilty. If it is said that the defendant is guilty because the trial judge has examined the evidence and come to that conclusion from his knowledge of life and the law, the decision he makes can be justified in the name of a more efficient judical system. Even though our notions of due process may be frustrated in the process, it might well be the price we must pay for a society of two hundred million people. At least the courts would be facing the real issue. But if it is said that the defendant is guilty because he has wisely and voluntarily chosen to plead that way, then the courts have closed their eyes to the realities of human nature. They have placed the judicial system upon a merry-go-round tempting all who dare, innocent and guilty alike, to grab for the brass ring.

JUDICIAL COMMENT ON GUILT OR INNOCENCE—A RIGHT WITHOUT A REASON

Howard P. Lucker

Traditionally, the constitutional right to a jury trial [1] in criminal cases has been viewed as a shield against government oppression.[2] While the concept remains inviolate, certain elements of it have been modified. Among these heretofore "untouchable" elements is the right of the trial judge to comment.[3] Two cases now pending in the Pennsylvania Supreme Court [4] involve the validity of one aspect of the right to comment; namely, the judge's right to express his opinion on the guilt or innocence of the defendant.

In the federal system, the right to comment empowers the judge to (1) state his recollections of the facts as they unfolded during the trial; (2) express his opinion on the credibility of the witnesses; and (3) to a limited extent,[5] voice his opinion on the defendant's guilt or innocence in any trial which he deems appropriate. Permissible comment in the above areas was limited to the extent that the judge must remark dispassionately, must not assume the role of an advocate, and must inform the jury that it alone is the final arbiter of fact and can disregard his judicial comments.[6]

In 1933, the Supreme Court in *United States v. Murdock*,[7] specifically qualified the judge's right to comment on guilt and innocence. Murdock was convicted under the Revenue Acts of 1926 and 1928 [8] for refusing

---

1. U.S. CONST. art. III; U.S. CONST. amend. VI.

2. Duncan v. Louisiana, 391 U.S. 145, 155 (1968); Singer v. United States, 380 U.S. 24, 31 (1965).

3. Patton v. United States, 281 U.S. 276, 288 (1930).

The remaining elements of a jury trial are a twelve man panel and a unanimous verdict.

The essentiality of these components has recently been questioned. Although most juries do consist of twelve members, in *Williams v. Florida*, 399 U.S. 78, 86 (1970), it was held that a twelve man panel is not a necessary ingredient of trial by jury. The *Williams'* court reasoned that the essential reason for a jury lies in the interposition between the accused and his accuser of the common sense judgment of a group of laymen. The proper performance of this role is obviously not conditioned upon the number of members composing the jury.

In the realm of criminal law, the requisite number of panel members has changed, while the unanimity concept has remained untrammeled. In *Hibdon v. United States*, 204 F.2d 834, 838 (6th Cir. 1953), the court viewed unanimity as an essential element of the right to a jury trial. Using the same approach as later articulated in *Williams*, it determined that protection against governmental oppression would be emasculated if the necessity of unanimity were altered.

4. Commonwealth v. Archambault, No. 469 (Pa. Jan. Term 1970). Commonwealth v. Motley, No. 659 (Pa. Jan. Term 1970).

5. United States v. Murdock, 290 U.S. 389 (1933).

6. Quercia v. United States, 289 U.S. 466, 469 (1933); Rudd v. United States, 173 F. 912 (8th Cir. 1909).

7. 290 U.S. 389 (1933).

8. Revenue Act of 1926, ch. 27, § 1114(a), 44 Stat. 116; Revenue Act of 1928, ch. 852, § 146(a), 45 Stat. 835. Under the Revenue Acts of 1926 and 1928, any individual making a payment to another must make an accurate report to the com-

TEMPLE LAW QUARTERLY, 1971, Vol. 45, pp. 73-80.

to supply information as required by the acts. The United States Supreme Court held that the trial judge erred in voicing his opinion on the defendant's guilt, and stated that:

> Although the power of the judge to express an opinion as to the guilt of the defendant exists, it should be exercised cautiously and *only in exceptional cases.* Such an expression of opinion was held not to warrant a reversal where upon the undisputed and admitted facts the defendant's voluntary conduct amounted to the commission of the crime defined by the statute. (Emphasis added.)[9]

While Murdock admitted to "voluntarily"[10] refusing to give information, he did not admit to acting "willfully".[11] The Court determined that since the element of willfulness was in dispute, *Murdock* was not an "exceptional case" and the trial judge should not have voiced his opinion on the guilt of the defendant.

Before we test the "exceptional case" theory, it is essential to discover the rationale underlying the right to comment generally. In *Billeci v. United States,*[12] the court of appeals articulated the following reason:

> The purpose of his comment is to aid, through his experience, the inexperienced laymen in the box in finding the truth in the *confusing conflicts of contradictory evidence.* (Emphasis added.)[13]

There is no difficulty in applying this rationale to the judge's statement of his recollection of the facts. Certainly, in view of the length and complexity of many trials, it is unquestionable that the judge can serve a valid guidance function by untangling the web of facts and refreshing the jury's mind.

However, the strength of the argument is not as obvious when applied to the judge's comment on credibility. In this area it can be contended that the judge is experienced in the art of cross-examination and can not be duped by a glib witness or a persuasive advocate. By permitting the judge to point out certain aspects of testimony, he may be able to help the jury avoid the shortcomings of naivety.

Notwithstanding the guidance function served by the judge's comments on credibility, it should be noted that a judge may unwittingly demonstrate his opinion on the guilt or innocence of the defendant in relat-

---

missioner has the power to examine all records and books of any individual to ascertain the correctness of all entries. The Acts also empower the Commissioner to administer oaths and take testimony. Any "willful" failure to supply required information is a violation of the Act.

9. 290 U.S. at 394.

10. A voluntary act is an intentional act exercised without "bad purpose". *Id.*

11. A willful act as used in criminal statutes means an intentional act done in "bad faith" or in complete disregard of its legality. *Id.*

12. 184 F.2d 394 (D.C. Cir. 1950).

13. *Id.* at 402.

ing such comment. If the judge accomplishes this in a case where the facts are in dispute, he has negated the effect of the "exceptional case". The unlawfulness of such circumvention is shown by the strain of cases stating that a judge may not do indirectly that which he has been forbidden to do directly.[14]

Although it can be argued that the judge serves a valid guidance function in his restatement of the facts and arguably in his remarks on credibility, it is difficult to rationalize his right to comment on guilt or innocence on this basis. Furthermore, in view of the essential reason for a jury trial, i.e., the interposition between the accused and his accuser of the common sense judgment of a group of laymen,[15] and the vast influence of the judge on the jury,[16] it seems that comment on guilt or innocence subtroverts the very essence of the right to a jury trial.

In addition to the guidance argument, academicians have attempted to rationalize the right to comment on other grounds:

> (1) [I]t saves time and expense in reducing the number of disagreements and the number of new trials granted for error by the trial judge; (2) it induces the judge to give closer attention to the incidents and developments of a trial until it is ended, and prevents

---

14. Buchanan v. United States, 244 F.2d 916 (6th Cir. 1957); Weare v. United States, 1 F.2d 617 (8th Cir. 1924).

15. Williams v. Florida, 399 U.S. 78 (1970).

16. Due to the nature of the jury system, particularly the secrecy surrounding the final decision, there is no empirical data to support the contention that the judge has vast influence over the jury. The Court in *Starr v. United States,* 153 U.S. 614, 626 (1894), was using common sense when it stated that: "It is obvious that under any system of jury trials the influence of the trial judge on the jury is necessarily and properly of great weight, and that his lightest word or intimation is received with deference, and may prove controlling."

However, there have been many studies in the field of social psychology which lend credence to that assumption. In one study, Lorge, *Prestige, Suggestion and Attitudes,* 7 J. SOCIAL PSYCHOLOGY 386-402 (1936), individuals were asked to read a statement by Thomas Jefferson and were later informed that the author was Lenin. It was demonstrated that their reaction changed. The second phase of the study was to have the individual indicate his degree of respect for the two men. They found that the change in reaction to the statements corresponded to the regard which the subject held the respective authors. The conclusions to this experiment were that the public figure is a stimulus to which the individual has attached a given response of a given strength; this represents the public figure's "prestige-value". The statement represents a second, weaker stimulus. Thus, when you attach a high-prestige source to the statement, the opinion changes positively and when you attach a low-prestige figure to the statement, the opinion changes negatively.

It is a small step from controlled studies, which indicate the opinions in a small group can be manipulated by a prestige figure, to the hypothesis that a judge can manipulate the jury. The role of a judge is obviously one of high prestige: the jury rises when the judge enters, the attorneys defer to the judge's rulings and, the judge is robed in black and radiates an aura of majesty.

In light of the judge's high prestige we must insure that his comments do not subtrovert the very purpose of his right to comment. His function is to guide the jury, not to "lead them by the nose". Norris v. Clinkscales, 47 S.C. 488, 510, 25 S.E. 797, 805 (1896). When the judge indicates his belief that a defendant is guilty he is no longer guiding. He has not said, here are the facts or here is a possibility to consider. Rather, he has "led" the jury by saying this is what I believe. *See also* Moore, *The Comparative Influence of Majority and Expert Opinion,* AM. J. PSYCHOLOGY 10, 16-20 (1921); M. SHERIF, THE PSYCHOLOGY OF SOCIAL NORMS (1925).

> him from becoming comparatively indifferent early in the trial after he has exhausted the human interest in the facts and grasped the main outlines of the legal situation . . . .[17]

These two reasons lack persuasiveness. There is no doubt that a judge who has the right to comment will not be overruled for commenting within the permissible limits. However, we can not substantiate the right to comment by arguing that if we deny the judge this power, he will exercise it without authority and thus be overruled. Certainly, by way of analogy, a judge who has the right to direct a guilty verdict would not be overruled for so doing.

While the first reason is self-serving, the second is transparent. A judge would not be inattentive in a proceeding simply because he is not permitted to comment. He always has a duty to rule on objections, admissibility of evidence and motions. In summary, none of the reasons given convincingly support the judge's right to comment on guilt or innocence.

It is noteworthy that the *Murdock* Court did not justify the classification of the "exceptional case" on any of the bases discussed above. The Court gave no reason. Rather, the Court may well have recognized the lack of validity of such comment. While it did not abrogate the right, it limited such comment to the "exceptional case". This classification is illogical. Assuming guidance is the only plausible reason behind any comment, the more disputed the facts, the greater the need for the judge's assistance in simplifying the problem. There can be no doubt that a just verdict is the desired goal of a jury trial. Based on the premise that the jury is not totally inept, there is no reason to believe that they would return the wrong verdict in the face of uncontroverted facts. Therefore, there does not appear to be any need for judicial assistance in the "exceptional case".

Notwithstanding the invalidity of the "exceptional case", it was a step in the right direction for this classification severely limits a prerogative which had existed without reason or restraint.[18] However, in view of the purpose for comment,[19] extension of the right to comment to guilt or innocence is unnecessary. Additionally, in light of the prohibition against directing a guilty verdict [20] and the undeniable influence of the judge on

---

17. Hon. M. A. Soper, C.A. 4th Cir., *The Charge to The Jury,* 1 F.R.D. 540, 544 (1940); *See also* Sunderland, *The Problem of Trying Issues,* 5 Tex. L.R. 18 (1927).

18. Quercia v. United States, 289 U.S. 466 (1933); Vicksburg & M.R.R. v. Putnam, 118 U.S. 545 (1886).

19. In *Billeci v. United States,* 184 F.2d 394, 402 (D.C. Cir. 1950) the court stated:

> The purpose of his comment is to aid, through his experience, the inexperienced laymen in the box in finding the truth in *the confusing conflicts of contradictory evidence.* (emphasis added).

20. Buchanan v. United States, 244 F.2d 916, 920 (6th Cir. 1957); Dillon v. United States, 279 F. 639, 643 (2d Cir. 1921).

the jury, *Murdock* should have held that this type of comment is never warranted. Notwithstanding the lack of justification for the "exceptional case", *Murdock* has never been questioned.[21]

A majority of the states have abrogated the right to comment entirely.[22] Generally, the states have rationalized their actions by stating conclusions rather than examining the purpose of comment as an element of a jury trial.

In the Washington Constitution the judge is not authorized to charge the jury as "to matters of fact, nor comment thereon, but shall declare the law." [23] The purpose of this section is to prevent the jury from being influenced by the judge's opinions.[24] Notwithstanding this clear, precise rule, the courts will not grant a new trial due to judicial comments unless they are "prejudicial".[25]

As Washington eliminates judicial comment by constitutional provision, so does Florida by way of statute.[26] Florida views the jury trial as two sided: The judge's sole function is to relate the applicable law to the jury and the jury has complete dominion as the fact finder.[27]

Illinois is another state that refused the judge the prerogative of comment. Under the state constitution, the guarantee to a jury trial encompasses the substantive rights included therein. As the right to comment is viewed as procedural rather than substantive, the denial of this right is not considered a denial of the guarantee to a jury trial.[28]

In 1879, California disallowed judicial comment.[29] However, in 1934 it amended its constitution, permitting the judge to "make such comment . . . as in [his] opinion is necessary for the proper determination of the cause." [30] This amendment was proposed to revitalize the role of the judge by entrusting him with sufficient power so that he would be more than a moderator.[31]

---

21. Davis v. United States, 227 F.2d 568, 570 (10th Cir. 1955). All cases that have considered *Murdock* have interpreted "exceptional cases" to be where the facts essential to guilt or innocence are virtually undisputed.

22. 9 J. Wigmore, Evidence §§ 2551, 2551(a) (3d ed. 1940); Johnson, *Province of the Judge in Jury Trials,* 12 J. Am. Jud. Soc'y 76, 77 (1928).

New Jersey is one of the remaining states that recognizes the broad power of comment. State v. Broxton, 49 N.J. 373, 230 A.2d 489 (1967); State v. Rudd, 49 N.J. 310, 230 A.2d 129 (1967); State v. Begyn, 34 N.J. 35, 167 A.2d 161 (1961).

Other states permitting some form of comment are: California, Connecticut, Maine, Maryland, Massachusetts, Michigan, New Hampshire, New Mexico, New York, Pennsylvania, Rhode Island, Utah, and Vermont. *See* Wright, *Instruction to Jury Without Comment,* Wash. U. L.Q. 177 (1954).

23. Wash. Const. art. IV, § 16.

24. State v. Mellis, 2 Wash. App. 859, 470 P.2d 558 (1970); State v. Crotts, 22 Wash. 245, 60 P. 403 (1900); State v. Surry, 23 Wash. 655, 63 P. 557 (1900).

25. State v. Williams, 68 Wash. 2d 946, 416 P.2d 350 (1966).

26. Florida Stat. Ann. § 918.10 (1945).

27. Simmons v. State, 160 Fla. 626, 36 So. 2d 207 (1948).

28. People v. Kelley, 347 Ill. 221, 179 N.E. 898 (1931).

29. Cal. Const. art. VI, § 17 (1879).

30. Cal. Const. art. VI, § 10.

31. People v. Ottley, 5 Cal. 2d 714, 56 P.2d 193 (1936).

Although Massachusetts has not abolished judicial comment, it has refused the judge the right to voice his opinion.[32] Under Massachusetts law, the judge may review the testimony and assist the jury by articulating guidelines.[33] However, he is restrained from stating his own judgment on conclusions upon matters of fact or credibility.

It is ironic that the states pass laws regulating the right to comment without analyzing its purpose. Those who advocate this prerogative do so under the guise of giving the judge more control over the trial.[34] Those who oppose the right do not question the underlying rationale, rather viscerally indicate that it is not an essential element[35] or that it invades the province of the jury.[36]

While the federal system has recognized the need for guidance through comment,[37] it has limited comment on guilt or innocence.[38] Pennsylvania is apparently aware of the need for guidance; however, its approach to judicial comment is less effective than the federal system's. In Pennsylvania, the judge has the right to comment on guilt or innocence in any case. Nevertheless, they are limited in the manner by which they articulate this right. In *Commonwealth v. Ott*,[39] the judge was reversed for charging the jury, "*that it's my duty* and it's my right to make a comment, under the law of Pennsylvania . . . ."[40] The court determined that the use of the word "duty" might be construed as a binding instruction on the jury. Following the *Ott* decision, a judge may comment on guilt with the single exception that he may not say that he has a "duty" to make such remarks. Aside from the court's handling of "duty", they reaffirmed the existing guidelines of permissible comment. Under this approach, a judge may comment on guilt or innocence,

> provided 1) that it is exercised fairly and temperately; 2) that there is reasonable ground for any statement the judge may make; and, 3) that he clearly leaves to the jury the right to decide all the facts and every question in the case, regardless of his opinion . . . .[41]

In *Commonwealth v. Young*,[42] the court carved out another exception from the judge's right to comment on guilt or innocence. The court held that it was reversible error for the trial judge to say:

---

32. MASS. GEN. LAWS ch. 231, § 81 (1932), "The courts shall not charge juries with respect to matters of fact, but they may state the testimony and the law."

33. Plummer v. Boston Elev., 198 Mass. 499, 84 N.E. 849 (1908).

34. *See* text accompanying note 31 *supra*.

35. *See* text accompanying note 28 *supra*.

36. *See* text accompanying notes 26, 27 *supra*.

37. Quercia v. United States, 289 U.S. 466 (1933); Vicksburg & C. R.R. Co. v. Putnam, 118 U.S. 545 (1886); Billici v. United States, 184 F.2d 394 (D.C. Cir. 1950).

38. United States v. Murdock, 290 U.S. 389 (1933).

39. 417 Pa. 269, 207 A.2d 874 (1965).

40. *Id.* at 271, 207 A.2d at 876.

41. *Id.* at 272, 207 A.2d at 876.

42. 418 Pa. 359, 211 A.2d 440 (1965).

> My comment, members of the jury, *and I have good reason for making it*, is that I think the defendant is guilty. (Emphasis added.)[43]

The reason behind this holding was that such a statement might lead the jury to believe that the judge is in possession of facts that they were not privy to. In light of *Ott* and *Young*, a judge may comment on guilt if he deletes the words "duty" and "reason" from his statement.

While it may appear that the Pennsylvania courts are attempting to stifle the exercise of this judicial prerogative, in *Commonwealth ex rel. Smith v. Rundle*,[44] the court reaffirmed the right of the judge to comment on guilt or innocence.

> In view of this record, particularly Smith's own trial testimony, we find no merit in the argument that the trial judge's comment, that a not guilty verdict would be a *miscarriage of justice*, was unwarranted or unfair. This is especially so, since it also appears that the jury received careful instructions that the determination of all factual questions was solely for its decision, and that a not guilty verdict could be returned. (Emphasis added.)[45]

Notwithstanding the *Smith* decision the court reversed a guilty verdict in 1968 due to the following charge:

> I'm not telling you what kind of verdict to bring in, but I'm telling you to stand up like men and women and do what you should do before your God to whom you will answer some day whether you answer to this court or not. You will answer to God some day for the way you conduct yourselves in this case. The chips will be down, and He will know everything you have done. You won't withhold one thing from Him.[46]

Although the judge never directly expressed his opinion on the defendant's guilt, the court determined that such language was coercive and may be interpreted as a binding instruction.

The Pennsylvania Courts are approaching the right to comment on guilt or innocence on a case by case method. Without explicitly saying that this right should be used in limited circumstances and defining those instances carefully, they find a different reason in each case as it is appealed. Such an approach lacks predictability.

The judge in Pennsylvania as in the federal system has the primary duty of clarifying issues and guiding juries.[47] He must be impartial and

---

43. *Id.* at 362, 211 A.2d at 441.

44. 423 Pa. 93, 223 A.2d 88 (1966).

45. *Id.* at 97, 223 A.2d at 90.

46. Commonwealth v. Holten, 432 Pa. 11, 18, 247 A.2d 228, 235 (1968). *See also* Commonwealth v. Wilmer, 434 Pa. 397, 254 A.2d 24 (1969).

47. Commonwealth v. Jordan, 407 Pa. 575, 587, 181 A.2d 310, 316 (1962).

not act as an advocate.[48] In light of the judge's function and the purpose of a jury trial, the Pennsylvania approach is weak. It is incumbent on the court to evaluate the purpose of the right to comment and to recognize the vast influence exerted by the judge.

After revaluating this area of judicial comment the court must then apply this new insight to the two cases which are now pending on this issue. In *Commonwealth v. Archambault,*[49] the defendant was convicted of first degree murder. In the course of the judge's charge, he indicated that he believed the defendant could not be found guilty of manslaughter or second degree murder, and then stated:

> I make comment again, but that comment can be totally disregarded by you, because it is entirely for you. I think it would be a miscarriage of justice to find this defendant not guilty. But again I say emphatically that it is entirely, completely, finally, unequivocally, for you, because yours is the power of a full, honest, impartial, intelligent consideration of the case to say what the verdict shall be.[50]

In *Commonwealth v. Motley,*[51] the defendant was convicted of first degree murder after the judge voiced a similar comment to that stated in *Archambault.* The Honorable judge stated:

> My comment is, Members of the Jury, that it would be a miscarriage of Justice, in my opinion, if you found this defendant not guilty.[52]

The court has several options: (1) it can follow the *Smith* case and affirm the convictions; (2) it can overrule *Smith* and say that the words "miscarriage of Justice" are too coercive; (3) it can take a half-way step and adopt the "exceptional case"; or (4) it can abolish the right of the judge to comment on guilt or innocence. In accordance with the above reasoning, the fourth choice is the only logical alternative.[53]

---

48. Commonwealth v. Bartell, 184 Pa. Super. 528, 546, 136 A.2d 166, 176 (1957); Commonwealth v. Garvey, 65 Pa. Super. 56, 62 (1916).

49. No. 469 (Pa. Jan. Term 1970).

50. No. 1710 (Phila. C.P., Sept., 1962); Notes of Testimony at 84.

51. No. 659 (Pa. Jan. Term 1970).

52. No. 142 (Phila. C.P., Dec., 1960); Notes of Testimony at 362.

53. Chapman v. California, 386 U.S. 18, 24 (1967), determined that federal courts will establish a harmless error rule for constitutional questions. They held "that before a federal constitutional error can be held harmless, the court must be able to declare a belief that it was harmless beyond a reasonable doubt." Certain constitutional rights are so basic, that any error relating to them is substantial. *See* Payne v. Arkansas, 356 U.S. 560 (1958) (coerced confessions); Gideon v. Wainwright, 372 U.S. 335 (1963) (right to counsel); Terry v. Ohio, 273 U.S. 510 (1927) (right to an impartial judge).

If the courts determined that comment on guilt or innocence would subtrovert the essence of a jury trial, any inadvertent statement relating to guilt would be a substantial error not subject to the harmless error rule. However, if it is determined that such comment does not infringe on the right to a jury trial, but is not necessary in the course of a trial, it would be subject to the normal harmless error rule.

THE JURY: A REFLECTION OF THE PREJUDICES OF THE COMMUNITY

Jennie Rhine

The Heterogeneous Culture

Bias in the Culture

The problem of selecting a "fair and impartial" jury recently received front page publicity in the San Francisco Bay Area during the trial of Huey P. Newton, a young black militant accused of murdering a white policeman.[1] Newton and his supporters charged that it was impossible for him to get a fair trial in the American judicial system. One objection was that the jury would be composed not of Newton's "peers" but of middle class whites, with racist attitudes, who would be predisposed to find him guilty. He explained that by a "jury of his peers" he meant not an exclusively black jury, but one consisting of people from and involved in his community, West Oakland, a lower class, primarily black, ghetto. People of similar economic status and language would be able to empathize with him, he felt, while middle and upper class whites would not.[2] Not one of the jury finally impaneled could be classified as a member of Newton's peer group.[3] This jury convicted Newton of voluntary manslaughter, a verdict which was virtually irreconcilable with the testimony.[4] It is felt the conviction was the result of an attitude on the part of the jurors that Newton should not get off scot-free, even though they had not been convinced of his guilt "beyond a reasonable doubt."

---

[1] People v. Newton, No. 41266 (Super. Ct., Alameda County, Cal., Sept. 27, 1968). Huey P. Newton is Minister of Defense of the Black Panther Party, a radical, black militant organization. In addition to murder, CAL. PEN. CODE § 187, he was also charged with assault with a deadly weapon, CAL. PEN. CODE § 245(b) (acquitted), and kidnapping, CAL. PEN. CODE § 207 (dropped).

[2] For a report of Newton's opinions as given at a press conference, see Boyle, *Notes on Jury Selection in the Huey P. Newton Trial*, THE PROGRESSIVE, Oct. 1968, at 29, 34.

[3] *Id.* at 34. Miss Boyle reports that the final jury, including alternates, consisted of one black (a loan officer in a bank), one person of Japanese ancestry, three with Spanish surnames (one a native of Cuba), a cosmetic saleswoman, a second banker, a machinist, two housewives, a bologna slicer, an engineer and property owner, and three employees of, respectively, a food packaging firm, a paper company, and an airline food caterer. *Id.*

Argument on a motion to quash the entire master panel and jury venire and the *voir dire* consumed the first three weeks of the trial. *Id.*

[4] *See, e.g.*, Good, *Verdict on Huey Newton: An Oversupply of Doubt*, NATION, Sept. 30, 1968, at 300.

HASTINGS LAW REVIEW, 1969, Vol. 20, pp. 1417-1445.

The bias present in a situation like Newton's can be contrasted with the common bias, most extreme in the South, in favor of a white man suspected of having committed a crime against a black person. Not infrequently, no jury will indict, much less convict, him.[5] In either case, the likelihood of justice going awry—the guilty going free or the innocent being convicted—is magnified because no jury selected by our present methods could possibly be called "impartial." The racist attitudes prevalent in white America today have been well documented.[6] It is not surprising that they also pervade the judicial system, including that "reflection of the conscience of the community," the jury.[7] Where jury deliberations have become known, overt prejudice toward blacks has been revealed.[8]

The existence of this bias places the black criminal defendant in a quandary. The chance of acquittal is generally twice as good before a jury as before a judge, and where juries *do* convict, they tend to convict on a lesser charge and sentence more lightly than a judge would.[9] Yet black people are more likely than whites to be convicted, and of a higher degree of crime;[10] if convicted, they also face more severe punishment.[11] On the other hand, black jurors, for reasons which should not need explanation, tend to favor the underdog.[12] This is not solely a racial phenomenon, but also a socio-economic one; juries of white collar workers (which would include few blacks) are preferred by prosecutors because they are more willing to convict.[13]

Cultural differences—ignorance of mores, language, life styles—compound the jury problem where defendants are not from the predominant socio-economic group, particularly where racial differences are present. One anthropologist tells of a recent homicide trial in which the defendant, the victim, and all witnesses except the police

---

5 L. MILLER, THE PETITIONERS: THE STORY OF THE SUPREME COURT OF THE UNITED STATES AND THE NEGRO 292-93 (1967).

6 *See, e.g.*, NATIONAL ADVISORY COMMISSION ON CIVIL DISORDERS REPORT (1968); G. MYRDAL, AN AMERICAN DILEMMA (2d ed. 1962).

7 Kuhn, *Jury Discrimination: The Next Phase*, 41 SO. CAL. L. REV. 235, 245 (1968) [hereinafter cited as Kuhn].

8 Broeder, *The Negro in Court*, 1965 DUKE L.J. 19, 21-24 [hereinafter cited as Broeder].

9 H. KALVEN & H. ZEISEL, THE AMERICAN JURY 58-61 (1966).

10 Broeder, *supra* note 8, at 23.

11 H. KALVEN & H. ZEISEL, THE AMERICAN JURY 210-11 (1966); G. MYRDAL, AN AMERICAN DILEMMA 550-54 (2d ed. 1962).

12 Broeder, *supra* note 8, at 29.

13 *Hearings on Miscellaneous Proposals Regarding the Civil Rights of Persons Within the Jurisdiction of the United States Before Subcomm. No. 5 of the House Comm. on the Judiciary*, 89th Cong., 2d Sess., ser. 16, at 1078 (1966) (testimony of Attorney General Katzenbach); Note, *The Congress, the Court and Jury Selection: A Critique of Titles I and II of the Civil Rights Act of 1966*, 52 VA. L. REV. 1069, 1095 (1966) [hereinafter cited as *The Congress, the Court and Jury Selection*].

were black ghetto residents.[14] Testimony brought out that before the homicide, the person who was killed had "put [the defendant] in the dozens."[15] Defense counsel's efforts to elicit clarification of this phrase were met with prosecution objections, which were sustained, that the witness was not an expert in semantics. As a result, neither judge nor jury learned that the death was a consequence of a "game" of verbal aggression and abusive namecalling, initiated by the deceased against the defendant.[16] In the same trial, when another witness was asked whether he had ever been convicted of a misdmeanor or a felony, he answered in the negative. When asked whether he had ever served time in a correctional institution, he replied, "No, sir, but I was a steward in the merchant marine for twenty years."[17] But when asked about specific convictions, he readily admitted them, and to having been imprisoned. Faced with questions in a vocabulary that was unintelligible to him, he had guessed (incorrectly) at the answers rather than reveal his ignorance of the words used. The jurors decided that the witnesses were either morons or liars, and the resulting verdict was a compromise out of confusion.[18] Other indications of cultural differences such as dress, demeanor, manner of speaking, and attitudes, as well as those of culture alone, also greatly influence jurors.[19]

The problem inherent in these differences is that while our society is culturally heterogeneous, with sharp differences among various groups, our legal system—including the jury system—functions as though we had a homogeneous culture—that of the dominant Anglo-Saxon middle class. The result is built-in prejudice against the culturally different.[20]

Representation on Juries

It has been said that the law cannot, as a practical matter, provide juries entirely free of prejudice, and that accordingly, "the defendant's hope and the law's faith have traditionally been that individual biases will somehow cancel each other out, if only the system of selection is fair and the jurors are free from overwhelming external influences."[21] It is the thesis of this note that we are incap-

---

14 Brief for D. Swett as Amicus Curiae on Defendant's Motion to Quash the Master Panel, People v. Newton, No. 41266 (Super. Ct., Alameda County, Cal., Sept. 27, 1968) (Built-in Biases in the American Legal System).

15 *Id.* at 5.

16 *Id.* at 4-5.

17 *Id.* at 6.

18 *Id.* at 5-6.

19 *Id.* at 12-13.

20 *Id.* at 4. Jurors themselves have occasionally indicated their awareness of this anomaly; where considering a case involving a black defendant, they have some times expressed a desire to have a black on the jury, or have used any black who perchance was a member, as an "expert" on black ghetto culture. *See* Broeder, *supra* note 8, at 30.

21 Kuhn, *supra* note 7, at 242.

able even of approaching this lesser goal of balancing the biases, at least in cases involving members of racial and cultural minorities (whether as victims or suspected perpetrators), unless and until our juries adequately represent those minorities. If the primary justification for the use of lay juries is that "they can reflect the conscience and mores of *the community* in applying punitive sanctions to individual cases,"[22] it should also be recognized that "the community" is an amalgam of heterogeneous "sub-communities." As will be shown, however, under present systems of jury selection, lay juries tend to represent only *one* "sub-community," the dominant white middle class.

If our juries "truly" represented, in rough proportion, the various racial, socio-economic and cultural groups within the geographic area from which they were drawn, they would more adequately represent the conscience of *the* community, an amalgam of all its parts. Biases of different groups would have, at most, only the proportional weight they carried within the community. Thus, although prejudices of the dominant class would not be cancelled out, they would at least be rendered less determinative of the verdict and perhaps less inflexible as well, simply because of the presence of minority group members on the same jury. Although a complete absence of biases may not be possible, a proportional representation of all biases is a practical possibility and would be preferable to the present overemphasis given the biases of the majority.

This note will discuss current methods of jury selection, emphasizing the selection of criminal juries in cases that have racial and/or socio-economic overtones, with a critical analysis of the steps commonly involved in such selection. Also given will be a synopsis of the current position of the law and the direction in which it is headed, and an analysis of the Jury Selection and Service Act of 1968.[23] Finally, some partial remedies will be suggested, aimed at accomplishing more proportional representation on our juries of the racial, cultural and socio-economic groups which exist in a given community.

The Selection Process

Since the method of selecting juries in the state courts is a matter of local law, usually left to the discretion of the local bench to work out within a very general statutory framework, and since there has not been until recently a uniform method of jury selection among the federal courts,[24] the systems used vary widely even within a single state. However, certain general steps are common to all. From

---

[22] *Id.* at 245 (emphasis added).

[23] 82 Stat. 53 (1968), *amending* 28 U.S.C. §§ 1861-69 (1964). The statute was passed on March 27, 1968 and became effective 270 days later.

[24] Until the passage of the Jury Selection and Service Act of 1968. *See* note 23 *supra*.

some source, a list of prospective jurors is drawn. These people are screened to weed out those who lack the "qualifications" required by local law, those who are "exempt," and those who are "excused." Panels of jurors are selected, generally by lot or some other chance method, from those who remain on the list. Finally, after *voir dire* examination and the exercise of "for cause" and "peremptory" challenges, jurors are selected out of the panel who will actually sit in judgment on the particular case.

The Population Pool

It should be apparent immediately that the initial determination of the pool of prospective jurors, the "population" from which the jury list will be drawn, is crucial in determining the nature of the jury that will finally be chosen. Depending upon the definition of "population," it is possible, and indeed most probable, that large groups or classes of people will be automatically excluded from jury service merely because they fail to fall within the definition. To illustrate, if prospective jurors are to be drawn from lists of registered voters, that determination eliminates all those not registered to vote. Obviously, any list of prospective jurors will not be representative of anything other than the "population" from which it is drawn. Thus the more nearly that "population" corresponds to the composition of the entire community, the more representative of that community the jury list will be.

"Key Man" System

The determination of the "population" from which prospective jurors will be drawn is almost universally entirely within the discretion of the local jury commissioners.[25] The method most widely used is the so-called "key man" system or one of its variations.[26] Under this system, the jury commissioner selects people from the community ("key men") to recommend others of their acquaintance for jury duty. Since people generally are acquainted primarily with others of similar interests, backgrounds, and socio-economic status, the "key men" will tend to recommend people like themselves. Unless they themselves are representative of all parts of the community, the prospective jurors they recommend will not be either. Since the same generality is likely to be true of the commissioner (that is, the "key men" he selects will tend to come from his own subculture), there is a great tendency towards uniformity of jurors and a con-

---

[25] *The Congress, The Court and Jury Selection, supra* note 13, at 1076. For a review of state statutes, see *id.* at 1072-76. This is no longer true for the federal courts, since the Jury Selection and Service Act of 1968 has become effective. See text accompanying note 158 *infra*.

[26] Lindquist, *An Analysis of Juror Selection Procedure in the United States District Courts*, 41 TEMPLE L.Q. 32, 33 (1967) [hereinafter cited as Lindquist].

sequent distorted reflection of the community.[27]

One common variation used either exclusively or primarily in a number of judicial districts, is the "key organization" system, where community organizations are requested to supply prospective jurors from their membership lists. Since over half the nation's adult population belongs to *no* voluntary organization, and there are economic, racial, educational and occupational correlations to the joining of organizations, this method is subject to the same criticism of distorted community representation.[28]

The "key man" method and its variations have been the subject of much criticism by legal writers as being productive of "blue ribbon" juries,[29] but generally have been upheld by the courts.[30] In one case, *Cassell v. Texas*,[31] the Supreme Court struck down a jury panel chosen by this system, but only because the jury commissioner admitted that no effort whatsoever had been made to find qualified people in the black community, which in this instance formed a significant portion of the population.[32] The system itself has been judicially condemned only by the Court of Appeals for the Fifth Circuit, and even there only for the federal courts of that circuit.[33]

Public List System

After the "key man" system, the second most common method of selecting potential jurors is by using public lists of one type or another—telephone directories, tax rolls, or voter registration lists.[34] The economic discrimination inherent in the first two types of public lists is obvious. Particularly in rural areas, but even in urban areas, poor people are less likely to have telephones. Similarly, tax rolls—especially if real property tax lists (the most common type of municipal taxation) are used—will exclude the poorest segment of the community.

The use of such economically discriminating sources has been held illegal only if some further element of discrimination which is

---

27 Kuhn, *supra* note 7, at 262.

28 Generally, those who are richer, more educated, employed as white collar workers or professional persons, and the white majority are more likely to belong to voluntary organizations. See Lindquist, *supra* note 26, at 35-36. Of course, the choice of organizations to serve as "sponsors" will also greatly affect the result.

29 *See, e.g., id.* at 37-47; Kuhn, *supra* note 7, at 260-64.

30 *See, e.g.*, Swain v. Alabama, 380 U.S. 202, 207-08 (1965); Billingsley v. Clayton, 359 F.2d 13 (5th Cir.), *cert. denied*, 385 U.S. 841 (1966); *cf.* Chance v. United States, 322 F.2d 201 (5th Cir. 1963), *cert. denied*, 379 U.S. 823 (1964); United States v. Hunt, 265 F. Supp. 178, 194-95 (W.D. Tex. 1967); United States v. Duke, 263 F. Supp. 828 (S.D. Ind. 1967).

31 339 U.S. 282 (1950).

32 *Id.* at 287-88.

33 Rabinowitz v. United States, 366 F.2d 34 (5th Cir. 1966).

34 Lindquist, *supra* note 26, at 34.

overtly based on race is involved. For example, in *Whitus v. Georgia*[35] the Supreme Court found that blacks had been systematically excluded from jury panels. The male population[36] of the county was 42.6 percent black, but only 27.1 percent of the taxpayers (from whom jurors were chosen) were black.[37] In spite of this disparity, the Court did not condemn the use of the tax lists. It merely held that the particular jury list involved was invalid because it was based in part on a previous list that had already been condemned by the Court, and because the race of the black taxpayer was noted on the lists.

The use of voter registration lists must be discussed in more detail; first, because the lists would appear to be nondiscriminatory in the northern and western states, and second, because their use for jury selection purposes has recently been given sanction by the Jury Selection and Service Act of 1968.[38] The use of such lists in the North has been upheld on the grounds that no "cognizable class," *i.e.*, a racial, economic, political or other identifiable group, was shown to have been excluded.[39] In the South, however, it has been recognized that voting lists which are themselves a product of discrimination may not be used.[40]

In 1964, of a voting age population throughout the nation of 114 million, only about 80 million were registered to vote.[41] Residence requirements are the most severe legal restriction upon registration, resulting in an estimated 8 million disenfranchised in 1960.[42] A large

---

[35] 385 U.S. 545 (1967).

[36] According to state law, women were qualified but not compelled to serve on juries; they were excused upon request. Whitus v. Georgia, 385 U.S. 545, 550 n.1 (1967), *citing* GA. CODE ANN. § 59-124 (1965).

[37] Out of 33 prospective grand jurors, three were black; one actually served on a grand jury of 19. Of 90 prospective trial jurors, seven were black; none actually served. Whitus v. Georgia, 385 U.S. 545, 550 (1967).

[38] See text accompanying notes 158, 163-64 *infra*.

[39] Gorin v. United States, 313 F.2d 641 (1st Cir. 1963); United States v. Greenberg, 200 F. Supp. 382 (S.D.N.Y. 1961); *cf.* United States v. Bowe, 360 F.2d 1, 7 (2d Cir. 1966) (validity conceded by appellants).

[40] United States *ex rel.* Goldsby v. Harpole, 263 F.2d 71, 78 (5th Cir. 1959); White v. Crook, 251 F. Supp. 401, 404-05 (N.D. Ala. 1966); Harper v. State, 251 Miss. 699, 171 So. 2d 129 (1965).

[41] Lindquist, *supra* note 26, at 47. According to the Gallup Poll, in the 1968 presidential election there were approximately 120 million people of voting age, of whom 72 million (60 percent) voted. By way of comparison, in 1964, 62 percent voted and in 1960, 63 percent voted. Projecting from polls, of the 48 million who did not vote in 1968, 4 million were ineligible because they were aliens or inmates of prisons and mental hospitals; 15 million were registered but were disinterested or did not like the candidates; 10 million could have registered but did not; 7 million were sick or disabled; 5 million were prevented from voting by residence requirements; 3 million were away from home; 3 million said they could not leave their jobs; 1 million failed to obtain absentee ballots. San Francisco Chronicle, Dec. 12, 1968, § T, at 9, cols. 1-2.

[42] Lindquist, *supra* note 26, at 48. In 1968, about 5 million persons were

proportion of these disenfranchised are from lower class cultural minorities, such as migrant farm workers or southern blacks who have recently immigrated to northern cities.[43] Extra-legal restrictions such as intimidation or apathy (which are also related to racial and/or socio-economic status) are largely responsible for the remaining failures to register.[44] "[I]n view of the fact that the lists exclude over 30 million people, a disproportionate number of whom are members of the lowest socio-economic strata of society,"[45] it is doubtful that voter registration lists, without supplementation, are capable of producing representative juries.[46]

The lower proportional voter registration among black people is not a peculiarly southern phenomenon. In the recent trial of Huey Newton, there was expert testimony to the effect that *all* recent studies of voting and voter registration, in the North as well as in the South, have shown that "poor persons and black persons and especially poor black persons are much less likely to register to vote . . . than are white persons or wealthy persons and especially white wealthy persons."[47] Evidence introduced in the trial concerning urban Alameda County, California, showed that while the county-wide registration rate of eligible voters was 82 percent, the registration rate in West Oakland, the predominately lower class black community in which the defendant was raised and lived, was 52.5 percent.[48] In

---

disenfranchised by this method. San Francisco Chronicle, Dec. 12, 1968 § T, at 9, cols. 1-2 (Gallup Poll). Residence of one year is required by 34 states and two years is required by Mississippi. Lindquist, *supra* note 26, at 48.

[43] *Cf.* Bureau of the Census, Voting and Registration in the Election of November 1966, at 3 (Population Reports, Series P-20, No. 174, 1968).

[44] *See* Lindquist, *supra* note 26, at 48. In the South only 28-39 percent of the eligible population is registered. *Id.*

[45] *Id.* at 49.

[46] *Id.*

[47] Record, vol. 1, at 260, People v. Newton, No. 41266 (Super. Ct., Alameda County, Cal., Sept. 27, 1968) (testimony of sociologist Sheldon Messenger).

[48] Exhibit in Support of Defendant's Motion to Quash the Master Panel, People v. Newton, No. 41266 (Super. Ct., Alameda County, Cal., Sept. 27, 1968). The following is a replica of the exhibit:

ANALYSIS OF CURRENT VOTING REGISTRATION IN ALAMEDA COUNTY

	1	2	3	4
Selected Areas of Alameda County	Percentage of Population Negro	Number of Persons 21 or Older	Number of Registered Voters	Rate of Registration (Col. 3/Col. 2)
Total: Alameda County	12.4	569,183	466,905	82.0
West Oakland[a]	71.3	20,680	10,862	52.5
South Oakland[b]	80.0	4,581	3,443	75.2
Montclair[a]	0.05	11,575	9,698	83.6
Hayward[b]	0.1	38,723	32,293	83.4
San Leandro[b]	0.02	39,957	32,995	82.6
Total Alameda County Negro Population			(approx.)	60.0

a. Figures for these areas are taken from Exhibit Y in People v. Craig, No.

contrast, suburban Montclair, with a black population of .05 percent, had the highest registration rate in the county with 83.6 percent.[49]

A sociologist testified in the Newton trial that the primary reason for the difference in registration rates was that

> low income people in general, and more specifically, the Negro population is more apathetic vis-a-vis the political process. It is a case of having less to gain from the political process. . . . [T]he political system . . . has been historically and remains contemporarily, although perhaps in a reduced amount, a relatively closed and foreign apparatus vis-a-vis the Negro population.[50]

He estimated that the overall registration rate of black adults was 60 percent.[51] Under circumstances like these, it is difficult to understand how one California court, while acknowledging that in its particular area the registration rate of blacks was 23 percent less than that of other racial groups, could state that the use of voter registration lists was not "*inherently*" discriminatory because qualifications and desire to register are factors "neutral to . . . national, racial or economic origin."[52] According to the court, the fact that blacks tend proportionally to register less than others was "*irrelevant*" to the defendant's right[53] to have a jury drawn from a fair cross section of the community.[54]

Notice

Regardless of the source from which the names of prospective jurors are drawn, the next step in the selection process is to send out notices to a given number,[55] asking them to complete forms establishing their "qualifications" and availability for jury service. Failure to follow up on the people who do not respond to the initial mailing is another cause of the disproportionate exclusion of the black and the poor. In the Huey Newton trial there was testimony that

---

41750 (Super. Ct., Alameda County, Cal., April 18, 1968).

b. Figures for these areas are derived from the collowing sources: Columns 1 and 2 are taken from BUREAU OF THE CENSUS, U.S. CENSUS OF HOUSING AND POPULATION: 1960 FINAL REPORT PUC (1)-137 (1966) (census track for San Francisco-Oakland). Column 3 is from the Registrar of Voters as of April 25, 1968.

49 Exhibit in Support of Defendant's Motion to Quash the Master Panel, People v. Newton, No. 41266 (Super. Ct., Alameda County, Cal., Sept. 27, 1968).

50 Record, vol. 1, at 88, People v. Newton, No. 41266 (Super. Ct., Alameda County, Cal., Sept. 27, 1968) (Assistant Professor Dizard, University of California, Berkeley).

51 *Id.* at 89.

52 People v. Tripp, No. CR 14790, at 2-3 (Super. Ct., San Diego County, Cal., Nov. 1, 1968).

53 For an analysis of this right see Fay v. New York, 332 U.S. 261, 299-300 (1947) (dissenting opinion); People v. White, 43 Cal. 2d 740, 278 P.2d 9 (1954).

54 People v. Tripp, No. CR 14790, at 3 (Super. Ct., San Diego County, Cal., Nov. 1, 1968).

55 Selected haphazardly, although perhaps weighted to balance the sexes.

the poor, and particularly the black poor, are more likely to move to an unknown address, to move out of the county, or to fail to respond for some other reasons than are whites or the relatively wealthy.[56] This was borne out by the evidence, which showed that of those to whom a notice of jury duty was sent, almost twice as many people from the ghetto community as compared to the white suburban community were eliminated because they failed to respond.[57]

The "Unqualified"

The third step in the selection process is the elimination of "unqualified" persons.[58] The required "qualifications" may be either objective (for example, being at least 21 and meeting residency requirements),[59] or subjective (for example, possessing "ordinary intelligence"[60] or being of "good character"). Either kind might be unduly discriminatory; the former by automatically excluding significant population segments, and the latter by giving the jury commissioner broad discretion, thereby permitting the exercise of any biases he may have.

The socio-economic discrimination inherent in objective residency requirements has already been noted in connection with the use of voter registration lists.[61] Another common type of objective disqualification is one against people with prior felony convictions,[62] although as Lawrence Speiser of the American Civil Liberties Union has pointed out, many times the people on trial are "the failures, the repeated failures, and . . . it would be desirable to have individuals [on the jury who, also being 'failures,'] perhaps would have a better understanding of the pressures, the problems . . . [of ghetto] situations. . . ."[63]

A third common criterion is one of minimum economic status. In New York, for example, a prospective juror must own at least two hundred and fifty dollars of personal property.[64] The discrimination here is apparent.

---

56 Record, vol. 1, at 256-57, People v. Newton, No. 41266 (Super. Ct., Alameda County, Cal., Sept. 27, 1968).

57 *Id.* at 257.

58 Drawing up a list of prospective jurors and eliminating the "unqualified" may be combined in one step, as where the key man system is such that those who make the recommendations select only "qualified" people.

59 *See, e.g.*, CAL. CODE CIV. PROC. § 198.

60 CAL. CODE CIV. PROC. § 198.

61 See text accompanying note 33 *supra*.

62 *See, e.g.*, CAL. CODE CIV. PROC. § 199(2).

63 *Hearings on S. 3296, Amendment 561 to S. 3296, S. 1497, S. 1654, S. 2845, S. 2846, S. 2923 and S. 3170 Before the Subcomm. on Constitutional Rights of the Senate Comm. on the Judiciary*, 89th Cong., 2d Sess., at 1132-33 (1966).

64 N.Y. JUDICIARY LAW § 504(3) (McKinney 1964); *see* Fay v. New York, 332 U.S. 261 (1947) (similar statute upheld). Economic status is frequently a nonstatutory qualification, as where tax rolls are used as the source of prospective jurors. See text accompanying notes 34-37 *supra*.

The use of subjective qualifications was considered by the Supreme Court in *Fay v. New York*.[65] In that case the so-called "blue ribbon" jury was upheld because the application of subjective standards—being intelligent, well-informed and literate in English—did not, according to the Court, result in the intentional exclusion of a recognizable class.[66] The application of subjective standards like "intelligence," "judgment," and "character" invariably will be discriminatory to the degree that the jury commissioner's or the "key man's" conception of those qualities is determined by his own educational, moral and socio-economic status. Moreover, the belief is widespread that the above listed qualities are rare among black people, not only because of less favorable educational and environmental influences, but also because of inherent shortcomings.[67] Additionally, subjective qualifications are sometimes given a veneer of nondiscriminatory application, as in the use of "objective" tests to measure "ordinary intelligence." Such a test was the reason for a recent dismissal of a jury panel in Alameda County because the test in question measured middle-class mores and vocabulary rather than intelligence.[68] The failure rate on the test was 14.5 percent in a white suburban community and 81.5 percent in a predominately black, lower class community.[69] The court refused to believe that "81.5% *of the registered voters* in a large section of Oakland are below the level of 'ordinary intelligence.' "[70]

The "Exempt" and the "Excused"

Some people are *exempt* from liability for jury duty by statute, usually because of their occupation.[71] Others are *excused*, generally

---

65 332 U.S. 261 (1947).

66 *Id.* at 290-92.

67 Kuhn, *supra* note 7, at 268.

68 People v. Craig, No. 41750 (Super. Ct., Alameda County, Cal., April 18, 1968). The court also considered the question whether the limitation of the jury panel to registered voters was itself too narrow, but decided that the percentage of adults otherwise qualified for jury service who failed to register in Alameda County "is probably small . . . since intensive voter registration drives take place before each state and national election and no group is discouraged from registering or voting." *Id.* at 8. However, no evidence on the issue was before the court. Defendant's Motion to Quash the Master Panel 8, People v. Newton, No. 41266 (Super. Ct., Alameda County, Cal., Sept. 27, 1968).

69 People v. Craig, No. 41750, at 5 (Super. Ct., Alameda County, Cal., April 18, 1968).

70 *Id.* at 7 (emphasis in the original).

71 *See, e.g.*, CAL. CODE CIV. PROC. § 200, which exempts, among others: Holders of public office; members of the Armed Forces while on active duty; teachers, physicians and dentists; telegraph and telephone company employees; attorneys, their clerks and secretaries; ministers; and persons who have recently performed jury duty. An exemption must be claimed by the person entitled to it. *See, e.g.*, CAL. CODE CIV. PROC. § 202.

on the basis of economic or physical hardship.[72] Usually the jury commissioner has the discretionary power to grant excuses, although he may be subject to judically determined procedures or rules.[73] Since the usual excuse is for financial hardship, the exercise of the commissioner's discretion commonly results in the exclusion of a disproportionate number of poor people, and therefore of blacks and other racial minorities.[74] The practice of systematically excusing *all* daily wage earners has been prohibited in the federal courts,[75] and the prohibition was recently extended by the Fifth Circuit to the state courts.[76] However, such decisions have curtailed the discriminatory effects of the discretion to grant excuses only in one flagrant form. The courts—while regretting that stipends for jury service are insufficient—have generally exercised little control over standards used to determine hardship, and have accepted unquestioningly the resultant economic and therefore, generally racial, discrimination.[77]

The Voir Dire

From the resulting list of qualified jurors (those from the original notified "population" not disqualified, exempt, or excused), some

---

[72] *See, e.g.*, CAL. CODE CIV. PROC. § 201.

[73] *See, e.g.*, CAL. CODE CIV. PROC. § 201(a). Judicial standards established in Alameda County permit hardship excuses for: Wage earners who are not paid while on jury duty and who have more than two children and a spouse who does not work; unemployed women with small children and no child care; and the operators of small businesses. Record, vol. 1, at 25-27, People v. Newton, No. 41266 (Super. Ct., Alameda County, Cal., Sept. 27, 1968). The court itself, rather than the commissioner, will grant excuses under other circumstances.

[74] In People v. Tripp, No. CR 14790 (Super. Ct., San Diego County, Cal., Nov. 1, 1968), the court granted defendant's motion to quash the petit jury panel. The court found that the commissioner departed from the statutory scheme in granting hardship excuses "for slight or trivial causes." *Id.* at 5, *citing* CAL. CODE CIV. PROC. § 201. This resulted in the use of standards that were "objectionably vague and subconscious," which effectively eliminated several large classes in the community, principally the unemployed, the impoverished, and the blue collar worker. People v. Tripp, *supra* at 5. The court also found that a prima facie case of discrimination had been established by showing that blacks comprised five per cent of the registered voters but less than one per cent of the jury panel; the presumption of discrimination was not overcome by the evidence, which showed that the disparity was related to the departure from the statutory standards governing economic hardship of jurors. *Id.* at 6.

[75] Thiel v. Southern Pac. Co., 328 U.S. 217 (1946). The Supreme Court based its decision on its supervisory power, but said that the exclusion "cannot be justified by federal or state law." *Id.* at 222.

[76] Labat v. Bennett, 365 F.2d 698 (5th Cir. 1966), *cert. denied,* 386 U.S. 991 (1967). See further discussion of case in text accompanying notes 134-39 *infra.*

[77] *See, e.g.*, United States v. Leonetti, 291 F. Supp. 461, 474-76 (S.D.N.Y. 1968). *But see* People v. Tripp, No. CR 14790 (Super. Ct., San Diego County, Cal., Nov. 1, 1968).

number is summoned for service on a particular panel. Prospective jurors are then subjected to a voir dire examination, which is intended to eliminate from the jury any who have preconceptions which will affect or prevent an unbiased judgment of the particular facts of the case. During the voir dire a prospective juror may be challenged by the court or by counsel, and thereby excused.[78] Challenges for cause may be made on the grounds either of implied bias—where an inference of bias is drawn from the existence of a relationship or other connection between the juror and an element of the case such as a party—or of actual bias—where the juror admits to a state of mind which would prevent him from being impartial.[79] The fact that the prospective juror admits to prejudice or bias is not necessarily sufficient to sustain a challenge for cause: If he asserts convincingly that he can overcome his feelings and judge the case with an open mind, the challenge is not allowed.[80]

The use of challenges for cause is hopelessly incapable of protecting the culturally or racially different criminal defendant from the racial prejudices of the jurors, the bulk of whom are drawn from the dominant white middle class. At the heart of the problem is the virtual impossibility of getting people to state their biases in the public voir dire. Most are reluctant to admit prejudice in the presence of strangers;[81] others are not consciously aware of their racist attitudes, or underestimate the impact of them on their ability to be objective.[82] The fact that in our society most if not all white people either consciously or unconsciously have attitudes of superiority toward other racial groups[83] has led one authority to state that the only way to eliminate white racism from a criminal case involving racial issues would be to have a jury of only black people, "a jury that would [in] the sociological sense . . . be a jury of the peers of the defendant."[84]

Peremptory challenges[85] are equally incapable of eliminating jurors with racist attitudes. While challenges for cause, used to excuse the rare juror who confesses to unalterable prejudice, are unlimited in number, the number of peremptory challenges which might be

---

78 Schuck, *Selection of a Jury*, in CALIFORNIA CIVIL PROCEDURE DURING TRIAL 93, 113 (Cal. Cont. Educ. Bar ed. 1960).

79 Title, *Voir Dire Examination of Jurors in Criminal Cases*, 43 CAL. ST. B.J. 70, 71-74 (1968).

80 *Id.* at 81.

81 Record, vol. 1, at 223, People v. Newton, No. 41266 (Super. Ct., Alameda County, Cal., Sept. 27, 1968).

82 Kuhn, *supra* note 7, at 243-44.

83 Record, vol. 1, at 283, People v. Newton, No. 41266 (Super. Ct., Alameda County, Cal., Sept. 27, 1968). *See generally* NATIONAL ADVISORY COMMISSION ON CIVIL DISORDERS REPORT (1968).

84 Record, vol. 1, at 285, People v. Newton, No. 41266 (Super. Ct., Alameda County, Cal., Sept. 27, 1968).

85 Some system of peremptory challenges is common to almost all jurisdictions.

used to eliminate those only suspected of racism is limited.[86] And because of the pervasiveness of racial prejudice, the excused juror is more than likely to be replaced by another with similar racial attitudes. However, where only a few minority members are on the jury panel, the peremptory challenge *is* an effective tool for eliminating *them*. It thus becomes an efficient device for the preservation of all-white juries.[87]

The use of peremptory challenges in this way by the prosecution has been the subject of many appeals,[88] only one of which has reached the United States Supreme Court. In *Swain v. Alabama*,[89] defense counsel showed that in the jurisdictional district no black person had survived the exercise of peremptory challenges over a fifteen year period, although blacks comprised 26 percent of the population and 10 to 15 percent of the jury panels. In a six to three decision, the Court held that the petitioner had failed to sustain the burden of proving that blacks were systematically excluded through the use of the challenges. Although a prima facie showing of discrimination would have been made had the discrepancy between blacks in the population and on the jury panels been sufficient,[90] such a prima facie rule of exclusion was not applicable to the peremptory

---

86 Where racial prejudice is "acceptable" to the community, defense counsel may do his client more harm than good by challenging an overtly biased venireman, even though he might be replaced by one less biased. Kuhn, *supra* note 7, at 244.

87 The manner in which blacks are totally eliminated from final juries because they constitute such a small percentage of the panels, even though the community has a large black population, has been demonstrated in many cases. *See* Swain v. Alabama, 380 U.S. 202 (1965); Watkins v. State, 199 Ga. 81, 33 S.E.2d 325 (1945); State v. Barksdale, 247 La. 198, 170 So. 2d 374 (1964), *cert.* denied, 382 U.S. 921 (1965).

88 *See, e.g.*, Swain v. Alabama, 380 U.S. 202 (1965); Watkins v. State, 199 Ga. 81, 33 S.E.2d 325 (1945); State v. Barksdale, 247 La. 198, 170 So. 2d 374 (1964), *cert. denied*, 382 U.S. 921 (1965).

89 380 U.S. 202 (1965). For criticism of the case, see L. MILLER, THE PETITIONERS: THE STORY OF THE SUPREME COURT OF THE UNITED STATES AND THE NEGRO 291-92 (1967); Kuhn, *supra* note 7, at 283-87; Note, *Peremptory Challenge—Systematic Exclusion of Prospective Jurors on the Basis of Race*, 39 MISS. L.J. 157 (1967); Comment, *Swain v. Alabama: A Constitutional Blueprint for the Perpetuation of the All-White Jury*, 52 VA. L. REV. 1157 (1966) [hereinafter cited as Comment, *Swain v. Alabama*]; 75 YALE L.J. 322 (1965).

90 The Court found that blacks were underrepresented by ten percent, an insufficient disparity for a prima facie case. 380 U.S. at 208-09. The deceptiveness of the Court's finding is apparent: the ten percent figure was apparently arrived at by subtracting ten to fifteen percent from twenty-six percent; but black representation on jury panels was in fact about fifty percent less than their proportion in the population (10-15 percent on panel/26 percent of population = ½ = 50 percent). See Finkelstein, *The Application of Statistical Decision Theory to the Jury Discrimination Cases*, 80 HARV. L. REV. 338, 346 & n.34 (1966); Kuhn, *supra* note 7, at 252. Criticism of the Supreme Court's mathematics is implied in Rabinowitz v. United States, 366 F.2d 34, 56 n.55 (5th Cir. 1966).

challenge procedure.[91] Rather, in order to satisfy the state action requirement of the equal protection clause, the defense would be required to show "when, why and under what circumstances"[92] the prosecution had removed blacks in the past.[93] A complementary ruling was that with respect to peremptory challenge cases, as with discriminatory selection of jury panels, equal protection would not apply to a particular case but only to a course of conduct over a period of time.[94] In short, *Swain* says that peremptory challenges are not subject to judicial scrutiny, and their use against those suspected of sympathy with an adverse party is common, legitimate, and beyond the reach of the equal protection clause in any given case.[95]

The impact of *Swain* is to isolate effectively from judicial review a device susceptible of extraordinarily efficient use, to perpetuate a totally white jury system in the South, and to prevent racially balanced juries in the North in cases in which race is an issue.[96] The basic supposition of the Court seems to be that the removal from jury panels of blacks who might possibly be sympathetic to a black defendant will result in their being replaced by jurors more probably impartial, albeit white.[97] The fallacy here is that, as previously noted, an all white jury is not neutral towards a black defendant, but hostile —particularly if the victim of the alleged crime is white.[98]

The Court's naiveté about racial attitudes also reveals itself in the requirement that the prosecution alone be shown to have been responsible for the systematic exclusion of blacks through the exercise of peremptory challenges. This burden is not only virtually insuperable, but also unjustifiable.[99] The requirement ignores the pervasiveness of racism throughout the legal system, for which state action is responsible since the state establishes and operates the legal system.[100]

A further result of *Swain* is that the use of peremptory challenges is given greater protection than the constitutional prohibition of discrimination.[101] Yet there is no constitutional right to peremptory challenges.[102] Where a constitutional claim conflicts with a nonconstitutional claim, the latter must yield.[103] Additionally, the

---

[91] Swain v. Alabama, 380 U.S. 202, 227 (1965).

[92] *Id.* at 226.

[93] *Id.*

[94] *Id.* at 221-22.

[95] Kuhn, *supra* note 7, at 285.

[96] *See* Comment, *Swain v. Alabama, supra* note 89, at 1174-75.

[97] *See* Kuhn, *supra* note 7, at 286-87.

[98] See text accompanying notes 1-20 *supra.*

[99] *See* Comment, *Swain v. Alabama, supra* note 89, at 1161-63.

[100] *See* Kuhn, *supra* note 7, at 296.

[101] *Accord,* Hall v. United States, 168 F.2d 161 (D.C. Cir.), *cert. denied,* 334 U.S. 853 (1948).

[102] Stilson v. United States, 250 U.S. 583, 586 (1919).

[103] Swain v. Alabama, 380 U.S. 202, 244 (1965) (dissenting opinion).

peremptory challenge appears to have developed as a protection for the defendant,[104] and therefore should not be available to assist the prosecution at the expense of other rights of the defendant.

The basis of the peremptory challenge is not that the challenge is without reason, but that the reason need not be made known.[105] This rationale could be preserved for most cases, yet yield to constitutional protection from discrimination, if the use of the challenge could be questioned when it gave rise to a reasonable inference of discrimination.[106] If challenges were consistently exercised against racial minorities in a case with no racial implications, their use presumably would not meet the test that racial classification must be shown to be "necessary to the accomplishment of some permissible state objective."[107] It would therefore be a denial of equal protection per se. If, on the other hand, race was relevant to the case being tried, consistent challenges of minority members would be subject to review, though not impermissible per se.

Challenges on strictly racial grounds would have to be distinguished from those for other, permissible reasons. A black jury member could still be challenged, for example, because he had the same kind of job as the defendant. However, a challenge solely on racial grounds would have the effect of replacing a possibly friendly juror with a probably hostile one. "It cannot be consistent with equal protection and with the principles of fair jury selection to permit the state to eliminate one element in the population deemed friendly to the defense in favor of another presumably hostile in precisely those cases where this disadvantages members of the minority race."[108]

This approach would require a change of the present rule, which does not allow the defendant to question the composition of his own particular jury, apart from past juries. But it is clear that even the prima facie rule of exclusion, if it were applied to the use of peremptory challenges, would be inadequate protection. The prosecution could easily avoid the rebuttable presumption of discrimination shown by the absence of black jurors over a period of time by keeping a few "safe" "Uncle Toms"[109] on the juries or by allowing blacks to sit unchallenged where race was irrelevant. The only effective safeguard against such "tokenism" is to allow the defendant

---

[104] *See* Comment, *Swain v. Alabama, supra* note 89, at 1170-73. *But cf.* Swain v. Alabama, 380 U.S. 202, 219-20 (1965).

[105] Note, *Peremptory Challenge—Systematic Exclusion of Prospective Jurors on the Basis of Race*, 39 MISS. L.J. 157, 160 (1967).

[106] *See* Kuhn, *supra* note 7, at 294; *cf.* Hall v. United States, 168 F.2d 161 (D.C. Cir.), *cert. denied*, 334 U.S. 853 (1948).

[107] Loving v. Virginia, 388 U.S. 1, 11 (1967).

[108] Kuhn, *supra* note 7, at 291.

[109] So-called by the Attorney General of Alabama, speaking of the blacks who helped acquit Eugene Thomas of the murder of Viola Liuzzo (a white civil rights worker killed in the South). *Id.* at 271.

to challenge the use of peremptories in his own case.[110]

The voir dire, with its peremptory and for cause challenges, is the last step in selecting the jury that will be impanelled to decide a particular case. As has been seen, the usual process begins with the definition of the population from which all prospective jurors will come. A group selected from that "population" is notified of possible jury service, and those who respond are screened to eliminate the "unqualified." Qualified jurors may claim an exemption or be excused either before or after being drawn to sit on the panel. This panel then will be subjected to the voir dire. Each step of the process is fraught with possibilities for discriminating, intentionally and unintentionally, against the less educated, the less fortunate, the less wealthy portions of the population—with their disproportionate numbers of racial minorities. The result is that few, if any, of our juries even approach being representative of the communities from which they are drawn.[111]

The Law—Its Status and Trends

The Case Law

Now that the common methods of jury selection have been analyzed, the current status of the law and its discernible trends can be further explored. Since juries in state courts are a matter of state law and a study of each state is beyond the scope of this note, discussion of legal controls on these juries will be confined to federal limitations on the exercise of the state's power. Juries in the federal system are subject to the supervisory powers of the federal appellate courts, as well as to constitutional and congressional control. Following a discussion of case law, the most recent congressional pronouncement, the Jury Selection and Service Act of 1968, will be analyzed.

The "Systematic Exclusion" Rule

The United States Supreme Court first enunciated a constitutional right to jury selection free from racial discrimination in 1879, when it held that the jury provisions of the Civil Rights Act of 1875 were constitutional under the 13th and 14th amendments.[112] From

---

110 *See id.* at 303; Comment, *Swain v. Alabama, supra* note 89, at 1173-74.

111 The reader is probably well aware that certain types of discriminatory jury selection are being ignored in this note, such as the discrimination which eliminates a disproportionate number of young people. They are outside the scope of this paper; there is no intent to slight their existence or importance.

112 *Ex parte* Virginia, 100 U.S. 339 (1879); Strauder v. West Virginia, 100 U.S. 303 (1879). The Civil Rights Act of 1875 provided, and still provides, that no otherwise qualified citizen "shall be disqualified for service as grand

this beginning developed the rule that the "systematic exclusion" of racial minorities from state jury panels was a denial of equal protection of the laws.[113] As a corollary, the Supreme Court developed the so-called "prima facie" rule: Where there is a *significant* disparity between the proportion of a racial group *chosen for jury duty* and the proportion of that group in the *eligible* population, the state has the burden of rebutting the presumption that racial discrimination is the cause.[114] As has been noted, the Court declined to extend the prima facie rule to the use of peremptory challenges.[115] The effect is that so long as the proportion of blacks (or other racial groups) on the panel is not too far out of line with their numbers on the lists from which jurors are to be chosen,[116] it makes no difference that none have in fact served on juries.

The theory underlying the systematic exclusion rule has been that when a traditionally oppressed group is arbitrarily excluded from serving on juries, the probability of prejudice to a defendant belonging to that group is so great as to make a showing of actual prejudice unnecessary.[117] The rule therefore clearly applies where the defendant and the excluded jurors all belong to a class traditionally subject to prejudice and oppression.[118] This has led some courts to adopt the so-called "same class" rule, requiring a showing of actual prejudice where the defendant does not belong to an oppressed class himself, or where the excluded class is different from his own.[119] Other courts have rejected the rule.[120] The Supreme

---

or petit juror" in any state or federal court because of "race, color, or previous condition of servitude." 18 U.S.C. § 243 (1964).

113 *E.g.*, Swain v. Alabama, 380 U.S. 202 (1965); Norris v. Alabama, 294 U.S. 587 (1935).

114 *See, e.g.*, Swain v. Alabama, 380 U.S. 202 (1965); Norris v. Alabama, 294 U.S. 587 (1935); *cf.* Hernandez v. Texas, 347 U.S. 475 (1954); Patton v. Mississippi, 332 U.S. 463 (1947); Smith v. Texas, 311 U.S. 128 (1940); Neal v. Delaware, 103 U.S. 370 (1880).

What constitutes a "significant" disparity has not been made clear, although in most cases where the Supreme Court has found such a disparity the exclusion of the racial group has been virtually total. *See* Kuhn, *supra* note 7, at 252-54. So far, the Supreme Court has not held unconstitutional any given method of defining the "eligible population," so long as it does not expressly exclude members of a particular racial group. See text accompanying notes 25-54 *supra.*

115 Swain v. Alabama, 380 U.S. 202 (1965).

116 See note 114 *supra.*

117 Note, *Jury Challenges, Capital Punishment, and Labat v. Bennett: A Reconciliation*, 1968 Duke L.J. 283, 300-01.

118 *See* Hernandez v. Texas, 347 U.S. 475, 477-78 (1954).

119 *The Congress, the Court and Jury Selection, supra* note 13, at 1097-98.

120 *E.g.*, Allen v. State, 110 Ga. App. 56, 137 S.E.2d 711 (1964) (white civil rights worker allowed to challenge exclusion of blacks); State v. Lowry, 263 N.C. 536, 139 S.E.2d 870 (1965) (white civil rights worker); *cf.* State v. Madison, 240 Md. 265, 213 A.2d 880 (1965) (defendant who believed in God

Court has never applied it,[121] but neither has the Court applied the systematic exclusion rule in favor of a person who did not belong to the excluded class.[122]

The "Cross Section" Rule

The systematic exclusion rule and its corollaries, based on the equal protection clause, until recently have been the major limitations imposed on state jury selection methods by federal law.[123] In the federal court system, however, the rule has prevailed that a jury must be drawn from a group which represents a "cross section" of the community:

> [T]here is a constitutional right to a jury drawn from a group which represents a cross-section of the community. And a cross-section of the community includes persons with varying degrees of training and intelligence and with varying economic and social positions. Under our Constitution, the jury is not to be made the representative of the most intelligent, the most wealthy or the most successful, nor of the least intelligent, the least wealthy, or the least successful. It is a democratic institution, representative of all qualified classes of people.[124]

The "cross section" rule was first applied by the Supreme Court

---

allowed to challenge exclusion of jurors who refused to state a belief in God).

[121] In Fay v. New York, 332 U.S. 261, 287 (1947), the Court discussed the rule without apparent disapproval.

[122] For criticism of the same-class rule, see Note, *Jury Challenges, Capital Punishment, and Labat v. Bennett: A Reconciliation*, 1968 DUKE L.J. 283, 300-01; Comment, *The Defendant's Challenge to a Racial Criterion in Jury Selection: A Study in Standing, Due Process and Equal Protection*, 74 YALE L.J. 919, 920-23 (1965).

The question has been asked in reverse: May there be systematic *inclusion* of minority groups? The Supreme Court has not ruled on the issue, having avoided it in both Akins v. Texas, 325 U.S. 398 (1945), and Cassel v. Texas, 339 U.S. 282 (1950). The fifth circuit held that systematic inclusion was constitutional in Brooks v. Beto, 366 F.2d 1 (5th Cir. 1966), *cert. denied*, 386 U.S. 975 (1967), *overruling* Collins v. Walker, 329 F.2d 100 (5th Cir. 1963), *aff'd on rehearing*, 335 F.2d 417 (5th Cir.), *cert. denied*, 379 U.S. 901 (1964). The court said in *Brooks* that the constitutional requirement that a jury represent a cross section of the community compelled the consideration of race, although this could not be permitted as a means of discrimination or to secure proportional representation or a predetermined or fixed limitation. 366 F.2d at 24.

Brooks is actually a due process case, which belongs with the discussion which follows. See text accompanying notes 146-49 *infra*. Whether the limitations it puts on the consideration of race are necessary, desirable, or even capable of being applied, should be considered.

[123] The due process clause of the Fourteenth amendment forbade only trial by a jury that was not impartial. Note, *Jury Challenges, Capital Punishment, and Labat v. Bennett: A Reconciliation*, 1968 DUKE L.J. 283, 299-300, *citing Moore v. Dempsey*, 261 U.S. 86 (1923).

[124] Fay v. New York, 332 U.S. 261, 299-300 (1947) (dissenting opinion).

in *Glasser v. United States*,[125] and further developed in *Thiel v. Southern Pacific Company*,[126] a 1946 case which held that the systematic exclusion of all daily wage earners from federal juries was unlawful. By imposing this rule on federal courts alone, the Supreme Court has treated racial and socio-economic discrimination as separate phenomena, requiring that federal courts be free of both while the state courts need rid themselves of only the most overt kind of racial discrimination. Thus, while the requirement that juries represent a cross section of the community has been ostensibly applied to *racial* exclusion in state courts,[127] the Supreme Court declined to apply it in a *socio-economic* context to a state "blue ribbon" jury in *Fay v. New York*.[128] The Court in actuality has applied only the systematic exclusion rule, a basically different concept, to the states, and even then only in a racial context.[129] The Court of Appeals for the Fifth Circuit, however, in a series of 1966 en banc decisions,[130] applied the "cross section" rule to juries in both the state and federal systems, and to both racial and socio-economic exclusion.

As the above quoted language suggests, the "cross section" rule is basically a due process doctrine, as opposed to the systematic exclusion rule, which is based upon equal protection. Thus in *Thiel*[131] (a cross section case), although the Supreme Court did not consider

---

125 315 U.S. 60 (1942). In that case, the Court held unlawful the practice of selecting jurors from lists supplied by public service organizations which conducted a jury service training program.

126 328 U.S. 217 (1946) (supervisory power).

127 *E.g.*, Smith v. Texas, 311 U.S. 128 (1940).

128 332 U.S. 261 (1947).

129 Some states have adopted the cross section doctrine on their own, although it is not clear to what extent. *See, e.g.*, People v. White, 43 Cal. 2d 740, 754, 278 P.2d 9, 18 (1954), *cert. denied*, 350 U.S. 875 (1955); State v. Ferraro, 146 Conn. 59, 147 A.2d 478 (1958), *cert. denied*, 369 U.S. 880 (1962); Allen v. State, 110 Ga. App. 56, 137 S.E.2d 711 (1964); State v. Lowry, 263 N.C. 536, 139 S.E.2d 870 (1965).

In the California case, the conviction was not reversed because there was no showing of prejudice to the defendant as required by the state constitution. People v. White, 43 Cal. 2d 740, 278 P.2d 9 (1954) (CAL. CONST. art. 6, § 4½). *But see* People v. Craig, No. 41750 (Super. Ct., Alameda County, Cal., April 18, 1968); People v. Tripp, No. CR 14790 (Super. Ct., San Diego County, Cal., Nov. 1, 1968) (no showing of actual prejudice required).

Exclusion of both racial and economic classes has become an issue in a current California trial which promises to become notorious, the trial of Sirhan B. Sirhan for the murder of Senator Robert Kennedy. Defense counsel argued a motion to quash the indictment, on the grounds that racial and economic classes were systematically excluded from the grand jury that brought it in. San Francisco Chronicle, Jan. 30, 1969, at 6, cols. 6-7; San Francisco Chronicle, Jan. 31, 1969, at 11, cols. 1-2.

130 Rabinowitz v. United States, 366 F.2d 34 (5th Cir. 1966); Brooks v. Beto, 366 F.2d 1 (5th Cir. 1966), *cert. denied*, 386 U.S. 975 (1967); Labat v. Bennett, 365 F.2d 698 (5th Cir. 1966), *cert. denied*, 386 U.S. 991 (1967).

131 Thiel v. Southern Pac. Co., 328 U.S. 217 (1946).

wage earners to be a class traditionally subject to discrimination and oppression, it held that a showing of actual prejudice was not required as it would have been under equal protection.[132] Also in *Thiel*, the petitioner's claim was recognized though he himself was not a member of the excluded class.[133]

The Court of Appeals for the Fifth Circuit was even more explicit in *Labat v. Bennett*,[134] a habeas corpus proceeding. The court held that where the records revealed a systematic exclusion of daily wage earners, the black defendants in a *state* prosecution were deprived of an impartial jury in violation of both due process and equal protection because the jury did not represent a cross section of the community. The court declined to base its holding solely on racial discrimination, although it noted that the excluded group, in violation of the equal protection clause, encompassed a large portion of the black community.[135] The court said:

> This exclusion [of daily wage earners] also goes to the fairness of the trial. The "very integrity of the fact-finding process" depends on impartial venires representative of the community as a whole. The undermining of the jury system's fact-finding process, the opportunity for unfairness, the risk that defendants who may be daily wage earners will be prejudiced by exclusion of jurors in the same class are dangers which would compel condemnation of the practice without the necessity of the court's finding actual prejudice affecting the outcome of the case. In this situation, as in the straight-out exclusion of Negroes, "the degree of prejudice can never be known."[136]

As noted above, the Supreme Court had declined to apply the "cross section" rule to state jury systems in *Fay v. New York*.[137] Although purporting to distinguish *Fay* on factual grounds, the *Labat* court in fact rejected both its restrictive approach and its requirement of a showing of actual prejudice. The court also removed, at least impliedly, any necessity for the excluded class to be traditionally oppressed. Furthermore, the court cited with approval state court decisions in which defendants had successfully challenged the exclusion of classes to which they themselves did not belong,[138] indicating that the fifth circuit will allow *any* defendant to challenge a jury selection process which excludes representation from significant community groups. The effect of *Labat* is to elevate claims for equitable jury selection procedures from restrictive equal protection considerations to due process rights.[139]

---

[132] *Id.* at 225.

[133] For the relationship of the "same class" rule to the equal protection clause, see text accompanying notes 117-22 *supra*.

[134] 365 F.2d 698 (5th Cir. 1966), *cert. denied*, 386 U.S. 991 (1967).

[135] *Id.* at 720.

[136] *Id.* at 723.

[137] 332 U.S. 261 (1947). See text accompanying note 128 *supra*.

[138] 365 F.2d at 723, *citing* Allen v. State, 110 Ga. App. 56, 137 S.E.2d 711 (1964); State v. Madison, 240 Md. 265, 213 A.2d 880 (1965). See note 120 *supra*.

[139] *See* Note, *Jury Challenges, Capital Punishment, and Labat v. Bennett: A Reconciliation*, 1968 DUKE L.J. 283, 302.

The results are strikingly different when jury selection procedures are treated as a matter of due process rather than equal protection.[140] The due pocess claim includes the equal protection claim, but goes much farther.[141] If having a jury which represents a cross section of the community goes to the fundamental fairness of the trial, the state has an *affirmative duty* under the due process clause to provide such a jury.[142] The equal protection claim, however, is denied if state action cannot be shown.[143] Because of the requirement that prejudice be shown except where the defendant belongs to a traditionally oppressed class, the equal protection claim is highly individualized, with limited value as precedent if upheld. A procedural due process claim which is accepted, however, is equivalent to a determination that the possibility of prejudice to *any defendant* receiving the same treatment is too great to be tolerated. Of course, the "same class" rule has no place in the "cross section" doctrine as based on the due process clause, because *every* defendant has the right to a representative jury.[144]

It is true that the courts have not yet defined "representative of a cross section of the community" to mean *proportional* representation; indeed, the cases have said that the defendant is *not* entitled to proportional representation.[145] However, it is submitted that the refusal to require proportional representation is neither necessary nor desirable. First, Supreme Court cases which have indicated that there is no right to proportional representation have considered the equal protection clause determinative, and can therefore be distinguished from attempts to define procedural due process rights. Second, as was recognized by the fifth circuit in *Brooks v. Beto*,[146] the cross section requirement *compels* consideration of race. Holding that the deliberate *inclusion* of some blacks on jury panels was not unlawful, the court noted that the Constitution must be color conscious, as well as color blind, to prevent discrimination from being perpet-

---

140 *See generally* Kuhn, *supra* note 7; Note, *Jury Challenges, Capital Punishment, and Labat v. Bennett: A Reconciliation*, 1968 DUKE L.J. 283, 301-02; Comment, *The Defendant's Challenge to a Raical Criterion in Jury Selection: A Study in Standing, Due Process and Equal Protection*, 74 YALE L.J. 919, 938-39 (1965).

141 Comment, *The Defendant's Challenge to a Racial Criterion in ury Selection: A Study in Standing, Due Process and Equal Protection*, 74 YALE L.J. 919, 938-39 (1965).

142 *Cf.* Gideon v. Wainwright, 372 U.S. 335 (1963); Griffin v. Illinois, 351 U.S. 12 (1955).

143 *E.g.*, Swain v. Alabama, 380 U.S. 202 (1965).

144 *See, e.g.*, Thiel v. Southern Pac. Co., 328 U.S. 217 (1946); Rabinowitz v. United States, 366 F.2d 34 (5th Cir. 1966) (white civil rights worker successfully challenged exclusion of blacks).

145 *E.g.*, Swain v. Alabama, 380 U.S. 202, 208 (1965); Akins v. Texas, 325 U.S. 398, 403 (1945); Billingsly v. Clayton, 359 F.2d 13, 18 (5th Cir.), *cert. denied*, 385 U.S. 841 (1966).

146 366 F.2d 1 (5th Cir. 1966), *cert. denied*, 386 U.S. 975 (1967).

uated.[147] Unfortunately, the *Brooks* court emphatically reiterates the proposition that representation may not deliberately be made proportional.[148] This seems inconsistent with the basic concept of the jury as "a democratic institution, representative of all qualified classes of people"[149] and in opposition to the plain meaning of the words, "representative of a cross-section of the community."[150]

The imposition on the states of an affirmative duty to provide proportional representation on jury lists as a requirement of due process would have a great impact on another inadequacy of our system of criminal justice—one of which both lawyers and laymen are aware but which has been given little attention by legal writers[151] or the courts. This is the propensity of totally or primarily white juries, particularly but not exclusively in the South, to acquit or refuse to indict white persons suspected of crimes against blacks or other minorities.[152] Under the equal protection concept,

---

[147] The apparent inconsistency here disappears if the *purpose* of the constitutional position under the circumstances is considered. That is, if the effect of considering race in a given situation is to discriminate, it is unlawful. If, however, *failing* to consider race results in the *perpetuation* of discrimination, *that* is unlawful.

[148] "[Awareness of race] must never, simply never, be applied to secure proportional representation. It must never, simply never, be applied to secure a predetermined or fixed limitation." 366 F.2d at 24. A rule that blacks (or any other minority) may be deliberately included, but not in deliberate numbers, seems unworkable. Note, *Constitutional Law—Jury Selection—Purposeful Inclusion of Negroes is Constitutional,* 13 WAYNE L. REV. 403, 409 (1967).

[149] Fay v. New York, 332 U.S. 261, 300 (1947) (dissenting opinion). For more complete quotation, see text accompanying note 117 *supra.*

[150] It should be noted that what is here proposed is not that *each jury* proportionately reflect the community, but rather that *each jury list,* from which prospective jurors are chosen at random, have proportional representation from each sub-community—socio-economic as well as racial.

[151] One exception is L. MILLER, THE PETITIONERS: THE STORY OF THE SUPREME COURT OF THE UNITED STATES AND THE NEGRO 120-22, 292-93 (1967).

[152] A former Ku Klux Klan leader, Samuel H. Bowers, accused of plotting to murder a black leader in Mississippi, reportedly told an ex-cohort shortly after the incident, "Don't worry . . . . No jury in Mississippi would convict somebody over killing a nigger." In two trials of Bowers, the jury was deadlocked each time. (The second jury consisted of 10 whites and 2 blacks.) San Francisco Chronicle, Jan. 26, 1969, § A, at 26, cols. 2-5.

A white San Francisco police officer was recently tried for having shot and killed a black man while off-duty. People v. O'Brien, No. CR 73512 (Super. Ct., San Francisco County, Cal., Mar. 20, 1969) (acquitted). The evidence as reported in the newspapers, although contradictory, would clearly have justified the prosecutor in asking for an indictment for first—or at least second—degree murder. The indictment was for manslaughter. San Francisco Chronicle, Nov. 2, 1968, § 1, at 1, col. 2.

It is not suggested that all white persons suspected of committing crimes against blacks have in fact committed them. But to the extent the correct result is reached in such cases, there would be more confidence in its

judicial review of jury selection is limited to those situations in which a party to the action chooses to challenge it. Where the discrimination in jury selection operates in favor of the defendant, he obviously has no reason to challenge it. If the white defendant is *convicted* by a white jury, he has no standing to challenge the exclusion of blacks from the jury where the "same class" rule has been applied. Even in the absence of the rule, there are strong social pressures against his challenging the system.[153] If, however, the state has an affirmative duty to include representation from all groups, once the due process standards are established they would prevail whether the defendant was white or black. Justice would then better serve the interests of a black victim (and a lawful society), as well as a black defendant.

Jury Selection and Service Act of 1968

The cross section requirement, already the law for at least the federal courts, has recently been given congressional sanction by the Jury Selection and Service Act of 1968.[154] The Act states:

> It is the policy of the United States that all litigants *in Federal Courts* entitled to trial by jury shall have the right to grand and petit juries *selected at random from a fair cross section of the community* in the district or division wherein the court convenes.[155]

The Act further provides that "all citizens shall have the opportunity to be considered for service . . . and shall have an obligation to serve . . . when summoned"[156] and forbids exclusion on grounds of "race, color, religion, sex, national origin, or economic status."[157] This declaration of policy is followed in the Act by a number of implementation provisions.

For the first time, a relatively uniform method of selecting juries is imposed throughout the federal court system. The Act requires that jurors be selected from lists of registered or actual voters, unless additional sources of names are "necessary to foster the policy and protect the rights" secured by the Act,[158] that is, where the voting lists[159] do not represent a fair cross section of the com-

---

correctness if the juries were not limited to whites and a few token "Uncle Toms."

153 *See* L. Miller, The Petitioners: The Story of the United States and the Negro 120-21 (1967).

154 82 Stat. 53 (1968), *amending* 28 U.S.C. §§ 1861-69 (1964).

155 82 Stat. 53 (1968), *amending* 28 U.S.C. § 1861 (1964).

156 82 Stat. 53 (1968), *amending* 28 U.S.C. § 1861 (1964).

157 82 Stat. 53 (1968), *amending* 28 U.S.C. § 1682 (1964).

158 82 Stat. 53 (1968), *amending* 28 U.S.C. § 1863(b)(2) (1964). *See also Report of the Commission on the Operation of the Jury System of the Judicial Conference of the United States*, 42 F.R.D. 353, 360-61 (1967). The reason for including actual voting lists was that registration lists are not required by all states or are out of date. *Id.* at 360.

159 Voter lists were chosen because they were thought to be "probably the most broadly based lists available." *Report of the Commission on the*

munity. This eliminates the "key man" system and its variations as the primary source of jurors. The Act also circumscribes the jury commissioner's discretion, by making selection criteria as objective as possible and by giving the commissioners no power to deviate from these criteria.[160] The enforcement provisions of the Act permit challenges to the composition of the panel by a criminal defendant, either party to a civil action, or the United States Attorney General before the voir dire stage of trial by motions to dismiss the indictment or to stay proceedings.[161]

While the 1968 Act should be somewhat successful in reducing discriminatory jury selection in federal courts, it falls short of being fully effective. By failing to define "fair cross section of the community," it leaves this definition to the courts. This is unfortunate because the current judicial definition is vague, but clearly something less than proportional representation.[162] The Act also condones the use of voting lists as the source of jury panels, at least where there are few overt restrictions on the right to register and vote. The Act thus ignores the de facto discrimination inherent in such lists.[163] It seems likely that courts in the North and West will continue to sustain the exclusive use of voter registration lists as "beyond reproach" under the new Act,[164] at least until a right to proportional representation is accepted. And although the Act restricts the jury commissioners' discretion, it still gives courts wide latitude to excuse or exclude.[165] Perhaps the most severe shortcoming of the Act is its failure to impose federal controls on the jury selection methods of the states.[166] In short, while the 1968 Act

---

Operation of the Jury System of the Judicial Conference of the United States, 42 F.R.D. 353, 361 (1967).

160 82 Stat. 53 (1968), *amending* 28 U.S.C. § 1865(b) (1964). The qualifications set forth by the Act are that the prospective juror: (1) be a United States citizen, at least 21 years old, and a resident of the judicial district for at least 1 year; (2) be able to read, write and understand English to the degree necessary to fill out the qualification form; (3) be able to speak English; (4) not be incapacitated by reason of mental or physical infirmity; and (5) not be a convicted felon or have charges pending. *See also The Congress, The Court and Jury Selection, supra* note 13, at 1139.

161 82 Stat. 53 (1968), *amending* 28 U.S.C. § 1867 (1964).

162 See text accompanying notes 125-49 *supra.*

163 See discussion accompanying notes 38-54 *supra.* That this discrimination was intentional may be inferred from a report of the Judicial Conference, where the "built-in screening element" of the lists is mentioned as a virtue because of the subsequent restrictions on grounds for disqualifying jurors. *Report of the Commission on The Operation of the Jury System of the Judicial Conference of the United States*, 42 F.R.D. 353, 362 (1967).

164 *See, e.g.,* United States v. Leonetti, 291 F. Supp. 461, 474 (S.D.N.Y. 1968). The court takes note of the new Act. *Id.* at 475 *passim*; *accord*, People v. Tripp, No. CR 14790 (Super. Ct., San Diego County, Cal., Nov. 1, 1968).

165 *See* 82 Stat. 53 (1968), *amending* 28 U.S.C. § 1866(c) (1964).

166 Congress has the power to pass legislation ensuring nondiscriminatory jury selection by the states under the thirteenth and fourteenth amend-

may correct some of the worst inadequacies of the federal jury system, it does not ensure nondiscriminatory selection even in the federal courts, and it completely ignores the state courts.

The 1968 Act has, however, supplied momentum to the current trend in jury selection. The systematic exclusion rule and its corollaries, based on equal protection, are giving way to the cross section doctrine, the due process implications of which are emerging. To date, though, the cross section doctrine has not been interpreted as requiring proportional representation of community groups, even though this appears to be its logical and necessary conclusion.

Some Suggested Remedies

The inadequacies and inequities of our present systems of jury selection and the legal restrictions on them are painfully clear. The systematic exclusion rule (which still applies in most states)[167] becomes even more ineffective as methods of token inclusion of minority groups become more sophisticated.[168] The cross section rule as presently interpreted by the federal courts is an improvement. What is imperative, however, is the imposition of an affirmative duty on the states to provide positive standards designed to ensure broadly based, nondiscriminatory jury selection methods. Requiring proportional representation on jury lists would probably be the most significant step toward an equitable jury system. However, weaknesses in jury selection systems could be at least partially rectified by other remedies, which might be accepted more readily and which would be desirable with or without proportional representation.

As has been noted, one of the major sources of discrimination in the present system is the virtually unlimited discretion vested in jury commissioners. It has been suggested that many of the stand-

---

ments. *See* Neal v. Delaware, 103 U.S. 370 (1880) (upholding constitutionality of jury selection provisions of Civil Rights Act of 1875); Strauder v. West Virginia, 100 U.S. 303 (1880); *Ex parte* Virginia, 100 U.S. 339 (1879). *See also* South Carolina v. Katzenbach, 383 U.S. 301 (1966) (sustaining Voting Rights Act of 1965 under section 5 of fourteenth amendment).

The Jury Selection and Service Act of 1968 in draft form did contain provisions affecting the states. See Title II of the proposed bill which prohibited discrimination in state jury selection. *Report of the Commission on the Operation of the Jury System of the Judicial Conference of the United States*, 42 F.R.D. 353, 381-86 (1967). However, Title II was an inadequate model for the legislation needed. It failed to impose the cross-section requirement of Title I, for example, or to contain effective means of enforcement. *See The Congress, the Court and Jury Selection, supra* note 13, at 1084-94.

[167] *But see* Labat v. Bennett, 365 F.2d 698 (5th Cir. 1966), *cert. denied*, 386 U.S. 991 (1967); Brooks v. Beto, 366 F.2d 1 (5th Cir. 1966), *cert. denied*, 386 U.S. 975 (1967) (imposing cross-section requirement on states in fifth circuit).

[168] *See* Labat v. Bennett, 365 F.2d 698 (5th Cir. 1966), *cert. denied*, 386 U.S. 991 (1967). *See also* Kuhn, *supra* note 7, at 237.

ards they apply are constitutionally objectionable as being impermissibly vague.[169] Unless guidelines are reasonably clear, it may be impossible to determine whether official action conforms to the standard and to secure effective review; official error and abuse are thus undetectible.[170] One writer thinks that there may be a stronger case for applying the "void for vagueness" doctrine to criteria for jury selection than to those for voter registration or school admission.[171] As he puts it:

> Misapplication of jury selection standards is less likely to be detected, objected to, and remedied. The Negro not selected for jury duty because of bias will rarely know of it and even more rarely sue for the privilege of spending two weeks in the jury room. . . . [H]is waiver [of his right not to be excluded on racial grounds] cannot be permitted to forfeit the right of litigants and the community to a jury system free of discrimination.[172]

Another weakness in the present system is the absence of sufficient guidelines for the determination of discrimination in a given case.[173] Statistical probability theory should be used to supply the needed guidelines, since it could be used to demonstrate mathematically the probability of a particular discrepancy resulting from chance.[174] There has been only one case in which the Supreme Court gave any recognition to probability theory. It noted in *Whitus v. Georgia*[175] that where 27 percent of a jury list was black, the mathematical probability of randomly choosing jury panels so that only 7 out of 90 veniremen were black (the actual composition of the panels) was 0.000006![176]

Another desirable application of contemporary mathematical methods would be to ensure representative jury lists by the use of population analysis and sampling techniques.[177] Such techniques could be used both as a means of procuring proportionally representative lists,[178] and as a check on the representativeness of present lists. To illustrate, the need to supplement voting lists in order to

---

[169] *E.g.*, Kuhn, *supra* note 7. at 276-82; *The Congress, the Court and Jury Selection*, *supra* note 13, at 1140-51; *cf.* People v. Tripp, No. CR 14790 (Super. Ct., San Diego County, Cal., Nov. 1, 1968).

[170] *Cf.* Yick Wo v. Hopkins, 118 U.S. 356 (1886); Davis v. Schnell, 81 F. Supp. 872 (S.D. Ala.), *aff'd per curiam*, 336 U.S. 933 (1949).

[171] Kuhn, *supra* note 7, at 281.

[172] *Id.* at 281-82.

[173] *Id.* at 254.

[174] A detailed discussion is outside the scope of this paper. *See generally* Finkelstein, *The Application of Statistical Decision Theory to the Jury Discrimination Cases*, 80 HARV. L. REV. 338 (1966).

[175] 385 U.S. 545 (1967).

[176] *Id.* at 552 n.2.

[177] Kuhn, *supra* note 7, at 263. For a more thorough discussion, see Mills, *A Statistical Study of Occupations of Jurors in a United States District Court*, 22 MD. L. REV. 214 (1962).

[178] Procuring lists through the use of these techniques would be more economical than the key man system. Kuhn, *supra* note 7, at 263.

have jury lists conform to a cross section of the community, as provided for in the 1968 Jury Selection Act,[179] could be determined by comparing the lists with a statistical sampling of the community. Any undue shortcomings in the former could then be remedied by selecting supplemental sources of jurors on the basis of the gaps indicated by the comparison.

An essential reform of the jury system is the elimination of financial hardship as an excuse from jury service, as it results in the disproportionate exclusion of poor people.[180] It is inconsistent with the requirement that a jury be representative of a cross section of the community to say, as some courts have said, that there is "no objection to excusing prospective veniremen for [economic] hardship."[181] The economic burden of administering justice in accordance with constitutional standards must be underwritten by the government.[182] The payment of higher fees to those performing jury service is only a partial solution.[183] To the person who would lose his job if he were absent for several weeks, the temporary receipt of jury fees will not prevent economic hardship.[184] It is thus also necessary that employers be required by law to keep the juror's job open for him.[185] If the law further required the employer to continue to pay wages to the absent juror,[186] adequate fees (probably at lower total government expense than at present) could then be paid to those who do not have regular jobs, such as workers who are employed on a daily basis, and housewives.[187]

Discriminatory jury selection results in loss of confidence in and respect for the administration of justice.[188] This is clearly true for

---

179 28 U.S.C. § 1863(b)(2) (1964).

180 See text accompanying notes 72-77 *supra*.

181 United States v. Leonetti, 291 F. Supp. 461, 475 (S.D.N.Y. 1968).

182 *Cf.* Gideon v. Wainwright, 372 U.S. 335 (1963); Griffin v. Illinois, 351 U.S. 12 (1955).

183 The Jury Selection and Service Act of 1968 doubled the basic jury fee from ten dollars per diem to twenty dollars per diem in federal courts. 82 Stat. 53 (1968), *amending* 28 U.S.C. § 1871 (1964).

184 Job protection is undoubtedly a major reason for the unduly small proportion of younger people on juries.

185 *Cf.* Day-Brite Lighting, Inc. v. Missouri, 342 U.S. 421 (1952) (state statute requiring that employees be given paid time off to vote held not to violate 14th amendment or contract clause of article I, section 10). *But cf.* Heimgaertner v. Benjamin Elec. Mfg. Co., 6 Ill. 2d 152, 128 N.E.2d 691 (1955).

186 *Cf.* Day-Brite Lighting, Inc. v. Missouri, 342 U.S. 421 (1952).

187 *But cf.* Heimgaertner v. Benjamin Elec. Mfg. Co., 6 Ill. 2d 152, 128 N.E.2d 691 (1955).

187 Although the states could adopt legislation to meet these needs, Day-Brite Lighting, Inc. v. Missouri, 342 U.S. 421 (1952), it seems highly unlikely that many of them will do so; federal legislation is probably a more effective and slightly more likely possibility. Congress would have power to pass such legislation under section 5 of the 14th amendment. See discussion note 166 *supra*.

188 *See* Kuhn, *supra* note 7, at 245-47.

members of minority groups who may confront a jury as criminal defendants or parties to a civil action. Exclusion of minority groups also deprives them as individuals from one of the very few opportunities available to them to directly participate in the processes of government.[189] As was said in a recent decision:

> The realities of our society emphasize the importance of jury panels drawn from a representative cross-section of the community. . . . Litigants and witnesses come into Court from all walks of life in a highly varied community. Unless jury panels represent the same walks of life and the same pattern of cultural differences, they will be less likely to understand fully the implications of the testimony they hear and the situations they must evaluate, and less likely to bring into their deliberations the background of experience and wisdom required for a just result. Similarly, the narrower the cultural spectrum of our jury panels, the less confidence the under-represented groups will have in the courts as temples of justice.[190]

Discriminatory selection also causes a breakdown in morality and increased lawlessness in the dominant culture.[191] When juries are not representative, "[t]he injury is not limited to the defendant—there is injury to the jury system, to the law as an institution, to the community at large, and to the democratic ideal reflected in the processes of the courts."[192] We thus have a vital interest in seeking radical improvement in our present methods of jury selection.

---

[189] *Id.*; Broeder, *supra* note 8, at 25-26. Broeder conducted a study of 23 jury trials, during which he interviewed, among others, the 3 black jurors on the juries. He writes that: "The account of the reactions of these [three black] jurors to their service is, for the most part, a dismal one. The chief bright spot consists in the immense gratification they derived simply from being selected to participate . . . ."

". . . [J]ury service democratizes, serving as a constant reminder that each of us has a say in the affairs of government." *Id.*

[190] People v. Craig, No. 41750, at 7 (Super. Ct., Alameda County, Cal., April 18, 1968).

[191] Kuhn, *supra* note 7, at 245-47. *See also* note 152 and accompanying text *supra*.

[192] Ballard v. United States, 329 U.S. 187, 195 (1946).

* Member, Third Year Class.

JUDICIAL RESPONSE IN CRISIS

National Commission on the Causes and Prevention of Violence

THE ACTIONS of the judicial system in times of large-scale mass protest—and especially civil disorder—are an important, if severe, test of a society's judicial system and its capacity to protect the rights and liberties of its citizens.[1] This chapter is a study of the judicial system and its response to mass protest. Because of the breadth of this topic—ranging from anti-war protest to black militancy and from the nature of political justice to the mechanics of processing thousands of cases during civil disorders—we have chosen to focus our inquiry more narrowly. So we begin this chapter with a survey of the actions of courts during the recent urban disorders. We then indicate some of the causes and implications of these actions, focusing primarily on themes that we feel have been developed inadequately elsewhere. In so doing we also indicate the broader implications of our analysis for the legal system and its functioning during periods of social unrest and mass protest, whether that be black militancy, student unrest, or anti-war protest.

To undertake even the study of the judicial response to the recent urban disorders, however, is far from easy, for there is little in the way of data. Indeed, there are far fewer studies in depth about even the *routine* operations of judges, prosecutors, and other court officials in the lower criminal courts than, for example, about police. Furthermore, judges are not as uniform in their views as police, and they are not organized

THE POLITICS OF PROTEST: A Task Force Report Submitted to the National Commission on the Causes and Prevention of Violence under the direction of Jerome H. Skolnick, 1969.

into guild organizations that have a sharp ideological character. So it is more difficult to generalize about judicial attitudes and actions.

Moreover, early governmental investigations of riots include few explicit comments on the operation of the judicial system. Reports of the 1919 Chicago riot, the 1935 Harlem riot, the 1943 Detroit riot, and the 1965 Watts riot offer, at most, cursory generalizations, without data on case processing, bail, or counsel. These early commissions evidently did not consider judicial actions as having any great importance; they were more or less taken for granted. This view was equally shared by government agencies and academics—even such classical studies of urban race relations as DuBois' study of *The Philadelphia Negro* [2] and Drake and Cayton's *Black Metropolis* [3] evaluated criminality without addressing its judicial context.

Official reports of riots during 1968, however, have given more attention to the judicial system. Undoubtedly this is in part because of an increased sensitivity in recent years to standards of judicial due process, largely because of the lead of the Supreme Court. Another reason for this recent concern is, of course, that during the urban disorders of the 1960's persons have been arrested in the thousands, straining the capacity of the courts to process and adjudicate cases in an orderly fashion. Almost 4,000 persons were arrested in Watts in August, 1965; [4] more than 7,200 persons were arrested in Detroit in a nine-day period in 1967; [5] 1,500 were arrested during a five-day riot in Newark; [6] in April, 1968, following the death of Martin Luther King,[7] over 3,000 persons were arrested in Chicago within a three-day period; during the week following Dr. King's death, 7,444 were arrested in Washington, D.C., and over 5,500 in Baltimore.[8] Thousands of other persons, including lawyers and media personnel, were, in the process, brought into contact with the lower criminal courts, persons who would not otherwise have been exposed to or even had secondhand knowledge about them. Responses ranged from anger at the injustices and callousness of the judicial system during periods of civil emergency to praise for overworked officials who did their best under trying conditions.

In these circumstances, it is not surprising that official attention has turned to assessing the administrative competence of the courts to cope with the volume of cases generated by civil disorders. The Kerner Commission Report devoted a chapter to problems of criminal justice during crises,[9] and the Chicago Riot Study Committee included a chapter on the courts in their report of August, 1968.[10] Other investigations have specifically focused on the courts; a District of Columbia committee reported on the courts in May, 1968; [11] a Baltimore committee reported in the same month; [12] a New York committee presented recommendations to Mayor Lindsay for court procedures during emergencies in August, 1968; [13] and the American Bar Association reviewed the problems of courts during civil disturbances in the spring issue of the *American Criminal Law Quarterly*.[14] We shall draw on these reports, as well as our own interviews and other materials, to describe judicial operations during civil disorders.

The Lack of Preparation: An Overview

The first major urban riot of the 1960's—in the Watts section of Los Angeles—was unanticipated by the judicial system, which understandably experienced severe administrative pressures. But even after the development of "emergency contingency plans" in some cities judicial systems continued to be unprepared for and overwhelmed by civil disorders.

The lack of preparation had an immediate practical impact. In Detroit, within two days of the beginning of the riot, 4,000 were incarcerated in makeshift jails. William Bledsoe, an Assistant State's Attorney General assigned to the Civil Rights Commission, reported that prisoners were "standing where there wasn't enough room to lie down. Or at least, people would take turns lying down. If you did find a place, you didn't dare get up. . . . Men and women were housed under these conditions together, without sanitary facilities, with perhaps one or two bologna sandwiches a day, if that. . . ." [15] In Newark, a large proportion of those arrested were held in an armory without proper food, water, and toilet or medical facilities until detention pressures finally forced authorities to release defendants on lower bails.[16]

Despite the Kerner Report's publication of lucid recommendations concerning the administration of justice in crisis, only New York had formulated a comprehensive emergency plan for the judicial system by April, 1968. Even in Washington, D.C., where the judicial system responded more fairly and efficiently than any other urban jurisdiction, "advance planning had been confined to discussion, making plans that were not operational by the time of the riot, or the drawing up of isolated plans that did not really resolve the central problems of mass arrest and detention." [17]

And in Chicago, for example, the Bar Association's Special Committee on Civil Disorders, which had been established almost ten months before the riot in April, 1968, had made no practical recommendations either to its constituency or the courts.

Thus, it is not so surprising that in Washington, D.C., cells built for eight were at times crowded with up to sixty persons.[18] And in Chicago, whose jail handles on an average day some fifty arrestees, on the weekend of the riots following Dr. King's death there were over five hundred cases per day without any corresponding increase in clerical and administrative personnel.[19]

In all cities studied, there was a serious shortage of professional and administrative personnel. The lack of a centralized and efficient record-keeping system meant that families and lawyers could not quickly locate defendants, nor could they always find an official who would accept bond.

These practical difficulties, which might have been predicted, often were aggravated by inflexible and hostile policies of court and correction officials. In Chicago and Baltimore, defendants were initially prevented from making phone calls to their families on the grounds that the security risk would be too great. In Detroit, men who were absent from their homes for as long as ten days could not be located by families or employers. In Baltimore, defendants were arraigned in courtrooms guarded by armed and helmeted soldiers. When lawyers were available there was little opportunity for lawyers to advise their clients, and some judges even refused to allow lawyers in their courtroom during the arraignment procedures. "The writ of habeas corpus," commented one Detroit defense lawyer, "was suspended and for several days there was a sign on the door of the Wayne County Jail that stated that no attorneys, either assigned or retained, could see their clients." [20]

The indignities to prisoners caught up in mass arrests were aggravated by the imposition of high bail, amounting to preventive detention, inadequate representation, and minimal observance of due process requirements.

The Role of Lawyers in Crisis

An important factor in shaping the judicial response was the absence of adequate defense lawyers in criminal court. During riots, the lack of experienced criminal lawyers becomes a major crisis, for the adversary system of justice depends upon defense attorneys to maintain its impartiality and integrity. When lawyers are either untrained, uninterested, or unavailable, the adversary system becomes a fiction and defendants are forced to rely on the good sense, professionalism, or benevolence of the courts—an outcome particularly undesirable in the stressful situation accompanying mass disorders.

One of the most severe deficiencies in the administration of justice under normal conditions is its failure to provide skilled defense counsel for defendants. Though lawyers are qualified to help strengthen the dignity, self-assertiveness, and power of the poor and disaffiliated, they have only recently begun to show organized interest in this task.[21] This becomes especially clear in times of civil disorders. The Kerner Commission found that the most serious legal problem during civil disorders is the "shortage of experienced defense lawyers to handle the influx of cases in any fashion approximating individual representation." [22] With the possible exception of some special interest groups, such as the American Civil Liberties Union and neighborhood legal agencies, the response by the organized bar to such emergencies has been, with very few exceptions, slow, insufficient, and ineffective. To make matters worse, the judiciary has at times restricted participation by volunteer groups, as in Detroit and Newark in 1967 and Chicago in 1968, where lawyers were denied access to courtrooms and jails.[23]

In Detroit, volunteer lawyers found it difficult to contact clients, and the organized bar made little effort to represent prisoners at arraignment, though they later responded after the riot was brought under control. According to a local law professor, "the legal profession in Detroit did not check the court of justice throughout most of the week in which the riot occurred. In fact, the profession was paralyzed." [24] By the middle of the second week of preliminary examinations it was difficult to secure the volunteer services of lawyers, since only 10 to 15 percent of the members of the Detroit Bar Association had offered their services.[25] While the bar associations in Chicago, Baltimore, and Washington, D.C., responded more quickly to the civil disorders in 1968, the results were by no means adequate. Little had been done to implement the Kerner Commission's recommendation that "the bar in each community undertake mobilization of all available lawyers for assignment so as to insure early individual legal representation to riot defendants." [26] Washington was the only city where the organized bar and judiciary cooperated in quickly recruiting and directing volunteer lawyers. In Chicago, the Bar Association offered assistance to the Chief Judge and Public Defender, who declined on grounds that extra resources were not needed. This response was taken at face value. The Bar Association refrained from criticizing the courts' actions during the riots, preferring instead to act as a broker between the courts and various legal defense organizations.[27] This was seen by representatives of these organizations as quiescent support of the courts' policies. Volunteer help was also initially refused by the Public Defender, who resented the interference of "outsiders" and regarded with suspicion their lack of experience in criminal courts.[28]

During the riots, courts in various cities often become armed camps, and some lawyers were intimidated by police and troops in and around the courtrooms. According to one volunteer in Detroit, "going into the court building was a devastating experience. It was surrounded by armed guards with machine guns. The building was practically a tomb and prisoners were being processed by some method I couldn't fathom."[29] In Chicago, lawyers were initially turned away from the courts by police guards. Those that demanded and received entry were ignored and, in some cases, met with hostility from bailiffs and court officials. At first, they were not allowed to enter the "bullpens" to interview prisoners. Even members of the Public Defender's Office were turned away from the jail by nervous sheriff's deputies. "I'm surprised that no one got shot there," commented an assistant public defender. "I remember walking up the steps [of the jail] with my public defender card in front and saw the Sheriff's police with a machine gun, with the safety off, pointed at me. . . ."[30]

Moreover, even when volunteer lawyers were present, they were all too often unfamiliar with criminal court practices. According to a survey in Detroit, 67 percent of the lawyers had spent less than 5 percent of their time in criminal court.[31]

Without organization or leadership, most volunteer lawyers found themselves facing chaotic situations in which they spent many frustrating hours waiting, petitioning officials, and wasting their considerable skills and resources. In Washington, D.C., according to Ronald Goldfarb:

> Lawyers converged on the Courthouse. Being unfamiliar with General Sessions, they groped for several hours trying to figure out the system. After doing so, they sat around, in many cases, waiting for appointments that were slow in coming because of the breakdown in the papering process.[32]

In Detroit and Washington, D.C., however, experienced criminal lawyers and law school interns established a briefing course for the volunteers.[33] There was no time for organization of similar programs in Chicago or Baltimore. Many inexperienced volunteers quickly left the courts out of feelings of frustration and incompetence.

With the exception of Chicago, black lawyers and criminal court "regulars" were generally absent from the ranks of volunteers. In Washington, the president of the predominantly black Washington Bar Association claimed that Negro defense lawyers had been purposely bypassed by the courts in favor of "uptown" lawyers.[34] In Chicago, the city's black Bar Association mobilized its members after the riot was over, held emergency meetings, and made public statements criticizing the court's expedient policies. This pressure helped to prod the court into holding bail hearings. In addition, these actions demonstrated sympathy by black lawyers with the "brothers on the street" and also helped to "reinstitute faith" in both black lawyers and the legal process.[35]

In general, riots have underlined the fact that the great majority of lawyers have little interest or experience in the legal problems of the poor. Bar associations have taken at best only a charitable interest in the criminal courts. This problem is compounded during riots by court officials who rarely extend cooperation to volunteers and maintain a veil of secrecy over proceedings. Legal agencies with special interest in judicial reforms also find that their efforts during a civil disorder tend to be frustrated in the interest of efficient rather than just proceedings. In Detroit and Chicago, members of the Lawyers' Guild and ACLU openly expressed their frustration with the courts. "We lent dignity to it last time by participating," said a spokesman for the Detroit Civil Liberties Union. "It was a farce." [36]

High Bail as Preventive Detention

Another serious problem in the judicial response to riots is found in bail. We have put together a city-by-city survey of bail practices during civil disorder in Detroit, Newark, Washington, D.C., Baltimore, and Chicago. The evidence is clear: the constitutional right to bail was almost invariably replaced by what in effect was a policy of preventive detention. This was particularly unfortunate. Not only did it work great hardships on the individuals involved—such as loss of employment because of absence—it also gave these persons an especially unfavorable experience with the practical workings of "the rule of law," an experience that was unlikely to persuade anyone of the merits of "working within the system for orderly change." In this way, the functioning of the judicial system during disorders may have contributed to the very grievances that lie at the roots of such disorders. Moreover, the implicit justification (if there was one) for these practices —that without preventive detention persons arrested would return to rioting—ignores two most important points. First, no evidence exists that this is true as a general proposition; indeed, it is surely untrue with respect to a great many of riot-related arrests—because of either the circumstances of the area or of the arrest, or the normal lapse of time involved in processing an arrested person. Thus, the "feedback to riot" justification for holding *large* numbers in custody is wholly lacking in evidence; and furthermore, it seems implausible to believe that following a court appearance, an arrestee charged with looting would return to the riot area, especially if his promise not to return was made a condition of his release. Second, the Kerner Commission correctly pointed out that alternatives exist to incarceration and suggested:

> That communities adopt station house summons and release procedures (such as are used by the New York City Police Department) in order that they be operational before emergency arises. All defendants who appear likely to return for trial and not to engage in renewed riot activity should be summoned and released.

In fact, all too often the constitutional right to bail seemed irrelevant. According to Judge Crockett of the Recorder's Court in Detroit:

> . . . hundreds of presumably innocent people, with no previous record whatever, suddenly found themselves separated from their unknowing families and jobs and incarcerated in our maximum security detention facilities . . . ; and all of this without benefit of counsel, without an examination, and without even the semblance of a trial.[38]

Whether this was because the courts were too overcrowded or because the courts intended to aid other public agencies in quelling the disturbances or were expressing distaste and fear of the participants in the disturbances, the effect was the same: punishment was applied before trial.

Detroit: In Detroit the use of bail as preventive detention was explicitly acknowledged by the judiciary. The twelve Recorder's Court judges met on the second day of the riot (Monday, July 27) and agreed to set bonds averaging $10,000; some were set as high as $200,000.[39] The *Detroit Free Press* noted that as a result of the decision, hundreds of persons were "railroaded through Recorder Court Sunday . . . night and Monday, slapped with high bonds and stashed away to await trial."[40] The high bail policy was applied uniformly—ignoring the nature of the charge, family and job status of those arrested, the prior record, and all other factors usually considered in the setting of bail. In response to criticism from black leaders, this policy was defended by one Recorder's Court judge: "We had no way of knowing whether there was a revolution in progress or whether the city was going to be burned down or what."[41] With the exception of one judge who gave individualized hearings but later said that even he had set bail too high, the judges of Recorder's Court carried out the high bail policy from July 23 to 30.

The impact of this policy was immediate. The detention facilities became severely overcrowded. The Wayne County Juvenile Home, with a capacity for 160 boys, housed more than 650 boys who could not make bond. Judge Lincoln, a Juvenile Court judge, dealt with this problem by declaring that "in spite of all the pressures, there has not been one boy released back to feed this riot."[42] Adult prisoners were incarcerated in maximum security prisons and police garages as the County Jail became overcrowded. Prisoners able to post bond were not always released. The overcrowded conditions did not prevent the Sheriff of the County Jail from refusing release of prisoners if he felt that the bond was "too low." The Sheriff claimed that the Executive Judge of the Recorder Court had ordered him to refuse release until the original judge reviewed the bail to see if it had been set too low.[43]

According to Judge Crockett, the situation had gotten so "far out of control that there was justifiable fear that if there were no riot then the Recorder Court's actions would surely have started one. We had hundreds of people in buses on Sunday for eighteen hours using a manhole as a latrine. This was prior to arraignment."[44] A week after the start of the riot, judges released hundreds of prisoners. Over 1,000 were released on their own recognizance. Yet, by Monday of the second week, 2,000 people were still confined, and on August 4, the end of the second week, 1,200 remained. Judge Crockett commented later that "even now there is [no real appreciation] of the full extent of the injustices we committed by our refusal to recognize the right to immediate bail and our objection to fixing reasonable bail." [45]

The arbitrariness of Detroit's high bail policy is further supported by a study made of 1,014 arrestees who were being detained awaiting trial in the Michigan State Prison.[46] Forty-four percent of those awaiting trial were married, and 86 percent had resided at the same address for one to five years. Eighty percent were employed, and 41 percent were employed at a major auto company. Moreover, 49 percent of those employed had worked at the same place for one to five years, and 14 percent had had the same employer for five to ten years. There was no consistent prior record. Sixty-seven percent had *no* prior convictions, 19 percent had one prior conviction, and 14 percent had previously been convicted two or more times. Thus from these statistics, one would have expected *less* stringent bail policies than usual; in fact the contrary was true.

Furthermore, the amount of bond showed little relation to the severity of the crime charged. The study concluded that "arrestees who were married, employed and without prior criminal records were treated virtually the same as were defendants who were single, unemployed, and had previous convictions and/or arrests." [47] Moreover, there are grounds to believe that future bail policies will have a similar effect. A former judge of Michigan's Supreme Court, for example, feels that the only lesson the Recorder's Court is likely to draw from the events is that "$15,000 to $20,000 bonds were unnecessary—next time bond will be $2,000 or so—to accomplish the same objective but to avoid the exposure. $2,000 bonds will keep them off the streets." [48]

Newark: In the summer of 1967, Newark courts employed a similar high bail-preventive detention policy until detention pressures forced a complete reversal. A "Release on Recognizance" program was initiated in the last days of the riot, with half of those arrested being interviewed and 65 to 80 percent of those being released. As in Detroit, public statements by high judicial officials showed a distinct lack of concern for those affected by a high bail policy. At the height of the riot, according to the *Newark Evening News* (July 14, 1967), the Chief Magistrate commented, "If they can't afford it, let them stay in jail."[49]

Chicago: In the April, 1968, disorders following the assassination of Dr. Martin Luther King, Chicago evidently took no notice of the Kerner Report's recommendations that

> . . . communities and courts plan for a range of alternative conditions to release, such as supervision by civic organizations or third party custodians outside the riot area, rather than to rely on high money bail to keep defendants off the streets. The courts should set bail on an individual basis and provide for defense counsel at bail hearings. Emergency procedures for fast bail review are needed.[50]

No emergency plans were made for release in a mass arrest situation. Rather, the courts continued the use of high bail to keep people off the streets. This policy had results similar to those in Detroit and Newark: detention facilities were overwhelmed and individualized justice was abandoned.

Yet the response of the Chicago courts to the April, 1968, disorders was consistent with plans made *after* Newark and Detroit. Soon after the disorders in those cities, the Chief Judge for the Circuit Court met at the Chicago Bar Association with the State's Attorney, Public Defender, Corporation Counsel, and representatives of the Chicago Bar and Legal Aid Society. They met to discuss "what lessons to draw from Newark and Detroit." At that meeting, the Chief Judge announced a high bail policy that would be followed in Chicago with the explicit intention of keeping those arrested off the streets during a riot.[51]

The April, 1968, riots were not the first time such a policy had been employed. In late January, 1967, Chicago experienced a snowstorm which immobilized the whole city, including the police. During this period, acts of looting and vandalism broke out on the predominantly black West Side. The courts responded to this crisis by imposing high bail on "looters." When the Chief Judge of the Circuit Court, John Boyle, was asked about the constitutionality of using high bond to keep a defendant in jail rather than to guarantee appearance at trial, he replied, "What do you want me to do—cry crocodile tears for people who take advantage of their city? Didn't I read . . . all about President Johnson's 'war on crime'?" [52] The Public Defender, in response to criticism from the ACLU that he was not challenging the courts' bail policies, commented that he was "not going to start fighting with judges because they set some bond that some people think is too high." [53]

According to an ACLU study in Chicago, the average bail for the charge of burglary under "normal" conditions is $4,300. Bail for the winter "looting" cases ranged from $5,000 to $30,000, with an average of $14,000. Bond hearings, as reported in official transcripts, typically took the following form: [54]

The Clerk:	Sam B.
The Court:	Branch 46. 1-31.
The Clerk:	Bond, Mr. State's Attorney?
The Court:	Bond for B . . . ?
State's Attorney:	On Sam B . . ., your Honor, the State will recommend a bond of $20,000.
The Court:	$20,000.

And in another case:

The Court:	What do you do for a living, son?
Defendant:	Sir, I work for the post office and for . . . two jobs.
The Court:	Can you afford to hire a lawyer?
Defendant:	Yes, I could, your Honor.
The Court:	All right. You hire yourself a good lawyer, sir. We will continue this case.
Defendant:	Your Honor, I have a wife and three kids and I only left them with twelve dollars in the house. Could I possibly get . . .
The Court:	Twelve dollars.
Defendant:	But I get paid from the post office this coming Thursday and I get my check at the other job, your Honor.

The Court:	You should have been on the job instead of out on the corner that night.
Defendant:	I had to get milk for my baby. I avoided this crowd as far as I could and then I was afraid they would rob me, your Honor; and my baby was crying. He is only 9 months old and I was going to—I was two blocks from my house avoiding these crowds because I am afraid they would rob me, but, your Honor, I got there and the police I saw—I could only see the top of the police car. Then I wasn't afraid any more because I thought the police wouldn't bother me. Then when the police got close the people went out of the store and dropped goods all over the ground.
The Court:	Someday you'll learn how order is in Chicago.
Defendant:	Sir, may I please have a personal bond?
The Court:	No, sir.
State's Attorney:	Motion State, February 20, 1967.
The Court:	I will not interfere with the bond. February 20, Bailiff.

Counsel was not permitted to represent defendants at the time bail was set, and the preliminary hearings were continued by the court for at least three weeks. This meant that defendants held under unusually high bail were incarcerated for three weeks before the court would even consider if there was probable cause to hold them. Almost all of the arrestees remained in custody unable to make bond. The city's judicial policies with respect to "looting" were well expressed by Magistrate Maurice Lee: "This type of crime during a citywide emergency is comparable to grave-robbing." [55]

It is perhaps not surprising, then, that the April, 1968, disorders found Chicago courts ready to impose bails which, though actually not "exorbitant," were nevertheless sufficiently high to prevent the immediate release of most prisoners. Moreover, there was no official mechanism for notifying families of the detention or amount of bond required for the release of those arrested. And volunteers were required to put tremendous pressure on the courts even to participate in such matters as notification during the bond hearings.

Problems of actually posting bail were endless. In most cases, the family of an arrested person knew only that he did not return home. The records department of the jail was closed in the evenings and, when open, rarely had information on the location of prisoners. Many prisoners who had money when arrested were initially unable to post bond since no bond clerks were available. At the jail and House of Correction, hundreds of concerned relatives were milling around with little idea of how to proceed. Several Sheriff's deputies guarded the jail, pointing their guns at the waiting crowd. Law students and legal aid lawyers performed the tasks that clerks should have performed if they had been assigned to the bond office.[56]

The bail policy was later justified by the Chief Judge of the Municipal Division. "When a man is sitting on the bench and he's looking out the window and he sees the city afire, big blazes here and there and everywhere, and he sees the people who are supposedly involved, it's very difficult for him to make a real considered judgment." [57] This inability to make a "considered judgment" inevitably favored the police over defendants. About 800 defendants were given bonds of $1,000 or over. Release-on-own-recognizance bonds were restricted for the most part to curfew violators, indicating that the gravity of the allegation tended to dictate the amount of bond. In determining bond, the courts paid little attention to such criteria as the background of those accused, despite the fact that over 70 percent of the defendants had never been previously arrested, 83 percent had never been previously convicted, and about 50 percent were arrested within six blocks of their homes. At least 37 percent of the arrestees spent over four days in jail pending the disposition of their cases. Ten days after the riot began, there were still over 200 people in jail who could not make bond.[58]

Baltimore: In Baltimore, according to a local blue-ribbon committee, bail for curfew violations was invariably set at $500, and few, if any, bondsmen were available at the courts. "Very few defendants were released on their own recognizance, and rarely was there time or inclination on the part of the judge to hear a defense plea for a bail geared to the circumstances of the individual defendant." [59] Of 345 curfew defendants who were not tried immediately, only 99 managed to make bail.[60] A significant number of curfew violators stood trial immediately under a stipulated prosecution; many reportedly pleaded guilty because of the "threat of incarceration implicit in the bail systems."[61] Of the 3,500 persons charged with curfew violations, all but 345 had been tried and sentenced during the riot:

> The mass trials of many defendants took place in an atmosphere akin to martial law. The disorders and the administration of the curfew generally made detention of defendants an incommunicado detention. Contact with those who might help in posting bail was problematic at best. Thus there was considerable pressure on defendants to agree to be tried summarily.[62]

Washington, D.C.: Bail policy in Washington, D.C., varied considerably. Compared with policies in other cities, it was certainly less oppressive and less arbitrary. Nevertheless, some judges set bond during the first two days of the riot with the express purpose of keeping defendants off the streets.[63] Other judges strictly adhered to the provisions of the Bail Reform Act, releasing many prisoners on their own recognizance and cooperating with volunteer lawyers to facilitate immediate release of their clients. Even so, fewer defendants were released on personal recognizance than is usually the case under normal conditions. According to Ronald Goldfarb:

> A check of Bail Agency records, and interviews with Bail Agency personnel, defense lawyers and prosecutors leads to one inescapable conclusion: defendants arraigned during the riot had more stable family ties, better employment records and far less serious criminal records than does the regular criminal defendant in the Court of General Sessions. . . . It is clear that many judges effectively discarded the liberal policies of the Bail Reform Act during the riot.[64]

Some Causes and Implications of Judicial Response

Routine Justice and Riot Justice

It is clear from the foregoing that the courts are ill prepared to cope with the volume of cases encountered in civil emergencies. When we ask why, the reason that is often given is strain—the added caseload simply is too much for the courts to handle. Any operating system, from a washing machine to a government bureau, breaks down from overload. Yet the "strain" explanation suggests an implicit assumption we believe to be unfounded: that the courts ordinarily offer services that are consonant with ideals of due process of law under an adversary system. By contrast, the evidence points to a direct relation between the way courts function during emergency situations and the way they function normally, and it is important that persons concerned with the shortcomings of the courts during emergencies not lose sight of the similar day-to-day shortcomings. Reform of the former necessarily should embrace the latter.

The courts are ordinarily understaffed and ill equipped; and the actions of courts during civil disorders may be seen as ordinary practices writ large, given public attention, and made vivid. In this section, we will examine routine justice as it proceeds in the same areas discussed previously. The similarities, we believe, will become evident.

It is in the lower courts that the quality of criminal justice must be measured, for as many as 90 percent of the criminal cases in this country are settled at this level.[65] Though the Supreme and Appeal Courts set precedents and receive wide publicity, it is the municipal courts that are the judicial system of most relevance for the vast majority of accused persons. It is thus of great significance that the President's Commission on Law Enforcement and the Administration of Justice found:

> It is clear that the lower courts are generally manned by less competent personnel than the courts of general jurisdiction. There are judges, attorneys and other officers in the lower courts who are as capable as their counterparts in more prestigious courts, but the lower courts regularly do not attract such persons. [66]

And the President's Commission on Crime in the District of Columbia recently observed that "abbreviated trials, disregard for witnesses, inadequate and shabby facilities—all contribute to an appearance of justice which weakens respect for law and order." [67] Again, according to the President's Commission on Law Enforcement and Administration of Justice:

> Every day in the courthouses of metropolitan areas the inadequacies of the lower courts may be observed. There is little in the process which is likely to instill respect for the system of criminal justice in defendants, witnesses or observers.[68]

Bail

If a defendant is charged with a noncapital offense, he generally has the right to be released on bail. Apart from the Eighth Amendment guarantee that bail cannot be "excessive," there are no strict guidelines, though the Supreme Court has ruled that the function of bail must be limited to guaranteeing the appearance of the defendant at subsequent proceedings; [69] thus it cannot be based on a desire to protect society from subsequent criminal conduct. In reality, however, the practices prevailing during riots also prevail in day-to-day bail-setting. Usually there is no evaluation of the factors, such as the accused's family and community ties, which may affect the likelihood of escape; more often bail is used *against* a defendant to "teach him a lesson," or to "protect the community," just as it is during a civil disorder.[70] The practical result of the system is that persons with money or access to money are able to obtain release on bail, while poor persons, who often cannot meet even the bondsman's fee, remain incarcerated.

A study of the administration of bail in Philadelphia showed that over 50 percent of persons held in lieu of bail were eventually released after trial, either through acquittal or on suspended sentence or probation.[71] Moreover, several studies have demonstrated that accused persons released on bail are able to put together a better defense and generally make a better appearance before the court, since they are able to get fresh clothes and do not enter the courtroom as prisoners.[72] The results of these opportunities are dramatic: persons released on bail are less likely to be convicted, and if convicted are more likely to receive shorter or suspended sentences.[73] Moreover, because the judge need not take account of this "dead time" in sentencing, the period awaiting trial often places pressure on the accused to plead guilty.

Ironically, then, the overcrowding of detention facilities during periods of civil crisis may work to the advantage of those so detained, as compared to the situation of the average poor arrestee charged with a felony. Overcrowded detention facilities put pressures on judges to release early—within a few days or a week—as compared to the weeks or months of jail time not uncommonly experienced in routine justice.

Counsel

Though the Supreme Court has held that the accused must be informed of his constitutional guarantees and his right to obtain or have counsel appointed, in day-to-day situations—just as in civil disorder situations—judges generally bypass or give little emphasis to these requirements.

> In theory the judge's duty is to advise the defendant of the charges against him and of his right to remain silent, to be admitted to bail, to retain counsel or to have counsel appointed, and to have a preliminary hearing. But in some cities the defendant may not be advised of his right to remain silent or to have counsel assigned. In others he may be one of a large group herded before the bench as a judge or clerk rushes through a ritualistic recitation of phrases, making little or no effort to ascertain whether the defendants understand their rights or the nature of the proceedings. In many jurisdictions counsel are not assigned in misdemeanor cases; even where lawyers are appointed, it may not be made clear to the defendant that if he is without funds he may have free representation.[74]

In Detroit, for example, counsel is rarely provided at the arraignment stage in Recorder's Court and, according to one expert, "ordinarily the accused is not informed that he has a right to have counsel 'appointed,' or that he can exercise this right 'immediately.' "[75] For the many who have been inadequately advised of their right to attorney, their first appearance in court is also likely to be their last. Most plead guilty without consultation, often under the implied threat of an additional stay in jail if a further hearing for a plea is required.

Even if an accused citizen obtains counsel, the reality of

what "counsel" means differs markedly from the abstraction envisioned in such Supreme Court decisions as *Gideon v. Wainwright* (1963), *Escobedo v. Illinois* (1964), *Miranda v. Arizona* (1966), and *In re Gault* (1967). In theory the right to counsel is perhaps the most important of rights because the presence of counsel should assure procedural regularity and the implementation of related principles. In fact, however, we find few defense attorneys who give to the role the attitude that Francis Allen has suggested as the mark of the qualified defense attorney: "a constant, searching, and creative questioning of official decisions and assertions of authority at all stages of the process." [76]

Studies of criminal defense lawyers suggest that "legal service" is characteristically too little and too late. The relatively few private lawyers available to the poor tend to be the least well trained and most inclined to violate the profession's code of ethics.[77] Criminal lawyers are predominantly general practitioners, unaffiliated with law firms, who make their livings from "small fee" cases and do a great deal of trial work.[78] According to Ladinsky, solo lawyers (most of whom handle the criminal matters of the poor) more often than firm lawyers come from lower-class backgrounds and from families having minority status. They "have quantitatively inferior education when compared to firm lawyers." [79] It is not surprising, then, that criminal lawyers on the average earn less from their work and outside sources than civil lawyers.[80]

Since most persons who appear in the lower courts are poor, where a defendant has counsel (and, again, a large proportion of defendants, particularly in misdemeanor cases, are not represented at all) that counsel is generally appointed without charge by the court. The quality of defense work by state-appointed attorneys is often even less distinguished than that by small-fee criminal lawyers.

Moreover, even in large cities the criminal bar is small and tends, along with the Public Defender's Office—which is usually more competent than appointed attorneys—to constitute a closed system. Given the pressures of the system to process vast numbers of cases, cooperation and accommodation are highly valued, with the result that most cases are negotiated on the basis of informal norms developed in response to administrative needs rather than legal principles:

> Most cases are disposed of outside the traditional trial process, either by a decision not to charge a suspect with a criminal offense or by a plea of guilty. In many communities one third to one half of the cáses begun by arrest are disposed of by some form of dismissal by public prosecutor, or judge. When a decision is made to prosecute, it is estimated that in many courts as many as 90% of all convictions are obtained by guilty pleas.[81]

Defense counsel is intimately involved in this process; his work comes to depend on cooperation with other officials in the system. The mass of clients may not be adversely affected. Yet the individual case may not be considered solely on its merits.[82] Moreover, there is no judicial review as to the fairness of the bargain, no guarantee that the defendant will receive what he has bargained for, and no control over the degree of pressure used to elicit acceptance of the bargain.[83] In this pretrial, publicly invisible method of dispensing justice, the defendant's guilt is generally assumed, a burden that ideally at least should be carried by the state.[84] The process comes to look less rational—subject to chance factors, to undue pressure, and sometimes to the hint of corruption.[85]

Faced with enormous caseloads, lacking financial and technical resources, and lacking especially the interest of the organized bar, the lower criminal courts should not be expected to generate a quality of distinction during emergencies that is fundamentally absent in its routine operations. Moreover, recommendations for improving the performance of courts during emergencies will be lacking unless they also address the problems found in these routine operations.

The Lower Court as an Agency of Law Enforcement

Although one may liken the functioning of the judicial system during mass disorders to its routine functioning, obviously something more dramatic is occurring. Not only are the problems faced during riots more severe than those confronted in the routine administration of justice; in addition, more varied and intense outside pressures are brought to bear on the courts.

During riots there is fear in the wider community, the courts come under scrutiny by the news media, and judicial authorities are in constant communication with political leaders. Under these circumstances, judicial actions and statements indicate that the courts usually cooperate by employing their judicial authority in the service of riot control, becoming, in effect, an agency engaged in nonjudicial forms of law enforcement.

In Detroit, for example, the Chief Judge of Recorder's Court made it clear in press releases that high bonds would be used to keep "rioters" off the street and that he would not release "thugs who would help to further [a] 'takeover-by-violence' plan." [86] The courts in Detroit refused to release prisoners until they were assured by the Mayor, a federal representative, and local military commanders that the city was secure.[87] The executive may tend to perceive judicial action as his responsibility. Regarding the Newark riot, the Governor proclaimed that "New Jersey will show its abhorrence of these criminal activities, and society will protect itself by fair, speedy and retributive justice." [88] The judges and magistrates in Newark were responsive to the Governor's direction that "the strength of the law . . . be demonstrated." [89] In Chicago, where the judicial system is routinely under tight political control, the courts cooperated with the Mayor's office and city prosecutors in detaining "rioters" until the emergency was declared over. The Chief Judge of Chicago's Municipal Division accurately reflected the political perspective of city hall: "I have seen tremendous progress for this particular minority group. They have come up so far and are progressing except for these civil disorders. Civil disorder . . . is the worst thing for the black race. It's bad; it's creating a cleavage in our society against them." [90]

In response to, and usually in agreement with, a desire for a quick restoration of order, the courts adopt a law enforcement perspective on riot control. Such a perspective may be summarized as follows: (1) civil disorders represent a time of extreme and dangerous emergency, requiring extraordinary measures of control and resistance; (2) the efforts of the police, military, fire department, and other public agencies must be actively supported to restore order as quickly as possible; (3) the presumption of guilt of defendants is made necessary by the presence of troops in the city, the sight of "fires on the horizon," and a common-sense appreciation of the danger and inherent criminality of a "riot" or "uprising"; (4) high bail is required to prevent rioters returning to the riot; (5) the nature of the emergency and the overwhelming number of defendants preclude the possibility of observing the niceties of due process; (6) due process will be restored as soon as the emergency has been terminated.[91] Both the courts and the police seek to prevent growth of the disorder, to distinguish the leaders, and to control the mob. The courts attempt to control the mob by detaining rioters until order is restored, by displaying power and resolve in the processing of defendants, by observing strict security precautions (having troops and police in court buildings and courtrooms, limiting access to prisoners, and checking credentials of lawyers), and by coordinating policies with other public agencies.

We have already suggested that the need for eliminating due process has not been documented. The evidence suggests that most "rioters" will not necessarily return to the riot area following a court appearance.[92] Moreover, when during crisis courts do become an instrument of order, rather than of law, communities find themselves without a tribunal for impartial judgment. This conclusion has two important consequences. First, as we have already noted, since the guilt of the accused is assumed, the adversary system and its attendant guarantees of due process are further eroded. Second, while there is ordinarily little control over the police and other agencies of government by courts, during riots there is active cooperation.

The criminal courts do more than arraign and try accused persons and sentence the guilty. When they operate properly, the courts insist on lawful standards of operation from other agencies of government. We do not have in mind here suits brought against governmental agencies, but rather what happens in the course of the routine criminal process. The courts have the responsibility to bring legal standards to bear on prosecutors, probation officers, police, lawyers, and other persons and agencies involved in law enforcement. In doing so, the courts are presumed to constrain these persons and agencies to adhere to law.

In order to perform this supervisory task, however, courts must in some degree be independent of other parts of the criminal justice system. The necessity for such independence —for a capacity to be both part of the law enforcement apparatus and in some degree stand apart from it—has long been recognized, for there are strong pressures on the criminal courts to be uncritical of other agencies of law enforcement. Recent Supreme Court decisions concerning the proper use of police power reflect an awareness of this tendency to erode the insulation between the criminal courts and other agencies of law enforcement. Under normal conditions, this tendency is occasionally halted by appellate court decisions and by professional standards of propriety. During periods of civil emergency, however, even stronger pressures are generated for expedient action, and the courts surrender much of what remains of their supervisory function; law enforcement agencies are encouraged, at least implicitly, to exert control by any means necessary. Moreover, the court's own actions—such as preventive detention through high bail—may be in violation of law. By condoning and following such policies, the courts contribute to the "breakdown of law" and to the establishment of an "order" based on force without justice. The implications of this situation are far-reaching. Some have been discussed earlier. To fully appreciate their gravity, however, one must examine the unique role that the courts play in our governmental system and the stresses that our legal system is undergoing in this time of widespread dissatisfaction and protest.

Disenchantment with Law

The criminal courts, like all legal institutions, are "political" in the sense that they engage in formulating and administering public policies.[93] The ties and differences between the political and judicial systems, however, are complex, and we must not overlook their distinctive characters.

The judicial system is tied to the political system in several obvious ways. Judicial personnel are sometimes elected; even more often they are appointed by political officeholders. Also, the enforcement of judicial decisions is often left to political officials. Finally, the laws the judiciary is empowered to interpret and apply are created and can be changed through political processes. In general, the closeness of the courts to the political system does much to ensure the flexibility of our legal system, its openness to change.

At the same time the judicial system is relatively insulated from politics. The selection of judicial personnel is guided in some measure by standards developed according to legal rather than political competence, and tenure arrangements have developed to protect judges from political interference. Moreover, judges are expected, and in considerable degree expect themselves, to be constrained by constitutional, statutory, and case law and by general principles of legality, in their assessment of evidence and their decisions. Such constraints are intended both to protect individuals against arbitrary state action and to prevent the courts from usurping powers more properly exercised by legislative and executive agencies.

In a constitutional democracy, then, the judiciary ideally functions as an impartial arbiter of conflict, relatively free from partisan interests—whether they be social, economic, or political. Our society recognizes that departures from that ideal are inevitable. However, it also views them with deep suspicion; for when the judiciary assumes a partisan role, the ideal of legality may seriously be undermined and the resolution of conflict reduced to the distribution and availability of force.

The evidence presented with respect to judicial behavior during the recent urban riots indicates a readiness by courts to lend their support to a system of preventive detention, to become an instrument of political needs relatively unrestrained by considerations of legality.[94] In the process, they undermine their own reputation as impartial arbiters of social disputes. Such actions lead to disaffection among those who have come into contact with a partisan judiciary, or who think they have. The importance of this cannot be underestimated, for the courts are our model for the "rule of law" to which we urge rioters to adhere. And lawlessness is precisely what we condemn in such dissidents.

Riot situations, however, are not the first instance of such disaffection. Yet the fact remains that the conduct of courts during riots reinforces the cynicism that many feel toward the legal system and converts others to similar views.

Because such disaffection decreases the likelihood of widespread acceptance of appeals to the "rule of law," it is important to examine briefly how this disaffection developed, prior to and after the recent urban disturbances. While it may be argued that much of this disaffection is due to naive and unreal demands made of the courts by the disaffected, it must be emphasized that the courts—and other branches of government—have themselves contributed to the decline of legal authority and, in some instances, to strengthening the resolve of dissenting groups. To the extent that this is true, the courts, like the police, may aggravate collective outbursts.

Political activity in the civil rights and anti-war movements was the first experience for many persons, both black and white, with the legal apparatus. In the early stages of the civil rights movement, especially in the South during the 1950's, the legitimacy of the legal system was assumed. People intentionally violated local laws, but they did so in the name of higher federal laws, which they believed would prevail in the courts. They had implicit faith in the justice of the legal system, if only it could be made to operate according to its own stated ideals.

The trouble was that even in theory, but especially in practice, the ideals of a federal system are ambiguous. Civil rights activists saw "the law" as federal law, the Constitution, the Supreme Law of the Land. White Southerners, at least those in political power, defied the federal law and interposed state law. Thus a paradox appeared: though federal law was declared by federal courts to be supreme, the hegemony of local laws and government—based on white supremacy—prevailed in practice. State judicial systems often actively participated in this erosion of legality. Moreover, federal courts, especially the lower federal courts, often facilitated or acquiesced in this process, or at best were powerless—whether for legal or political reasons—to do anything about it. As a result, the stature of all law—state and federal, legislative and executive and judicial—suffered. As Tom Hayden testified before this commission on October 23, 1968:

> The major issue that shaped our political outlook . . . was domestic policy and particularly the problem of civil rights in the South which came to the attention of northern students in 1960 through the direct action of voter registration campaigns. . . . Working in the South brought us face to face for the first time with the reality that we had never known, the direct reality of the police state. . . . The crucial discovery of that experience for many students, however, was that the South was not an isolated and backward region but was an integral part of the whole country. . . .
>
> An elementary lesson began to dawn on us, a lesson that never was taught us in our civics classes, and that lesson was simply that law serves power. . . .[95]

Although the importance of experiences in the South cannot be overestimated, disaffection was not merely a product of the civil rights struggle in the South.

Two points are of particular importance in this respect. First, lower-class blacks, whether in the North or South, have always been skeptical of the courts' capacity to administer fair and equal criminal justice.[96] As long ago as 1903, W. E. B. DuBois noted that "the Negro is coming more and more to look upon law and justice, not as protecting safeguards, but as sources of humiliation and oppression." [97] In recent years, most militant blacks have come to believe, along with one SNCC leader, that "the legal system is bankrupt. There is no such thing as justice for black folks in this country." [98] Thus, the Kerner Commission was correct in concluding that "civil disorders are fundamental governmental problems, not simply police matters." [99] We will enlarge on that perspective in our concluding chapter.

Second, among protesters outside the South there was also a deterioration of respect for the legal system. To understand why this occurred, one must examine (1) the expectations of these protesters, and (2) the suitability of the courts for the role they are forced to play in protest situations.

In the early 1960's, students, blacks, and civil rights workers had much faith in the courts, and early experiences in the civil rights movement at least held out the hope that the judiciary might be a progressive governmental ally. Indeed, the courts were often far ahead of the other branches of government in upholding the notion of legality. Moreover, legality —with its corollaries of consistency and impartiality—was often found to coincide with justice, and this nurtured the expectation that some element of "social justice" could and would emerge through the judicial process. Even when civil rights activists became disillusioned with the legal system and the courts in the South and began to focus their attention on the North, they still had faith in the legal processes in the North—after all, it was not the South. Profound disillusionment, however, soon occurred in the North also.

An extensive literature exists on the role that courts play in our democracy. Some of this has already been sketched, but the functioning of courts is obviously much more complex than this. The importance of precedent, the doctrine of "political questions," the scope of appellate review, the distinction between "pure speech" and "conduct," the roles of the jury and the judge, and similar nuances—which often prevent courts from reaching the "just" result or even from deciding a case on its substantive, as opposed to procedural, merits—are all important to a sophisticated evaluation of the courts. However, for better or worse, it is a fact that the vast majority of our citizens—and protesters—do not have such refined notions concerning the courts.

Thus at least some of the disillusionment with the legal system might have been avoided if a more "sophisticated" appreciation of our judicial and governmental system had existed. Such an appreciation would have recognized the limitations "inherent" in the judicial process and would not have been disappointed by actions of courts which were consistent with a strict standard of "neutrality" and "legality" but did not meet broader notions of social justice. Indeed, it would have been recognized that, in other contexts (such as the South), judicial neutrality had been thought desirable.

However, such understanding of the limitations of the judiciary was not widespread in the civil rights movement (as Tom Hayden's testimony suggests), and increasingly courts were perceived as and resented for acting in a manner contrary to the movement's conceptions of social justice. For example, the Chief Judge of the Court of General Sessions in Washington, D.C., has defended "neutrality" and "objectivity" by saying:

> When faced with a mass civil disorder, there will be great pressure to disregard the particular violation—especially if the activity is nonviolent; especially when it is in support of a cause which is obviously just; and especially when you happen personally to agree with some of the basic aims of the demonstrators. We, the judges, cannot afford to succumb to that kind of temptation.[100]

So, activists soon perceived "neutrality" at least a strict judicial interpretation of it—as an obstacle to social justice. Ironically, even those with "more sophisticated" views are likely to agree with such a short-run analysis. They, however, point to the long-run necessity of a neutral judiciary. It is this point that the disenchanted activists either did not see or rejected on grounds that social needs were too urgent.

But that was only part of the problem. An authority can manage a claim of "neutrality" provided it is also consistent. Yet an increased exposure to the courts, especially the lower courts, seemed to those involved to reveal inconsistency. An observer of civil rights activity in San Francisco in the summer of 1964 commented:

> Scores of defendants all accused of the same crime are being tried by different departments of one system. There are variations in rulings on the admissibility of evidence, variations in the attitudes of judges toward the cases and, most importantly, great variations in outcome. Some jurors have complained that attempts have been made to "gag" them in the deliberation process. I know of one instance of three boys who alleged that they were sitting together that night at the Sheraton Palace. One of the boys was acquitted, one of the boys was convicted, and one of the boys will be tried again because of a hung jury. The boys expressed in amazement to me: "And we were sitting side by side!" [101]

Clearly, the reality was out of line with expectations. Defendants are less likely than officials to view the system in overall terms.[102]

As important, perhaps, was the fact that students more and more tended to view the courts as enforcers of rules that were themselves arbitrary. For example, students during the

1964 Free Speech Movement at the University of California challenged the administration's attempt to end a long tradition of political activity near Sather Gate. Judge Robert Kroninger, when faced with sentencing students arrested during the Free Speech Movement, made the following evaluation: "Resistance to the rule of law whether active or passive is intolerable, and to describe criminal conduct as civil disobedience is to make words meaningless."[103] Yet from the perspective of the student protesters, *merely* to describe their civil disobedience as criminal conduct is equally meaningless. As they saw it the alternative was to acquiesce to an administration which, according to the report of its own prestigious investigative committee, had "displayed a consistent tendency to disorder in its own principles."[104]

Similarly, the courts have come to be seen as enforcing laws that are technicalities either designed or used to suppress dissent. Such a view in many instances was not without factual basis. For example, after the April, 1968, peace march in Chicago, a distinguished commission reached the following conclusion:

> By attempting to discourage protest by withholding [parade] permits, the City invites disaster at some time when it may have constitutional reasons for prohibiting a particular assembly. . . . The First Amendment is meaningless unless dissenting individuals attempt to take advantage of the rights it affords. If such individuals do not make the attempt, it is true that there is no violence, no conflict, no overt repression of speech; there is also no freedom. . . . In a democracy, it should not require courage to defy authorities in order to express dissenting views.[105]

Moreover, congressional enactment and judicial enforcement of a law specifically aimed at draft card burning—after this was already used as a means to voice dissent—was widely seen as a blatant attempt to stifle dissent, as were many of the policies promulgated by General Hershey, Director of the Selective Service System. Finally, anti-war protestors and blacks have seen themselves charged with criminal offenses—often of an omnibus nature such as "mob action"—to which police actions have contributed.

It is obviously true that the courts, as such, should not be the object of blame in many of the foregoing instances; under any realistic theory of judicial responsibility they had no option open to them. At the same time, however, it is true that judicial enforcement of these laws heightened the bitterness of protesting groups and lessened their respect for the legal system. Perhaps, then, any lessons to be drawn from this experience should be addressed to the other branches of government. And central to any such lesson is the recognition that during periods of protest the legal and social system, fragile in the first place, is by definition undergoing unusual stress, precisely because of the importance of the issues involved and depth of feelings involved. To the extent that the courts are required to enforce laws that are not particularly necessary or which place unnecessary stress on the legal system, the legal system itself suffers.

Related to this is another manner in which the recent escalation of protest has resulted in an enormous burden on traditional disciplinary and criminal procedures and thus contributed to the growing disenchantment with the legal system. This derives not so much from the larger number of cases, but rather from the courts being asked to perform tasks for which they are inherently unsuited. And this becomes increasingly true as protest increases, and it becomes more difficult to draw lines between dissent and criminality.[106]

The criminal process is based on the implicit assumption that crime, by and large, is an individual enterprise, or at most an enterprise encompassing only a small proportion of any community. The lower criminal courts are designed to handle a large volume of misdemeanor cases in which most defendants plead guilty and do not contest the authority and legitimacy of the courts. Moreover, the process assumes that those activities defined as "crimes" are disapproved of by a large proportion of the community. This, however, is not true of contemporary mass protest, if the community in which the protest occurs is taken to be the most relevant.

Often a significant segment of the protesting community is involved in protest "crimes"—as, for instance, in Watts, Detroit, Berkeley, and Columbia—and a large proportion do not define the activity as "crime." Moreover, protesters do not accept the court's authority to decide the disputes. This situation is one in which even further disenchantment and erosion of the concept of legality are likely; as such it presents a crisis for the courts and the legal system. By being required to pass judgment over communities that do not support the judgment, courts are placed in an extremely difficult political and thus legal situation.

The federal courts have faced this type of situation in the South; municipal courts in the North face what is perhaps an even more difficult situation with respect to the black communities. The black communities are black, and they are segregated as a result of a history of white domination going back to slavery. So perhaps more accurate than this analogy to the South is one to the colonial court, for the black communities of America—segregated communities providing the maids and janitors and carwashers for more affluent whites—come close to being internal colonies. And to the extent that a lack of political and social change forces the courts to deal with these problems, the legal system itself is placed in a difficult and dangerous position.

Recommendations

To those who seek recommendations for improving the performance of the courts during civil crises, we can offer no simple—or even difficult—*solutions*. When the courts become a central political forum, it seems reasonable to infer that the traditional political machinery is malfunctioning. For the courts, the fundamental problem is that they are organized to do one sort of task—adjudicating—and that in civil disorders they are asked to deal with the outcome of political conflict as if it were *only* a criminal matter. Under such conditions, they often become and are perceived as an instrument of power rather than of law.

Given the fact that the courts will probably continue to be burdened with the responsibility of handling mass protests, every effort should be made to improve the ability of the courts to administer justice efficiently and fairly, with full regard to the civil liberties of defendants. Several reforms are needed in this respect:

1. The criminal courts are in serious need of thorough re-

organization so that they may be capable of meeting even minimal standards of justice, decency, and humanity under normal conditions. Such reorganization would help to eliminate some of the more flagrant abuses of legal rights during a civil disorder. More significantly, it would help to eradicate one of the causes of such emergencies, for there is good reason to believe that injustice and the ensuing loss of faith in the authority of the law may move rational persons toward extralegal action. It is especially tragic that those who have most reason to be disenchanted with our society—particularly the poor and ethnic minorities—are treated most unjustly by the courts. Our criticism is not primarily aimed at court officials, for in an important sense the personal competence of such officials is the least of our problems. Much more important is the fact that we have not furnished the courts with financial, administrative, and jurisprudential resources commensurate with their importance in a society aspiring to constitutional democracy.

2. The actions of the courts during a civil disorder should be lawful, sympathetic, and respectful. It seems clear from the evidence that during periods of civil crisis pressures on the courts for expedient action are inevitable. Despite these pressures, the courts must make every effort to encourage the *lawful* operation of the entire law enforcement system, including the police and prosecutors, as well as themselves. The Kerner Report made several important suggestions with respect to this problem. Among its recommendations are:

> That communities adopt station house summons and release procedures (such as are used by the New York City Police Department) in order that they be operational before emergency arises. All defendants who appear likely to return for trial and not to engage in renewed riot activity should be summoned and released.
>
> That recognized community leaders be admitted to all processing and detention centers to avoid allegations of abuse or fraud and to reassure the community about the treatment of arrested persons.
>
> That the bar in each community undertake mobilization of all available lawyers for assignment so as to insure early individual legal representation to riot defendants through disposition and to provide assistance to prosecutors where needed.

Legal defense strategies should be planned and volunteers trained in advance. Investigative help and experienced advice should be provided.

That communities and courts plan for a range of alternative conditions to release, such as supervision by civic organizations or third-party custodians outside the riot area, rather than to rely on high money bail to keep defendants off the streets. The courts should set bail on an individual basis and provide for defense counsel at bail hearings. Emergency procedures for fast bail review are needed.

That no mass indictments or arraignments be held and reasonable bail and sentences be imposed, both during or after the riot. Sentences should be individually considered and pre-sentence reports required. The emergency plan should provide for transfer of probation officers from other courts and jurisdictions to assist in the processing of arrestees.[107]

We support these recommendations of the Kerner Commission, which were adopted in detail by the District of Columbia and other Committee reports, with the following reservation. Clearly some emergency measures are needed to permit the courts to operate in an orderly fashion during a civil crisis. The danger is that such "temporary" measures may become permanent and "emergencies" become routine. We are especially concerned with the trend toward devising "emergency measures" which are not addressed to needed fundamental reforms in the routine criminal justice system. For example, recent official investigations of the operation of the courts in crisis have sought new laws and new judicial techniques for controlling "rioters." Thus, many cities are presently exploring the possibility of preventive detention legislation,[108] and a blue-ribbon commission in Baltimore has recommended the passage of a "scavenging" law in anticipation of future riots.[109] Moreover, these trends lead us to believe that preparations are being made to deal efficiently with future civil disorders while little is being done to remedy the social and political grievances that motivate such disorders. This is a fundamental error.

Finally, we believe that a number of assumptions, both in social psychology and in official conceptions, have served to obscure and undermine the political character of contemporary protests. In our concluding chapter, we intend to assess those assumptions.

JOHN P. FRANK

Conflict of Interest and U. S. Supreme Court Justices

Conflict of interest wears two faces. In a narrow sense, it is the disqualification of a judge from hearing a particular case because of some interest, bias, or relationship to the case. This is a concept which has grown greatly with the years. In the broader sense, the phrase is applied loosely but generally to any situation in which the judge in his capacity as a citizen or, merely, as a human being, involves himself in matters which the community feels are incompatible with his role as a judge. Here, too, there has been vast change. John Marshall felt free to take an active role in political gatherings of his party. Peter V. Daniel, a federal district judge in Virginia from 1836 to 1841 and a Supreme Court Justice from 1841 to his death in 1860, was an active supporter of President Van Buren. He assisted Van Buren in getting the nomination in 1836, and helped win his election. He was conspicuously involved in party affairs thereafter, and supported the President in letters to the newspaper.[1] Today no judge can maintain an active political role.[2]

These shifts in the perception of conflicts of interest in general and disqualification in particular come partly by common law development, partly by statute, rule, or canon, and partly by what might be described as political or public opinion jerks or jumps from especially newsworthy episodes. For illustration, when Andrew Carnegie died, he left $10,000 a year to Chief Justice Taft, the annuity to continue throughout the Chief Justice's life and his wife's. Taft fully considered whether he could accept the sum, and after consultation with Elihu Root, concluded to do so; the first press response was favorable. But the Hearst press attacked the annuity, and Taft quickly divested himself of it, assigning it to Yale University; he was "profoundly concerned that the usefulness and influence of the Court should not be lessened on this account. . . ."[3] As a precedent, the Taft episode is

JOHN P. FRANK is a member of the bar at Phoenix, Arizona. He wishes to acknowledge the assistance in preparing this essay of John McLamb, a student at Yale Law School.

[1] See generally, J. Frank, *Justice Daniel Dissenting* (1964).

[2] ABA Special Comm. on Standards of Judicial Conduct, *Preliminary Statement and Interim Report* 7 (1970). This special committee, headed by Chief Justice Roger J. Traynor, is preparing a proposed revision of the Canons of Judicial Ethics on conflicts of interest. As of midsummer, 1970, this preliminary draft has been distributed for comment. It will be referred to hereafter as the *Traynor Report.*

[3] A. Mason, *William Howard Taft* 274 (1964). Taft had previously declined to receive a $25,000 a year pension to all ex-Presidents tendered by Carnegie. H. Pringle, *The Life and Times of William Howard Taft* 847 (1939).

THE AMERICAN JOURNAL OF COMPARATIVE LAW, 1970, Vol. 18, pp. 532-548.

clouded. It surely cannot mean that Supreme Court Justices may not receive bequests; it probably does mean that they would be unwise to accept them from Titans.

Laced with a little partisanship, an episode which might otherwise not be regarded as involving any conflict may suddely become momentous and have long consequence. The retirement of Justice Clark when his son became Attorney General, the appointment of Abe Fortas as Chief Justice and his later resignation, the Burger, Haynsworth, Carswell and Blackmun appointments, and the inquiries into Justice Douglas have caused wholesale reconsideration of both the law of disqualification in particular and of conflict of interest in particular.[4]

I. Types of Conflict

A. Conflict by Involvement

As everybody knows, babies may come from storks, lower court judges may come from senators (with a bit of midwifery help from the Department of Justice and the American Bar Association), but Supreme Court Justices may really be chosen by Presidents. This does not always happen; I once described Joseph Rucker Lamar, a Justice from 1911 to 1916, as "the choice of a President who had run out of ideas." [5] Nonetheless, generally speaking, unlike the other federal judicial appointments, a Supreme Court appointment is usually not simply a parchment with a presidential autograph but represents an actual judgment in which a President really participated. In such an instance, the one chosen is really and truly someone in whom the President reposes trust and confidence.

Inevitably Presidents use many men, but there are not many in whom they truly repose trust and confidence. Particularly in view of the propinquity of the Court to the White House, Presidents very frequently ask their appointees for advice on a variety of matters. Because the association is so personal, the practice normally does not much outlast the term of the appointing President; that is to say, succeeding Presidents usually but not always find other advisers. Nonetheless, appointing Presidents frequently look for advice to their appointees, because in many instances they were dependent upon those same appointees for advice before the appointment.

This practice was brought into sharp controversy when in June, 1968, President Johnson appointed Associate Justice Abe Fortas as Chief

---

[4] The two subjects are too large for single law review article treatment, and I am therefore dividing them by discussing conflict in the broad sense here, and disqualification with precise reference to pending legislation in *Law and Contemporary Problems,* Winter, 1970, issue. For extensive earlier discussion of disqualification, see my "Disqualification of Judges," 56 *Yale L. J.* 605 (1947).

[5] Frank, "Supreme Court Justice Appointments," 1941 *Wis. L. Rev.* 343, 378 (1941).

Justice of the United States. Fortas had been the President's personal counsel at the time of his appointment, and Johnson continued to consult him on some matters between his appointment as an Associate Justice by Johnson in 1965 and the date of his appointment to the Chief Justiceship.

Fortas attended some White House meetings, and he was consulted on some phase of the 1966 State of the Union message. He was called in to consider some specific issues on problems related to the war in Vietnam, and was also consulted in two or three instances of emergencies in the early urban riots. He later published a pamphlet against violence.[6] His association with the President was not disguised and was used by Senator Griffin to plague him on the Chief Justiceship.[7]

Fortas' opponents, particularly those with a desire to hold the vacancy until after a new President should be inaugurated in 1969, vigorously attacked Fortas' role as a Presidential adviser, contending that this was a conflict of interest.

The advisory relationship of the Justices to the President was first presented in the administration of John Jay, the first Chief Justice. President Washington was accustomed to relying upon Jay for advice and counsel. During his administration he did from time to time ask Jay for advice, and he received it.[8]

Jay did not always satisfy the administration's requests. On July 18, 1793, Thomas Jefferson, as Secretary of State, forwarded to Chief Justice Jay and the full Court some twenty-nine strictly legal questions, relating to problems of the administration arising from the Napoleonic Wars. These were questions essentially of a sort which might very well arise in a lawsuit, as for example, the twenty-seventh question, which was: "Is the principle, that free bottoms make free goods, and enemy bottoms make enemy goods, to be considered as now an established part of the law of nations?"

On August 8, 1793, Chief Justice Jay and the Court wrote the President. The letter referred to the division of the government into three separate departments and said,

> "These being in certain respects checks upon each other, and our being judges of a court in the last resort, are considerations which

---

[6] A. Fortas, *Concerning Dissent and Civil Disobedience* (1968).

[7] *Hearings on the Nomination of Abe Fortas to be Chief Justice of the Supreme Court Before the Sen. Comm. on the Judiciary,* 90th Cong., 2d Sess. 103, 106, 125-28, 1348-49, 1363 (1968).

[8] For illustrations see 6 D. S. Freeman, *George Washington,* 269-70 (New York 1954). Thus, in one instance, Washington said in connection with British relations and Spanish activities on the Mississippi, "I requested Mr. Jefferson and Colonel Hamilton, as I intend to do the Vice President, Chief Justice, and Secretary at War, to revolve this matter in all its relations in their minds."

afford strong arguments against the propriety of our extra-judicially deciding the questions alluded to. . . ."[9]

The distinction Jay made between general advice on matters of policy and precise legal advice on specific questions has somewhat irregularly been maintained in practice ever since.

Chief Justice Taney advised President Jackson, who had appointed him, both in writing and orally.[10] Justice David Davis, Lincoln's campaign manager, executor, and friend, advised Lincoln on martial law problems which were later to be the subject of his greatest opinion.[11] The extent to which Chief Justice Fuller advised President Cleveland on policy is unclear, but he counselled him directly on running for a second term, and was requested by the President for advice on appointments.[12]

Justice Brandeis was an administration adviser during the crises of World War I. An important distinction he made was that he would not go to the White House to discuss a political matter, such as an appointment, unless expressly requested to do so by the President. His biographer includes a colorful account of how, on December 9, 1917, President Wilson came to the Brandeis apartment to request advice on certain railroad problems.[13] Chief Justice Taft was so occupied as an adviser to Presidents Harding, Coolidge, and Hoover that a biographer includes a chapter, "Presidential Adviser," in the most recent work on this Justice.[14] Justice, later Chief Justice, Stone was a frequent adviser of President Hoover, as well as his fellow exerciser in what was called the Medicine Ball Cabinet; his biographer tells of Stone making "comments on drafts or speeches and executive messages."[15]

Justice Frankfurter, who had been a Roosevelt adviser before his appointment, continued to be so thereafter. He is credited with responsibility for the appointment of Secretary of War Henry L. Stimson, and took an active interest in the affairs of the War Department.[16] Justice Byrnes was so deeply involved in Presidential counselling and service during his one year on the Court that he named a chapter in his autobiography, "Extracurricular Activities."[17]

---

[9] The documents of the Washington-Jay correspondence are collected in F. Frankfurter and H. Shulman, *Cases on Federal Jurisdiction and Procedure* 38 (rev. ed. 1937).

[10] See C. B. Swisher, *Roger Taney* 329-30 (1936). The episodes following were discussed by Justice Fortas: *Fortas Hearings,* supra note 7, at 164-65 (1968).

[11] Ex parte Milligan, 4 *Wall.* 2, 18 *L. Ed.* 281 (1866); D. Donald, *Lincoln's Manager, David Davis* 204 (1960).

[12] W. King, *Melville Weston Fuller* 164, 181 (1950).

[13] A. Mason, *Brandeis* 521-22 (1946), and for other administration counselling, see pages before and after.

[14] A. Mason, *William Howard Taft* 138 (1964).

[15] A. Mason, *Harlan Fiske Stone* 270 (1956).

[16] H. Stimson and McG. Bundy, *On Active Service* 334 (1948).

[17] J. Byrnes, *All in One Lifetime* 147 (1958).

President Truman's high regard for Chief Justice Vinson has been fully documented by the ex-President. This was a close relationship which, President Truman says, developed "after I moved to the White House." There, for a year, Vinson was a top war economics official before his appointment as Chief Justice. Thereafter the President talked to Vinson about Russian affairs, discussed a possible foreign mission, and later requested Vinson to succeed him as President.[18]

The examples listed have not been instances of advice on cases in the Court. Several Justices did advise President Buchanan shortly before his inauguration in 1857 on the problems of slavery in the territories about to be decided in the *Dred Scott* case; indeed, Justice Grier told him all about the case before it was decided so that he could have the knowledge for use in his inaugural address.[19] This conduct is universally regarded as aberrational and improper.

The foregoing enumeration is a sampling from readily available materials. I would estimate that at least twenty-five percent of the Justices have at some time advised with the President after their appointment; Justices Murphy and Douglas are other examples during the Roosevelt period. To this must be added the Justices who have undertaken, at the reqeust of a President, some extra-judicial duty which necessarily involved advice for the President, as for example, Justice Roberts on Pearl Harbor; Justice Jackson on war crimes; and Chief Justice Warren on the Commission which bears his name.

This relationship tends to wither as the service of the Justice extends and he grows apart from succeeding administrations. The whole concept of informal advice is derivative of that peculiar trust and confidence which the appointing President had in the Justice, and with the passage of time the Justices become merely affable strangers in relation to the White House. It may be that this phase of Supreme Court conflict of interest is about to take a new historical turn. As an aftermath of the failure of Justice Fortas to be confirmed as Chief Justice, President Nixon has affirmatively excluded the possibility of appointment of Justices from among the circle of his trusted advisers and friends, choosing virtual strangers instead; and his choices as made from among lower court judges necessarily exclude those who are his direct and traditional counselors. Yet if one may tender a guess as to the future course of events, this burst of isolating virtue will not last; another President will find another Jay, or Taney, or Fuller, or Taft, or Stone, or Vinson, or Fortas.

There are other types of involvement than counselling Presidents; a Justice may feel an impulse to counsel the country in general or some subdivision of it. When this impulse to lead and counsel is confined

---

18 H. Truman, *Years of Trial and Hope* 213, 489-90 (1956).

19 Scott v. Sandford, 19 *How.* 393, 15 *L. Ed.* 691 (1856); and for details see C. Warren, *The Supreme Court in United States History,* II: 293-98 (Boston 1926).

essentially to the operation of the legal system, it is not regarded as conflict of interest and is universally admired unless carried to such an extent that it distracts from the Justice's capacity to perform his primary labors. Justice Tom Clark was the most active national leader in the improvement of judicial administration of any figure in the Court's history.[20] Justice Rutledge was equally available, though less mobile than Justice Clark for old friends in the world of legal education, as well as for old friends in general; he may well have been so generous in this regard as to have unduly burdened himself. Justices have also very commonly lectured or written on law; Justices Story and Miller are among the greats, to name only the dead; and the practice, in small or large degree, is almost universal. All these practices are endorsed in the Traynor Report.[21]

Controversy arises when a Justice involves himself beyond the traditional law orbit to enter other areas of policy. These judicial interests may well over from the law into the polite arts, for example, involvement in the Smithsonian Museum or the Mellon Gallery. One more far-ranging member of the Court is Justice Douglas. Douglas is a man of extraordinary breadth of interest and of extraordinary energy, and while the business of being a Supreme Court Justice may be a backbreaking load for some—retired Justice Whittaker is a good illustration of a man who found it simply too much—Justice Douglas cannot be kept busy by these demands. His interests take him around the world and into print on topics of conservation of natural resources;[22] and his interests have on occasion led him to express himself on matters of war and peace.

In 1970 a substantial number of members of the House of Representatives asked for an investigation leading to possible impeachment of Justice Douglas. The matter progressed in an odd fashion, without the critics giving any clearcut and incisive list of official complaints so that the defense, headed by former Judge Simon H. Rifkind, was compelled to devise first what it thought the charges were, and second to make some answer to them. These related to a half-dozen items which can be approached in terms of conflict of interest. Put briefly:

(1) The critics complained of points of view expressed by Justice

---

[20] For full details, see Frank, "Justice Tom Clark and Judicial Administration," 46 *Tex. L. Rev.* 5 (1967).

[21] *Traynor Report,* supra note 2 at 1-2.

[22] "One of the most dynamic books of the 1960's was Rachel Carson's *Silent Spring.* The book tells of man's unwitting, careless, and devastating destruction of his world by the chemicals and poisons that he puts into the air, the water, and the ground. The book cites no Presidents of the United States, no Senators. It does quote from Charles Darwin; a doctor from the citrus experiment station in Riverside, California; from scientists at the British Royal Navy Physiological Laboratory; and four times from Mr. Justice Douglas." J. Frank, "William O. Douglas," in L. Friedman and F. Israel (eds.), *The Justices of the United States Supreme Court 1789-1969,* IV, 2447 (1969).

Douglas in a recent book, *Points of Rebellion,* a discussion of violence in the world today. The Justice's critics charge that he advocates violence. Justice Tom Clark, reviewing the book, expressly rejects this view, and says the book "cries out with much truth." [23] I put this aside without further comment since the dispute does not involve conflict of interest in any conventional sense.

(2) The second charge concerns the fact that an extract from the book was allowed by Random House Publishers, the publishers of the work, to appear in *Evergreen Review,* a magazine which also included wholly unrelated but offensive photographs. Here the charge is less conflict of interest than conflict with propriety, the critics feeling that a Supreme Court Justice should not allow his works to be caught in such company. The defense is that the republication of the extract is something over which Justice Douglas had no control and as to which he was not consulted.

(3) Douglas published an essay in a magazine known as *Avant-Garde* on folk singing for which he received a fee of $350. Subsequent to the making of those arrangements, including the submission of the article, the Justice discovered that the magazine was in fact published by a Ralph Ginzburg, who was actively involved in federal courts as a defendant both for pornography and libel. Justice Douglas promptly disassociated altogether from *Avant-Garde.* Subsequently thereto a case involving Ginzburg did come to the Supreme Court. Certiorari was denied, *Ginzburg v. Goldwater,*[24] without Justice Douglas being aware that this is the same Ginzburg as the one connected with *Avant-Garde* in which the publication had appeared two years earlier.

Judge Rifkind contends that even had Justice Douglas been aware of the Ginzburg-*Avant-Garde* connection, he would not have been obligated to disqualify on the theory that a single isolated article in a publication does not require one to disqualify in matters which may relate to the financial affairs of that publication or someone associated with it.[25] Justice Douglas has disqualified when he had an extensive relationship with a publication. Having written a dozen times for *Look* magazine since 1951, he regularly disqualifies in matters relating to the owner of that publication or the publishing house.[26]

(4) The fourth charge is that Douglas engaged in the practice of law as a counselor for the Albert Parvin Foundation, of which he was for some time the president. In the interest of reasonable brevity, I can

[23] Clark, "Book Review," 83 *Harv. L. Rev.* 1931, 1933 (1970).

[24] 396 *U.S.* 1049 (Jan. 26, 1970).

[25] Letter from Judge Simon Rifkind to the Honorable Emanuel Celler, May 18, 1970.

[26] See Polizzi v. Cowles Magazines, Inc., 344 *U.S.* 853, 73 *S. Ct.* 94, 97 *L. Ed.* 662 (1952); 345 *U.S.* 663, 73 *S. Ct.* 900, 97 *L. Ed.* 1331 (1953); 344 *U.S.* 988, 73 *S. Ct.* 1128, 97 *L. Ed.* 1397 (1953); Cowles Communications, Inc. v. Alioto (No. 1985 *Misc.,* Apr. 27, 1970).

note only that had he done so it would have been a violation of law.[27] Any lawyer looking at any document is likely to respond in terms of the cast of mind which a lawyer has, but the Rifkind documentation indicates quite clearly that the "law practice" aspects of the Parvin Foundation affairs were left entirely to others.

The Canons of Ethics have never altogether excluded judges from giving some legal advice. For example, present Justice Harry Blackmun, when a Federal Circuit Judge, served as co-executor of several estates and received fees in three years of some $8,500. Perfectly obviously he was giving some legal opinions about the matters with which he dealt. This was entirely proper; Canon 27 of the American Bar Association Canons of Judicial Ethics expressly permits a judge to hold executorships and trusteeships.[28] Hence, Judge Rifkind concludes that a member of the federal judiciary is engaged in the practice of law only where he is specifically engaged to perform legal services as a lawyer.

(5) Apart from the matter of the alleged law practice, complaint is made of the Justice's association with the Albert Parvin Foundation. The charges suggest that the association in itself is intrinsically invidious because of the source of the funds. These are said to come from the "international gambling fraternity," because Parvin has a fairly remote connection with a Nevada hotel. Judge Rifkind in response said, "In serving as a director of the Albert Parvin Foundation, and receiving modest compensation for such services, Mr. Justice Douglas followed long precedent—as, for example, did Chief Justice Warren Burger and Justice Harry Blackmun with respect to the Mayo Foundation and the Kahler Corporation."[29]

(6) The final Douglas charge is of association with the Center for the Study of Democratic Institutions. The essential response of the Douglas defenders is that this is a good thing to do and involves no conflict of any kind.[30]

Another type of conflict of interest from possible outside involve-

---

[27] 28 U.S.C. § 454 provides that a Justice "who engages in the practice of law is guilty of a high misdemeanor."

[28] The Traynor Report proposes that a judge should only act as an executor or trustee for the estate or person of a member of his family. *Traynor Report,* supra note 2 at 3.

[29] Judge Rifkind added by way of general description that the foundation had made grants of three-quarters of a million dollars, which was all of its income, over a nine-year period to support fellowship programs at Princeton University and at the University of California at Los Angeles, and for efforts to improve American relations with Latin America, and for peace. Other participants in the affairs of the foundation were the president of Princeton, a former dean of the Yale Law School and former president of the University of Chicago, a former Pulitzer prize winning newspaper man, and a former editor-in-chief of the Encyclopedia Britannica. Letter from Judge Simon Rifkind to the Honorable Emanuel Celler, May 18, 1970.

[30] Judge Rifkind's statement acknowledging that Douglas associated with the Center says, "So have Chief Justices Warren and Burger, George Romney, and Robert Finch, and scores of other distinguished Americans. His [Douglas'] services to the Center in an

ments arises when Justices undertake some special non-judicial duty in the service of the government. In the beginning, when Justices had very little to do, this was easier than it has become. Chief Justice Jay, for example, was also Ambassador to Great Britain where he negotiated a major treaty. Five Justices served on the Electoral Commission of 1876; two arbitrated a boundary dispute between Venezuela and British Guiana. Justice Brandeis was an adviser to the delegation to the 1919 Peace Conference. Justice Roberts was in charge of the Pearl Harbor investigation. Justice Jackson was the prosecutor of the Nuremberg War Crimes trials and Chief Justice Warren headed the investigation into the assassination of President Kennedy.

The propriety of these activities is subject to vigorous dispute. Chief Justice Stone, who had to carry the administrative burden caused by Jackson's absence at Nuremberg, referred bitterly to his colleague's "lynching party." [31] There is a considerable view that no justice should be involved in a substantial outside activity other than judging. Chief Justice Warren solved the problem through Herculean effort, by performing both his task as Chief Justice and his task as head of the Warren Commission at the same time.

B. The Conflict of Ambition

The basic theory behind lifetime appointment of judges is that the judge will best do an independent job if he is not concerned about the continuity of his employment. That continuity can be affected by factors other than removal; the Justice may voluntarily go somewhere else. If he is an Associate, he may have hopes of becoming Chief Justice; if he is a member of the Court, he may aspire to the Presidency.

No Justice of the Supreme Court has ever been corrupted by money; but I, at least, feel that the corroding effect of ambition has on occasion done damage. To put the thing in a summary way, I have personally gone through the enormous collection of boxes of the papers of John McLean at the Library of Congress. There was no day between his appointment in 1829 and his death in 1860 in which McLean was not aspiring to be someone's choice at the next Presidential election. The ambitions particularly of Justice Field and Justice Jackson seem to me to have blighted performance. Prior to 1910, no Associate Justice had been appointed Chief Justice, and the tradition might have hardened to the point at which this would never occur. President Taft, by

---

executive capacity have been uncompensated. His occasional honoraria for participation in seminars and symposia averaged less than $1,000 per year, and are the same paid to other judges, senators, and congressmen." Letter from Judge Simon Rifkind to the Honorable Emanuel Celler, May 18, 1970.

[31] A. Mason, *Harlan Fiske Stone* 716 (1956). For strong criticism of the use of judges for nonjudicial purposes, see *S. Exec. Rep. No. 7 on Use of Judges in Nonjudicial Offices,* 80th Cong., 1st Sess. (1947).

the selection of Associate Justice White as Chief Justice in that year, broke that growing tradition irretrievably, so that now White, Hughes (after a long break in service), Stone, and Fortas have all been nominated as Chief Justices, having been Associate Justices, and perhaps Associate Justice Potter Stewart would be Chief Justice today had he not expressly renounced the possibility to President Nixon. Of the seven Chief Justice appointments since 1910, four have gone to Associates.[32]

I make no complaint on the merits of these appointments. Nonetheless, Justice Roberts once urged the adoption of a constitutional amendment making any person who thereafter accepted an associate or chief justiceship ineligible for the Presidency or the Vice-Presidency.[33] I support this and more; a country with two hundred million people can afford to immobilize nine of them.

II. Recent Developments

More attention has been paid to conflict of interest in the United States Supreme Court between July, 1968 (the nomination of Justice Fortas as Chief Justice), and June, 1970 (the seating of Justice Blackmun), than in any time in its history; and while the big guns are now silent, the end is not yet.

A. The Fortas Episode(s) and the Rules of the Judicial Conference

In June, 1968, President Johnson appointed Associate Justice Abe Fortas to the vacancy created by the resignation of Chief Justice Earl Warren; and the President also nominated Judge Homer Thornberry for the vacancy which would have been created had Justice Fortas become Chief Justice. The Fortas nomination was withdrawn at his own request before it was voted upon, and the Thornberry nomination was never seriously considered. The appointment was immediately opposed by Senator Robert Griffin of Michigan, Republican whip, because of its timing. As he forthrightly said, a Republican victory was in prospect and the new President should have the choice. Senator Griffin thereupon set the pattern for the almost two years of turmoil which were to follow by focusing opposition upon claimed conflicts of interest. From the beginning, he and his allies contended that it was improper for Fortas to have been a Johnson adviser after his appointment. The concept was reduced to the ugly-sounding word "cronyism"; the facts and their relation to precedent have been considered earlier.

[32] The Hughes with a fifteen-year break and the Fortas without confirmation.

[33] O. Roberts, "Now is the Time: Fortifying the Supreme Court's Independence," 35 *A.B.A.J.* 1 (1949). Justice Roberts also believed that no Associate Justice should become Chief Justice. He had accepted two Presidential appointments for outside services and thought that both had been mistakes.

In the course of the appointment's consideration by the Senate, a new controversy arose stemming from the fact that Fortas, while a Justice, had given a fifteen-week law course at American University in the District of Columbia. This was not unusual, nor was the fact that he was compensated; the compensation, $15,000, was larger than usual for a lectureship, but it also included the preparation of a set of materials which were turned over to American University for its use. The compensation was part of a $30,000 sum raised through personal solicitation by Fortas' former partner, Paul Porter, among five former clients of the firm, a matter as to which Fortas was not informed. In their matters, if any reached the Court, Fortas would presumably have disqualified anyway.[34] The balance was used to subsidize students, who were gathered from several law schools, and for other University purposes.

The controversy really went to the appearance of the matter. The episode was suggestive of one which had embarrassed President Nixon when he was a Senator from California and a candidate for Vice President in 1952; it had developed that he had received money in cash contributions to supplement his income or meet his expenses from various of his constituents. Differences were substantial; Nixon's was a pure income supplement, while Fortas in fact was performing the duties of a lectureship. Nonetheless, Nixon had vindicated himself before the country in the famous "Checkers" speech.[35] But a combination of factors—the urge to hold the appointment over, the objections from those who opposed Fortas on the merits of his judicial performance, and the circumstance of the lectureship—all contributed to force hearings, take time, and finally compel the withdrawal of the nomination.

In the spring of 1969, Fortas resigned from the Supreme Court in the aftermath of a direct charge of conflict of interest. Fortas had been appointed to the Supreme Court in 1965 at the strong instance of President Johnson. In so doing he relinquished a practitioner's income many times that of a Supreme Court Justice. Louis Wolfson, a former client, had been extensively involved in the construction industry and was a utility executive. He had a charitable foundation of his own, particularly interested in problems relating to civil rights. An arrangement was made with Fortas whereby he would undertake extensive work in the field of racial and religious tolerance, including some writing which would have become the property of the Foundation, and would receive an income of $20,000 a year for his life, with a similar amount to his wife should she outlive him. The bequest of Andrew Carnegie to Chief

[34] For a full discussion, see testimony of Dan B. J. Tennery, Washington College of Law, American University, *Fortas Hearings,* supra note 7 at 1286. The *Traynor Report* states that "compensation should be no more than reasonable in amount, no more than a non-judge would be paid for the same activity, and from a proper source." *Traynor Report,* supra note 2 at 5.

[35] For background and text, see E. Mazo, *Richard Nixon* 122-35 (1959).

Justice Taft and his wife mentioned earlier is similar, except that Taft had no duties. Presumably, Fortas was unaware of the criticism leveled at Taft by the Hearst press almost fifty years before.

When this arrangement was made, Wolfson, though he fell considerably short of being an esteemed public figure, was in no legal difficulties; by the end of the year he had been indicted for securities law violations. Prior to the indictment, Justice Fortas resigned his connection with the Wolfson Foundation and relinquished his future compensation agreement. After the indictment, he returned the 1966 compensation.

These episodes—the arrangement and its termination—were wholly outside the public view. Subsequently Wolfson was convicted. In May, 1969, *Life* magazine published a substantially accurate account of the episode. A giant wave of public attention and criticism followed, and Fortas resigned from the Court.

The resignation was one of the most spectacular chapters in the history of the Supreme Court. It is so recent that not enough historical documentation has as yet been discovered to make a completely clear account of the matter possible.[36] The question of judgment became so entwined with the question of conflict of interest as to make the two inseparable. On the point of judgment alone, the Taft-Carnegie parallel fails in three vital respects: first, Wolfson really was a shabby fellow and Carnegie was not, although sizeable elements of the public could reasonably be expected to be distressed at the prospect of a Justice of the Supreme Court receiving a sizeable sum from either; second, strong forces of institutionalized respectability backed Taft and Carnegie. Third, Fortas renounced his arrangement years before any public question arose and returned the one installment received; Taft was pushed into his renunciation by newspaper opinion and, it is believed, retained the first installment. Even more fundamental, Carnegie was dead and could not be suspected of making any further demands upon this earth; Wolfson was in a very different position.

But all of the foregoing matters go to judgment. As a matter of straight conflict of interest Fortas had violated no rule then existing. Prior to 1963, federal judges had been free to be associated both with corporations for profit and corporations not for profit. Justice Story, for example, was on the board of directors of a bank. In 1963, the Judicial Conference, with the whole matter before it, adopted a resolution that "No Justice or Judge of the United States shall serve in the capacity of an officer, director, or employee of a corporation organized for

[36] Attorney General Mitchell and Chief Justice Warren met on the subject, but there is no information on the factual scope of this conference. *New York Times,* May 13, 1969, at 23, col. 1.

profit."[37] This had left judges free to associate themselves with non-profit corporations and foundations, and a great many had done so; as has been previously noted, of the present Court, Chief Justice Burger had been associated with such a foundation and Justice Blackmun with a related body, and each received compensation for his time. The 1964 edition of *The Foundation Directory* lists more than a dozen federal judges associated with foundations. What happened in the Fortas case is that Wolfson's subsequent extreme legal troubles—as to which Fortas disqualified when they came to the Supreme Court—were read back into the earlier arrangement to give an appearance of impropriety whether in reality it existed or not. Because of the peculiar position which the Supreme Court occupies in American life, the appearance of wrong became more important than reality, and Fortas resigned in the belief that the Court would suffer in the work it had to do, heavily dependent as it is on public trust and confidence, if he continued.

The resignation came in May, 1969. Chief Justice Warren, whose resignation had precipitated the first Fortas controversy, was still on the bench because his successor, while then confirmed, had not yet taken his oath and would not do so until the end of the term approximately a month later. Warren caused the Judicial Conference to adopt a resolution on June 10, 1969, which precluded judges from accepting "compensation of any kind, whether in the form of loans, gifts, gratuities, honoraria or otherwise" for any services apart from their salaries. Special exemptions were allowed only "upon a determination that the services are in the public interest or are justified by exceptional circumstances and that the services will not interfere with his judicial duties."[38]

This resolution would have created a new and rigid standard which would have knocked out the participation of judges in the most benign of activities, as, for example, writing or teaching. It ran into severe criticism, one of the foremost critics being Judge Irving R. Kaufman, the presiding judge of the Second Circuit and the President of the Institute of Judicial Administration. Kaufman stressed that no activities should be permitted which interfered with the primary judicial job, nor should he engage in any activity which would "plant seeds of doubt in the mind of the public." On the other hand he felt the judges must be in the world; they should not be isolated; their knowledge and their skills should be available for the building and enrichment of the community; and that to the extent that reasonable remuneration may be required to

---

[37] *Reports of the Proceedings of the 1963 Judicial Conference of the United States* 62 (1964).

[38] *Reports of the Proceedings of the 1969 Judicial Conference of the United States* 42 (1970).

make these things possible, it is altogether proper.[39] Professor Delmar Karlen, the Director of the Institute of Judicial Administration, feeling that the Judicial Conference resolution represented what he described as "over-reaction to the Fortas incident" also wrote and testified on the need of a more relaxed and workable standard.[40]

In June, 1969, Chief Justice Burger succeeded Warren and so came to preside over the Judicial Conference. He had a long and close background of association with the Institute of Judicial Administration himself. In November, 1969, the Warren resolution was suspended pending further study, but provisions were retained requiring the reporting of outside income of judges. Meanwhile, in the declining days of the Warren administration, a last flurry occurred related directly to the Supreme Court. On June 17, 1969, the Court voted to defer consideration of Chief Justice Warren's proposal that the Court adopt for itself the standards of the Judicial Conference resolution, preferring to hold the matter until the new Justices (*i.e.,* Burger for Warren and an unnamed replacement for Fortas) might be seated.[41] A few days later the Chief Justice announced that Justices Brennan, Stewart, White and Marshall would follow the code adopted by the Judicial Conference, Justices Black, Douglas and Harlan declining to make comment.[42]

After the suspension of the Warren resolution, the whole subject went to a special American Bar Association Committee headed by Chief Justice Roger Traynor, recently retired from the Supreme Court of California, with a distinguished membership including Supreme Court Justice Stewart. The Traynor Committee did make recommendations still pending in the summer of 1970 which kept the accounting features of the Warren plan, but otherwise did generally relax its strictures. The Committee report allows for compensation and reimbursement of expenses for outside activities such as writing and teaching and participation in civic and charitable associations.[43]

It is too soon to know what the actual practice of the Supreme Court will be for the future. Justice Douglas has withdrawn as head of the Parvin Foundation, and Justice Brennan disassociated from a New York University program with which he had been connected. With the Traynor policy probably to be adopted, these rigors will not last; but it is extremely unlikely that any Justices will in the near future see fit to receive any significant outside earned income except from activities closely related to the judicial function, such as lecturing or writing.

---

[39] Address by Judge Irving R. Kaufman, Institute of Judicial Administration, in Dallas, Texas, Aug. 12, 1969.

[40] See *Report of the Director, Institute of Judicial Administration,* Sept. 26, 1969 (to be published).

[41] *New York Times,* June 18, 1969, at 1, col. 2.

[42] *New York Times,* June 24, 1969, at 24, col. 3-4.

[43] *Traynor Report,* supra, at 1-2, 5.

B. *The Post-Fortas Appointments*

1. *Chief Justice Burger.* The hearing on Chief Justice Burger was more an accolade than an inquiry; it was over in less than two hours. The only allusion to possible conflict of interest was an exchange with Senator Tydings. Tydings asked for a list of all professional corporations, business firms or enterprises in which Burger had been an officer, director, proprietor, or partner during the time that he had been on the bench. Burger responded that, apart from his strictly professional associations, he had been a trustee of the Mayo Foundation for some eleven years. Although this was not developed in the record, he had received a fee of $2,000 a year for some portion of that service, an arrangement which was perfectly appropriate under the governing 1963 Judicial Conference Resolution previously discussed. At the same time, the matter suggested possible comparison with the Wolfson Foundation. Burger recognized a duty on the part of a Chief Justice "to try to see that the judicial system functions more efficiently." To that end he would commit "every energy and every moment of the rest of my life," believing that "all matters not relating to judicial work and the improvement of the administration of justice would have to be eliminated."[44]

Chief Justice Burger did, subsequent to his confirmation, relinquish his position with the Mayo Foundation.

2. *Judge Haynsworth.* The major conflict aspect of the Haynsworth appointment was over disqualification, a matter put aside here.[45]

The only area of inquiry of a more general sort related to Haynsworth's role as director and officer of Carolina Vend-A-Matic, a company which he had helped to found and which achieved great prosperity in the sale of coffee, sandwiches and other refreshments in southern industrial plants. When Haynsworth went to the court, he was an officer and director of that company, as well as several others. He then relinquished his official connection with all except Vend-A-Matic and one other.[46] He continued to serve with the company from 1957 to 1963, when the Judicial Conference adopted the Resolution that judges should not serve as officers or directors of concerns conducted for profit.

The Vend-A-Matic directorship and officership, assuming that they were held until 1963, involved no violation of any Canon or precept of

[44] *Hearings on the Nomination of Warren E. Burger to be Chief Justice of the Supreme Court Before the Sen. Comm. on the Judiciary,* 91st Cong., 1st Sess. at 5, 9 (1969).

[45] See my companion essay in *Law and Contemporary Problems,* supra, n. 4, for a comprehensive account of the disqualification aspects of the Haynsworth, Carswell, and Blackmun appointments.

[46] *Hearings on the Nomination of Clement F. Haynsworth, Jr. to be Associate Justice of the Supreme Court Before the Sen. Comm. on the Judiciary,* 91st Cong., 1st Sess. at 42 (1969).

the Judicial Conference, much less a statute, and the relationship drew its toxic effect from two other circumstances. First, the enterprise had been splendidly profitable—the Judge parlayed a $2,400 investment in 1950 into the better part of a half million dollars in 1964 when the enterprise was sold. This spectacular increase could be given a certain tone. Apart from this, Haynsworth had had an earlier failure of memory concerning the association. The enterprise was so closely held that its affairs were considered from time to time over the lunch table rather than by any parliamentary or formal procedure. In testimony before another committee in 1969, prior to his nomination for the Justiceship, he had said casually and incidentally that he had been disassociated from all corporate offices when he went to the bench. When he was in fact nominated as a Justice, he rechecked the record with care. He was then surprised to find that he had been, according to the minutes, elected as vice president each year from 1957 to 1963, although it was his recollection that he had resigned in 1957. He told all this to the Judiciary Committee.[47] These lapses were insignificant insofar as conflict of interest was concerned because it was immaterial when the Judge disassociated from the company management so long as it was promptly after the 1963 Resolution. The relationship may or may not be significant in terms of candor; I think not, but Senator Griffin thought otherwise. In a chronicle of conflict of interest, the matter is mentioned only to be put aside.

3. *Judge Carswell.* The Carswell appointment did not, in any normal usage of the term, involve any serious question of conflict of interest. There were no stock problems as to Carswell for he had never held any corporate stock, although his wife had some.[48] Carswell became a United States Attorney for the Northern District of Florida in July, 1953. Some six months later, he was an incorporator of an all-White country club in Tallahassee. After an intervening Supreme Court decision requiring that municipal golf courses be desegregated, a municipal golf course in Tallahassee was put into private hands, obviously to avoid desegregation; again, Carswell was one of the incorporators and directors of this new club. In 1957, Carswell became the District Judge in Tallahassee, and in 1963, he bought in on a racially restricted resort area. There is some suggestion in the views of those who opposed his confirmation that these activities were in violation of his constitutional oath.[49]

The dissenting Senators did not present these episodes as a matter of

---

[47] This episode is discussed in the dissenting opinion of Senator Griffin, *Exec. Rep. No. 91-12,* 91st Cong., 1st Sess. at 40-43 (Nov. 12, 1969).

[48] *Hearings on the Nomination of George Harrold Carswell to be Associate Justice of the Supreme Court Before the Sen. Comm. on the Judiciary,* 91st Cong., 2d Sess. at 15 (1970).

[49] See memorandum attached to "Dissenting Report of Four Senators," *S. Exec. Rep. No. 91-14,* 91st Cong., 2d Sess. at 13, 14, 29-30 (Feb. 27, 1970).

conflict of interest so much as they felt them to indicate an insensitivity to human rights, and the episodes may fairly be put aside in a survey of conflict of interest.

As with Judge Haynsworth, an unfortunate bobble on an answer to a question gave Carswell more trouble than a correct answer could possibly have given; in answer to a direct question, he stated that he was not an incorporator of the 1956 country club when in fact he was; the response in context appears to have been a plain lapse of memory or mis-speaking rather than a deliberate falsehood.[50]

4. Justice Blackmun. It was an uncomfortable witness chair for nominees Haynsworth and Carswell, but for Judge Blackmun, the whole brief business was a love feast. Like Judge Haynsworth, Judge Blackmun, after he became a judge, had received income from a private corporation for profit, the Kahler Corporation. This enterprise, which was a hotel keeping concern organized in conjunction with the Mayo Clinic at Rochester, Minnesota, paid Blackmun an annual fee of $1,500. Following the adoption of the Judicial Conference Resolution of 1963, he promptly disassociated from that corporation. He also received some $8,500 in executor's fees between 1962 and 1965, all of which was in accord with existing Canon 27 of the American Bar Association Canons of Judicial Ethics as interpreted in the opinions of the ABA.[51]

Four Senators who had voted against both Judges Haynsworth and Carswell elicited this information from the Department of Justice in response to written questions:

(1) Blackmun never heard a case involving a corporation or other entity for which he was then serving as an officer, director, or in a similar capacity. He had sat in four cases involving corporations in which he had a stock interest. (In the light of the Haynsworth controversy, Judge Blackmun had abandoned this practice.)

(2) Blackmun had sat in no cases involving his own former clients; he had sat in six cases involving his former partnership, which under the accepted Canons was quite proper.

(3) The nominee simply didn't know whether he had sat in any case involving any parent, subsidiary, affiliate or major supplier or customer of any corporation in which he had an interest.[52]

Putting aside the matters of disqualification, it was swiftly and conclusively apparent that there was not even a plausible conflict of interest which could be linked to Blackmun's name.

III. A Robust and Independent Judiciary

An unhappy by-product of the Fortas and Haynsworth matters may

---

[50] *Carswell Hearings,* supra note 48, at 12.

[51] For details, see *Hearings on Nomination of Harry A. Blackmun to be Associate Justice of the Supreme Court Before the Sen. Comm. on the Judiciary,* 91st Cong., 2d Sess. at 12, 17 (1970).

[52] Letter, Richard G. Kleindienst to Senator Eastland, Apr. 28, 1970, *Blackmun Hearings,* supra, at 18-21.

be a swing of the pendulum too far toward restriction. We should not require that only eunuchs may guard the sanctuary of justice. When an administration feels pushed from millionaire Haynsworth to genteelly limited Carswell so as to get a nominee who has no stock, it is pushed too far; choices should not be narrowed so severely. Of course a rich man may be a just judge as Brandeis and Stone bear witness, and their money has to be somewhere. More broadly, judges are bound to be in activities which may affect their pocketbooks, and it is frequently a very good thing that this is so. From Justice Story, the first great legal writer in America who was a full-time professor of law at Harvard and wrote nine major legal works, to Chief Justice Burger, who in 1969 along with other distinguished American judges attended an administrative law conference at Oxford, England, leading judges have participated in activities. Justice Black, who is as close to the perfect model of ethical probity as has ever sat, has, within recent years, published an article in the Encyclopedia Britannica, published lectures at Columbia University, and participated in the production of a television film on the Constitution. Eight Justices have participated in the annual James Madison Lectures at New York University.

Not only are these good things, but the efforts to control them may be far more dangerous than any ill thought to lurk in the practices. The post-Fortas Judicial Conference resolution, now happily suspended, would have kept a judge from giving a law lecture or writing a book except with the approval of some committee of his fellow judges who must decide that the services are in the public interest or are justified. As Justice Douglas (Justice Black concurring) has said, "All power is a heady thing as evidenced by the increasing efforts of groups of federal judges to act as referees over other federal judges." Terming the practices, or their potential, "monstrous" he says, "Federal judges are entitled, like other people, to the full freedom of the First Amendment. If they break a law, they can be prosecuted. If they become corrupt or sit in cases in which they have a personal or family stake, they can be impeached by Congress. But I search the Constitution in vain for any power of surveillance which other federal judges have over those aberrations." [53]

The polygamous societies of Mohammedan countries sought to maintain the virtue of their women by veiled incarceration from the public eye. This may or may not secure virtue, but it is too high a price to pay. The benefits of having the judges in the community are too great to forego, and the benefits of their independence of judgment are the greatest of all. On the Supreme Court at least, conflicts of interest have been managed with overwhelming success by an occasional statute, the process of decision, and a very high measure of individual discretion.

[53] Chandler v. Judicial Counsel, 90 *S. Ct.* 1648, 1677-82 (1970).

MILITARY JUSTICE IN THE CONSUMER PERSPECTIVE

Daniel H. Benson

American military justice is under constant attack. It is distrusted by civilian lawyers, detested by the ordinary serviceman who is subject to it, and criticized by military legal officers who administer it.[1] The following comment by Robert Sherrill is typical of current criticism of military law:

> Because the military has been so singularly unconscious of its defects and so inept at correcting those it does recognize, countless attorneys, millions of servicemen and ex-GIs, some civilian jurists and even some politicians are now convinced that there is no use to wait longer for internal reforms and that the best thing to do is simply to take away the judicial process and return jurisdiction to the civilian courts.[2]

---

1. *See* Brown, *The Crowder-Ansell Dispute: The Emergence of General Samuel T. Ansell,* 35 MIL. L. REV. 1 (1967); Schiesser, *Trial by Peers: Enlisted Members on Courts-Martial,* 15 CATH. U.L. REV. 171 (1966); Schiesser & Benson, *Modern Military Justice,* 19 CATH. U.L. REV. 489 (1970); West, *A History of Command Influence on the Military Judicial System,* 18 U.C.L.A.L. REV. 1 (1970).

2. R. SHERRILL, MILITARY JUSTICE IS TO JUSTICE AS MILITARY MUSIC IS TO MUSIC 217 (1970). A former military judge advocate has stated:

> Under this system of 'justice' military defendants for almost two hundred years have been subjected to despotic military judicial actions. To name only a few of the more common travesties that are or have been visited on victims of the system: denial of legal counsel, increase of adjudged sentences, rigged verdicts and sentences, reversal of acquittals, and outrageous intimidation of both assigned military defense counsel and members of the court.

West, *Command Influence,* in CONSCIENCE AND COMMAND: JUSTICE AND DISCIPLINE IN THE MILITARY 73 (J. Finn ed. 1971) [hereinafter cited as CONSCIENCE AND COMMAND]. Another author has expressed his criticism of the system in this manner:

> To be court-martialed, in Army lingo, means to be convicted. More than ninety percent of all courts-martial result in 'Federal Court conviction'—an insurmountable stigma in landing most civilian jobs. During the course of the Vietnam war there have been annually seventy thousand courts-martial, service-wide; in addition, some thirty thousand men receive general or undesirable discharges through 'board actions' every year. These are run by three-officer panels.

F. GARDNER, THE UNLAWFUL CONCERT 220 (1970). Regarding the gross abuses

ARIZONA LAW REVIEW, 1971, Vol. 13, pp. 595-617.

The Supreme Court of the United States has recognized that "[a] court-martial is not yet an independent instrument of justice but remains to a significant degree a specialized part of the overall mechanism by which military discipline is preserved."[3]

Criticism of military justice is not new. Within a few years after enactment of the *Uniform Code of Military Justice*,[4] the actual functioning of the new Code was brought under sharp attack.[5] Thirty years earlier, a high-ranking Army judge advocate, Brigadier General Samuel T. Ansell, ruined his military career when he vigorously attacked the harsh system of military justice that existed during and after World War I.[6] There are even indications that some members of the committee appointed by Congress in 1776 to study and revise the Articles of War were not entirely satisfied with the result of their labors. The committee simply adopted, with minor modifications,[7] the British Articles of War. It was a choice based on expediency, as John Adams forthrightly acknowledged:

> There was extant one system of articles of war which had carried two empires to the head of mankind, the Roman and the British; for the British articles of war were only a literal translation of the Roman. It would be in vain for us to seek in our own inventions, or the records of warlike nations, for a more complete system of military discipline. . . . I was, therefore, for reporting the British articles of war, *totidem verbis*.[8]

Whatever the intent of the committee members, the continuing current criticism is easier to understand when it is realized that, in essence, the fundamental principles of the American system of military justice are those of ancient Rome. In view of the composition of the committee it is astonishing that the American system of military justice reflects the char-

---

involved in administrative discharge proceedings, see Custis, *Due Process and Military Discharges*, 57 A.B.A.J. 875 (1971).

3. O'Callahan v. Parker, 395 U.S. 258, 265 (1969).

4. 10 U.S.C. §§ 801-940 (1970) (originally enacted as Act of May 5, 1950, ch. 169, § 1, 64 Stat. 108).

5. *See, e.g.*, Keeffe, *JAG Justice in Korea*, 6 CATH. U.L. REV. 1 (1956).

6. *See* Ansell, *Some Reforms in Our System of Military Justice*, 32 YALE L.J. 146 (1922); Ansell, *Military Justice*, 5 CORNELL L.Q. 1 (1919); Brown, *supra* note 1; Morgan, *The Existing Court-Martial System and the Ansell Army Articles*, 29 YALE L.J. 52 (1919). General Ansell was reduced from Brigadier General to Lieutenant Colonel on March 4, 1919. *Hearings on S. 64 on the Establishment of Military Justice Before a Subcomm. of the Senate Comm. on Military Affairs*, 66th Cong., 1st Sess. 160-64 (1919).

7. For instance, expressions of allegiance to the Crown and reference to the colonists as "His Majesty's most faithful subjects" were deleted. *Compare* American Articles of War of 1775 *with* American Articles of War of 1776, in W. WINTHROP, MILITARY LAW AND PRECEDENTS 953-71 (1920 reprint, 2d ed. 1895). The committee members were John Adams, Thomas Jefferson, John Rutledge, Benjamin Franklin and William Hooper. 3 WORKS OF JOHN ADAMS 69 (C.F. Adams ed. 1851). The Articles are set forth at 5 JOURNALS OF THE CONTINENTAL CONGRESS 1774-1789, at 788-807 (Lib. Cong. ed. 1906). They replaced Articles adopted a year earlier. 2 *Id.* 111 (1905).

8. 3 WORKS OF JOHN ADAMS 68 (C.F. Adams ed. 1851).

acteristics of a monarchial, rather than a republican, form of government. As one commentator observed: "[O]ne would have anticipated that a distinctive American democratic flavor would be instilled into any code which it recommended for the government of men who were created equal. Nothing could be further from what occurred."[9]

In any event, the American system of military justice has been the subject of hostile criticism for years, and the intensity of the criticism is mounting rapidly. This is especially true among rank-and-file servicemen.[10] Gardner suggests that the rights of rank-and-file servicemen are undergoing such critical scrutiny today because

> GIs are demanding [their rights]. More than three million men and women find themselves subject to the UCMJ—most of them involuntarily. Some five percent of the draftees are college graduates. They are young in a country where young people are questioning their parents' values. Many of them are black and figure their primary fight is for equality at home. Others are downright political—by virtue of their education or background on the streets—and consider the war wrong as well as futile. Some are poor and see no connection between the war and their own needs. Among the WAC and nurses are innumerable women who joined the service because they felt oppressed by small towns, the dullest of jobs, meager pay; now they find their oppression has deeper roots. And there are hundreds of thousands of Vietnam returnees who are antiwar because they have seen war.[11]

This article will examine critically the military's official perspective of military justice, including the affirmative deceptions practiced consciously or unconsciously by the military to reinforce that perspective. Military justice will then be viewed from an entirely different perspective, that of its most frequent consumer, the rank-and-file serviceman. This latter examination will demonstrate the gross inequities of the present system of military justice. Finally, an alternative system of justice for military personnel will be proposed.

The title and approach[12] of the present work are based on a 1963 article by Edmond Cahn, entitled *Law in the Consumer Perspective*.[13] It

---

9. Schiesser, *supra* note 1, at 172.

10. F. GARDNER, *supra* note 2, at 217: "Many GIs feel they need an ombudsman. Currently, Congressmen receive about five hundred letters a day from soldiers. These have no political impact, since they are never collated, never perceived or presented to the public as anything but random incidents."

11. *Id.* at 225.

12. In his foreword to an anthology of Cahn's works, the late Justice Hugo L. Black said of Cahn:

> A major purpose of his books, and indeed of his life, was to promote, through analysis and discussion, governmental processes that would achieve justice. I find in his writings the same kind of inspiring arguments for equal justice for all people that is found in those enduring books which contain the maxims and precepts of the great religions and philosophies of the world.

Black, *Foreword* to E. CAHN, CONFRONTING INJUSTICE, at xi (L. Cahn ed. 1966).

13. Cahn, *Law in the Consumer Perspective*, 112 U. PA. L. REV. 1 (1963).

is unnecessary to expand upon Cahn's concepts;[14] all that is needed is to apply them to military justice. Although the consumer perspective is of primary concern, an understanding of the philosophy of the official perspective is essential to a proper appreciation of the consumer perspective.

THE OFFICIAL PERSPECTIVE

The armed services, perhaps in the hope that the criticism will dissipate, steadfastly refuse to recognize the problem. They officially view military justice as a superb system of modern criminal law and procedure. This view is evidenced by the praise usually lavished on the entire system by military lawyers.[15] There have been, however, some exceptional and courageous military officers, such as Ansell[16] and Lieutenant Colonel Charles W. Schiesser,[17] who have recognized the system for what it is and, even in the midst of the military career milieu, have done their best to reform it. Unfortunately, men of this nature are the exception, and their efforts have been slow to bear fruit. Although the United States Court of Military Appeals was intended by Congress to exercise close and skeptical supervision over those few military cases reaching it for review,[18] it has adopted the viewpoint of the military.[19]

Surprisingly, one of the early spokesmen for the official viewpoint of military justice was none other than Professor John Henry Wigmore, who adopted this position on military law: "The prime object of military organization is Victory, not Justice. . . . If the Army *can* do justice to its

---

14. For discussion of an important additional factor in military law which is not present in civilian law, affirmative deception, see text accompanying notes 32-64 *infra*.

15. *See, e.g.*, Birnbaum, *Rights of the Convicted*, 4 TRIAL, Feb.-Mar. 1968, at 14; Hodson, *"Is There Justice in the Military?"*, 15 ARMY RES. MAG., Nov.-Dec. 1969, at 22; O'Malley, *Mapp, Miranda and the Accused*, 4 TRIAL, Feb.-Mar. 1968, at 10; Ward, *UCMJ—Does it Work?*, 6 VAND. L. REV. 186 (1953); Westerman, *Court of Military Review*, 24 ARMY DIGEST, Oct. 1969, at 10, 11.

16. *See* Brown, *supra* note 1.

17. *See generally* Schiesser, *supra* note 1; Schiesser & Benson, *supra* note 1. Lieutenant Colonel Charles W. Schiesser is presently on active duty as a career Army legal officer, the status that he occupied when he authored the cited articles. Justice Douglas, writing for the majority in O'Callahan v. Parker, 395 U.S. 258 (1969), noted Schiesser's 1966 analysis of the unfairness of the military "jury" in trials of enlisted personnel. *Id.* at 263 n.2.

18. Most of the court-martial cases tried under the present system of military justice can never reach the Court of Military Appeals for appellate review, because they do not come within the narrow limits of that court's jurisdiction as set forth in 10 U.S.C. § 867(b) (1970). Of the 72,243 Army court-martial convictions in 1969, the Court of Military Appeals had jurisdiction for direct review in only 2,323 of such cases; 464 petitions for grant of review, which are similar to petitions for a writ of certiorari in the Supreme Court of the United States, were processed in 1969, but review was granted in only 61 cases. *See* ANNUAL REPORT OF THE U.S. COURT OF MILITARY APPEALS AND THE JUDGE ADVOCATES GENERAL OF THE ARMED FORCES AND THE GENERAL COUNSEL OF THE DEPARTMENT OF TRANSPORTATION 17-18 (1969).

19. *See* Benson, *The United States Court of Military Appeals*, 3 TEX. TECH. L. REV. 1 (1971). This is somewhat similar to the Interstate Commerce Commission's adoption of the industry viewpoint rather than a watchdog outlook. *See* R. FELLMETH, THE INTERSTATE COMMERCE OMISSION (1970).

men, well and good. But Justice is always secondary; and Victory is always primary."[20] Wigmore continued:

> Military justice wants *discipline*—that is, action in obedience to regulations and orders; this being absolutely necessary for prompt, competent, and decisive handling of masses of men. The court-martial system supplies the sanction of this discipline. It takes on the features of Justice because it must naturally perform the process of inquiring in a particular case, what was the regulation or order, and whether it was in fact obeyed. But its object is discipline.[21]

The present official perspective, which is not significantly different from Wigmore's primitive approach, was expressed quite accurately as follows: "The aims of [the American and French] systems of military justice are the same—swift enforcement of military order and discipline while guaranteeing to the accused the maximum legal protections *reasonably available under the circumstances*."[22] The *Army Staff Judge Advocate Handbook* (SJA Handbook) states: "Military justice in a very real sense represents the correctional side of military discipline."[23] This, then, is the official approach to military justice, the official perspective.

Philosophy of the Official Perspective

The definitive explanation of the official perspective of law was set forth by Edmond Cahn who said: "All the modern legal systems have inherited a single characteristic way of viewing the problems of society. We may call it the 'imperial or official perspective' because it has been largely determined by the dominant interests of rulers, governors, and other officials."[24] According to Cahn, the official perspective "has a typical rhetoric which, when expertly manipulated, can seem very persuasive."[25] This rhetoric is persuasive because it makes use of phrases and maxims that would be reasonable if restricted to their proper uses. All too frequently, however, such language is misused by those promoting the official perspective.[26] Cahn concluded that while it may be true in

---

20. Address by Professor Wigmore to the Maryland Bar Association, June 28, 1919, in 24 MD. ST. B. ASS'N TRANS. 183, 188 (1919), *reprinted in* Wigmore, *Lessons from Military Justice*, 4 J. AM. JUD. SOC'Y 151 (1921). Wigmore was a reserve colonel in the Army Judge Advocate General's Department.

21. *Id.*

22. Ryker, *The New French Code of Military Justice*, 44 MIL. L. REV. 71, 93 (1969) (emphasis added).

23. DEPARTMENT OF THE ARMY, STAFF JUDGE ADVOCATE HANDBOOK 7 (Pamph. 27-5, 1963) [hereinafter cited as SJA HANDBOOK].

24. Cahn, *supra* note 13, at 4.

25. *Id.* at 5.

26. Cahn gave some examples, *id.* at 6:

> Some of the familiar phrases are: the public interest in getting things finally settled; the duty to abide by established principles and precedents; the necessity of showing respect for expert judgment and administrative convenience; the dominant need for certainty in the law; the obligation to preserve the law's predictability so that men will know how to order their affairs; the danger of opening the gates of penitentiaries

some instances that "hard cases make bad law," frequently, as a result of the rationalizations put forth by advocates of the official perspective, "bad law makes hard cases."[27] It is traditional for jurists of the official perspective, Cahn noted, "to justify the legal system in terms of averages, wholesale statistics, and overall performances."[28]

Cahn's philosophy of the official perspective of law is consistent with the rationalizations employed by the official supporters of the present system of military justice. In military justice, as in the law generally, those who support the official perspective are the "rulers, governors, and other officials." They are the judge advocates general, the senior commanding officers, the judges of the United States Court of Military Appeals, and the judges of the various courts of military review.[29] They employ a rhetoric which seems extremely persuasive when "expertly manipulated." Furthermore, as Cahn pointed out, the persuasiveness of such rhetoric is based upon the reasonableness the phrases and maxims have when restricted to their proper uses. The problem is that in military law, as in other areas of the law using the official perspective, they are not so restricted.[30] Military authorities also seek to justify the present system of military justice in terms of "averages, wholesale statistics, and overall performances."[31] The points made by Cahn about the official perspective of civilian jurisprudence and courts, therefore, are applicable with equal force to military law and courts-martial.

Affirmative Deception

An additional factor, insofar as military justice is concerned, is the affirmative deception engaged in by advocates of the official perspective in military law. It is a delicate matter, but its examination is fundamental to a correct understanding of the actual functioning of American military justice.[32] If properly understood, the matter of affirmative deception may have a significant impact on reform legislation in the future.

. . . and (by way of solace to the man on his way to the electric chair) the undeniable right to petition for executive clemency.

27. *Id.* at 8.

28. *Id.* at 16.

29. These are the intermediate appellate courts in the American military justice system. *See* 10 U.S.C. § 866 (1970).

30. See text accompanying note 64 *infra.*

31. Cahn, *supra* note 13, at 16. *See generally* articles cited *supra* note 15 for examples of such justifications.

32. The question of affirmative deception on the part of advocates of the official perspective in military justice apparently has not been raised in the literature of the legal profession. It has been discussed to some extent in nonlegal books and articles concerning military justice. *See, e.g.,* F. GARDNER, *supra* note 2; R. SHERRILL, *supra* note 2; West, *supra* note 1. See also Henry B. Rothblatt's trenchant account of the vast difference between military justice in theory and in practice as he experienced it while acting as defense counsel in the Green Berets' case. Rothblatt, *Why the Army Tried to Railroad the Green Berets,* TRUE, Mar. 1970, at 29-33, 96-97. Affirmative deception, however, has never been precisely delineated as such or considered specifically as a significant individual phenomenon in our system of military law. Although some aspects of this deception were dis-

Neither the motives of those who engage in such deception nor the extent to which they are aware of their conduct is raised here. They may have been so deeply indoctrinated with the military viewpoint that they simply do not perceive the divergence between the official perspective and the objective facts of military justice as it functions. A senior career Army officer has said:

> [T]he whole Army structure is pervaded with fear of reprisals that stifles any whisper of dissent. Reprisal can come in many forms—the 'efficiency report,' secret 'security' investigation, character assassination, professional ostracism and humiliation. The consequence is to keep many good officers gagged in obedience to the Army's protective self-deceptions, and frees the less observant to get away with anything. One self-deception is that the end justifies the means . . . .[33]

Regardless of the motives or awareness of those who utilize the deceptions of the official perspective, the question of affirmative deception must be closely examined to appreciate its significance in military justice. It is beyond the scope of this article to catalog and discuss all of the deceptions practiced by advocates of the official perspective in military law. Accordingly, three typical examples—the nature of the military judge, the alleged abolition of command influence, and the role of the staff judge advocate—will be set forth.

The military judge is an appropriate example with which to begin. With the enactment of the Military Justice Act of 1968,[34] the position of "military judge" was created. In an early article a senior Army judge advocate wrote that the military judge "has been given functions and powers more closely allied to those of a federal district judge, except that in a trial with court members [the military jurors], the members still determine the sentence."[35] A senior military judge of the United States Air Force Court of Military Review, stated that a military judge has "functions and powers more closely aligned with those of Federal district judges."[36] Former Chief Judge Robert Quinn of the Court of Military Appeals expressed the view that the provisions relating to the military judge in the Military Justice Act of 1968 "will conform military procedures more closely to that of the Federal civil courts."[37] In addition, there has

---

cussed peripherally in Schiesser, *supra* note 1, and Schiesser & Benson, *supra* note 1, the matter was not isolated for special consideration. *See also* Benson, *We are the Casualties,* 21 REFORMED J. 3 (1971); Benson, *The Christian and Military Justice,* 20 REFORMED J. 6 (1970).

33. King, *Making it in the U.S. Army*, NEW REPUBLIC, May 30, 1970, at 19-21.

34. 10 U.S.C. §§ 801-936 (1970). The presiding legal officer at a court-martial was formerly designated a "law officer."

35. Westerman, *supra* note 15, at 11.

36. Goldschlager, *The Military Judge: A New Judicial Capacity,* 11 A.F. JAG L. REV. 175 (1969). The author was as well a senior judge advocate prior to August 1969.

37. Letter from former Chief Judge Robert E. Quinn of the United States Court of Military Appeals to Philip J. Philbin, Chairman of the Committee on Armed Services, Subcommittee No. 1, *quoted in* Goldschlager, *supra* note 36, at 180.

been "widespread undiscriminating comparison of military judges with federal district judges"[38] in the literature of the legal profession.[39]

The truth about the status and functioning of the military judge renders such widespread comparison with a federal district judge ludicrous. A military judge has no tenure; he is merely a judge advocate officer who can be assigned to judicial duties by his judge advocate general or by the personnel branch within his particular judge advocate general's corps. He can be removed from judicial duties without cause, advance notice, or a hearing.[40] Some military judges are assigned to armed services headquarters in Washington, D.C., and then located for duty purposes in various posts, bases and stations around the country and the world. The vast majority of military judges, however, are assigned directly to the local senior commanding officer of the particular post, base or station.[41]

The ruling of a military judge dismissing a specification before a court-martial, where the ruling does not amount to a finding of not guilty, can be set aside by the military officer who convened the court-martial and ordered the charges to trial.[42] Unlike a federal district judge, a military judge has no power to order the confinement and release of an individual under any circumstances. A military judge "finds" an accused guilty, but that finding and the ensuing sentence have no legal effect until and unless the lay military officer who convened the court approves it.[43] If the lay convening authority disapproves all or any part of the finding of guilt or the sentence, which he may do with or without reason, the military judge is absolutely powerless to alter that determination.[44] A military judge has certain very limited powers to hold a service member in contempt of court, but that determination and any sentence imposed have no legal effect until and unless the military commander who convened the court approves them.[45]

---

38. Schiesser & Benson, *supra* note 1, at 498.

39. *See, e.g.*, Cutler, *The Right and Duty of the Law Officer to Comment on the Evidence*, 35 MIL. L. REV. 91 (1967); Grimm, *Criminal Justice in the Military Establishment*, 37 J. AM. JUD. SOC'Y 14, 19 (1953); Miller, *Who Made the Law Officer a "Federal Judge"?*, 4 MIL. L. REV. 39 (1959); O'Connell, *Independent Judiciary of the Army*, 5 BOSTON B.J. 21, 22 (1961).

40. Both the Code and the *Manual for Courts-Martial* are silent on the matter of tenure for military judges. Compare the provisions of the Administrative Procedure Act, 5 U.S.C. § 7521 (1970), which allow removal of a federal hearing examiner only after an opportunity for a hearing and upon a showing of good cause.

41. Army Reg. 27-10, ¶ 9-2(c-d) (change 8, Sept. 7, 1971); *cf.* Douglass, *The Judicialization of Military Courts*, 22 HAST. L.J. 213 (1971).

42. DEPARTMENT OF DEFENSE, MANUAL FOR COURTS-MARTIAL ¶ 67f (rev. ed. 1969) [hereinafter cited as MANUAL]. *See also* DEPARTMENT OF THE ARMY, ANALYSIS OF CONTENTS [OF] MANUAL FOR COURTS-MARTIAL, UNITED STATES, 1969 REVISED EDITION (Pamph. 27-2, 1970).

43. 10 U.S.C. §§ 860, 864 (1970).

44. *Id.* § 864. *See also* United States v. Kirsch, 15 U.S.C.M.A. 84, 91, 35 C.M.R. 56, 63 (1964); United States v. Massey, 5 U.S.C.M.A. 514, 520, 18 C.M.R. 138, 144 (1955).

45. 10 U.S.C. § 848 (1970); MANUAL, *supra* note 42, at ¶ 118.

A military judge has no power to enforce the orders of his court; for example, all orders for the production of evidence and witnesses depend upon the response, or lack of it, by lay military commanders.[46] The court over which a military judge presides does not come into existence until the order of a military commander gives it life. Similarly, the military commander can abolish it by a military order whenever he wishes.[47] No court-martial exists until a military commander creates it with a military order,[48] and indeed the Army Court of Military Review recently noted that courts-martial "are not a portion of the Judiciary of the United States. They are part of the Executive, rather than the Judicial, branch of our Government."[49] There are other significant ways in which a military judge differs from a federal district judge, but the foregoing specific items should suffice to make it abundantly clear that whatever a military judge is, he differs in many important respects from a federal district judge.

A second affirmative deception is the assertion that command influence on military justice has been virtually abolished in the armed services. Nothing could be further from the truth. The extensive study by Luther West, a former career Army judge advocate, plainly shows and adequately documents the widespread extent of improper command influence throughout the legal branch of the Army today.[50] Military commanders still frighten, intimidate, and thoroughly control legal functionaries in the American system of military justice, whether the legal functionary is a prosecutor, defense counsel, court member ("juror"), staff judge advocate (senior legal adviser to a commander), or Judge Advocate General. Henry Rothblatt's article on the Green Berets' case,[51] although written for popular consumption, is the first-hand report of a veteran criminal trial lawyer and author of several books on criminal trial work. Rothblatt details thoroughly the almost incredible degree to which General Creighton Abrams, Jr., was able to control, influence, and ultimately determine the final disposition of the Green Berets' case, notwithstanding the requirements of procedure, the *Uniform Code of Military Justice*, or other aspects of military law. Both Robert Sherrill and Fred

46. Control over military personnel rests with military commanders of various units, posts and stations; only they can order military personnel to attend trials as witnesses, in response to the "order" of a military judge. Similarly, such commanders control official military records, and may or may not produce them on demand by a judge. *See, e.g.,* Army Reg. 195-10, ¶ 4-4f (Jan. 8, 1968), which requires the express approval of the Provost Marshal General for release of military police investigation reports.

47. MANUAL, *supra* note 42, at ¶ 5a.

48. *See* United States v. Robinson, 13 U.S.C.M.A. 674, 33 C.M.R. 206 (1963).

49. United States v. Bowman, 42 C.M.R. 825, 828 (1970). *See* C. WRIGHT, LAW OF FEDERAL COURTS 34 (2d ed. 1970).

50. West, *supra* note 1; West, *Command Influence,* in CONSCIENCE AND COMMAND, *supra* note 2.

51. Rothblatt, *supra* note 35. Henry Rothblatt recently served as defense counsel in the trial of Colonel Oran K. Henderson for his conduct in connection with the events at My Lai.

Gardner list incident upon incident of unlawful command influence in the trial of recent court-martial cases.[52] Command influence remains a powerful and corrupting influence throughout military justice.

By contrast, the position of advocates of the official perspective is that command influence, as a significant problem in military law, is a thing of the past. They cite the provisions of the Military Justice Act of 1968 which "strengthen"[53] the prohibitions against command influence.[54] The amendments to the Code, however, merely list and prohibit various kinds of unlawful command influence not specifically mentioned under the prior Code. Despite these new provisions, unlawful command influence persists.

The Court of Military Appeals apparently views command influence as almost nonexistent, since it has seen fit to consider the issue so infrequently. The *Uniform Code of Military Justice* was in existence for 10 years before the first significant case of alleged command influence reached the court in 1961, and another 6 years passed before the court again acted on the issue.[55] This record says little about the actual existence of command influence in the armed services, but it speaks clearly about the extent to which the Court of Military Appeals may be divorced from the reality of the situation. Former Judge Latimer once said: "[I]f anyone now believes that a court-martial is merely an agency of the commander, and governed solely by his whims, then he is too blind to see what has clearly been spelled out by members of Congress."[56] Apparently the trial of Lieutenant William Calley made a believer out of Latimer, now in private practice, who defended Calley. He insisted that command influence in the *Calley* case started with President Nixon and worked its way down through the Army's chain of command.[57]

A third deception may be found in the provisions of the *Manual for Courts-Martial*, the *Uniform Code of Military Justice*, and the assertions of apologists for the official perspective: the chief legal officer of a command, the staff judge advocate, is a detached and impartial quasi-judicial official.[58] The staff judge advocate has the duty of providing legal advice

---

52. F. GARDNER, *supra* note 2; R. SHERRILL, *supra* note 2.
53. Simpson, *How the MCM, 1969 (Rev.) Provides for: I. Improvements in Trial by Special Court-Martial, II. Increased Safeguards Against Command Influence, III. Simplified Procedures on Oaths and Records of Trial,* 11 A.F. JAG L. REV. 181, 193 (1969).
54. 10 U.S.C. § 837(b) (1970). *See* Comment, *The Military Justice Act of 1968: Congress Takes Half-Steps Against Unlawful Command Influence,* 18 CATH. U.L. REV. 429 (1969).
55. *See* United States v. Kitchens, 12 U.S.C.M.A. 589, 31 C.M.R. 175 (1961); United States v. DuBay, 17 U.S.C.M.A. 147, 37 C.M.R. 411 (1967).
56. Commencement address by George W. Latimer, former judge, U.S. Court of Military Appeals, to the Judge Advocate General's School, U.S. Army, Charlottesville, Virginia, Jan. 18, 1952, *quoted in* Landman, *One Year of the Uniform Code of Military Justice: A Report of Progress,* 4 STAN. L. REV. 491, 508 (1952).
57. *See* R. SHERRILL, *supra* note 2, at 217.
58. *See generally* 10 U.S.C. §§ 834, 861 (1970); MANUAL, *supra* note 42, at

to the commander on all military justice matters.[59] Moreover, the staff judge advocate is the immediate commanding officer of all prosecutors and defense counsel in the particular command; he renders their military efficiency reports, assigns them to various cases, determines their role in a given case, and otherwise controls their functioning in his office. In the broadest sense, he closely resembles a civilian district attorney. Yet he is the official who must perform the conflicting functions of advising the senior military commander whether to refer a case to trial, and then, after trial of the case, of *impartially and objectively* preparing a review of the matter and advising the commander what action should be taken to affirm, alter or reject the findings and sentences. Merely to state the proposition upon which his functioning is based is to refute it; no man can judge his own work impartially. That impossible task, in effect, is what the spokesmen of the official perspective in military justice are advocating.

The result of this particular deception has been tragic, for it is largely through the staff judge advocate that most of the unlawful command influence in the military justice system is perpetrated. Former Judge Advocate West states:

> Neither the concept nor practice of military justice could have developed as they have within the Armed Forces of the United States were it not that the Supreme Court and the American people have been tragically indifferent to the plight of the military defendant. Neither our people nor our courts acknowledge that military commanders and military staff judge advocates are not fair-minded men in the judicial sense of the word; that they are, basically, incapable of operating a system of justice along democratic principles.[60]

Indeed, the SJA Handbook—which is a practical manual for the operation of a staff judge advocate's office rather than a publication designed to bolster the image of the military justice system—bluntly informs all staff judge advocates that they are representatives of the command first, and lawyers second.[61] The Handbook also informs the staff judge advocate that since "his efficiency report will usually be prepared by the chief of staff . . . [he] must be a working and cooperative member of the staff."[62] He is pointedly reminded that he "must acquaint himself with the personality and the policies of his commander."[63] These instructions are un-

---

¶ 85; West, *supra* note 1, at 106-07; West, *Permissible Bounds of Staff Judge Advocate Pretrial Activity*, 23 MIL. L. REV. 85 (1964).

59. *See generally* SJA HANDBOOK 7-53.

60. West, *Command Influence*, in CONSCIENCE AND COMMAND, *supra* note 2, at 73-74.

61. SJA HANDBOOK at 75: "First, the staff judge advocate of a command is a staff officer and, as such, has the duty to assist the commander to command effectively and to accomplish the assigned mission. Second, as a judge advocate, he is the military legal advisor to the commander."

62. *Id.* at 76.

63. *Id.* at 8.

likely to foster the development of independent legal officials who can function with courage and impartiality. They serve as warnings to the staff judge advocate that his first loyalty is to his commander, even to the detriment of his legal judgment.

Many additional deceptions could be described, but the three examples set forth are sufficient to demonstrate that the official military perspective relies on more than mere exaggeration of the merits of the system in order to sustain itself. The way in which apologists of the official perspective in military justice use language to accomplish such deception raises serious linguistic questions and borders on the Orwellian. Linguistic analysis seeks to clarify the meaning of statements by investigating the way in which they are ordinarily used.[64] The same methodology might be used profitably in the field of military justice, where advocates of the official perspective misapply words having specific connotations. The term "independent" when applied to a military judge is one example. When used to describe a federal district judge, the word "independent" has certain well-understood, accepted connotations. A federal district judge is appointed for life on good behavior and cannot be removed from office on the basis of unpopular decisions. This independence tends to promote a certain fearlessness and integrity commonly associated with the federal judiciary. It is a misuse of language, however, to refer to a military judge as independent and to compare him with a federal district judge. Furthermore, it is deceptive to attempt to qualify the use of the word "independent" when talking about a military judge, for it must be qualified to the point where it no longer retains any vestige of its original meaning.

The foregoing analysis of affirmative deception is essential since the official perspective in military justice cannot be fully understood without an appreciation of the extent to which deception is practiced to make palatable the grosser inequities of the present system.

The Consumer Perspective

Edmond Cahn explained that the consumer perspective in law looks at the targets of the law's impacts:

> In the consumer perspective, the significance of any principle, rule, or concept, however exalted, is investigated by observing the specific human targets of its impacts and the occasions when it becomes material to concrete experiences of the members of the community. It was this method that disclosed that the sense of injustice—rather than a purported sense of justice—exerted vital influence within the operations of law.[65]

---

64. Linguistic analysis has been brought to bear in recent years in the field of religious language. *See* P. van Buren, The Secular Meaning of the Gospel 81-106 (1963); New Essays in Philosophical Theology (A. Flew & A. MacIntyre eds. 1955).

65. Cahn, *supra* note 13, at 14.

Most of the defendants tried by American courts-martial, the specific human targets of military justice, are enlisted men in the lower ranks and grades of the armed forces. Trials of officers and senior noncommissioned officers are comparatively rare. This fact is of great significance in an examination of any aspect of American military justice.

The system of military justice is under officer control which begins with an enlisted man's immediate commanding officer and culminates in the almost unlimited power of the officer who is the convening authority. Charges are usually preferred by the serviceman's immediate commanding officer, transmitted to officers for processing through trial and conviction, and then given to the convening authority, who alone can refer charges to trial by court-martial.[66] After trial the case may go to the court of military review of the particular service, where once more officers pass upon the legal and factual sufficiency of the case.[67] Since they do not have the money to retain civilian counsel, the overwhelming majority of military defendants have officers for defense counsel at all trial and appellate levels. The case eventually may reach the United States Court of Military Appeals where, for the first time, there are no officer-judges.

Most military "jurors" are officers; at most, a military defendant can expect only one-third of his court members to be enlisted personnel, and even for that proportion he must make a written demand prior to trial.[68] Furthermore, the armed services again have managed to practice a cruel deception on the Congress, the Court of Military Appeals, and the enlisted personnel subject to court-martial jurisdiction: if an enlisted service member demands enlisted court members, senior noncommissioned officers (sergeants) will usually be appointed by the convening authority.[69] Senior sergeants are among the least sympathetic and the most

---

66. 10 U.S.C. § 834 (1970).

67. An exception is the Navy Court of Military Review which permits civilian judges to sit with officers.

68. 10 U.S.C. § 825(c) (1970).

69. Joseph W. Bishop, Jr., now Richard Ely Professor of Law at Yale, and in 1952-53 Deputy General Counsel and Acting General Counsel of the Army, said in a 1970 article: "The code entitles an enlisted man to demand that enlisted men be among the members of the court-martial that tries him, but he knows that what he will probably get are first and master sergeants, who are likely to be rougher than commissioned officers." Bishop, *The Quality of Military Justice,* N.Y. Times, Feb. 22, 1970, § 6 (magazine), at 38. It was the intent of Congress that an enlisted soldier should be tried, if he so desired, by a panel consisting of at least one-third of his *peers* rather than senior sergeants. See *Hearings on H.R. 2498 Before a Subcomm. of the House Armed Services Comm.*, 21st Cong., 1st Sess. 1140 (1949). Judge Homer Ferguson, of the Court of Military Appeals, dissenting in United States v. Crawford, 15 U.S.C.M.A. 31, 35 C.M.R. 3 (1964), noted that the Army practice of always appointing only senior noncommissioned officers has "rendered valueless" the right envisioned by Congress and commented that the still existing technical right "to have enlisted personnel on one's court-martial has become a relatively dead letter throughout the armed services." *Id.* at 55, 35 C.M.R. at 27. This is the natural result of placing senior noncommissioned officers on court-martial panels when enlisted men are requested.

conviction-oriented of all the members of the armed forces, with the exception perhaps of the senior officers.[70] A low ranking enlisted service member has little hope of being tried by a "jury" of his peers, and, regrettably, the Court of Military Appeals has actually sanctioned that result.[71]

The sense of injustice mentioned by Cahn arises when the largest single segment of the military population is denied the right to participate in the military judicial process except as criminal defendants. Theoretically, any member of the armed services can prefer charges against any other member,[72] but in practice, throughout the American system of military justice, officers are in full control. The right of a private to prefer criminal charges against a commanding general is, therefore, largely illusory.

Perhaps the best way to summarize the general inequities of the entire American military justice system is to consider the stark powers of the convening authority, which are vastly greater than those vested in any single official in any civilian judicial system[73] and include the exclusive right to refer a case to trial. Most of the courts-martial tried in the armed forces are special courts-martial,[74] which require no formal pretrial investigation. In order to refer a case to a general court-martial,[75] however, the convening authority must first order a formal "Article 32 Investigation," so designated because it is required by that article of the Code.[76] The Article 32 Investigation is praised by advocates of the official perspective who compare it to and extol its superiority over grand jury investigation.[77] There is a catch, however, in the best tradition of Joseph Heller's *Catch 22*. The catch is that no matter how thorough or satisfactory the investigation, the convening authority is not bound to follow the recommendations made by the officer who conducted it.

---

70. Edward Sherman points out that "non-commissioned officers . . . are usually considered even more disciplinarian and severe than officers." Sherman, *Justice in the Military*, in CONSCIENCE AND COMMAND: JUSTICE AND DISCIPLINE IN THE MILITARY, 21, 48 (J. Finn ed. 1971). *See also* Bishop, *supra* note 69.

71. United States v. Crawford, 15 U.S.C.M.A. 31, 35 C.M.R. 3 (1964). *See* Benson, *The Military Jury: An Unrepresentative Tribunal?* 7 TRIAL, Sept.-Oct. 1971, at 40; Higley, *Flawed Justice,* 7 TRIAL, Sept.-Oct. 1971, at 45.

72. 10 U.S.C. § 830 (1970).

73. See authorities collected in note 47 *supra.*

74. Special courts-martial have jurisdiction to try military personnel for any noncapital offense punishable under the *Uniform Code of Military Justice* (UCMJ). They are empowered to adjudge any punishment not forbidden by the UCMJ except death, dishonorable discharge, dismissal, confinement for more than six months, hard labor without confinement for more than three months, forfeiture of pay exceeding two-thirds pay per month, or forfeiture of pay for more than six months. 10 U.S.C. § 819 (1970).

75. General courts-martial have jurisdiction to try military personnel for any offense punishable under the UCMJ. They are empowered to adjudge any punishment not forbidden by the UCMJ, including the penalty of death where specifically authorized. *Id.* § 818.

76. *Id.* § 832.

77. *See, e.g.,* Moyer, *Procedural Rights of the Military Accused Over a Civilian Defendant*, 22 ME. L. REV. 105, 109-14 (1970).

Gardner illustrated perfectly this basic flaw in the Article 32 Investigation by describing how the convening authority in the Presidio "Mutiny" Cases completely overruled the investigating officer's report recommending no mutiny court-martial, and referred the cases to trial.[78] Furthermore, during the trial the convening authority has the power to overrule decisions of the military judge on issues of law,[79] and after the trial to approve all, part, or none of the findings and sentence, as he sees fit. All this is in addition to his power to appoint judge, "jury," prosecutor, and defense counsel in every case.[80]

The armed services are apparently unconcerned that the great majority of American servicemen have no opportunity to participate in the judicial system to which they are subject during their period of military duty.[81] Edmond Cahn would have disagreed, believing as he did that when it comes to justice one cannot merely classify the consumers of law as facets or fragments of men, but must consider them as whole men: "[The law] puts the whole man in jail, hangs the whole man, takes away money, status, and property that affect the life of the whole man. When it imposes guilts, they pervade the whole man."[82] Our system of military justice regularly and systematically deprives whole men of the right to participate in the judicial system under which they must live for a significant part of their lives. It imposes guilt upon these same whole men, and they resent and chafe under the arbitrary functioning of such a system. This situation is not only unsatisfactory, but also unnecessary.

First, it is not necessary to deprive lower ranking enlisted men of their rights as American citizens. Other nations treat their soldiers differently and more humanely:

> Soldiers in the West German Army can now join unions and negotiate with the government as to living and working conditions; also, the German Army has recently junked the appellation 'sir' in addressing superior officers. The East German Army did away with sirring long ago. France, shocked by the obedience of junior officers to rebellious generals in Algeria, has rewritten its code of justice to permit much more independence of thought and action. And in some respects the Israeli Army is almost a classless society.[83]

Similarly, our ordinary enlisted personnel should be allowed to participate in the system of justice to which they are subject.

Second, there is likely to be a harmful long-term effect on Ameri-

---

78. *See* F. GARDNER, *supra* note 2, at 106-10.
79. MANUAL, *supra* note 42, at ¶ 67f.
80. 10 U.S.C. §§ 825-27 (1970).
81. The basic, consistent position of the armed forces is that the present officer-controlled system of military justice is virtually without flaw. See authorities collected *supra* note 15, and note that no discussion of the opinions or reactions of enlisted personnel to the present military law system is presented.
82. Cahn, *supra* note 13, at 15.
83. R. SHERRILL, *supra* note 2, at 220.

can society as a whole if a large segment of the population are deprived of their legal rights for a period of two to four years of their lives. As Robert Sherrill correctly stated: "Justice is too important to be left to the military. If military justice is corrupt—and it is—sooner or later it will corrupt civilian justice. Perhaps this has already begun."[84] Sherrill further noted that when one-fifth of all adults have had some military service, it is no longer possible to separate military life from civilian life. The lessons and experiences of the one are carried over into the other. It is unhealthy for rights—indeed, to deprive them of justice itself—during the period of their our society to deprive large numbers of our younger citizens of substantial military service, and then expect them to resume their places in civilian society with an attitude of trust toward our courts and faith in our civilian judicial system. In view of the teachings of Edmond Cahn about the consumer perspective, this is folly of a very serious nature, and its effects upon us are likely to be long-lasting.

Reform of Military Justice

Past reforms of the *Uniform Code of Military Justice* have been ineffective in correcting the defects inherent in the American system of military justice. As West expressed it in his definitive analysis of unlawful command influence:

> The military judicial setting is still dominated by military commanders, from the inception of charges to the completion of appellate review, with the exception of the handful of cases each year that are subject to review by the United States Court of Military Appeals, and in these cases only a semblance of constitutional protection against command control is afforded the military defendant.[85]

Further piecemeal reform would be inadequate so long as real control of the military legal system remains in the hands of the nonlegal military commanding officers.

In 1970, Lietuenant Colonel Charles W. Schiesser and the author proposed specific reforms considered essential to an adequate overhaul of the present military justice system.[86] It was recommended that military judges be given the tenure and independence necessary to make them comparable to federal district judges, and urged that military convening authorities be divested of the power to overrule military judges on issues of law.[87] It was also suggested that military appellate judges be given sufficient tenure and independence to enable them to discharge their responsibilities, and that the various armed forces courts of military review be provided with specific statutory authority to issue extraordinary writs

84. *Id.* at 213.
85. West, *supra* note 1, at 151.
86. Schiesser & Benson, *supra* note 1, at 518-19.
87. *Id.*

in aid of their jurisdiction.[88] It was further proposed that convening authorities be divested of their power to determine the membership of the courts-martial that they convene, and recommended that defense counsel for all court-martial cases be granted full independence and insulation from the pressures that may now be exerted upon them by military commanders.[89] An independent, central defense organization to which all military defense counsel would be assigned was suggested as a possible method of providing adequate protection for those military lawyers who defend the consumers of military justice.[90] Beneficial as these changes might be, however, they would still constitute mere patchwork reform, and this, unfortunately, is characteristic of the reforms proposed by other concerned observers of our military justice system.[91]

Although the American military justice system was altered by reform legislation in 1920, 1950 and 1968, "the basic court structure, the method of selection of the court, the commander's control of the court machinery, the statement of certain crimes, and the heavy reliance on administrative reviews rather than judicial appeals have not been substantially altered."[92] West even goes so far as to question whether the changes made by such legislation were, in any meaningful sense, reforms at all.[93]

If this is true, then what is the solution? West proposes to transfer all military justice functions from the armed forces to a civilian agency:

> With only minor exceptions, the system of military justice in this county must be completely removed from the operational control of the military departments, and placed in the hands of civilian administrators, preferably under the control of the Attorney General of the United States.[94]

That step in the right direction constitutes the minimum reform that should be undertaken, but more is required.

The United States may look to Germany for an example of what is needed in the American system of military justice. In spite of traditional German militarism, military justice in the Federal Republic of Germany has been returned to civilian control. Criminal offenses committed by German armed forces members are tried in the civil rather than military courts.[95] Although this represents a radical departure from the immediate past, the Germans are quite satisified with their new system.[96]

---

88. *Id.* at 519.
89. *Id.* at 518.
90. *Id.* at 508.
91. *See, e.g.*, Sherman, *The Civilianization of Military Law*, 22 ME. L. REV. 3, 86-87, 96-100, 102-03 (1970).
92. *Id.* at 59.
93. "Our lesson from history is that lesser reforms, designed to leave the military judicial system in the operational control of military commanders, or to leave the punishment of military commanders who overreach the system in military hands, *are reforms in name only*." West, *supra* note 1, at 154 (emphasis added).
94. *Id.* at 153-54.
95. *See* N.Y. Times, Apr. 11, 1969, at 12, col. 1; *id.*, Apr. 9, 1969, at 3, cols. 1-2.
96. When the West German army was established in 1955, it was constructed

Legislation should be enacted withdrawing jurisdiction from the military justice system for all offenses other than crimes against the military, such as absence without leave, refusal to obey orders and desertion. All other jurisdiction, including crimes created by the common law and state and federal statutes, should be vested exclusively in the state and federal courts having subject-matter jurisdiction for those crimes and within whose geographical jurisdiction the crime was committed.

The Supreme Court, by its 1969 decision in *O'Callahan v. Parker*,[97] adopted this general approach and divested the military of some of its prior court-martial jurisdiction. The defendant in *O'Callahan* had been convicted by a court-martial of nonmilitary offenses committed in a civilian community while he was on leave.[98] A majority of the Court held that the military was without jurisdiction to try such offenses under the circumstances, since there was no "service connected" crime involved. The majority opinion noted that the petitioner was properly absent from his military base when he committed the crimes with which he was charged, the crimes were not committed on a military post or enclave, the situs of the crime was not an armed camp under military control, there was no connection between the crimes charged and the defendant's military duties, the victim was not performing any duties related to the military, the crimes were peacetime offenses and were committed in American territory rather than in a foreign country, the civil courts were open and functioning, and the crimes did not involve any flouting of military authority.

Due to the careful enumeration of factors which removed this case from court-martial jurisdiction, the opinion's scope is somewhat uncertain. It is at least arguable that if one or more of the listed characteristics were not present, the same court would have found that the exercise of military jurisdiction was proper.[99] This uncertainty is heightened by the recent appointment of two new associate justices to the Supreme Court of the United States. It appears, therefore, that further limitations on court-martial jurisdiction are more likely to be enunciated by Congress than by the Court.

---

on democratic principles, and troops were made subject to civilian courts for discipline. There have been no military courts in West Germany since the collapse of Hitler's regime in 1945, and there has been general satisfaction over the absence of courts-martial. Sherman, *supra* note 91, at 92.

97. 395 U.S. 258 (1969). Held to have prospective application only, Gosa v. Mayden, 450 F.2d 753 (5th Cir. 1971).

98. O'Callahan was charged with attempted rape, housebreaking, and assault with intent to rape in violation of 10 U.S.C. §§ 880, 930, 934 (1970), respectively. It is interesting to note the breadth of section 934:

> Though not specifically mentioned in this chapter, all disorders and neglects to the prejudice of good order and discipline in the armed forces, all conduct of a nature to bring discredit upon the armed forces, and crimes and offenses not capital, of which persons subject to this chapter may be guilty, shall be taken cognizance of by a general, special, or summary court-martial, according to the nature and degree of the offense, and shall be punished at the discretion of that court.

99. *Compare* 395 U.S. at 273, *with id.* at 283 (Harlan, J., dissenting).

Some problems inhere in the approach suggested in this article. Jurisdiction would overlap in some cases, as it does now with respect to state and federal courts, where a particular act by a serviceman violated a combination of military, state and federal criminal statutes. The same offenses may be punishable under both state and federal laws, in which case state and federal courts will have concurrent jurisdiction over them. Prosecution and conviction by both federal and state courts for the same acts which violate federal and state laws, regardless of which court convicts the defendant first, do not constitute double jeopardy in violation of the fifth amendment of the Constitution.[100] Double jeopardy is not involved because the prosecutions are by two different sovereigns. Separate prosecutions would not be permitted, however, in federal and military courts even when the same conduct violated both federal and military laws, since both courts are arms of the same, single sovereign.[101] Thus the only priority which would have to be established is between military and federal jurisdiction when an act violated both military and federal laws.

Cases raising serious jurisdictional conflicts, however, would be exceptional rather than commonplace, and most cases could easily be classified as military, federal or state. In any event, the difficulties would be far outweighed by the advantages of transferring jurisdiction over all nonmilitary offenses from the military to the civilian courts.

A more serious problem is presented by those cases involving criminal offenses committed by military personnel outside the territorial limits of the United States. The United States district court for the district in which the offender is arrested or is first brought upon return to the United States,[102] presently has jurisdiction to try American citizens for criminal offenses begun or committed on the high seas or in aircraft flying over the high seas.[103] Present federal statutes could be expanded to cover comparable situations involving offenses committed by armed forces personnel on or over the high seas.

Offenses committed by American service personnel within the territorial limits of foreign countries present even more difficult problems. It is doubtful whether federal district courts could be given jurisdiction over such offenses. First, there is the settled principle that every sovereign nation has the right, and the jurisdiction, to try all persons who commit criminal offenses within the territorial limits of that nation. As a general

100. Abbate v. United States, 359 U.S. 187, 195 (1959) (state conviction followed by federal conviction); Bartkus v. Illinois, 359 U.S. 121, 139 (1959) (federal acquittal followed by state conviction); *see* Moore v. Illinois, 55 U.S. (14 How.) 13 (1853); United States v. Marigold, 50 U.S. (9 How.) 560 (1850); Fox v. Ohio, 46 U.S. (5 How.) 410 (1847); *cf.* Waller v. Florida, 397 U.S. 387 (1970). The federal district courts have original jurisdiction over all offenses against the laws of the United States. 18 U.S.C. § 3231 (1964).

101. Waller v. Florida, 397 U.S. 387, 394 (1970); Grafton v. United States, 206 U.S. 333, 354-55 (1907).

102. 18 U.S.C. § 3238 (1970).

103. *Id.* § 7. *See* United States v. Bowman, 260 U.S. 94 (1922).

rule, that right can be modified only by treaty provisions, and in the absence of a specific treaty the United States would have no legitimate authority to exercise jurisdiction over American citizens who commit offenses in a foreign country.[104] Second, substantial constitutional questions involving due process would be raised by trial in the United States of a service member who had committed an offense thousands of miles away in a foreign country.[105] It requires little imagination to anticipate the almost insurmountable problems that would be created pertaining to investigation of the facts, preparation of the case, and securing the presence of essential witnesses on behalf of an accused. Without adequate provision for government payment of the expenses that would necessarily be involved, defendants who could not personally bear such expenses would be denied due process. Furthermore, it would be expensive to transport military defendants from foreign countries to the United States for trial.

One possible solution, where the civil courts of the foreign country are open and functioning, would be to allow those civil courts to try American military personnel for crimes committed in the foreign country involved. This arrangement is presently in effect in several countries where American troops are stationed, pursuant to treaty provisions and status of forces agreements.[106]

Perhaps a better solution would be to allow the military to continue to exercise its present jurisdiction over American service personnel who commit offenses in foreign countries. It is unsatisfactory to allow the present injustices to pervade any category of cases, but continuation of the military's present court-martial jurisdiction may be the only practical way to deal with military offenders who commit crimes in foreign countries.

Return to the Original Intention

Whatever the problems, the time has come to terminate the military's jurisdiction over nonmilitary criminal offenses. Although, as the Supreme

---

104. *See* Schooner Exchange v. McFaddon, 11 U.S. (11 Cranch) 116, 136 (1812), where Chief Justice Marshall restated the general principle of international law that a nation possesses and exercises within its own territory an absolute and exclusive jurisdiction, and that any exception to this jurisdiction must be traced to the consent of the nation, either express or implied.

105. The Supreme Court has said, however, that Congress has the power to provide for federal district court trials of discharged soldiers accused of offenses committed while in the armed services, presumably regardless of where the offenses were committed. Toth v. Quarles, 350 U.S. 11, 21 (1955).

106. *E.g.*, North Atlantic Treaty Organization Status of Forces Agreement, June 19, 1951, art. VII, 4 U.S.T. 1792, T.I.A.S. No. 2846; Protocol Agreement with Japan, September 29, 1953, 4 U.S.T. 1846, T.I.A.S. No. 2848, *concluded pursuant to* Administrative Agreement, February 28, 1952, art. XVII, ¶ 1, 3 U.S.T. 3341, T.I.A.S. No. 2492; Security Treaty with Japan, September 8, 1951, art. III, 3 U.S.T. 3329, T.I.A.S. No. 2491.

For a discussion of the history, validity and operation of such treaty provisions, see Wilson v. Girard, 354 U.S. 524, 526-30, 544-48 (1957).

Court observed in *Reid v. Covert*, "[t]he tradition of keeping the military subordinate to civilian authority may not be so strong as it was in the minds of those who wrote the Constitution,"[107] early American practice gave no broad, general criminal jurisdiction to courts-martial. Justice Douglas, speaking for the majority in *O'Callahan v. Parker*, noted:

> It was, therefore, the rule in Britain at the time of the American Revolution that a soldier could not be tried by court-martial for a civilian offense committed in Britain; instead military officers were required to use their energies and office to insure that the accused soldier would be tried before a civil court.[108] [Footnote omitted.]

In 17th century England the practice of court-martialing soldiers in peacetime evoked strong protests from Parliament.[109] Lord Chief Justice Hale wrote that trial by military courts "may not be permitted in time of peace, when the King's Courts are open for all Persons to receive Justice according to the Laws of the Land."[110] Hale commented that military justice is not a true system of law at all, but is "something indulged, rather than allowed as a law"[111] because of the need for order and discipline in the army. Sir William Blackstone agreed.[112]

Departure from that general principle by the British colonial troops and those in authority over them was among the grievances protested by the American colonists.[113] It is not surprising, therefore, that the Declaration of Independence included the complaint that George III had "affected to render the Military independent of and superior to the Civil Power." The Continental Congress emphasized in the Articles of War adopted in 1776 that it was important for the military authorities to ensure that soldiers who committed crimes would be brought to justice. Nevertheless, it is clear from the context of the provision that it was expected that the trials would be conducted in the civil courts.[114]

Although the practice followed was not always consistent, court-martial convictions for ordinary civilian crimes were set aside during the 19th century by military convening authorities on the ground that the charges alleged only a violation of the general criminal law and failed to state a military offense.[115] During the Civil War, Congress provided for trial

---

107. 354 U.S. 1, 23 (1957).
108. 395 U.S. 258, 269 (1969).
109. See Justice Black's excellent and thorough discussion of this area in Reid v. Covert, 354 U.S. 1, 25-27 (1957).
110. M. HALE, HISTORY AND ANALYSIS OF THE COMMON LAW OF ENGLAND 41 (1713).
111. *Id.* at 40.
112. 1 W. BLACKSTONE, COMMENTARIES 400, 413 (Dawson reprint 1966).
113. See Justice Black's historical examination, in *Reid v. Covert*, of the protests of John Adams, Thomas Jefferson and others, against British abuses in the exercise of military jurisdiction. 354 U.S. at 23-30.
114. *See* 1776 ARTICLES OF WAR, art. 1, § 10, in W. WINTHROP, MILITARY LAW AND PRECEDENTS 1494 (2d ed. 1896, reprinted 1920).
115. *Id.* at 1124 nn.82, 88.

by court-martial of some civil offenses without regard to their effect on good order and discipline in the military forces, but this exception applied only "in time of war, insurrection, or rebellion."[116] It was not until 1916, just prior to American entry into World War I and comparatively late in the history of American military justice, that the Articles of War were revised to provide for military trial of certain specific civilian crimes in peacetime if committed by persons subject to military law.[117]

Thus, instead of being a radical departure from the historic British and American view of military justice, return of jurisdiction over soldiers who commit civilian offenses to the civil courts would be a return to sound original practice. It would also be consistent with the true intent of the authors of the Constitution. As the Supreme Court pointed out in *Reid v. Covert,* "the jurisdiction of military tribunals is a very limited and extraordinary jurisdiction derived from the cryptic language"[118] in article I, section 8 of the Constitution, and was intended to be only a narrow exception to the normal and preferred method of trial in civilian courts. The Supreme Court went on to say that "[e]very extension of military jurisdiction is an encroachment on the jurisdiction of the civil courts, and, more important, acts as a deprivation of the right to jury trial and of other treasured constitutional protections."[119] In *O'Callahan v. Parker* the Court adhered to this general view of the matter, noting that, in addition to being "singularly inept in dealing with the nice subtleties of constitutional law,"[120] courts-martial apply a body of substantive military law that is probably too vague to satisfy the standards developed by the civil courts.[121] The Court thus made it clear that in light of these and similar deficiencies in military law and trial practice, the historic principle of allowing the civil courts to try soldiers whenever possible is sound and should not be abandoned in favor of broad court-martial jurisdiction.[122]

In this article, military justice has been considered primarily from the consumer perspective, that is, the perspective of "the specific human targets of its impact."[123] It is important to remember, however, that society as a whole has a significant interest and stake in the extent to which military jurisdiction is controlled and limited. In *Toth v. Quarles*, the Supreme Court pointedly warned:

---

116. Act of Mar. 3, 1863, ch. 75, § 30, 12 Stat. 736.
117. Act of Aug. 29, 1916, ch. 418, § 3, 39 Stat. 651.
118. 354 U.S. at 21.
119. *Id.*
120. 395 U.S. at 265.
121. *Id.* at 265-66. Justice Douglas, writing for the majority, noted that "[o]ne of the benefits of a civilian trial is that the trap of Article 134 may be avoided by a declaratory judgment proceeding or otherwise." *Id.* at 266. Article 134 of the *Uniform Code of Military Justice*, 10 U.S.C. § 934 (1970), punishes as a crime "all disorders and neglects to the prejudice of good order and discipline in the armed forces" as well as "all conduct of a nature to bring discredit upon the armed forces."
122. 395 U.S. at 268-72.
123. Cahn, *supra* note 13, at 14.

> There are dangers lurking in military trials which were sought to be avoided by the Bill of Rights and Article III of our Constitution. Free countries of the world have tried to restrict military tribunals to the narrowest jurisdiction deemed absolutely essential to maintaining discipline among troops in active service.[124]

Justice Douglas reached the heart of the matter when he observed that a civilian trial is held in an atmosphere conducive to the protection of individual rights, "while a court-martial is marked by the age-old manifest destiny of retributive justice."[125] It is unhealthy to permit such a system to be extended unduly and unnecessarily into what is properly the realm of the civil courts. For this reason the American people, as well as individual military defendants, have a vital interest in narrowing military jurisdiction to its proper limits. Only by such reform can the consumers of military justice become consumers of that substantially superior form of justice which is available to their nonmilitary fellow citizens.

---

124. 350 U.S. 11, 22 (1955).
125. O'Callahan v. Parker, 395 U.S. 258, 266 (1969).

CALIFORNIA'S PRISON SYSTEM:
WE MUST BRING IT INTO THE TWENTIETH CENTURY

By WALTER KARABIAN

ASSEMBLYMAN WALTER KARABIAN, B.A., M.S., J.D., is the Majority Leader of the California State Assembly. A graduate of University of Southern California Law School in 1963, he is a member of the California Bar. Mr. Karabian was a Los Angeles County Deputy District Attorney prior to his election to the Legislature in 1966.

The author gratefully acknowledges the assistance of Mrs. Anne Chiarenza, a member of his staff. A member of the Massachusetts Bar, Mrs. Chiarenza is a graduate of Boston University Law School and former Special Assistant Attorney General, Commonwealth of Massachusetts.

California operates the largest penal system in the nation, and the best. Yet, if you were to enter this progressive system as a misfit in 1971, you would be virtually certain to emerge in 1975 not only less able to function on the outside, but much more defeated and dangerous than you were when you entered.

The California correctional system, praised by no less a penal authority than Karl Menninger as "far out in the lead among the states, with excellent programs of work, education, vocational training, medical services, group counseling, and other rehabilitative activities,"[1] is critically close to failure. If it does indeed represent the optimum to be found in the 50 states, one despairs to imagine what conditions are like in the other 49.

Anyone remotely connected with criminal justice in California will tell you that the system itself is in dire need of rehabilitation. The only question is how —and how quickly — this can be done. Can we solve the problems besetting our criminal and correctional procedures with money, more trained personnel, a more humane and far-sighted treatment program for the men in our prisons? Of course we can. But given the temper and priorities of the times, these resources are not likely to be forthcoming. Yet, from a purely pragmatic point of view, much can be done by simply beefing up existing programs and putting into practice inexpensive but highly promising ideas for penal reform.

There are nearly 30,000 felony offenders in California's prisons. Roughly half this number are non-white. The prototypal inmate is young, undereducated and was chronically unemployed on the outside. His life experiences have been predominantly negative. His self-image is low, his sensitivity to injustice high. He is vulnerable at every point and he knows it.

From this man and his counterparts behind bars, one hears an almost unanimous litany of trouble. Facilities are 50 percent overcrowded. To survive at all, he must endure a pitiless assault on the last vestiges of his identity and individuality: homosexual rape, hours of idleness, inadequate or nonexistent medical and psychiatric care, smouldering racial tensions often fired to flashpoint by untrained and openly hostile guards, bad food, filth — the list is long. But, as degrading as these conditions are, the overwhelming concern of this man is the unyielding and mindless nature of the bu-

1. At a recent news conference, however, following his address before a NAACP Legal Defense Fund seminar in Los Angeles, Menninger referred to all American prison systems as a "shambles—beastly, unworkable and expensive." Their sole effect, he said, is "to degrade and humiliate people and rob them of their human dignity." *Los Angeles Times*, May 23, 1971.

THE BLACK LAW JOURNAL, 1971, Vol. 1, pp. 145-151.

reaucracy that manipulates his life, not only while he is in custody, but after he has been released on parole.

For him, the twin symbols of this bureaucracy are the indeterminate sentence and a wholly deficient rehabilitation program.

California pioneered the adoption of the indeterminate sentence, whereby a felony offender is remanded to prison for "the time prescribed by law" rather than a time certain. The Legislature sets minimum and maximum terms for each offense. As conceived by early reformers, the indeterminate sentence was basic to rehabilitation and early release, providing the flexibility necessary for weeding out of the prison population those persons who, but for the time certain of their commitment, could be leading useful lives on the outside. In theory, at least, it transfers the sentencing function from the courts to the professional prison staff, persons trained to observe the inmate at close range and make a judgment as to his fitness for parole not on the basis of his crime, but on the circumstances surrounding it and the subsequent "modification of anti-social behavior" he demonstrates in prison. It allows the "rehabilitated" inmate to be released sooner than would be possible under a fixed sentence.

In practice, however, prison administrators have found the indeterminate sentence to be a formidable disciplinary weapon, a weapon against which there is virtually no defense. As applied today, the indeterminate sentence assures much longer sentences than would be imposed by the courts for all but the most docile inmates. It comes down hardest, of course, on "trouble-makers," a group variously described as religious and political nonconformists, ethnic "leaders," psychotics, "writ-writers" in pursuit of due process, and behavioral deviants, depending upon the bias of the decision-maker. "From the vindictive guard who sets out to build a record against some individual, to the parole board, the indeterminate sentence grants Corrections the power to play God with the lives of inmates."[2]

That prison officials should seek discretion over sentencing is not surprising. They are, after all, saddled with the job of managing the prisons, and "from the official's point of view a first requisite is effective influence over inmate conduct. So long as inmates desire freedom, restrictions on freedom — threatened or actual — will provide a possible strategy for control, for effective influence; and the Correctional Establishment as a whole is premised on the desire of inmates for freedom."[3]

In fact, of course, the actual length of an individual's sentence is determined by the Adult Authority, a nine-member board consisting of the Director of the Department of Corrections and eight gubernatorial appointees. While the Penal Code states that members should "have a varied and sympathetic interest in corrections, sociology, law, law enforcement, and education,"[4] the present board is made up primarily of former policemen, prosecutors, FBI and Corrections personnel. This body serves as the parole board, charged to "determine and re-determine" the length of time a man must serve. It has the power to make a judicial determination of sentence, to retract that determination and refix sentence, to grant parole and to revoke parole, and its decisions are rarely subject to review or appeal.

Dividing into two-member panels, assisted by case-hearing representatives, the Adult Authority renders 30,000 to 40,000 determinations yearly. The inevitable result of this crushing caseload is that an inmate's hearing before the Adult Authority, the outcome of which will determine whether or not to fix sentence and grant parole,[5] generally lasts a scant 10 minutes. And these 10 minutes are not exclusively his—while one member listens to the proceedings, the other

2. Jessica Mitford, "Kind and Usual Punishment in California," *The Atlantic Monthly*, May, 1971.
3. Sheldon Menninger, *Strategies of Control*, University of California, Center for the Study of Law and Society, 1968.
4. California Penal Code, Section 5705.
5. The Adult Authority is under no legal obligation to set the sentence and generally does not do so until it is ready to grant parole.

is reading the dossier on the next inmate.

The panel's decision is based on information to be found in the prisoner's file,[6] a collection of material, little of it sworn, consisting of whatever the authorities know about the man: comments of the trial judge and the prosecutor, the probation officer's report, psychiatric evaluation, reports by guards of "deviant" behavior (which can run the spectrum from refusal to eat breakfast to attempted suicide)[7] and disciplinary infractions. While the guards and other prison personnel are encouraged to familiarize themselves with the prisoner's folder, the prisoner is at no time permitted to see it. Further, if parole is denied, the prisoner is not entitled to know why it is denied, nor is his attorney. No transcript is made of the hearing; family members, the press and legal counsel are all excluded from the proceedings.

Should an inmate's case for parole survive an examination of his folder, it remains vulnerable to the whims and biases of the parole panel. Lacking any guidelines of an official nature, California's parole policy is subjective rather than scientific. Inmates find that as the parole panels rotate, so do the indicia of "rehabilitation."[8]

Thus, determination of sentence parole is almost totally discretionary, and its arbitrary exercise has resulted in abuses of every kind. Examples abound of parole denials in clear violation of constitutional guarantees.

THE RESULT of the indeterminate sentence has been that the median time served in prison has risen dramatically in the past decade. In 1960, the median time served in California was 24 months; by 1968 it had risen to 36 months, an increase of 50 percent in eight years, and it continues to rise.[9] Yet, the 1970 report of the Assembly Select Committee on the Administration of Justice confirms what modern criminologists have been saying for years, that the character of convicted felons does not alter appreciably from one year to the next, that "persons committed to prison in 1960 . . . were essentially the same type of person as those committed for a similar offense in 1968."

The man committed to prison today is no more dangerous, hostile or menacing to society than the felon committed last year or the year before. There is, therefore, no logic to justify the increase in time served. It should be noted that the reluctance of the Adult Authority to release men from custody has not reduced California's increasing crime rate.

Longer sentences are costly to the State;[10] but far worse, they do not result in good behavior after release. On the contrary, persons serving longer terms are less likely to readjust on the outside than those serving short terms.

In fact, studies show that persons serving longer terms recidivate at a rate 10 percent higher than short termers.

---

6. There is no procedural guarantee that the parole board will review all the facts concerning an individual case: "At present, a counselor spends from five to 15 minutes with the inmate in evaluating his 'progress' of the previous *year*. (Inmates) wonder, what kind of an accurate evaluation even a qualified person could make in that length of time?" Institute for the Study of Crime and Delinquency, (45) p. 78.
7. The Caucus of Black Elected Officials of the California State Legislature, in its 1970 report on conditions at Soledad, made the following recommendations: "We strongly urge that accusations of improper behavior brought against inmates for minor offenses — like refusal to shave when no mirror is available — *be excluded from an inmate's permanent dossier and that no indication of such accusations reach the eyes of the Adult Authority* (emphasis theirs). Black Caucus Report, "Treatment of Prisoners at California Training Facility at Soledad Central," The California Legislature, p. 11, 1970.
8. ". . . the time an individual spends in prison seems to depend on three factors: (1) The values and feelings of individual parole board members. (2) The 'mood' of the public. (3) Institution population pressures." California Legislature, Assembly Criminal Procedure Committee, *Deterrent Effects of Criminal Sanctions*, p. 40, May, 1968.
9. See Adult Authority Manual of Statistics for 1945 through 1966, March, 1967, Table 1, and *Analysis of the Budget Bill, 1969-70*, p. 131.
10. According to the California Assembly Office of Research, the institutional cost per year of maintaining an inmate is $3,012. As we have noted, the average sentence is 36 months, which raises this figure to $9,036, per commitment episode. (These figures represent the saving to the State per inmate if the institution were closed.)

    More compelling, since 30 percent of this population returns to prison within two years, the cost of an average "unsuccessful" commitment episode, based upon a return to prison for 18 months on a technical violation, is more than $13,000. The average cost for those returned to prison from parole with a new felony conviction is more than $18,000. Such offenders usually spend 36 months in prison before being re-paroled.

In effect, California's parole policy acerbates the problems it was designed to solve. It operates as a mindless, moving conveyor belt upon which our felons are tossed with total disregard for the human pileup at the other end.

The cost to the individual in prison, however, is beyond measure. He does not know how much time he will serve until the end of his sentence, since his sentence is not fixed until that time. If parole is denied he has no recourse. The meting out of an indeterminate sentence amounts to summary injustice to him, a major source of anger, resentment, bitterness and defeat. Psychologically, he faces more uncertainty than most in our society. He cannot plan or prepare for the future. He is in every way the pawn of a swollen bureaucracy. It is no wonder that a crisis in our prisons is upon us.

The legislation I introduced in the 1971 Session of the Legislature will buy time, time to devise and expedite criminals and correctional procedures to reduce permanently our prison population, an essential first step to long-range penal reform. It includes a measure that would require parole of most prisoners at the completion of the minimum sentence.[11] Under this proposal, the Adult Authority would continue to determine sentence length, but a felon would serve only the legal minimum behind bars, and the balance on parole. Further, if parole were denied, the burden of proof would rest with the parole board, and grounds for denial would be reduced to clearly discernible facts relating to the nature of the original crime and the prisoners' history of excessive criminality or violence. This proposal also reduces to five the members of the Adult Authority and specifies that, in addition to the Director of Corrections, they shall consist of an experienced criminal attorney, a behavioral scientist, a person trained in the education of disadvantaged persons, and a law enforcement administrator, all "with substantial records of achievement."

A second measure[12] provides that the Adult Authority officially "show cause" whenever the automatic parole is denied by submitting a written report of each denial which meets specifications to be determined by the Bureau of Criminal Statistics.

This proposal would bring our parole policy under critical scrutiny and eliminate irregularities inherent in any purely arbitrary exercise of authority.

An equally important component of this legislative package seeks to put some economic bone and tissue on the Department of Corrections' rehabilitative arm, California Correctional Industries.[13] Established to provide "training in work habits and work skills to the inmates as a means of improving employment opportunities after release" and "prevent idleness," this program is self-supporting and even modestly profitable. Yet, the entire program employs barely 10 percent of the State's prison population.

According to a recent estimate, there is at least a nine-month waiting period to get into Industries. And, for the fortunate few who make it, many of the jobs are sadly ill-suited to prepare them for life on the outside. At Soledad prison, for instance, where more than half of the 2,787 inmates will be returned to the urban centers, only 400 are working. Of the 400, nearly half work in dairy and hog ranch programs. At Folsom, about 150 inmates of the 600 employed are learning to make license plates, a skill which cannot be utilized outside prison.

In addition, many jobs being done on prison equipment by inmates are automated on the outside; thus, men train for obsolete work. But to automate in prison would further reduce the number of jobs in Correctional Industries, so inmates continue to do busy work on outdated equipment for an outrageously low pay scale that ranges from two cents to 16 cents an hour.

Finally, prison-made goods are often inferior to those manufactured in private industry. Recently, the State requested

11. Assembly Bill 2064. A similar provision is included in Assembly Bill 483, introduced by Assemblyman Leo J. Ryan.
12. Assembly Bill 2816.
13. Assembly Bill 2062.

clothing manufacturers to submit, along with their bid, assessments as to the durability of their shorts, T-shirts and denims. These estimates revealed that the quality of prison-made clothing was so low and frequency of replacement so high that the State paid 12 percent more because it used Correctional Industries clothing.

Since the Correctional Industries program must be self-supporting, and the productivity per inmate is as little as one-sixth of that of a worker in private industry, the profit margin is slim indeed. At that, where private industry might use a portion of its profits to expand operations or purchase new equipment, much of the Correctional Industries are turned over to the States' General Fund.

Recently the textile mill at San Quentin was closed; so was the cannery at Folsom. Yet, the most innovative proposal in last year's Correctional Industries report, was for a "vast plan for providing several new laundries consistent with the long-range needs of Mental Hygiene."

Corrections officials are not unaware of the deficiencies of the Industries program. They know that there are too few jobs. But, they also know that inmate participation in other rehabilitative programs, such as vocational training and academic courses, is also woefully inadequate. These efforts, well-intended though they are, are failing. They reach only a fraction of the State's inmates. They occupy less than four hours a day of the prisoners they reach.

The inadequacy of Correctional Industries reflects both political pressure and economic reality. Within the 103 million dollar prison budget, there is no allocation for the subsidy of this program. (Only five cents of every prison dollar is now spent on rehabilitation.) Even if the economy were stronger and funds available, it is unlikely that the non-voting prison population would receive them.

To make matters worse, private industry has generally opposed measures which might increase Industries' production or place Industries on a more competitive footing — this in spite of the fact that the total Industries output comprises only 0.1 percent of total manufacturing and wholesale sales in California.

As it is, prison-made products may be sold only to tax-supported agencies, and total production is limited by law. Yet, when Folsom sought to reduce losses in its metal-stamping industries by expanding to metal desks, private industry lobbied against it so vigorously that it succeeded in limiting the sale of those desks to State offices only. Similarly, fear of competition has prompted organized labor to lobby against efforts to develop prison industry.

The legislation I have proposed would neutralize the conflict between Correctional Industries and private industry. It would expand employment and training opportunities for inmates by providing financial incentives to private industries to expand their operations to include the State's prisons. Among these incentives are tax deductions to participating firms for a percentage of the training costs and wages of inmates; payment by the State of a portion of inmate wages for a fixed period of time while training; and a provision entitling a participating firm to a 10 percent price preference over out-of-state businesses on purchases made by the State.[14]

Participating firms would be required to hire their inmate employees upon their release if their performance while in prison had been satisfactory.

Products and profits from a participating firm's prison branch would, of course, belong to the firm, but inmates would be included within any labor contract between the private firm and its other employees. Inmates would also be entitled to join unions as dues-paying members.

Inmates in the program would reimburse the State from their earnings for the reasonable cost of their confinement.

14. By judicial determination, the California Preference Law, Section 4330, which entitled California firms to a five percent price preference over out-of-state businesses, was declared unconstitutional in 1970 (53 Ops. Atty. Gen. 72, 2/11/70), but contracts entered into by the State of California prior to this ruling are legal and binding on all the parties to the contract.

The balance of an inmate's earnings would be applied to pay any personal debt or other obligations, the remainder to be held in trust in a savings account until the inmate is released.

This plan would create a productive environment within the prisons. It would revitalize the concept of rehabilitation by providing inmates with realistic training for work on the outside, a marketable skill, the capability of providing for his family while he is confined, and money in the bank when he is released.

Nearly 80 percent of California's convicts go to prison for non-violent crimes. Before their prison experience, they are not unlike their counterparts on the outside. But, once in prison, dehumanizing pressures rapidly corrode any ties that remain with the outside, to the end that most convicts re-enter civilian life full of rage and bitterness toward the system that locked them up.

If we can begin to stimulate in the men inside the walls the rhythm and routine of life and work on the outside,[15] we might be able to restore some semblance of balance and reason to life inside. At the very least, the system will cease to destroy men as inexorably as it does now.

Currently, there are nearly 100 bills pending in the California Legislature, touching almost every aspect of prison reform. But in the final analysis, the most enlightened measures can only bring cosmetic relief to a system which has simply grown too large to be adequately or intelligently administered.

We are, as I have said, buying the time necessary to achieve fundamental prison reform. A basic requisite to that reform is a reduction in the prison population.

Ironically, while there is little disagreement among penal experts that prisons fail as a means of punishment or as instruments with which to change criminal behavior, prison overcrowding, rather than humanitarian concern, emerges as the most compelling liberalizing force in the correctional field.

Nationwide, new programs are being developed to relieve the crush of prison population by the treatment and control of offenders in the community rather than in prison. (In Los Angeles County, 2,000 probation officers supervise 61,300 adults and juveniles in the community, and the results, in terms of recidivism, have been impressive.)[16] In addition to release under supervision, reformers are advocating — and trying — weekend leaves, work-release programs, outside classes and halfway houses as alternatives to simple incarceration.

In my view, however, a permanent reduction in prison population can only come about through a careful redefinition of the criminal law to exclude offenses against private morality and taste. Assuming the essential function of the criminal law to be the protection of our persons and property, the American tradition of using it also to regulate the moral conduct of the individual citizen is a major cause of prison overpopulation. Worse, this "overreach" of the criminal law has so overloaded our entire criminal justice system, that it is wholly defective as a means of protecting us against those activities which are the proper concern of the criminal law — crimes of violence, serious depredations of property, and the exploitation of the defenseless and the young.

Judges, corrections officers and policemen agree that they could serve with far greater efficiency if the system were relieved of that class of offense known as "victimless crime," offenses such as prostitution, abortion, homosexuality, drunkenness, vagrancy, gambling and drug use. According to the President's Commission on Law Enforcement and the Administration of Justice, these offenses account for fully half of the six million non-traffic arrests of adults per year in the United States. Because these crimes lack victims, that is complainants who seek the protec-

15. Another proposal in this legislative package, AB 2063, would provide facilities to enable inmates to spend two-day visits, at least three times a year, with those persons who have been approved on the inmate's visitation or corrspondence list. The inhuman sexual deprivation endured by prison inmates has produced a prison environment where homosexual rape is commonplace; in addition, prolonged separation has resulted in the destruction of the marriages of countless convicts.

16. "Justice on Trial," *Newsweek*, March 8, 1971.

tion of the criminal law, there is growing sentiment among the experts that they are not the legitimate concern of the criminal law.

In his excellent book on the control of crime, Norval Morris states, "In this country we have . . . a long tradition of using (the criminal law) as an instrument for coercing men to virtue. It is a singularly inept instrument for that purpose. It is also an unduly costly one, both in terms of harm done and in terms of the neglect of the proper tasks of law enforcement."[17]

Most of our legislation concerning narcotics, gambling and sexual behavior is based on the erroneous assumption that the criminal law has the capacity to alter human proclivities. Yet, there is no evidence that the incursion of the criminal law into the spheres of social welfare and private morality has brought about the Millenium. We do not drink less alcohol or take less drugs, nor are we sexually more strait-laced by dint of criminal sanction.[18]

As a case in point, examine what happened in California after the Legislature had imposed a mandatory sentence of one to 10 years in prison for the possession of marijuana. In 1961, the Legislature removed the sentence of 0-12 months in county jail as an optional penalty for possession, and imposed the stiffer sentence. At the same time, it also increased penalties for sale and for offenders with prior convictions.

Did these sanctions limit the sale or possession of marijuana? On the contrary. In 1961, the year the sanctions were imposed, there were 3,500 arrests for marijuana offenses. By 1966 this figure had increased to 18,000, a rise of 400 percent.

By 1970, 43 percent of *all* felony arrests in California were drug arrests.

Statistics relating to arrests and convictions for other "victimless" crimes seem to support the proposition that criminal sanctions serve almost no deterrent purpose. In fact, the overreach of the law contributes to the crime problem. We have only to remember that the "Noble Experiment" of 1913 spawned more than the romantic era of bathtub gin and speakeasies. It also helped to finance the largest criminal industry in the modern world.

I am not unmindful of the fact that a review of the criminal law raises many legal and administrative issues; there are legitimate objections to the repeal of certain criminal statutes. My point is that inevitably we will have to undertake such a review as an alternative to the penal approach, which is both wasteful and futile. As Myrl Alexander, director of the Federal Bureau of Prisons noted, "We all recognize that the traditional institutions of the past haven't produced the desired results . . . imprisonment is a failure."[19]

Our resources in manpower and money are by no means infinite. We have a clear responsibility to apprehend and confine the dangerous offender, and to rehabilitate him when possible. We cannot hope to succeed in even this limited pursuit if we remain wedded to a concept of criminal law which does not distinguish between the felon who steals property and endangers lives, and the non-violent offender who violates private codes of social conduct. Imprisonment is not the answer to the national problems such an offender creates or the social displacements which spawn his behavior. We can no longer afford to pay the heavy concomitant costs of perpetuating a system which fails to come to grips with this reality.

---

17. Morris, Norval and Gordon Hawkins, *The Honest Politician's Guide to Crime Control,* Page 5.
18. There is some evidence that the extensive use of criminal sanctions may actually *decrease* the public safety. A recent study by Herbert Packer concluded, in a chapter on drug use, abortion, gambling, alcoholism and "white-collar" crime, that, "It is by no means clear that we can persuade the public to view conduct as wrongful by making it criminal. Law, even criminal law, simply is not that potent a weapon for social control. Our experience with the use of the criminal sanction during the Prohibition period suggests that the reverse is true . . . There is indeed some reason to fear that sensitivity toward the criminal sanction has decreased as the formal apparatus of the criminal law has been called on to deal with a wide variety of morally neutral conduct . . ." Packer, Herbert L., *The Limits of the Criminal Sanction,* page 359, 1968.
19. *Los Angeles Times,* November 17, 1968.